ORGANIZATIONAL
STRESS

Sara Miller McCune founded SAGE Publishing in 1965 to support the dissemination of usable knowledge and educate a global community. SAGE publishes more than 1000 journals and over 800 new books each year, spanning a wide range of subject areas. Our growing selection of library products includes archives, data, case studies and video. SAGE remains majority owned by our founder and after her lifetime will become owned by a charitable trust that secures the company's continued independence.

Los Angeles | London | New Delhi | Singapore | Washington DC | Melbourne

SECOND EDITION

ORGANIZATIONAL STRESS

A Review and Critique of Theory, Research, and Applications

CHRISTINA G.L. NERSTAD, INGVILD M. SELJESETH,
ASTRID M. RICHARDSEN, CARY L. COOPER,
PHILIP J. DEWE & MICHAEL P. O'DRISCOLL

Los Angeles | London | New Delhi
Singapore | Washington DC | Melbourne

Los Angeles | London | New Delhi
Singapore | Washington DC | Melbourne

SAGE Publications Ltd
1 Oliver's Yard
55 City Road
London EC1Y 1SP

SAGE Publications Inc.
2455 Teller Road
Thousand Oaks, California 91320

SAGE Publications India Pvt Ltd
Unit No. 323–333, Third Floor, F-Block
International Trade Tower, Nehru Place
New Delhi 110 019

SAGE Publications Asia-Pacific Pte Ltd
3 Church Street
#10-04 Samsung Hub
Singapore 049483

Editor: Donna Goddard
Editorial assistant: Emma Yuan
Production editor: Martin Fox
Marketing manager: Lucia Sweet
Cover design: Wendy Scott
Typeset by: TNQ Technologies
Printed in the UK

**Library of Congress Control Number:
2022944485**

British Library Cataloguing in Publication data

A catalogue record for this book is available from the British Library

ISBN 978-1-5297-2472-1
ISBN 978-1-5297-2471-4 (pbk)

At SAGE we take sustainability seriously. Most of our products are printed in the UK using responsibly sourced papers and boards. When we print overseas, we ensure sustainable papers are used as measured by the PREPS grading system. We undertake an annual audit to monitor our sustainability.

CONTENTS

About the Authors   vii

Preface   ix

1 What is Stress?   1

2 Organizational Stress and the Brain   29

3 Job-Related Sources of Strain   45

4 Assessing Job-Related Strains   65

5 A Special Form of Strain: Job-Related Burnout   79

6 Moderators of Stressor-Strain Relationships   105

7 Coping with Job Stress   137

8 Organizational Interventions   153

9 Methodological Issues in Job Stress Research   173

10 The Changing Nature of Work: Implications for Stress Research   193

References   211

Index   269

ABOUT THE AUTHORS

Cary L. Cooper is the 50th Anniversary Professor of Organizational Psychology and Health at the Alliance Manchester Business School, University of Manchester. He is a Founding President of the British Academy of Management, Immediate Past President of the Chartered Institute of Personnel and Development (CIPD), former President of RELATE, and President of the Institute of Welfare. He was the Founding Editor of the *Journal of Organizational Behavior*, former Editor of the scholarly journal *Stress and Health* and is the Editor-in-Chief of the *Wiley-Blackwell Encyclopaedia of Management*, now in its 3rd Edition. He has been an advisor to the World Health Organization, ILO, and EU in the field of occupational health and well-being, was Chair of the Global Agenda Council on Chronic Disease of the World Economic Forum (2009–2010) (then served for 5 years on the Global Agenda Council for Mental Health of the WEF) and was Chair of the Academy of Social Sciences (2009–2015). He was Chair of the Sunningdale Institute in the Cabinet Office and National School of Government (2005–2010). Professor Cooper is currently the Chair of the National Forum for Health & Wellbeing at Work (comprised of 40 global companies e.g. BP, Microsoft, NHS Executive, UK government (wellbeing lead), Rolls Royce, John Lewis Partnership, etc.). Professor Cooper is the author/editor of over 250 books in the field of occupational health psychology, workplace well-being, women at work, and occupational stress. He was awarded the CBE by the Queen in 2001 for his contributions to occupational health, and in 2014, he was awarded a Knighthood for his contribution to the social sciences.

Philip Dewe is an Emeritus Professor at Birkbeck, University of London. He has written widely on work stress and coping. He is a Fellow of the Academy of Social Sciences, the European Academy of Occupational Health Psychology, and Birkbeck, University of London.

Christina G. L. Nerstad is Professor of Organizational Psychology/Organizational Behavior at the Department of Leadership and Organizational Behavior, BI Norwegian Business School. Her research activities are in the areas of occupational health psychology, organizational psychology/organizational behavior, and human resource management focusing on the motivational determinants of achievement, stress, health, and well-being at work. Her work has been published in journals such as *Academy of Management Journal*, *Journal of Organizational Behavior*, *Journal of Occupational Health Psychology*, and *Human Resource Management*, and she has written several book chapters which are published by both national and international publishers. She is involved in research collaboration projects with a number of organizations, and she teaches various topics at Ph.D., executive, Master of Science, and bachelor programs.

Michael P. O'Driscoll is Emeritus Professor of Psychology at the University of Waikato, Hamilton, New Zealand, where he taught courses in organizational psychology and organizational research methods for over 35 years. His primary research interests were job stress and coping, including workplace bullying and work-life balance, and more generally the relationship between work and health. Since his retirement in 2017, he has actively contributed to Grey Power, an organization which advocates for the health and well-being of older people in New Zealand.

Astrid M. Richardsen is Professor Emerita at BI Norwegian Business School, where she was Head of Department of Leadership and Organizational Behavior from 2007 to 2015. She was founder and Associate Dean for the MSc program in Leadership and Organizational Psychology from 2003 to 2016. Her research interests have been mainly in the area of occupational health, focusing on job stress, burnout, work engagement, and work and organizational outcomes, and she has held several research grants to study these issues. Her work encompasses papers in international and national journals, as well as several edited books and book chapters. She has been an advisor to private and public organizations on the antecedents and consequences of occupational stress and how to confront such problems. She now lives in Canada and divides her time between grandchildren, creative pursuits, and academic work.

Ingvild M. Seljeseth is a Clinical Psychologist graduated from the University of Oslo in 2008. She earned her Ph.D. in Leadership and Organizational Behavior from the Norwegian Business School BI in 2018. Seljeseth is currently an Associate Professor at the Department of Leadership and Organization, Kristiania University College, and an Adjunct Professor at the Department of Communication and Culture, BI Norwegian Business School. Seljeseth's academical work centers on social hierarchies, leadership, and stress. Earlier, Seljeseth worked as an organizational psychologist assisting clients in selecting and developing leaders and management teams.

PREFACE

The last 20 years have seen fundamental changes to the nature and structure of work, where and how people work, the sector they work in, their employment relationship or psychological contract, the way they develop careers, balance their working lives, and achieve satisfaction and well-being (Dewe & Cooper, 2021). The main forces or drivers of these changes are globalization, advances in technology, and the changing nature and structure of work (Dewe & Cooper, 2017, 2021; Dewe et al., 2010). These changes have had an impact on the structure of organizations, work practices and the skills needed, how modern organizations are managed and led, and the blurring boundaries between work and home. Workers' stress, strain, and thriving at work have also been affected by the changing nature of work. Studies have found that the incidence of stress-related absence and presenteeism is increasing globally, and that the average duration of absence days due to stress-related illnesses was longer than for physical illnesses (Dewe & Cooper, 2017).

Globalization or the rise of multinational and global corporations is a result of global competition, growing economies and developing markets, and technological advances (Dewe & Cooper, 2017). Organizations have restructured through mergers and acquisitions in order to enhance profitability or survive global competition, but also through capital and production movements and the demands for rationalization. However, such restructuring is often met with apprehension and fear of the unknown by employees, often associated with stress, especially job insecurity, although reactions depend on how these changes are managed.

The pressures toward globalization constitute the new reality of work and have major implications for the structuring of work and organizations all over the world. The result is a growth in complex organizational networks and structures that require different approaches to management, working and employment arrangements, culture and values. The new reality of work also has resulted in more complex human resource strategies including career management, performance management, work-life balance and well-being, and in demands for work arrangements that can deal with constant change, and alleviate job insecurity, negative job stress, and strain. The rapid advances in technology have been transformational in terms of the shift to knowledge work (Dewe & Cooper, 2021). The transformation to a knowledge economy came about as a result of the rise in knowledge intensive industries and high-tech manufacturing, a shift away from investments in physical assets to intangible assets such as software, design, human capital, research, and development (Dewe & Cooper, 2017). The role of the computer has been a central force in the transformation of work life, together with cell phone use, the internet and social media. The growth of knowledge work has created demands for a knowledge intensive and highly skilled workforce with more flexibility in terms of how work is organized, the time and location of work, and for new ways of working that emphasize collaboration, facilitation, and networking. At the same time, the technological advances challenge the role of well-being for knowledge workers.

Jobs are no longer for life, due to downsizing there are fewer people with higher workloads, and people are working longer hours than ever before, despite early predictions that technology would transform our work and produce shorter workweeks. Technological advances have made it possible to work remotely, but have led some to conclude that the long hours culture has given way to the 'always-on' culture (Worral & Cooper, 2016). In the latest Quality of Working Life Survey, Worral and Cooper (2016) showed the impact of the changing nature of managerial work: over 90% of mangers worked for longer than contracted hours, the long hours have a negative effect on their stress levels, almost 80% reported that the volume of work has increased substantially, over 60% report that technology has contributed to not being able to switch off which is adversely affecting family life, and almost all report change fatigue resulting from constant and major changes in the workplace.

Also, work-life balance considerations are increasing the demand for the development of flexible working arrangements. Over the past decades, more and more people work from their homes. Technological advances have made this possible, and the recent pandemic has made it a necessity. The concept of 'the flexible workforce' is upheld as an ideal, although in family-friendly terms it can at times be anything but flexible, instead blurring the boundaries between work and family. We are increasingly creating 'virtual organizations', and it will be interesting to see how the virtual organization will manage this dispersed workforce in the future.

The purpose of the second edition is, consistent with the first edition, to review research in the field of organizational stress in order to reflect upon what this research can tell us about the current and future state of the workplace and its impact on the health of all employees. The forces of change in the workplace – globalization, advances in technology and the changing nature and structure of work – will change the direction of and present challenges for research into work stress and coping. While a number of potential stressors in the workplace have received less attention from the stress perspective, including terrorism, poor leadership, organizational politics, and workplace violence, the focus on the more traditional stressors – role stressors, overload, cross-over and work-life balance – is still highly relevant. The changes in the workplace also lead to the need to refine and make relevant the measures used to study people's work experiences. It helps to focus our efforts on the future of work, where it is going, and the role industrial and organizational psychologists can play in better understanding the dynamics of occupational stress. Hopefully, this book will provide the groundwork for master students, Ph.D. students, and academics alike in their efforts to identify future areas of fertile research in the field of workplace stress and coping, stress management interventions, and what can be done to minimize or eliminate the sources of negative stress that exist in the workplace.

REFERENCES

Dewe, P., & Cooper, C. (2017). *Work stress and coping: Forces of change and challenges*. SAGE.

Dewe, P., & Cooper, C. (2021). *Work and stress: A research overview*. Routledge.

Dewe, P., O'Driscoll, M., & Cooper, C. (2010). *Coping with work stress: A review and critique*. Wiley-Blackwell.

Worral, L., & Cooper, C. (2016). *Quality of working life survey*. C. M. Institute.

1

WHAT IS STRESS?

To the individual whose health or happiness has been ravaged by an inability to cope with the effects of job-related stress, the costs involved are only too clear. Whether manifested in minor complaints of illness, serious ailments such as heart disease, or social problems such as alcoholism and drug abuse, stress-related problems exact a heavy toll on individuals' lives (Campbell Quick & Henderson, 2016; Eddy et al., 2017). In addition, it has long been recognized that families suffer directly or indirectly from the stress problems of their members – suffering that can be manifested in unhappy marriages, divorces, and spouse and child abuse. But what price do organizations and nations pay for a poor fit between people and their environments? Stress has been seen as a contributory factor to the productivity and health costs of companies and countries, but, as studies of stress-related illnesses and deaths show, stress imposes a high cost on individual health and well-being as well as organizational productivity (Hassard et al., 2018). Productivity-related losses have been found to represent the majority of the total cost of work-related stress to society (between 70% and 90%), while medical costs and health care constitute the remaining 10%–30% (Hassard et al., 2018). Based on data from several countries (Sweden, Denmark, France, Switzerland, the United Kingdom, the EU-15, Australia, and Canada), the costs of work-related stress have been found to range between 221.13 and 187 million US dollars (Hassard et al., 2018). Thus, the economic burden imposed by work-related stress on society seems to be significant. However, stress can also be adaptive for individuals and subsequently lead to individual growth (Meurs & Perrewé, 2011).

By integrating the adaptive characteristics of stressful experiences with the previous models of occupational stress we hope that this book can provide a balanced and complete picture to examine the concept of stress and its application in organizational contexts. In the following chapters, we review the sources and outcomes of job-related stress, the connection between occupational stress and neuroscience, the methods used to assess levels and consequences of occupational stress, and the strategies that might be used by individuals and organizations to confront stress and its associated problems. We also devote one chapter to examining a very extreme form of occupational stress – burnout, which has been found to have severe consequences for individuals and their organizations. Finally, we discuss scenarios for jobs and work in the new millennium, as well as the potential sources of stress that these scenarios may generate.

The major focus of this volume is research on stress arising in job-related, organizational contexts. In each chapter, we examine critical issues concerning stress research and some of the challenges facing researchers in this broad and complex field. Our aim is not to provide a total review of all relevant studies on job stress but to stimulate awareness and critical thinking about a selection of significant theoretical and empirical issues. The present chapter begins with a brief overview of a selection of influential historical origins and early approaches to the study of stress, discusses the strengths and weaknesses of these early approaches, and describes the evolution of more contemporary and popular models of stress. We conclude the chapter with an exploration of emerging themes in the delineation of stress and related concepts.

OVERVIEW OF STRESS DEFINITIONS

One difficulty in conducting research on stress is that the concept has multiple meanings and wide discrepancies exist in the way that stress is defined and operationalized (Bliese et al., 2017). For instance, the concept of stress has variously been defined as both an independent and a dependent variable and as a 'process'. This confusion over terminology is compounded by the broad application of the stress concept in medical, behavioral, and social science research over the past 50–60 years. Each discipline has investigated stress from its own unique perspective, adopting as a guideline either a stimulus-based model (stress as the 'independent' variable) or a response-based model (stress as the 'dependent' variable). The approach taken is dictated by the objectives of the research and the intended action resulting from the findings. What is clear from the different ways in which stress has been defined is that there has been considerable debate and discussion as to what stress really means.

As we discuss in this chapter, the importance of this debate can be established by way of two points. First, theoretical definitions of concepts determine the nature and direction of research, as well as the possible explanations that can be proffered for research findings. Definitions provide researchers with theoretical boundaries that need to be constantly extended and reviewed to ensure that what is being defined reflects the nature of the experience itself (Newton, 1995). Second, the definitional debate gives a sense of time and historical perspective, shedding light on why a certain focus or approach prevails, and a mechanism for considering the explanatory potential of current research.

Almost all research on stress begins by pointing to the difficulties associated with and the confusion surrounding the way in which the term stress has been used. Kagan (2016) states that the ambiguity inherent in the concept of stress limits its utility, although useful when applied to events which constitute a serious threat to individual well-being. As has already been noted, stress has been defined as a stimulus, a response, or the result of an interaction between the two, with the interaction described in terms of some imbalance between the person and the environment (Campbell Quick & Henderson, 2016; Meurs & Perrewé, 2011). As empirical knowledge has developed, particularly that surrounding the person–environment (P-E) interaction, researchers have considered the nature of that interaction and, more importantly, the psychological processes through which it takes place (Dewe & Cooper, 2017).

From this debate has emerged a belief that traditional approaches to defining stress (i.e., stimulus, response, interaction) have, by directing attention toward external events, diverted researchers away from considering the processes within the individual through which such events are appraised (Duckworth, 1986). This is not to say that such ideas have gone unresearched or that earlier definitional approaches are inadequate. However, as knowledge and understanding of stimulus, response, and interaction definitions and their associated meaning have advanced, the debate about how stress should be defined has shifted ground. Rather than singling out and focusing separately on the different elements of the stress process, it is today more common to examine the nature of that process itself and to integrate stimulus and response definitions within an overall conceptual framework that acknowledges the dynamic linkages between all elements of the stress process.

Before considering the different stress definitions in more detail, it should not be assumed that different approaches to defining stress have followed in some logical sequence. A range of factors, including the discipline of the researcher, the direction of the research, and the research questions asked, will influence whether a particular definitional approach is adopted. Furthermore, at the conceptual level many researchers believe that stress should be defined in process oriented (e.g., transactional) terms, but empirical research has often adopted definitions that emphasize a particular part of the stress process rather than the nature of the process itself. Despite the confusion in terminology, the important message to emerge is that defining stress is not just an exercise in semantics: The way in which stress is defined has a fundamental impact on how research is conducted and results are explained, and definitions must capture the essence of the stress experience rather than simply reflect a rhetoric (Newton, 1995). The existing models and definitions of stress represent various traditions of studying stress. Of these, the most prominent and emphasized are the *biological* (e.g., Selye's theory of stress), *epidemiological* (e.g., stimulus-based models of stress), and *psychological* (e.g., transactional theory of stress; conservation of resources theory) traditions (Cohen et al., 2016). The *biological tradition* is concerned with brain-based systems which are essential for metabolic control including monitoring the effects of enzyme activity and normal homeostatic regulation of body temperature, etc., that the body maintains to keep individuals alive (Cohen et al., 2016). The *epidemiologic tradition* concerns objective stress levels which are produced by individuals' exposure to life events like unemployment, economic strain, and divorce. The *psychological tradition* assumes that the same event, such as holding an oral presentation at work, may not be stressful for all individuals. For example, individuals appraise the potential threat of a certain event and to what extent they have the resources needed to cope (Lazarus & Folkman, 1984). If they perceive that they have the sufficient resources to cope, the event may not be experienced as stressful. A group of researchers have more recently proposed stress as a beneficial heuristic, facilitating the incorporation of biological, epidemiological, and psychological traditions to study stress and disease (Cohen et al., 2016). As can be seen in some of the theories we will present in this chapter, the mentioned traditions for studying stress have been applied in a more integrative way (e.g., cognitive activation theory of stress; CATS).

Given the variety of ways in which stress has been defined and its multiple meanings (Bliese et al., 2017), stress research and also this book differentiates between *stressors* – the events or properties of events (stimuli) that are encountered by individuals and which may cause subsequent reactions; *stress* – the overall process of perceiving and appraising stressors as well as related expectancies; *strain/thriving* – the individual's psychological, physical, and behavioral responses to stressors, where the stress response may lead to strain (i.e., sustained activation which has strain effects) or thriving – i.e., when short-term activation has thriving effects in terms of vitality, positive adaptation and learning (Porath et al., 2012; Spreitzer et al., 2005) – depending on the type of activation; and *outcomes* – the consequences of strain/thriving at both the individual, group, and the organizational level (Beehr, 1998; Beehr & Franz, 1987; Bliese et al., 2017; Meurs & Perrewé, 2011). Further, moderators also play an important role in shaping the strength of the relationships between stressors, appraisal, expectancy, stress, strain/thriving, and outcomes (see Figure 1.1). In terms of stress, we have included appraisal and expectancies in the organizational stress process model (Figure 1.1). First, *appraisal* is a process of evaluating whether and in what way a certain encounter with the environment is relevant to a person's well-being (Folkman et al., 1986). Second, individuals' appraisals determine their *expectancies*, that is, what is stored in the brain based on previous stressful encounters (this is explained to a greater extent in Chapter 7), and which may influence what kind of stress response individuals anticipate (Meurs & Perrewé, 2011). We include stress response anticipation in the model to emphasize the importance of considering what potentially may prolong a work stress experience and affect future expectations and thinking (i.e., perseverative cognition) about stressful situations (Brosschot et al., 2005; Meurs & Perrewé, 2011).

As illustrated in Figure 1.1, stressors are the antecedent conditions, and strain/thriving is the person's response(s) to those conditions. Partly in line with Beehr, we suggest that the term stress should be used to denote the overall process incorporating stressors, appraisal, expectancy/coping responses, perceived stress, strain/thriving as well as accounting for potential moderators, such as job resources, in the process. In addition, by drawing on models encompassing a more positive view on stress, we distinguish between two stress processes. That is, one is more adaptive than the other and may facilitate thriving and in turn adaptive outcomes rather than strain and maladaptive outcomes (see Figure 1.1). Also, the dotted reciprocal arrows leading from strain/thriving to appraisal in Figure 1.1 illustrate that the experienced outcomes of stress in turn may influence how employees appraise future stressors, thus creating potential maladaptive or adaptive reciprocal relationships.

In practice, it may be difficult to integrate the various stress theories because they pertain to different elements of the stress process and thus have the capacity to explain different things. Further, not all theories would agree upon the inclusion of appraisal

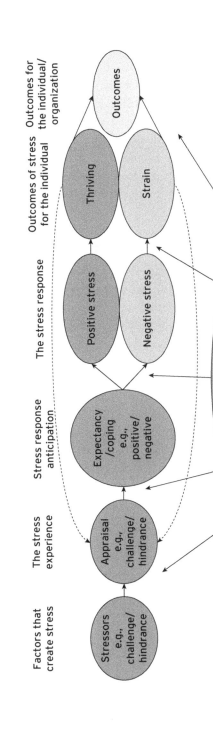

Figure 1.1 Organizational stress process

(e.g., conservation of resources theory) or expectancy (e.g., transactional model of stress) in such a model. It should also be noted that coping is defined differently in several theories and can therefore be argued to serve as a mediating or moderating variable in the organizational stress process, depending on the theory one draws upon (see Chapter 7). With all of this in mind, we still attempt to incorporate parts from several of the most popular and contemporary stress models today in an integrative way. We propose that the various theories are more likely to complement each other, rather than being at odds (cf. Locke, 1996; O'Brien & Beehr, 2019). Although popular stress theories seem to explain stress and the stress process somewhat differently, as argued in this chapter, what they say about the same phenomenon does not seem to be directly contradictory. By considering the components of the various stress theories, we may become better able to understand the nature of job-related stress.

RESPONSE-BASED DEFINITIONS OF STRESS

The phrase 'being under stress' is one that most people can identify with, although it can mean different things to different individuals. This expression focuses not so much on the nature of stress itself but on its outcomes or consequences. A response-based approach (see Figure 1.2) views stress as a dependent variable (i.e., a response to disturbing or threatening stimuli).

The origins of response-based definitions can be found in medicine and are usually viewed from a physiological perspective – a logical stance for a discipline trained to diagnose and treat symptoms but not necessarily their causes. The work of Hans Selye in the 1930s and 1940s marks the beginning of this approach to the study of stress. In 1936, Selye introduced the notion of stress-related illness in terms of the general adaptation syndrome (GAS), suggesting that stress is a nonspecific response of the body to any demand made upon it (Selye, 1956). Selye's focus was medical: General sickness was characterized by loss of motivation, appetite, weight, and strength. Evidence from animal

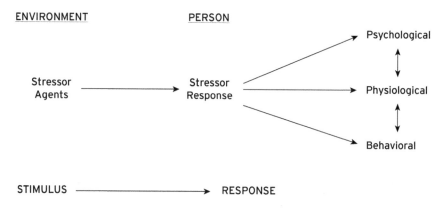

Figure 1.2 A response-based model of stress

Source: Reproduced from Understanding Stress, Sutherland and Cooper (1990), Nelson Thornes Ltd.

studies also indicated internal physical degeneration and deterioration. Responses to stress were considered to be invariant to the nature of the stressor and therefore to follow a universal pattern.

Three stages of response were described within the GAS. The alarm reaction is the immediate psychophysiological response, when the initial 'shock' phase of lowered resistance is followed by 'countershock'. At this time, defense mechanisms are activated, forming the emergency reaction known as the 'fight or flight' response (Cannon, 1935). Increased sympathetic activity results in the secretion of catecholamines, which prepare the body physiologically for action: For example, heart rate and blood pressure increase, the spleen contracts, and blood supplies are redirected to the brain and skeletal muscles. The second stage is resistance to a continued stressor, in which the adaptation response and/or return to equilibrium replace the alarm reaction. However, resistance cannot continue indefinitely, and if the alarm reaction is elicited too intensely or too frequently over an extended period, the energy needed for adaptation becomes depleted, and the third stage (exhaustion, collapse, or death) occurs (Selye, 1983).

Although the nonspecificity concept of stress-related illness and the GAS have had far-reaching influence and significant impact on the conceptualization and under-standing of stress, they have been challenged (Cox, 1985). Research indicates, for instance, that responses to stimuli ('stressors') do not always follow the same pattern and can be stimulus specific and dependent on the type of hormonal secretion. For example, anxiety-producing situations are associated with adrenalin, whereas noradrenalin is released in response to aggression-producing events. Also, the GAS approach does not address the issue of psychological responses to stress, nor that a response to a potential threat may in turn become the stimulus for another response. In sum, the model is too simplistic. As Christian and Lolas (1985) suggested, the framework of the GAS is still valid for some typical stressors (e.g., the physical factors of heat and cold), but it is not adequate to explain psychosocial stress.

An additional problem associated with the response-based approach is that disagree-ment exists about the actual manifestations of stress, as well as about where in the organism or system stress is manifested: 'Is it in the single cell, in an organ or throughout the entire organism?... Biochemical, physiological or emotional functioning?... At the endocrine, immunological, metabolic or cardiovascular [level]?... Or in particular dis-eases, physical and psychological?' (Pearlin et al., 1981, pp. 341–2). Clarification of this issue is problematic because the findings of replication research are likely to be confounded. Individuals may adapt to any potential source of stress, so the response will vary over time (e.g., in the assessment of noise on hearing and performance).

Although the word stress usually has negative connotations, Selye (1976) emphasized that stress reactions are not automatically bad and that they cannot be avoided because being alive is synonymous with responding to stress. In fact, a certain level of stress is necessary for motivation, growth, development, and change and has been referred to as eustress. However, unwanted, unmanageable stressor situations are damaging and can lead to distress, or what we will refer to in this book as strain.

Because of their medical focus, which emphasizes the organism's response, Selye's approach and response-based definitions in general have also been criticized because they appear not to consider environmental factors in the stress process. In other words, there has been a tendency to ignore the stimulus dimension of stress experiences. The difficulties associated with the GAS prompted studies where the focus shifted to exploring the external conditions that lead to stress. The result was the formulation of a stimulus-based approach to defining stress, with the emphasis on identifying those events or aspects of events that might cause stress.

STIMULUS-BASED DEFINITIONS OF STRESS

Identification of potential sources of stress is the central theme of the stimulus-based model of stress (Goodell et al., 1986). The rationale of this approach is that some external forces impinge on the organism in a disruptive way. Stimulus-based definitions of stress have their roots in physics and engineering, the analogy being that stress can be defined as a force exerted, which in turn results in a demand or load reaction, hence creating distortion. If the organism's tolerance level is exceeded, temporary or permanent damage occurs. The aphorism 'the straw that breaks the camel's back' encapsulates the essence of stimulus-based definitions of stress. An individual is perpetually bombarded with potential sources of stress (which are typically referred to as stressors), but just one more apparently minor or innocuous event can alter the delicate balance between coping and the total breakdown of coping behavior (Cohen et al., 2016; Holmes & Rahe, 1967). In short, this model of stress treats stress as an independent variable that elicits some response from the person.

Rapid industrialization provided the initial impetus for this approach, and much of the early research into blue-collar stress aimed to identify sources of stress in the work environment in order to provide optimal working conditions (Cooper & Smith, 1985). Considerable attention was paid to physical and task circumstances (such as heat, cold, noise, and social density). However, it is now realized that focusing solely on objective measures of environmental conditions is inadequate. Individual differences, such as variability in tolerance levels and expectations, can account for the fact that two individuals exposed to exactly the same situation might react in completely different ways. This is a major weakness of the stimulus model. In fact, Lazarus (1966) stated that no objective criterion is sufficient to describe a situation as 'stressful' and that only the person experiencing the event can do this. Nevertheless, although the stimulus model has limitations, it is useful in identifying common stressor themes or patterns that might affect the majority of the workforce. In Chapter 3, we provide an overview of some of the more prevalent and pervasive stressors that are encountered in organizational contexts. However, as we shall discuss in more detail in later chapters (see especially Chapter 6), attention to the individual's perceptions and appraisal of the stressors is essential for determining whether the person is experiencing distress or 'strain'.

SHORTCOMINGS OF RESPONSE AND STIMULUS DEFINITIONS

Both the response and stimulus definitions of stress are set conceptually within a relatively simple stimulus-response paradigm. It is now recognized that they largely ignore individual differences and the perceptual and cognitive processes that might underpin these differences (Cox, 1990; Sutherland & Cooper, 1990). In short, response and stimulus definitions have proved to be taxonomic in nature, providing researchers with an opportunity to establish what are essentially lists of responses and situations (or events) that may fall under each definitional heading. Such definitions are important and necessary; however, as research into stress has advanced, approaches to defining stress have often failed because they are unable to provide a comprehensive 'theory of stress' or a context for considering the nature of the stress experience itself.

Specifically, three criticisms can be leveled at stimulus-response definitions. The first has already been mentioned – they reflect only one component of the stress process and say little about the process itself. Embedded within this criticism are concerns that in an attempt to explore the range of situations and responses that may give rise to stress, little attention (at least at the empirical level) has been given to the inherent properties of the different stimuli and responses themselves. For example, stimulus definitions have been important in identifying different categories of events that have the potential for causing stress (e.g., 'acts of God', 'critical life events', and 'daily hassles'). As a result, properties of the events themselves (such as their frequency, duration, demand, intensity, and severity) have been somewhat overlooked in the understandable drive to explore relationships between the mere occurrence of these different events and a range of stress responses.

Much the same can be said for response-based definitions. Because almost any response can be classified as a 'stress response', often responses are regarded as homogeneous, and little consideration has been given to the duration of the response or its pattern. Nor, for that matter, has much attention been paid to the idea that certain events may give rise to very specific responses. Therefore, to suggest that an event is not stressful may overlook the fact that researchers must pay more attention to the specificity of responses and their nature rather than simply concluding (perhaps erroneously) that no stress is present in such an encounter. Because stimulus-response definitions each focus on a single aspect of a relationship, it is only ever possible to conclude that an event has the potential to be stressful or that a response may be a stress response. A stimulus or a response can be declared as 'stressful' or a 'stress response' only when the two components are considered in relation to one another and the impact of one on the other has been determined. For this reason, as we shall see later in this chapter, contemporary stress definitions have focused first on the interaction between the stimulus and response and then on the process nature of stress itself.

The second problem that emerges when stress is defined simply in terms of a stimulus or response has also been alluded to. It is that these frameworks fail to account for individual differences. This criticism stems from the argument that knowledge of a stimulus condition, for example, does not necessarily allow exact prediction of a response because whether a stimulus is likely to produce a response depends on the moderating influences of individual differences (e.g., personality attributes, expectations, values, and goals), the context (e.g., levels of social support, control, and appraisal), and the person's role and status within the organization (e.g., tenure, function, level in the hierarchy, and job attributes). Much of this criticism can be summed up in the view that what is stressful for one individual may not be stressful for another. Chapter 6 further discusses potential moderators of job-related stress, including individual differences.

The third criticism is directed more toward the impact that such definitions have on understanding the stress process. This criticism is best expressed by the view that arbitrarily limiting the definition of stress to only one dimension of a process draws attention away from the nature of the process itself. As we have already discussed, stress involves both a stimulus and a response in relation to one another, and it is the relational nature of stress that should be the focus of any definition (Lazarus & Launier, 1978). When considered in these terms, the aim should be to point researchers toward those processes that link the individual with the environment. To accept that stress resides, not in any one component, but in the nature of the relationship itself should be the integrating point of any definition. Early efforts to examine this relationship built upon the notion of interaction between environmental stimuli and individuals' responses.

STRESS AS AN INTERACTION

The interactional approach to defining stress focuses on the statistical interaction between the stimulus (e.g., work overload) and the response (e.g., strain). This approach, described as 'structural' (Stahl et al., 1975) and 'quantitative' (Straus, 1973), is one where a relationship, usually correlational, is hypothesized between a stimulus and a response. This approach is essentially static (cause and effect), with any consideration of process being limited to inferential explanations when the interaction fails to materialize or is different from that predicted. A definition like this, which focuses only on the interplay between two variables, means that attempts to explain the complexity of such a relationship are limited to 'structural manipulations', such as the influence of a third moderator variable (e.g., social support), which again do not provide an explication of the stress process.

The above comments are not intended to imply that moderator analysis is not worth pursuing. However, as we shall see in Chapter 6, job stress research has investigated a very large array of moderator variables, sometimes with little theoretical rationale for their inclusion in a study's design, resulting in inconsistent and frequently ambiguous findings about the role of these variables. We suggest that it is important now to move beyond the simple identification of potential moderator variables to more comprehensive theories that attempt to also explain the mechanisms in the stress process. For example, job stress could rather be viewed as a transaction – an ongoing relationship between the individual and the environment. The interactional approach is limited in its ability to expose the causal pathways inherent in that relationship. In contrast, the transactional model of stress endeavors to explore the essential nature of stressor–response–outcome relation-ships and to encapsulate an understanding of the dynamic stress process itself, not merely the statistical relationship between variables.

STRESS AS A TRANSACTION

The transactional approach draws researchers toward identifying those processes that link the individual to the environment. What distinguishes this approach from earlier approaches is the emphasis on 'transaction' – identifying the processes that link the different components, recognizing that stress does not reside solely in the individual or solely in the environment but in the conjunction between the two, and accepting that no one component (i.e., stimulus, response) can be said to be stress (Lazarus, 1990) because each is part of, and must be understood within, the context of a process.

Whereas the interactional definition of stress focuses on the structural features of the person's interaction with his or her environment, transactional definitions are more concerned with the dynamics of the psychological mechanisms of cognitive appraisal and coping that underpin a stressful encounter (see Figure 1.3). As illustrated in Figure 1.3 there are two types of appraisal. From a transactional perspective (Lazarus, 1966), the experience of stress is defined first by the person's realization that something is at stake (primary appraisal). In the primary appraisal process, the individual gives meaning to an encounter. The meanings that best express this appraisal process are those involving harm, the threat of harm, or challenge. Once an encounter is appraised as being in some way a threat to the person's well-being, the secondary appraisal process begins. This process is concerned with the identification and availability of coping resources to deal with the threat, harm, or challenge (Lazarus, 1991). These two appraisals are the key to the stress-coping process (Dewe & Cooper, 2012).

Stress is, therefore, not a factor that resides in the individual or the environment; rather, it is embedded in an ongoing process that involves individuals transacting with

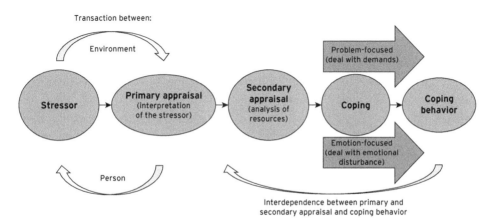

Figure 1.3   Transactional theory of stress

their environments, making appraisals of those encounters, and attempting to cope with the issues that arise (Bliese et al., 2017). At the heart of the transactional definition is the idea that stress is a dynamic cognitive state. It is a disruption in homeostasis or an imbalance that gives rise to a requirement for resolution of that imbalance or restoration of homeostasis (Dewe et al., 1993). What distinguishes this approach from other definitions is its emphasis on the process – on meaning, adjustment, and coping as core defining elements – and its focus on understanding the adaptive process itself.

The term 'transaction' implies that stress is neither in the person nor in the environment but in the relationship between the two (Lazarus, 1990). Stress arises when the demands of a particular encounter are appraised by the individual as about to tax or exceed the resources available, thereby threatening well-being (Lazarus, 1991) and necessitating a change in individual functioning to 'manage' the encounter. The transactional definition points to three important themes – a dynamic cognitive state, a disruption or imbalance in normal functioning, and the resolution of that disruption or imbalance (Dewe et al., 1993; Holroyd & Lazarus, 1982; Meurs & Perrewé, 2011; Newton, 1989). These themes provide a popular framework for modeling stress – particularly in general psychology – and for capturing what is believed to be the essence of the stress experience (Dewe & Cooper, 2017).

Thinking of stress in this way reveals a 'number of profound implications' (Lazarus, 1991, p. 6) for the way stress is researched and stress interventions are designed. It requires researchers to consider which research methods are appropriate for understanding the complexities of the stress process, how such knowledge should be applied, and the responsibilities we have to those whose working lives we research. Although the application of the transactional perspective to work settings is not without its critics (e.g., Brief & George, 1991; Hobfoll et al., 2018), and although it is not free of methodological concerns, job stress research 'can only benefit from the careful and thoughtful application' of this approach (Harris, 1991, p. 28).

It is clear that there is a gap between interactional and transactional approaches to defining stress and that the transactional perspective introduced a fundamental shift in how stress was conceptualized and researched. From an interactional standpoint (see Coyne & Gottlieb, 1996), constructs such as causes (stimuli) and consequences (responses) are 'detachable entities' capable of being described independently of each other and, when entered into a causal relationship, maintain a conceptual distinctiveness. From a transactional perspective, on the other hand, such constructs are defined relationally and ultimately become inseparable from the context within which the stressful encounter takes place. As Lazarus (1990) has illustrated, no one variable can be said to be 'stress', as they are all part of the transaction process, and an independent variable at one time may (as the encounter unfolds) be considered at another time as a dependent variable. For example, trying to predict what factors influence how people cope at one time makes coping a dependent variable, whereas other research may explore coping as a predictor of an individual's well-being and hence treat coping as an independent variable.

THEORETICAL MODELS OF JOB-RELATED STRESS

As early as 1970, McGrath (1987) urged researchers to approach the investigation of stress using theoretical models that would reflect the sequence of events in stress transactions as well as their interrelationships. The first step in determining how robust current models of work stress are in aiding our understanding of the stress process requires that we consider the context – the theoretical frameworks – out of which such models have emerged. These frameworks should provide not only a platform upon which research can be built but also a stimulus to research and theory building as we differentiate and elaborate the relevant constructs (Leventhal, 1997).

Much of the research on work stress has been carried out using an interactional framework, even though, as we will see later, attempts have been made to at least recognize within this context the dynamic-adaptational nature of stress. The issue here is the same as has already been discussed in relation to defining stress: that is, that the interactional perspective may not provide a sufficiently comprehensive framework to enable a full understanding of the stress process (Lazarus, 1990). Nevertheless, this approach has clearly been important in drawing attention to the separate constructs that play a significant role in understanding stress. Indeed, many of the studies described in this volume have been based upon this interactional perspective.

As outlined by Tetrick and LaRocco (1987), the work stress model that best characterizes the interactional framework postulates that the perceived presence of certain work conditions (see Chapter 3) may be associated with a number of stress responses (Chapter 4). This model also predicts that various organizational characteristics, situational factors, and individual differences can influence (moderate) this stimulus-response relationship (see Chapter 6). Generally, the model has resulted in three types of research applications (Dewe, 1991; Dewe & Cooper, 2017). These include (a) identifying, describing, and categorizing different stimuli; (b) demonstrating a relationship between the different categories of stimuli and responses; and (c) exploring the nature of that relationship by investigating the moderating influence of different organizational, job-specific, and individual-difference variables.

The aim of the discussion that follows is to briefly review a number of these models and to examine their contribution to our understanding of the stress process. Whether they can be categorized as 'interactional', 'transactional', 'balance', 'cognitive activation', and/or 'process' models is not of concern in the present context. Rather, we hope to illustrate the major thrust of each theory/theoretical model, the ways in which it has enhanced our knowledge of job-related stress, and which elements of the nature of stress it incorporates. Our selection of models is not exhaustive, but it does draw attention to a number of common features that reflect the domain within which work stress research takes place. Similarly, the intention here is not to engage in a detailed critique of these models but rather to consider the notion of person environment (P-E) fit, which is either implicitly or explicitly common to most models of work stress, and to consider how far the notion of fit can be taken as embodying the nature of the stress process.

A number of specific models have been identified to play an important role in developing the theoretical context for investigating work stress (e.g., Bliese et al., 2017; Dewe & Cooper, 2017; Meurs & Perrewé, 2011). Among others these include McGrath's (1976) stress cycle model, the P-E fit approach (French et al., 1982), Karasek's (1979) job demands-control model, the job demands-resources model (Bakker & Demerouti, 2007; Schaufeli & Taris, 2014), the conservation of resources model (COR; Hobfoll, 1989; Hobfoll et al., 2018), the challenge-hindrance model of stress (CHM; Cavanaugh et al., 2000), the effort reward imbalance model (ERI; Siegrist, 1996, 2010), and the cognitive activation theory of stress (CATS; Ursin & Eriksen, 2004, 2010).

There are several points of convergence among different frameworks, in particular the notion that stress entails a sequence of events that includes (a) the presence of a demand, (b) a set of evaluative processes through which that demand is perceived as significant and taxing in terms of its impact on individual resources or requiring from the individual something other than normal functioning, and (c) the generation of a response that typically affects the well-being of the individual (Kahn & Byosiere, 1992).

Despite general consensus on several of the above issues, there is less than complete agreement about the conceptualization and measurement of even the most well-established and researched constructs, such as demands and responses. Where there is agreement, however, it is most likely to be along the lines that (a) demands and responses can be understood only within the context of the evaluative processes that give significance and meaning to encounters; (b) it is through these processes that the individual and the environment are linked; (c) it is these processes that best express the nature of work stress; and (d) strain occurs when there is an imbalance between the demands of the encounter and the resources of the individual to manage those demands. Unfortunately, agreement on these points occurs mainly at the conceptual level, and there still seems to be considerable wrangling among researchers over how these evaluative processes should be defined and measured, how they should be incorporated into a work setting, and whether current methodologies can ever adequately capture their qualities.

McGraths Stress Model

The idea of a sequence of events and the concept of 'fit' can best be understood by considering the approaches adopted by the different models. For example, McGrath (1976) proposed a sequence of events where the demands of an encounter and its outcome(s) are linked through three processes: appraisal, decision making, and performance. The first of these (appraisal) concerns how the encounter is interpreted, the second (decision making) involves the selection of a response, and the third (performance) involves how well the encounter is managed. McGrath also referred to an 'outcomes process', which he described as the feedback mechanism through which the encounter is reappraised. In this model, 'imbalance' or 'misfit' occurs as a result of the individual's appraisal of events and occurs when the consequences of not meeting the demands are perceived as being significant.

The Person-Environment Fit Model of Stress

The P-E fit model of stress is perhaps the one that has been most widely discussed in the literature (Dewe & Cooper, 2017; Edwards & Cooper, 2013). In brief, this model proposes that strain occurs when the relationship between the person and the environment is out of equilibrium. That is, a lack of fit between the characteristics of the person (e.g., abilities, values) and the environment (e.g., demands, supplies) can lead to unmet individual needs or unmet job demands. These unmet needs or demands can in turn result in strain. The main point is that subjective P-E misfit – that is, how individuals perceive the encounter – increases the likelihood that strain will occur. Implicit in the notion of misfit is the individual's ability to manage an encounter, and elements like values, supplies, demands, and abilities, all of which help to determine the perceived misfit, could be described as representing aspects of a transactional process. The difficulty is that there is little in the way of empirical evidence to support this model, due to different forms and versions of fit, problems in clarifying the exact nature of misfit and appropriately measuring the constructs involved (Dewe & Cooper, 2017; Edwards & Cooper, 2013; van Vianen, 2018).

The Job Demands-Control (Support) Model

The job demands-control (JDC) model (Karasek, 1979) has been characterized as a leading model of work stress (de Lange et al., 2003; Meurs & Perrewé, 2011). The model is based on the proposition that the interaction between job demands and job control – referred to as job decision latitude and defined in terms of decision authority and skill level – is the key to explaining strain-related outcomes. In this model, strain occurs when high job demands, or pressures are combined with low decision latitude – a perceived inability to influence tasks and procedures at work. The concept of control has long been recognized as an important facet of the stress process. However, debate over how control should be operationalized, questions about how the interaction should best be measured, the lack of accounting for individual characteristics, as well as limited longitudinal research have generated mixed results (Kain & Jex, 2010; Taris et al., 2010). Karasek and Theorell (1990) further updated the model by adding social support (referred to as the job demands-control-support model; JDCS) as another relevant resource to determine individuals' responses to job demands (see Figure 1.4).

This extended model has received some support in being related to strain outcomes, although the buffering effect of control has only been modestly supported (e.g., de Lange et al., 2003; Dewe & Cooper, 2017; Häusser et al., 2010). A possible explanation may be that control has to be matched with the demands placed on employees in order to have a buffering effect (Häusser et al., 2010; Kain & Jex, 2010; Meurs & Perrewé, 2011). Another meta-analysis including 141 studies and 145,424 respondents, spanning three continents, 15 countries and 40 different occupations found that gender, nationality, and occupation also serve as moderators in the JDCS interrelationships (see Fila et al., 2017). We refer the reader to Chapter 6 for a further discussion of evidence concerning Karasek and Theorell's model and the role of control and support in the stressor–strain relationships.

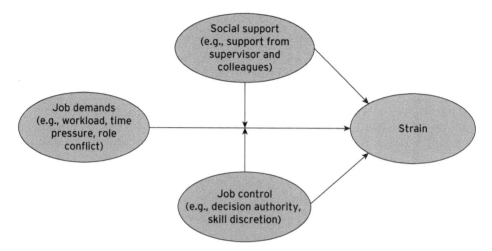

Figure 1.4   The job demands-control-support model

Source: Based on Fila et al. (2017) and Häusser et al. (2010).

The Job Demands-Resources Model and the Challenge-Hindrance Model of Stress

Another more recent extension of the job demands-control model is the *job demands-resources (JD-R) model* developed by Demerouti et al. (2001) and later revised by Schaufeli and Bakker (2004), Bakker et al. (2014), and Bakker et al. (2023). The model (see Figure 1.5) initially brought together two research traditions, namely work stress and job design (Bakker & Demerouti, 2007; Demerouti et al., 2001; Schaufeli & Bakker, 2004; Schaufeli & Taris, 2014) and the model matured to become a theory in the period between 2011 and 2016 (Bakker & Demerouti, 2017; Bakker, Demerouti & Sanz-Vergel, 2023). In this book we therefore interchangeably refer to the JD-R model, theory and/or framework. The main idea behind the model is that the specific work condition can be classified as either job demands (e.g., job insecurity, work overload, interpersonal conflict, time pressure) or job resources (e.g., social support, feedback, job autonomy), and any resource or any demand can influence employee health and well-being. Thus, the JD-R model is different from other stress models, such as the JDC model, which only include a limited number of job demands and resources as antecedents of job stress (Bakker & Demerouti, 2017; Bakker et al., 2023).

According to the JD-R framework, job demands are characterized as any 'physical, social, or organizational aspects of the job that require sustained physical or mental effort and are therefore associated with certain physiological or psychological costs' (Demerouti et al., 2001, p. 501). Demerouti et al. (2001, p. 501) describe job resources as any 'physical, social, or organizational aspects of the job that may do any of the following: (a) be functional in achieving work goals; (b) reduce job demands and the associated physiological and psychological costs; (c) stimulate personal growth and development'. According to JD-R, there are two psychological processes which play a part in the development of stress (see Figure 1.5) – the health impairment and the

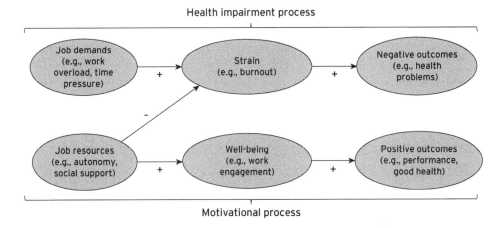

Figure 1.5   The job demands-resources model

Source: Based on Lesener et al. (2019), Schaufeli (2017), and Schaufeli and Bakker (2004).

energetic/motivational process (Bakker & Demerouti, 2017; Schaufeli & Bakker, 2004). In the health impairment process, the cost of high job demands are predicted to deplete employees' resources, which in turn facilitates energy impairment (disengagement and exhaustion) and health problems (Dewe & Cooper, 2017; Lesener et al., 2019; Xanthopoulou et al., 2007). On the contrary, in the energetic/motivational process, the benefits of job resources are theorized to foster development and growth as well as prevent energy depletion (Bakker & Demerouti, 2007; Lesener et al., 2019; Schaufeli, 2017; Schaufeli & Taris, 2014). Further, job resources are also proposed to diminish the negative influence of high job demands on energy depletion (Schaufeli & Taris, 2014). In the JD-R model, resources become particularly significant when the circumstances become more demanding; then the motivational potential of the resources is more likely to be applied as a strategy of coping (Bakker & Demerouti, 2017; Demerouti & Bakker, 2011). Personal resources such as self-efficacy and optimism have also been proposed to play a similar role to job resources, and based on the extensive JD-R research longitudinal studies have shown how the relationships between job demands, resources and well-being are both causal and reversed causal (see Bakker & Demerouti, 2017 for a review). In addition, personal demands (i.e., the requirements employees themselves set for their behavior and performance and which requires effort and may have certain costs), such as personal expectations, personal health threats, or workaholism have also been proposed to play a relevant role in the health impairment or motivational process (Britt et al., 2021; Demerouti & Bakker, 2022). Meta-analytical evidence focusing on longitudinal studies concludes that the JD-R model represents 'an excellent theoretical basis to assess well-being for a broad range of organizations' (Lesener et al., 2019, p. 1). The empirical evidence so far indicates support for both the motivational/growth process and the health impairment process (Bakker et al., 2023; Lesener et al., 2019; Schaufeli & Taris, 2014). Also, based on the theory and related research, a more complex version of the model (see Bakker & Demerouti, 2017) has been presented which incorporates both causal effects and reverse causal effects in both the motivational and health impairment processes. In the motivational process, job crafting (i.e., proactive changes employees do in terms of their job demands and resources) has been proposed and found to play a role in creating a gain spiral of resources (Bakker & Demerouti, 2017). In the health impairment process, self-undermining (i.e., behavior generating difficulties which impairs performance) has been proposed and found to create a loss spiral (Bakker & Demerouti, 2017). More recently, with the purpose of broadening the predictive value of the JD-R model to crisis situations (e.g., COVID-19), the scope of the model was expanded again (Bakker et al. 2023). Propositions concerning the role of various life domains including organizational, work, personal, and family demands and resources have been developed (see Demerouti & Bakker, 2022 and Bakker et al., 2023). According to the expanded JD-R theory and model, these life domains are interconnected, and constantly need to be regulated to ascertain a form of balance.

Another theory of stress has also been influential in the further development of the JD-R model (Bakker & Demerouti, 2017). This framework, referred to as the *challenge-hindrance model of stress (CHM)*, emphasizes – in line with scholars such as Selye (1956) and Ursin and Eriksen (2004, 2010) – that job stress also has beneficial qualities and that it is important to consider and understand the duality of stress (Cavanaugh et al., 2000; LePine, 2022; Mazzola & Disselhorst, 2019; O'Brien & Beehr, 2019; Podsakoff et al., 2023). Originally, the CHM draws on a resource theory referred to as the conservation of resources theory (COR; described below) (Hobfoll, 1989). However, later the focus of the model turned more toward the transactional theory with its emphasis on appraisal (O'Brien & Beehr, 2019; Webster et al., 2011). According to CHM workplace, stressors can be divided into two distinct categories. Challenge stressors (e.g., time demands, responsibility, workload) characterize demands which facilitate a sense of accomplishment and performance opportunities (Cavanaugh et al., 2000). Hindrance stressors (e.g., role conflict, political barriers, role ambiguity) describe demands which are likely to thwart performance or interfere with the individual's goals (Cavanaugh et al., 2000). These stressors have found to relate differently to various outcomes – challenge stressors predict some positive outcomes (e.g., job satisfaction, commitment, engagement), while hindrance stressors predict negative outcomes (e.g., turnover intentions, turnover, withdrawal behaviors) (e.g., Lepine et al., 2005; Pod-sakoff et al., 2007; Webster & Adams, 2020). However, in a recent meta-analysis, Mazzola and Disselhorst (2019) found that although challenge and hindrance stressors were similarly related to performance and engagement, they were both consistently negative for physical health, counterproductive work behavior, and psy-chological strains. The authors therefore concluded that embracing this model as a prominent stress model may be premature, particularly given this lack of consistency in results patterns. Another issue is that the same stressor has been found to be both slightly hindering and slightly challenging (LePine, 2022; Webster et al., 2011). Thus, arguing for the existence of either challenge or hindrance stressors may be risky

(O'Brien & Beehr, 2019). This is also the case with respect to stressor appraisal; the same stressor may be appraised as both challenging and hindering (Webster et al., 2011).

With respect to the JD-R model and the CHM, there are several areas that need further attention in future research. For example, there is a need to further clarify whether demands are perceived as challenging (positive) and/or hindering (negative), whether demands and resources are valued similarly, and whether particular demands or resources interact with each other (e.g., Bakker & Demerouti, 2017; Cavanaugh et al., 2000; Crawford et al., 2010; Dewe & Cooper, 2017; LePine, 2022; Lesener et al., 2019; O'Brien & Beehr, 2019). Also, the emphasis on distinguishing between job resources/demands and personal resources/demands (e.g., workaholism, perfectionism) and how they may be interrelated, how employees craft and shape their jobs, and how this may affect perceptions of demands and resources and their application, as well as the existence of dynamic relations (reverse and reciprocal relationships) in the JD-R model, all illustrate central areas for additional research (Bakker & Demerouti, 2017; Lesener et al., 2019; Schaufeli & Taris, 2014). Additionally, how available resources may liberate high levels of motivation or may not necessarily be motivating in highly demanding conditions requires further research (Bakker & Demerouti, 2017). Webster et al. (2011) found that stressors relate to various outcomes (i.e., turnover intentions, strains, and job dissatisfaction) through challenge and hindrance appraisals (i.e., primary appraisal). Accordingly, they suggest extending the CHM framework to include the role of challenge and hindrance appraisals, which contradicts the initial idea of COR. Still, the role of secondary appraisal (i.e., evaluation of personal coping capabilities in a certain situation) in the CHM framework is not yet clear and could facilitate a starting point for future research questions (Webster et al., 2011). Furthermore, by drawing on the transactional theory of stress (Lazarus & Folkman, 1984) and its emphasis on threat appraisal (when situations are perceived to potentially cause personal loss or harm), Tuckey et al. (2015) proposed the importance of introducing a distinction between *threat* (anticipated harm or loss to the self) and hindrance (obstacles to goal attainment) stressors and appraisals to the CHM framework. Such an approach is referred to as a *three-dimensional challenge-hindrance-threat framework* for stressors and stress appraisals. Based on two studies, the authors (Tuckey et al., 2015) found support for a distinction between threat, hindrance, and challenge stressors and appraisals. Also, these stressors and appraisals were found to predict distinct outcomes. This underlines the relevance of applying various theoretical approaches (i.e., transactional theory and CHM) to stress in an integrative way to achieve potentially more accurate knowledge on the nature of the stress process (see also Podsakoff et al. 2023 for a review).

The Conservation of Resources Theory

The *COR theory* (Hobfoll, 1989; Hobfoll et al., 2018) focuses on the gain and loss of resources, where resources are the personal characteristics – such as personal traits and key skills; energies – such as money, time, and knowledge; objects – such as tools for work and vehicles; and conditions – such as tenure, having an appreciated work role, and employment – which are valued by individuals (Hobfoll et al., 2018). The basic emphasis of the model is that 'individuals strive to retain, protect and build resources and that what is threatening to them is the potential or actual loss of these valued resources' (Hobfoll, 1989, p. 516). According to COR, resources are the main necessary units to understand stress. Environmental events are suggested to threaten or trigger depletion of individuals resources, where COR emphasizes the objectively stressful nature of events and how these are complicated sequences which may occur over time (Hobfoll et al., 2018). Stress is regarded as a result of an actual or threatened loss of resources or lacking resource gain following an investment of resources. COR theory offers an understanding into the opportunities resources offer for individuals' adaptation and growth, the importance of and how resource pools facilitate development, how experience fosters learning, how resources engender goal achievement, the role of resources as coping strategies, and their relevance with respect to crossover (resource exchange), as well as stress management and interventions (Dewe & Cooper, 2017; Hobfoll, 2002; Hobfoll et al., 2018). With respect to stress and strain, empirical evidence has shown that individuals are more likely to experience strain (e.g., burnout, depression, physiological outcomes) when they lose their resources at work (Halbesleben et al., 2014). Still, the motivational component of COR also suggests that employees tend to try to avoid resource loss as well as cope by investing in resources, which also has been supported by empirical evidence (e.g., Halbesleben, 2007; Hobfoll, 2001; Whitman et al., 2014).

There is still a need for future research to clarify aspects such as how employees determine the value of their resources, how resources fluctuate, what characterizes resource conservation and acquisition processes, what role individuals themselves and those surrounding them play in the development of resources, how resource focused interventions can result in employee resource change and subsequent outcomes, as well as time dynamics – e.g., amount of time of resource gain or loss (Halbesleben et al., 2014; Hobfoll et al., 2018).

What is not clear in the theories presented so far is the duration of the stress experience and the role of previous confrontations with a stressful situation (Meurs & Perrewé, 2011). Also, the importance of future expectations related to stress experiences may play a vital role. This has been neglected in models presented so far.

The Effort Reward Imbalance Model

Another theoretical stress model – the effort reward imbalance (ERI) model (Siegrist, 1996) – has achieved considerable attention in the organizational stress literature (e.g., Eddy et al., 2016; Eddy et al., 2017; Meurs & Perrewé, 2011; van Vegchel et al., 2005). The ERI model (see Figure 1.6) builds on the idea of social exchange and social reciprocity which is the core of the work contract imposing particular efforts (job demands/ obligations) on employees which are to be executed in exchange of rewards (e.g., money, career opportunities, and esteem) (Siegrist, 2010).

The main concerns of the ERI model are the stressful features of the work contract (Siegrist et al., 2004). An example is when the excessive effort invested by an employee is not reciprocated by equitable rewards, thus creating an ERI. Such imbalance evolves

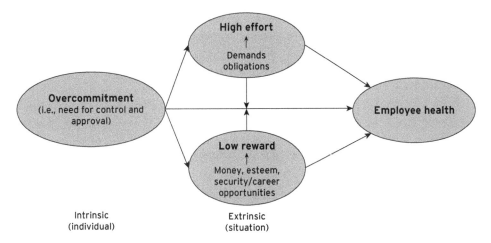

Figure 1.6 Effort reward imbalance (ERI) model

Source: Based on van Vegchel et al. (2005).

when employees gain fewer rewards than they thought they deserved (Siegrist, 1996). In such a *high cost-low gain* condition, employees are likely to experience strong negative emotions due to the perceived reward deficiency (Siegrist et al., 2004). If recurrent, such conditions are likely to create negative stress reactions and subsequent sustained strain (Siegrist, 2010; van Vegchel et al., 2005). This situation becomes even more intense for individuals who are characterized to have a high need for approval and a motivational pattern of extreme work-related commitment, also referred to as *overcommitment* (Siegrist et al., 2004; van Vegchel et al., 2005). This is because the overcommitted individuals have a greater inclination to exaggerate their efforts beyond what is formally expected/needed or to more commonly expose themselves to high job demands (Siegrist et al., 2004). As shown in Figure 1.6, overcommitment influences employee's perception of high effort and low reward, and indirectly employee health. Because overcommitment can be very exhausting in the long run, it is also thought to predict employee health directly (van Vegchel et al., 2005). ERI theory predicts that the highest risk of poor health is when ERI (extrinsic) interacts with overcommitment (intrinsic).

The ERI model of work-related stress has been applied to predict several outcomes such as behavioral outcomes (e.g., absenteeism, alcohol consumption, smoking), job-related well-being (e.g., burnout, job satisfaction, work motivation), physical health outcomes (e.g., cardiovascular disease), and psychosomatic health symptoms (e.g., depression) (Eddy et al., 2017; van Vegchel et al., 2005).

It should be noted that the ERI model may be explained by *cognitive activation theory of stress* (CATS; Ursin & Eriksen, 2004), which we describe in the next section. CATS offers an explanation for why we may expect negative health outcomes from an ERI (Eriksen, 2017). According to CATS, ERI concerns a discrepancy between *normal situation (set) values* and what is *happening in reality (actual) values* (see Chapter 2 for more explanation). This discrepancy is likely to result in sustained activation (brain arousal) and may in turn result in various maladaptive health- and work-related consequences (Reme et al., 2008). This is only expected when the reward has high affective value and the ERI is long-lasting (Reme et al., 2008).

The Cognitive Activation Theory of Stress

What is intriguing about *CATS* (Ursin & Eriksen, 2004) is that it addresses aspects which other organizational stress theories have struggled to explain. These include how stressful experiences can be potentially favorable, whether and how experiences of stress facilitate learning, how time plays a role in stress experiences and how individuals' responses to stressors are directed by their expectancies (Meurs & Perrewé, 2011). CATS defines stress based on four components (Eriksen, 2017; Ursin & Eriksen, 2004); (1) *the stress stimuli (stressor)* – these are demands or threats which the individual is exposed to in a given situation; (2) *the stress experience* – this is the demand/stressor/situation (threatening or pleasant) experienced and appraised by the individual and beliefs about how to respond; (3) *the (nonspecific) general response to the stress experience* – this is the alarm response which increases brain arousal, enhancing wakefulness to prepare problem/stressor solving; (4) *the experience (feedback) of the stress response* – following a response to a stressor individuals receive feedback regarding the results of their response; this feedback affects the feeling of being stressed and can adjust perceptions of the stressor and/or consequence expectancies concerning future experiences.

According to CATS stress is not necessarily assumed to be detrimental. Rather the experience of stress can have both *negative* (straining effects) and *positive* (training effects) *consequences* for the individual, and these are driven by individuals' expectancies (Meurs & Perrewé, 2011; Ursin & Eriksen, 2010). To what extent a stressor is perceived as pleasant or threatening depends on the individual's appraisal. This appraisal is contingent upon previous experiences and the expectations the individual has of the outcome – that is how they believe that they will cope with the particular situation (Meurs & Perrewé, 2011). One of the most important reasons for a reduction in a stress response is *learning* from the situation. For example, a study of employees facing downsizing showed that the survivors of previous organizational changes, developed positive outcome expectancies based on their past experiences (Svensen et al., 2007). This suggests that learning facilitates reduced uncertainty and either positive or negative *expectancies* for future outcomes of potentially stressful situations. In addition, and related to learning, the stress response progresses over *time*. When an employee is unable to cope with stressors, arousal levels become prolonged and the impact of a stressful situation is likely to become extended (Meurs & Perrewé, 2011). On the other hand, employees with effective ways of coping with stress are likely to only experience brief arousal (Meurs & Perrewé, 2011). Empirical evidence suggests that individuals who have a poor ability to recover from stressors may experience prolonged arousal and ill health (Harris et al., 2007). In line with the transactional model of stress, appraisal is an important aspect of CATS, because employees develop expectations through appraisal. These expectations regulate whether a stimulus becomes a stressor and whether employees contemplate that they can cope (Meurs & Perrewé, 2011; Ursin & Eriksen, 2004).

The theoretical propositions of CATS have so far mainly been tested and supported in nonorganizational domains (Meurs & Perrewé, 2011), except for a study on the role of goal clarity and organizational stress conducted by Arnetz (2005). Future research therefore needs to clarify the relevance and features of the theory in organizational settings. Perhaps an integration of the other organizational stress models with CATS can facilitate a more complete picture not only of the maladaptive characteristics of stressful experiences, but also the adaptive characteristics.

Is It Relevant to Incorporate Various Stress Theories and Models?

Hobfoll's critique of Lazarus and Folkmans (1984) transactional stress theory is specifically related to the relevance of appraisal – where what is stressful is suggested to be what is perceived as stressful. According to Hobfoll and colleagues (2018), such an understanding will require waiting until after an event to recognize what is stressful. They therefore argue that stress appraisal theories, which also includes CATS, are either nonpredictive or idiographic. They even go so far as to state that 'arguing that stress is that which is appraised as stressful is classist, sexist, and racist' (Hobfoll et al., 2018, p. 104). In our view, the incompatibilities between COR theory and the transactional theory (see Hobfoll, 2001; Lazarus, 2001) may instead contribute to pose interesting research questions, in which other theoretical stress frameworks may be helpful. For example, one may question what makes an individual appraise a stressor as a hindrance or a challenge, what initiated this discrepancy (O'Brien & Beehr, 2019) – how much is a result of individual differences in perception and how much is a result of the situational stressor? Drawing on CATS could for example also help to answer such questions by more closely investigating what is going on in the brain when individuals experience various stressors (see Chapter 2). Therefore, the various theories we have presented so far are not necessarily competing, rather there may be aspects of all of these theories which may be helpful in increasing our understanding of the nature of stress (see Figure 1.1). Following Lock's (1996) suggestion to incorporate multiple theories in an integrative way can be beneficial to future organizational stress research, accumulation of organizational stress related knowledge, and a more complete and balanced understanding of the nature of stress.

The models presented so far draw attention to a number of themes that may provide a common pathway for research and a better understanding of the stress process and its application to work settings. The first theme is that of a misfit, mismatch, or imbalance between the person and the environment. All of the above models are based upon a fundamental premise that strain occurs when there is a misfit, mismatch, or imbalance between the demands of the situation and the resources of the individual. The issue facing researchers is agreeing on what exactly the nature of that misfit is. Three factors are crucial: The misfit must be perceived (by the individual) as salient and significant, it must represent a threat to the person's well-being, and it must require actions over and above normal functioning. One criticism that can be aimed at many of these models is that although they identify some of the structural components that precipitate a misfit, they frequently fail to identify those elements that characterize the nature of the misfit and that link the person and the environment. Agreeing on the nature of that mismatch is important because it forces researchers to focus on process issues.

How Can We Understand the Stress Process and Its Implications?

Although the pervasiveness of references to stress in the popular media as well as in academic publications may help in drawing attention to the issues involved, some of the discussion and suggestions that have emerged have made it almost impossible at times to separate findings from fiction and research from anecdote, to the extent that to the casual observer it is questionable whether being under stress is any different from simply being alive. For those engaged in research, it is not difficult to identify a sense of frustration growing out of the fact that it always seems necessary to spend so much time defining stress when there are far more important issues to confront (Beehr & Franz, 1987; Bliese et al., 2017). Some researchers have even contended that stress is too large a phenomenon and too all-encompassing to investigate (Schuler, 1980).

This has not deterred research interest in the phenomenon. However, it is also clear that the current level of interest and popularity that surrounds the idea of stress is not always helpful. Defining stress is not meant to be a tortuous academic exercise in semantics far removed from the 'real world', nor should it be viewed as some sort of initiation process that all researchers have to go through. Definitions provide a context, a sense of coherence, and a framework for understanding research findings. More importantly, as researchers we have a moral obligation to those whose working lives we wish to explore. This obligation requires that we give thought to how stress can best be defined so that research captures the reality of the stressful encounter and is relevant to and reflects the experience of those who are being researched. In short, to fail to give careful consideration to what we mean by stress may well trivialize encounters that 'affect adversely the psychological well-being of most persons exposed to them' (Brief & George, 1991, p. 16).

It is important to tread a middle ground, where stress is not regarded as causally linked to all ills and is not seen as the root cause of all social problems. When it does occur, however, stress can leave individuals emotionally drained and often more vulnerable to other illness and disease. However, stress can also facilitate learning and growth and lead to adaptive outcomes such as well-being. The real issue is not whether there is too much or too little stress in people's lives but how we can understand the stress process and its implications for the management of stress. The complexities involved in developing this understanding should not be oversimplified by inadequate consideration of what we are trying to research, nor should they be trivialized by exaggeration of the issues involved.

There is an extensive body of research working to redress this balance. Sophisticated techniques have been developed to obtain data on biochemical, neuroendocrine, and electrical systems of the body, and computer-based statistical analysis enables simultaneous investigation of many parameters and variables. As we shall discuss further in Chapter 4, researchers should explore both the subjective and objective measurement of stress. Understanding the explanatory potential that resides in both types of methodologies would allow a more balanced approach to emerge that aims to establish the most appropriate methods for unraveling the stress process. Longitudinal and multilevel analysis has increasingly been applied and may also become an even greater feature of future research. Continual refinement of traditional research methods and exploration of the utility of new methods will enable job stress researchers to evaluate the appropriateness of different methodologies for understanding and exploring the totality of the stress process.

EMERGING THEMES IN STRESS RESEARCH

How stress should be defined should by now be recognized as important. Definitions provide a framework for understanding why different approaches have been adopted, the results that have emerged, and, as knowledge has accumulated, their relative strengths and weaknesses and how future research may be directed. Contemporary definitions point to the relevance of identifying those processes that link the individual with the environment. This approach, though accepted at the theoretical level, has yet to receive a more complete treatment at the empirical level.

Adopting a more balanced perspective means that no one variable can be said to be stress (as in the more traditional approach to defining stress) because, as Lazarus (1990) has articulated, stress 'has been defined as a continually changing relationship between person and environment' (p. 4). This book draws attention to critical issues in the conceptualization, measurement, and understanding of job stress in the context of people's working lives and their lives overall. In particular, when considering stress research, contemporary practice and procedures may need to be reviewed, taking into account the following issues.

What is being measured? Two questions stem from consideration of this issue. The first is, 'Whose reality is being assessed?' and the second asks, 'Do measures actually assess what they purport to?' By considering these questions, attention is drawn not just to how adequate current measures are in expressing the nature of stress but also to whether existing methods can capture the complexities of the stress process. Following from this is the more complex (and perplexing!) question of how the stress process should be investigated.

How appropriate are current methodologies? This, as will be discussed later, is not about whether one methodology is better than another but rather about what methods should be used to best capture the stress process. This issue inevitably requires some discussion of the roles of qualitative and quantitative methodologies. Here we need to consider two questions (which are raised in Chapter 9): 'Where are current methodologies taking us?' and 'What can alternative methodologies provide?' For instance, qualitative methods reflect a richness in their approach to data gathering and analysis and should be viewed as offering a number of insights into interpretation and understanding separate from those provided by quantitative methods. If a distinction is made between description (quantitative) and meaning (qualitative), then the convergence of both approaches offers a balance and draws on the strengths of both approaches to unravel the complexities of the stress process.

What does all this mean in practice? Specifically, what are the measurement implications of considering stress research from various theoretical perspectives? This question can be answered in a number of different ways. At the construct level, there is a need to develop measures that capture important facets of the stress process and to ensure that all key facets of that process are assessed appropriately. At the systems level, the question is, 'How can we capture the changing person-environment relationship?' (Lazarus, 1990, p. 4). Although we will address these two issues in more detail later, they are raised here to draw attention to the need for a two-phased strategy in stress research. Phase 1 entails getting the construct measurement right. Researchers should resist the temptation of wanting to measure the process before adequate consideration has been given to construct measurement. Phase 2 requires consideration of the role that a construct plays within a complex system that encompasses reciprocal causality and contains changing moderating and mediating relationships. This is a much more difficult task. In the following chapters, we reflect upon some of the critical issues involved.

In summary, adopting one of the more contemporary theoretical perspectives (e.g., COR, JD-R, CATS) requires reconsideration of traditional measurement practices and research designs. At the heart of the matter is the need for theory-based measurement (Bliese et al., 2017; Meurs & Perrewé, 2011) aimed at capturing the nature of the stress process itself. Researchers must acknowledge that this aim may be achieved only following a period of 'quiet reconstruction' during which accepted traditions are critically examined in terms of how best they express that process. They must also consider how appropriate different methodologies are in describing the subtleties of the stress process. This consideration may differ depending on whether the focus of the research is at the construct or the systems level, whether the aim is to describe events or determine their meaning. Whatever the level of analysis, stress research can no longer stand apart from such issues if advances are to be made in our understanding of the stress process. With this view in mind, the remaining chapters are designed to stimulate thought about what needs to be done and how best that may be achieved.

Chapter 2 addresses how stress is acknowledged to be an important matter in neuroscience research (Godoy et al., 2018). The aim of the chapter is to briefly introduce the reader to organizational neuroscience (e.g., Becker et al., 2011; Waldman et al., 2017) in connection with organizational stress, i.e., the implications of brain science for workplace behavior with an emphasis on stress. We will discuss how theories of organizational stress phenomena can benefit from incorporating empirical findings, methodologies, and overarching themes from neuroscience, particularly the networks of brain systems and processes responsible for organizational stress and related attitudinal and behavioural outcomes. We also attempt to present some directions for future research concerning organizational stress and the application of neuroscientific techniques (Murray & Antonakis, 2019).

We begin in Chapter 3 with a review of environmental factors that may function as sources of stress. As noted above, these variables are referred to as stressors, and it is important to be aware of the impact of various kinds of stressors on individuals in the workplace. Equally important, however, is an understanding of individuals' reactions or responses to these stressors, which we discuss in Chapter 4. Following other theorists (e.g., Beehr and his colleagues), we refer to these reactions as strains. They represent the physiological, psychological, and behavioral response of individuals to threats upon their well-being. In Chapter 5, we outline the phenomenon of burnout, a special form of strain that has been studied particularly in relation to human service occupations, although in recent years it has also been investigated in other occupational groups. Factors that induce burnout and potential consequences of burnout are examined in this chapter.

Chapter 6 identifies several variables that may serve as either buffers (alleviators) or exacerbators of stressor–strain relationships. Job stress research has explored a number of these moderator variables, and in Chapter 6 we review the findings of this research and discuss mechanisms that may be responsible for moderator effects.

In Chapters 7 and 8, we turn to the issue of stress management. Chapter 7 analyzes the stress-coping behaviors of individuals and reviews research that has been conducted on the use and effectiveness of coping strategies. Chapter 8 is based on the premise that organizations share the responsibility for stress management and that interventions at the organizational level may be needed to address the effects of certain kinds of stressors, especially those over which individuals may have little control. Methodologies for evaluating the effectiveness of stress management interventions are discussed in this chapter.

Chapter 9 focuses attention on a range of methodological issues that confront researchers of job-related stress. We review various research designs, their strengths and limitations, and examine whether existing methodologies are capable of providing a satisfactory assessment of the stress-coping process. In this chapter, we also raise suggestions on how the outcomes of job stress research may be optimized.

The final chapter in this volume, entitled 'The Changing Nature of Work', reflects upon the ever-changing context in which individuals' function, in particular how technological, environmental, economic, political, and sociocultural forces shape the way in which work arrangements (and hence jobs) are being restructured. Here we posit that changes in workplace environments have tended to be dominated by technological and economic imperatives and that there is a need for greater application of perspectives that also emphasize psychological and sociocultural dimensions of work experiences. Ultimately, the design and maintenance of workplace environments that enhance individual well-being, as well as contribute to organizational productivity, is a major challenge that confronts practitioners and researchers alike.

We hope that this volume, and the issues explored within it, will stimulate debate and discussion among the community of stress researchers. Job stress research is embarking upon an exciting period in its history as we move into a century that promises to open up new, and perhaps very different, workplace arrangements. We do not purport to hold all the answers – rather, our aim is to raise some significant questions about research in this field and to challenge researchers to reflect upon their theories, frameworks, and empirical activities.

2

ORGANIZATIONAL STRESS AND THE BRAIN

Why is the brain important for understanding organizational stress processes? An answer to this question is that the brain is considered to be 'the master controller of the interpretation of what is stressful and the behavioral and physiological responses that are produced' (McEwen, 2000, p. 172). Thus, the brain represents the 'cognitive machinery' (Becker et al., 2011, p. 934) behind our work related experiences, whether they are stressful or not.

This chapter about organizational stress and the brain is brand new and was not included in the first edition of the book. We have decided to include this new chapter because as stated above, the human brain plays an important role in understanding the organizational stress process (cf. Lovallo, 2016; McEwen & Gianaros, 2010; Meurs & Perrewé, 2011; Waldman et al., 2017). The brain is involved in both the perception and interpretation of stressors, the physiological, emotional, cognitive, and behavioral responses to stressors, and the brain may itself be altered, both structurally and functionally, by stressors (Lovallo, 2016; McEwen & Gianaros, 2010; O'Connor et al., 2021; Ursin & Eriksen, 2010). Another reason is that stress is acknowledged to be an important matter in neuroscience research (Godoy et al., 2018) which more recently has been emphasized as an important area for organizational scholars and research to embrace (e.g., Becker et al., 2011; Murray & Antonakis, 2019; Waldman et al., 2017).

The aim of this chapter is to introduce the reader to organizational neuroscience (e.g., Becker et al., 2011; Waldman et al., 2017) in connection with organizational stress. Neuroscience is the in-depth study of the nervous system and in particular the human brain. An underlying framework under the 'umbrella' of social cognitive neuroscience (Lieberman, 2007) is the so-called organizational neuroscience (Becker et al., 2011). Organizational neuroscience can broaden the understanding of organizational processes and individuals at work (Butler et al., 2016; Waldman et al., 2017). In terms of organizational stress, organizational neuroscience contributes by bringing in an additional level of analysis, to the organizational, group/collective, and individual levels, that is individuals' discrete brain processes (Becker et al., 2011), to better understand the central role the brain plays in explaining the organizational stress process and potential outcomes of it. For example, organizational neuroscience can contribute to the understanding of how events at work can influence employees' internal bodily states (e.g., appraisal processes) during stress responses (Lovallo, 2016).

It should be noted that this chapter will not cover all biological aspects which are part of the field of neuroscience (e.g., synapses, neurons etc.). Rather, the chapter gives a basic and simplified introductory overview of the human brain in terms of the particular networks of brain systems and processes, which are responsible for and associated with organizational stress processes. We will present a selection of theories that emphasize the important role of the brain in understanding organizational stress, as well as discuss how theories of organizational stress phenomena can benefit from incorporating overarching themes, methodologies, and empirical findings from neuroscience. Particularly we focus on the networks of brain systems that are associated with organizational stress and related affective, cognitive, attitudinal, and behavioral outcomes. We also attempt to present a brief overview of research conducted on organizational stress and the brain, as well as present directions for future research concerning organizational stress and the application of neuroscientific techniques (Murray & Antonakis, 2019). Although the field of neuroscience has been embraced by several social science fields (e.g., marketing, economics, and more recently organizational behavior), we believe there is great potential for organizational stress research to explore the implications of brain science for organizational stress and stress/strain-related outcomes. Bridging organizational neuroscience with psychological theories of organizational stress can be an interesting future direction, particularly when it comes to nonconscious processes and their relevance for the organizational stress process (cf. Becker et al., 2011).

ORGANIZATIONAL STRESS AND ORGANIZATIONAL NEUROSCIENCE

In line with an organizational neuroscience perspective, the brain perceives stressors (e.g., work overload, destructive leadership, time pressure) and determines physiological and behavioral responses to these (McEwen & Gianaros, 2010). Therefore, the brain is considered to be the central organ of organizational stress and organizational stress adaptation (McEwen, 2019). The brain contributes to decide what is stressful to the individual by supporting stress appraisal processes, both conscious and unconscious. As a result of the stress appraisal, the brain controls health promoting or health inhibiting behavior (McEwen & Gianaros, 2010; Ursin & Eriksen, 2004).

Multiple systems and areas in the brain are involved and interact with each other in the stress process with the aim of restoring balance and dealing with the threat. Notable areas of the brain that have received attention by researchers in the stress process are the prefrontal cortex, the amygdala, the hypothalamus, the hippocampus, and more recently the thalamus.

The prefrontal cortex is part of the cerebral cortex and is located at the front of the frontal lobes. In the evolution of the brain, the prefrontal cortex has shown a massive and disproportionate high expansion (e.g., higher number of cortical neurons) compared to other areas of the brain (Kaas, 2013). The primary function of the prefrontal cortex is 'the representation and execution of new forms of organized goal-directed action' (Fuster, 2015, p. 8). The prefrontal cortex is essential in the executive control of the brain and is involved in functions such as working memory, planning, decision-making, inhibitory control, and priming brain structures to perform an act (Fuster, 2015). To accomplish this, the prefrontal cortex has the capacity to flexibly integrate information from both cortical and subcortical areas due to extensive functional neural network connections across the brain. The prefrontal cortex is suggested to have a top-down modulation of attention, in so doing applying prior knowledge and memory, more than strictly sensory driven attention (Fuster, 2015; Sneve et al., 2019). The prefrontal cortex is thus a central area in the brain that both makes sense of the stressor and is involved in deciding the response to the stressor.

The *amygdala is* a group of nuclei (i.e., cell groups) that is located in the medial temporal lobe and considered to be part of the limbic system of the brain. The amygdala receives multiple connections from across the brain and is involved with processing of emotional information, as well as regulation of other cognitive functions such as attention and memory (LeDoux, 2007). Endocrinological changes in response to stressors may lead to increased consolidation of threatening or emotionally loaded experiences through the activation of amygdala (Roozendaal et al., 2009). Thus, threatening experiences, such as giving a job talk in front of a non-supportive audience, are remembered more vividly and longer than are mundane experiences, such as walking to the coffee machine.

The *hypothalamus* comprises less than 1% of the total volume of the brain and thus is a small subcortical brain structure which is recognized to be a target of stress hormones (e.g., cortisol; McEwen & Gianaros, 2010). By coordinating the so-called endocrine system and autonomic nervous system (ANS), the hypothalamus (and the brainstem) can regulate the individual's internal environment (e.g., heart rate) to cope with a certain stressor (Reeve, 2015).

In addition to the hypothalamus, the *hippocampus* (see Figure 2.1), located in the medial temporal lobe, often known as the brain system which supports different forms of memory and mood (McEwen, 2016), was one of the first, besides the hypothalamus, to be recognized as important for the regulation of stress hormones (McEwen et al., 1968). The hippocampus has receptors for glucocorticoids (i.e., hormones), which may have both protective and damaging effect on the hippocampus (McEwen, 2001). The hippocampus is highly interconnected to other areas of the brain, such as the prefrontal cortex and the amygdala.

The *thalamus* is considered to have many important functions by acting as a sensory center between other subcortical nuclei (augment cortical processes; located beneath the

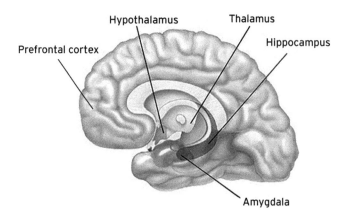

Figure 2.1   Midsagittal view of the human brain

cerebral cortex) and the cortices (i.e., cerebral cortex), contributing to cognition, wake and sleep awareness, as well as motor control (Lovallo, 2016; Yoshii, 2021). The thalamus is considered unique in terms of being involved in stress responses and stress recovery (Reinelt et al., 2019). In addition to receive information about the arousal state of the individual, the thalamus receives inputs from the hypothalamus and brainstem. The connectivity with cortical regions and the activation in the thalamus have been linked with learning processes that underlie behavioral flexibility (Wolff & Vann, 2019; Zhu et al., 2018). Therefore, it is speculated that the thalamus may be involved in stress-based learning processes (Reinelt et al., 2019). A recent study found that stress-related changes in the thalamus were more pronounced in participants with stronger stress responses in subjective stress (Reinelt et al., 2019).

Two physiological systems that have received extensive attention in the stress process is the *sympathetic-adreno-medullar (SAM)* axis and the *hypothalamic-pituitary-adrenal (HPA) axis*. While the SAM response to stress is instant, the HPA initiates a more delayed response. An extensive review of these two systems is beyond the scope of this chapter, thus, interested readers are referred to for instance *The Handbook of Stress: Neuropsychological Effects on the Brain* edited by Cheryl D. Conrad (2011).

The SAM axis is an autonomic response system activated by several brain regions, including the amygdala and the hypothalamus, resulting in the release of catecholamine hormones (i.e., epinephrine and norepinephrine) by the adrenal medulla and the secretion of norepinephrine from sympathetic nerves. The effect of these hormones is immediate and pervasive throughout the body, and often referred to as the 'fight-or-flight' response. The response of the SAM involves among other things dilation of pupils, increased respiration and heart rate, and the postponing of digestion and colon activity to permit more blood to the muscles.

The hypothalamic–pituitary–adrenal (HPA) axis is activated by the secretion of corticotrophin releasing factor by the hypothalamus, resulting in the release of adrenocorticotrophic hormone (ACTH) by the pituitary gland. ACTH is transported by the blood supply to the adrenal cortex, where it initiates the production of the glucocorticoid cortisol. Research has suggested that cortisol has a prominent and sophisticated role both in adapting to stressors and to the normal functioning of the body (McEwen, 2018). In the stress process, cortisol release results in the organism's increased access to excess energy and decreased inflammation. The activation of the HPA axis may be prolonged over extended amounts of time. Together, the SAM and HPA allow the body to respond to stressors in an adaptive way.

In the next sections, we will present a selection of theories, some of them presented in Chapter 1, to illustrate how some stress theories have embraced and incorporated the neuroscience perspective to understand stress.

THE TRANSACTIONAL THEORY OF STRESS

The transactional theory of stress, which we also described in Chapter 1, elegantly explains how employees' transactions with the work environment can engender emotions, which trigger particular work-related stress responses. Through appraisal processes (primary appraisal – evaluation of a work event as threatening or challenging; secondary appraisal – evaluation of available coping resources) employees evaluate to what extent the work events (e.g., holding a public presentation) that they experience are threatening or not, as well as whether they are familiar or not. Based on the appraisal process, behavioral strategies are generated which may be successful or not.

Lazarus and Folkman (1987) did not initially address the role of brain systems in the appraisal process. Still, by drawing on the transactional theory of stress, Lovallo (2016) has attempted to specify plausible brain system mechanisms involved in the various aspects of the transactional stress model, particularly related to appraisal processes. In relation to primary appraisal, it is relevant to consider the path of sensory information which is sent from the sense organs to the thalamus (Lovallo, 2016). In terms of stress responses and recovery, the thalamus acts as the dominant coordination center for most incoming information which in turn is directed to the primary cortical projection areas – i.e., receive information/input from the sense organs (Zhang et al., 2019). Most likely through a sensory arousal effect, the thalamus is also involved in memory and sleep regulation which can be affected by stress (Yoshii, 2021; Zhang et al., 2019). Incoming visual and auditory information pass from the primary cortical projection areas through a series of association areas of the cortex (Lovallo, 2016). Accordingly, raw sensory information is progressively expounded and connected with stored memories. In combination with memories, the amplifications of sensory input are accountable for giving individuals' perceptions of object-like qualities which are recognized as either familiar or unfamiliar (Lovallo, 2016). Furthermore, different streams of sensory information (auditory and visual) converge, and an elaborated stream is transmitted to the inferior temporal gyrus – i.e., involved in high cognitive functions, including emotion regulation, language and visual awareness; one of three gyri of the temporal lobe (Lin et al., 2020). The affective side of the primary appraisal involves the amygdala – the emotional center of the brain – which is essential as a memory system for emotionally laden and fearfully laden events (McEwen & Gianaros, 2010). The memory system will influence the individual's evaluation of a work-related event as threatening or challenging. Thus, both cognitive and affective sides of the appraisal process are essential to understand psychological stress reactions.

During secondary appraisal, the hippocampus and amygdala, which have complementary and parallel functions, are involved. The hippocampus plays an active role in learning and remembering declarative information, while the amygdala helps individuals outline emotional memories and based on experience adjust responses (Lovallo, 2016). Together with the hippocampus, the amygdala is crucial in building up and storing familiar experiences and their motivational meanings (Lovallo, 2016; McEwen & Gianaros, 2010). Specifically, the hippocampus helps individuals to recall what happened with respect to a previously stressful work-related event (e.g., I lost my voice while holding an important presentation at work), while the amygdala facilitates the recall of what previously stressful work-related experience felt like (e.g., I felt anxious). Thus, recalling what previously happened and how it felt is likely to influence the secondary appraisal where individuals evaluate available coping resources, the subsequent plan of action, and evaluation of potential costs or benefits in the evaluation of potential outcomes.

In sum, the highest level of control over individuals' homeostatic functions (i.e., striving to self-regulate and adjust to stressful events) is exercised through psychological appraisal processes. We believe that future research may clarify and explain organizational stress by combining theories such as the transactional stress model and organizational neuroscience. This may broaden our understanding of positive and negative organizational stress, and how to enhance work related health and well-being.

In the next section, we discuss allostatic load theory which highlights the brain as a central mechanism in stress processes.

ALLOSTATIC LOAD THEORY

Allostasis refers to the organism's active process of adapting to stressors by the adjustment of various physiological systems (such as autonomic, metabolic, and immune system) that act together in complex and non-linear ways to restore equilibrium (balance). Thus, allostasis is the process of maintaining stability and balance through change. Physiological agents and hormones mediate the effects that stress can have on the body (McEwen, 2000). In the short run they may have adaptive and protective effects, but a mismanaged, over-produced, or prolonged physiological activation in response to stressors can also have a cost by leading to allostatic load, often referred to as the 'wear and tear' on the body. Thus, allostatic load may be the result of both the repeated response to stressors, lack of adaptation of the response, prolonged response activation, or inadequate response to stressors (McEwen, 2007). Allostatic load is understood as 'the cumulative pathophysiology that can result from this dysregulation and excess stress' (McEwen et al., 2015, p. 1353). Allostatic load may speed up disordered physiological processes associated with disease (McEwen, 2000). In Chapter 4, we discuss various strain indicators of the allostatic load process.

The adequate secretion of hormones involved in the stress process promotes adaption and protects the body in the initial stage of stress. However, prolonged elevations or imbalance of these hormones may potentially have maladaptive and damaging effects on the brain together with other bodily systems. Thus, while the brain is involved both in the perception and physiological activation when confronting stressors, the brain is also shaped by the stress experience. Seminal research beginning with McEwen and colleagues in the 1960s showed that glucocorticoids (e.g., cortisol) had receptors in the hippocampal area of the brain, a region involved with memory and mood regulation, suggesting that this specific area was also affected by the secreted glucocorticoids (McEwen et al., 1968). Early research suggested that exposure to severe stress may lead to shrinkage and loss of dendritic spines in the hippocampal area (McEwen et al., 2015). The line of research that ensued has shown that stress experiences, if encountered at developmental vulnerable years or if they are pronounced in magnitude or time, may have both structural and functional effects on several regions of the brain (McEwen & Morrison, 2013; McEwen et al., 2015).

Several areas of the brain are changed by stress through multiple mechanisms. Importantly, these mechanisms often interact in nonlinear ways, where the effect of one mechanism might depend upon the effect of multiple other mechanisms or distort the responses of other mechanisms (McEwen et al., 2015). Neuroscience research has relied upon both animal studies and human studies (both clinical studies and neuroimaging studies) to understand how the brain is altered by the experience of stress. A review by Arnsten (2009) suggested that while even mild uncontrollable stress impairs the functionality of the prefrontal cortex, structural changes of the prefrontal cortex may follow after chronic exposure to stressors. These architectural changes of the prefrontal cortex involve both areas within, but also the signaling pathways to other areas of the brain such as the hippocampus (Cerqueira et al., 2007). Initially, researchers suggested that chronic forms of stress may lead to atrophy, or cell death, especially in the hippocampal area through the cascading toxic effects of glucocorticoids in the brain (Sapolsky et al., 1986). Research on healthy subjects also suggests that perception of high levels of chronic stress is related to decreased hippocampal volume (Gianaros et al., 2007; Gray et al., 2014). Thus, exposure to stressors may have degenerative effects such as reduction of the brain volume. More recent research also suggests that exposure to stressors may have toxic effect on the hippocampal and the prefrontal cortex, and possibly suppress their interconnectivity (Lucassen et al., 2014). There is also evidence suggesting that ordinary stress, such as preparing for an important exam, negatively affects the functional connectivity of the frontoparietal network, but that these changes are reversible after a period of recovery (Liston et al., 2009). Thus, students should allow themselves a relaxing summer holiday when possible!

While the exposure to stressors may lead to cell death in some parts of the brain, it may also lead to hypertrophy, or cell growth, in other parts. One area of the brain that experiences a morphological change is the amygdala, which in response to repeated stressors may respond with increased number of spines, dendritic growth, and neuronal remodeling (Roozendaal et al., 2009). The enhanced amygdala activation may lead to improved consolidation of affective memories, which is highly beneficial in the short term given the importance of remembering threatening situations to learn to avoid them in the future. However, the structural changes in the amygdala in response to intense or chronic stressors may lead to malfunctioning neural pathways (such as the hippocampus and the prefrontal cortex) involved in the regulation of the stress response (Arnsten, 2009). Furthermore, while the structural changes in the hippocampal area is suggested to be reversible, the amygdala does not seem to readjust or change back to its original morphology, suggesting more permanent changes (Roozendaal et al., 2009). However, research that examines the effect of interventions (mindfulness-based stress reduction) suggest that when perceived (negative) stress is reduced, so is the grey matter density of the amygdala (Hölzel et al., 2010).

Another potential mechanism is that stress impairs both cell proliferation and adult neurogenesis (i.e., generation of neurons from the neural stem cells) in parts of the hippocampal area, more specifically, the dentate gyrus. Thus, stressors inhibit the production of new neurons in the hippocampus and thus reduces the plasticity and functional properties (e.g., memory consolidation and mood regulation) of the brain (Toda et al., 2019). A functional adult neurogenesis is also shown to be important for an adaptive regulation of the HPA axis, which involve endocrine and behavioral responses to stressors (Snyder et al., 2011).

Lastly, stress has also been shown to affect the expression of genes, either by temporary changes or more enduring ones. Animal studies suggest that characteristics of the stressors, such as novel or successive, affect how genes are expressed in the hippocampus. Or as Gray et al. (2014, p. 1171) stated 'a history of stress exposure can permanently alter gene expression patterns in the hippocampus and the behavioral response to a novel stressor'.

To summarize, multiple brain areas and circuits are involved both in processing and responding to a stressor. Further, research suggests that the brain itself is a dynamic organ that shows structural plasticity and is shaped in multiple ways by stressors. There is a reciprocal feedback system, where areas of the brain instigate a response and may over time also be changed by the response. While some of the changes may sound irreversible and maladaptive, most research notes that the immediate responses in themselves constitute an adaptive process that in the long run may be taxing for the brain (and the body). It is important to note that most of these studies examine profound or chronic stressors, and there is little evidence that normal stressors experienced in daily life affect the brain in equal magnitude (McEwen, 2018). Nevertheless, in some jobs or for some people, job stressors may be of such a character that the functionality and structure of the brain are modulated in response.

In the next section, we will address cognitive activation theory of stress (CATS) and how CATS explains the role of the brain in explaining the stress process.

COGNITIVE ACTIVATION THEORY OF STRESS (CATS)

CATS does not share the concerns emphasized by *allostatic load theory* where the repetition of brief exposures to allostatic load (alarm and arousal) is expected to have detrimental effects on the healthy individual (Ursin & Eriksen, 2010). CATS rather proposes that essential elements of all complex brains are arousal and stress, and that stress assumedly is an adaptive response (Ursin & Eriksen, 2004). Therefore, while individuals handle difficult tasks, alarm and arousal that are short lasting, do not have a detrimental effect on the healthy individual. According to CATS, the real concern appears when arousal occurrence is sustained with no solution as it may lead to disease (Ursin & Eriksen, 2010; Wyller et al., 2009). Stress responses represent normal activation responses which result in an increase in arousal and subsequent somatic (i.e., bodily) and behavioral change. These are mediated by mechanisms described in psychoendocrinology (i.e., the study of the relationship between endocrine function and mental states/mental illness), psychophysiology (i.e., the study of the relationship between physiology and psychology), and psychoimmunology (i.e., the study of the relationship between the mind, the nervous system, and the immune system) (Ursin & Eriksen, 2004). CATS does not add new insights related to those mechanisms; instead, CATS contributes to a systematic understanding of the *psychological mechanisms* that explain *when* the alarm arises and when it may become maladaptive (Ursin & Eriksen, 2004). In the next sections, we therefore present the theoretical arguments presented by CATS and the role of the brain in understanding the stress process from a CATS perspective.

As briefly explained in Chapter 1, CATS defines stress based on four aspects, (1) the stress stimuli, (2) reports of the stress experience, (3) the nonspecific general stress response (increase in arousal), and (4) the experience of the stress response (feedback to the brain from the response) (Ursin & Eriksen, 2004, 2010). The *stress stimuli* or so-called stressors are the demands and threats that individuals are exposed to in various situations, and these are evaluated by the brain (Ursin & Eriksen, 2004). To what extent work-related stressors (e.g., high workload, change processes, long working hours, time pressure, unemployment etc.) are appraised as threatening, hindering, or positively challenging depends on how the individual appraises the situation. The appraisal of for example high workload (stressor) will according to CATS be based on employees' previous *experiences* – i.e., what they have previously learned – as well as their expectations of how they believe they will be able to cope with the situation (the outcome) (Eriksen, 2017). CATS emphasizes that demands and thoughts related to conditions outside of the work setting will also contribute to affect whether a certain situation (stressor) at work will trigger a stress response or not.

In terms of the *stress experience*, the brain stores relations between stressors as well as between stressors and responses, and it is this learned information which CATS refers to as expectancy (Ursin & Eriksen, 2004). For example, when an employee's brain has established that a high workload precedes feelings of exhaustion and lacking professional accomplishment (see Chapter 5), the brain 'expects' such responses (i.e., feeling exhausted, feelings of lacking accomplishment) after situations of high workload. The brain filters all stressors before they get access to the response system, which explains why individuals can react very differently to the same stressor (Eriksen, 2017; Ursin & Eriksen, 2004). CATS describes two such *filters in the brain*, one in relation to stimulus expectancies (i.e., defense mechanisms) and the other in relation to response outcome expectancies (i.e., coping, helplessness, hopelessness). *Stimulus expectancies* in the form of psychological defense mechanisms have the purpose of protecting individuals from becoming overwhelmed and they are proposed to be unconscious (Eriksen, 2017; Meurs & Perrewé, 2011). Under threating conditions, defense mechanisms may keep the threat unconscious and subsequently buffer the stress response or maintain low levels of activation (arousal). Psychological defense mechanisms can be both positive – e.g., keeping cool under a crisis/catastrophe – but also negative – e.g., being too relaxed in a critical work situation in which one should be stressed to mobilize action (Eriksen, 2017).

Coping behavior (see also Chapter 7) is produced by the alarm. According to CATS, *response outcome expectancies* in the form of coping (the individual feels able to handle the threatening situation with a positive result) dampen the stress response, while helplessness (no relationship between what the individual can do and the outcome) and hopelessness (all action leads to devastating results) sustain it (Ursin & Eriksen, 2010). When coping behavior is expected to facilitate positive results, the alarm is either reduced or removed. However, when there is no coping, the two expectancies helplessness or hopelessness occur (Meurs & Perrewé, 2011; Ursin & Eriksen, 2004). In terms of the arousal effects of hopelessness and helplessness, the amygdala and its connections with the hypothalamus are involved (LeDoux, 1993; Ursin & Eriksen, 2004). Through sustained arousal and/or lacking motives for engaging in a positive lifestyle, the states of hopelessness and helplessness may lead to somatic disease (Ursin & Eriksen, 2004). In that way, CATS may contribute to explain social differences in work-related health.

The *stress response* is a general alarm in the homeostatic system which is responsible for creating a general increase in wakefulness and brain arousal (activation), as well as specific responses to handle the reasons for the alarm (Meurs & Perrewé, 2011; Ursin & Eriksen, 2004). This occurs in a very fast process when there is a divergence between what is expected (normal situation values) and what really exists (what is happening in reality-values), i.e., current sensory information is compared with stored brain information (Ursin, 2009). All brains have many such normal situation values with corresponding actual values (Ursin & Eriksen, 2004). Finally, the alarm (or stress response) gives feedback to the brain through a feedback loop. One source of information is feedback to the brain from the individual's arousal (Eriksen, 2017).

Short-term arousal (phasic activation) is likely to have training effects (Meurs & Perrewé, 2011). However, if the stress response is sustained, sensitization (i.e., a psychobiological mechanism explaining why some individuals get more sensitive than others to a variety of stimuli such as work related stressors), extreme fear-based learning, and changes in functional brain networks are potential consequences, subsequently leading to strain (Meurs & Perrewé, 2011; Munk et al., 2021). Therapeutic cognitive techniques (change ways of thinking and behaving, e.g., learning to accept that one gets nervous and that it may be a good thing when performance is at stake) may be helpful in the process of influencing how the feedback to the brain is interpreted and subsequently reduce arousal (Eriksen, 2017; Ursin & Eriksen, 2010).

CATS theory has mainly been applied in other fields than organizational stress research, and there is still a need to clarify its application and relevance in organizational settings (Meurs & Perrewé, 2011). We believe that there are several avenues for future research considering the CATS theory and organizational neuroscience. Given that organizational stress is not viewed as detrimental to the individual by default, it is relevant to clarify the long-term consequences of adaptations to organizational stress and positive results of organizational stress. From a neuroscience perspective, we may question what characterizes the brain areas and circuits involved in both processing and responding to a work-related stressor in positive versus negative organizational stress processes? Further, how do negative appraisals become positive experiences and how does learning influence long-term organizational stress activation and future appraisals of work-related stressors? How can organizational neuroscience help clarify these issues as well as the role of anticipatory organizational stress (e.g., worry) which is so far less commonly researched?

To our knowledge, there are no studies in the organizational psychology field which draw upon CATS theory and organizational neuroscience. We see great potential for bridging these perspectives to understand more clearly the positive and negative organizational stress processes and the involved brain areas. Perhaps most importantly, CATS may be an intriguing theory to draw upon to further clarify the role of unconscious processes from an organizational neuroscience perspective (Becker et al., 2011). An extension to the original CATS theory, proposed by Brosschot et al. (2005), is to account for the mechanism that causes negative expectancy to be prolonged. Perseverative cognition, defined as 'the repeated or chronic activation of the cognitive representation of stress-related content' (p. 1045), is such a mechanism which may explain prolonged arousal or activation (Brosschot et al., 2005). We discuss this matter further in the section about future research directions.

METHODS OF ORGANIZATIONAL NEUROSCIENCE

Basic methods of organizational neuroscience (e.g., electroencephalogram–EEG; functional magnetic resonance imaging—fMRI) may be helpful for organizational stress research. The methods use various techniques to facilitate detailed information on how the brain works. Such methods are well described in a recent special issue on organizational neuroscience (Murray & Antonakis, 2019), and we refer the interested reader to the articles published there for more details and a thorough discussion. We will however briefly present two of the most commonly applied approaches for the study of brain activity including some of their strengths and weaknesses.

One of the oldest method to study brain activity is the electro-encephalogram (EEG) in which electrodes are attached to the scalp of individuals to measure electrical activity in the brain, that is brain wave patterns (Camerer et al., 2005; Jack et al., 2019). Another popular, and more recent, imaging technique is functional magnetic resonance imaging (fMRI) which measures blood flow in the brain by applying changes in blood oxygenation level of bold – blood oxygenation level dependent (BOLD) signal (Jack et al., 2019;

Loued-Khenissi et al., 2019). Both EEG and fMRI allow the comparison of brain activity among individuals performing an experimental task and a control task. Different brain activity in response to different tasks provides an indication of the brain regions that are activated by the experimental task (Camerer et al., 2005).

These methods have strengths and weaknesses. For example, a strength of EEG is that it directly can screen neural activity; however, a limitation is that it only can measure outer activity in the brain (Camerer et al., 2005). Compared to fMRI, EEG does not have the same sensitivity to neural activity in all brain regions (Jack et al., 2019). The strength of the fMRI method is that it facilitates better spatial resolution (i.e., number of pixels utilized in image construction) than EEG, however a limitation is that the temporal resolution (i.e., duration of time) is poorer because the blood flow to active brain areas occurs with a time lag (Camerer et al., 2005; Jack et al., 2019). Jack et al. (2019) propose that fMRI should be the preference, particularly for exploratory research designs.

In sum, organizational neuroscience methods may help inform existing organizational stress theory, although researchers must learn from previous errors conducted in the field of organizational neuroscience and make mindful and informed choices with respect to the appropriate neuroscientific techniques to apply. Hybrid approaches which draw on the strengths of various neuroscientific techniques may have great potential (Camerer et al., 2005).

RESEARCH ON ORGANIZATIONAL STRESS USING EEG AND FMRI METHODS

For the purpose of this chapter, we searched for published research on organizational stress and organizational neuroscience research applying EEG and fMRI methods. We applied Google scholar and various databases (e.g., EBSCO host, PsycINFO, etc.) for our search. It was hard to come across such studies, particularly studies that were conducted in real work settings. We also reached out to the Academy of Management Organizational Neuroscience community to ask for guidance. We received very helpful responses from three scholars.[1] They referred us to various interesting studies, although a review of all of them goes beyond the scope of this chapter. In this section we emphasize some examples of research and the information from our literature search and what these scholars directed us to. However, it should be noted that there seems to be a need for more research bridging organizational stress and organizational neuroscience. As emphasized by one of the scholars, the challenge with investigating organizational stress by applying methods such as fMRI and EEG is how the measurement platform influences stressor perception and the stress response. He gave the illustrating example of how it is impossible to put a police officer in an fMRI scanner while dealing with a difficult arrest.

---

[1]We thank Nina Nesdoly, Dr. George Christopoulos, and Gareth Shackleton for their very helpful and kind responses.

Therefore, experimental stressors may be more convenient to apply while studying organizational stress.

Combining brain imaging techniques and common experimental stressors is not without problems. For example, the Trier Social Stress Test (TSST; Kirschbaum et al., 1993) is an experimental stressor developed for the application in standard laboratory settings. TSST induces stress by asking participants to make an interview-style presentation. The presentation is followed by a surprise arithmetic test that is to be conducted in front of an interview panel. The panel members do not give encouragement or feedback. The TSST was developed over a long time to make sure that it would produce a consistent HPA axis response in human participants, particularly given the significant role the HPA axis plays when experiencing stress and also because HPA axis dysfunction is associated with various health related disorders. Although this test is considered to be the gold standard of experimental stress research (Allen et al., 2017), it should be noted that the test mainly gives information on the participants neurobiological response to *acute* stress. It is argued to not be well suited to brain imaging approaches, such as fMRI that requires the participant to lie inside a scanner (see Allen et al., 2017 for an overview of other limitations). Thus, the main focus on acute stress may also be a limitation, particularly when one is interested in investigating forms of stress that are not acute. As a better opportunity to combine with fMRI (and positron emission tomography; PET), the Montreal Imaging Stress Task (MIST; Dedovic et al., 2005) has been developed, in which the participants in the stress condition are asked to complete an arithmetic task which is somewhat above their mathematical skill (Allen et al., 2017). The MIST has been found to be useful for studying effects of stress perception and processing on brain activation changes in fMRI studies (Dedovic et al., 2005). However, from the interest of understanding organizational stress, one may ask if the application of such tests in fact can capture organizational stress?

Based on our literature search, at least one study was conducted in a real work setting. That study investigated construction workers and measured workers stress in construction sites by applying EEG (Jebelli et al., 2018). The study showed that a field stress recognition procedure, where they used a wireless and lightweight wearable EEG device and an EEG signal processing framework which reduces noises, can be applied for an early detection of workers stress under various work-related stressors. The strength of the study was that it was conducted in a real work setting, and the fact that it was not only focusing on acute stress. A potential limitation was the very limited sample size and also that different brain wave patterns were evident among the participants while they faced the same stressors. Also, a clear organizational stress theoretical framework did not seem to be evident. This may question the practical implications of the study and may also pose the question whether it is at all possible to generalize the findings and practical implications from the study. Still, what is intriguing about this study is that it illustrates that it possible to measure workers stress in a real work setting with affordable equipment. Thus, is future research may draw on this approach and connect it more clearly to organizational stress theory.

In another experimental study (using fMRI) of participants struggling with chronic stress (attributed to working 60–70 hours per week over several years), Golkar et al. (2014) found that compared to a control group (i.e., healthy volunteers with no history of chronic stress), participants who suffered from chronic organizational stress showed an impaired ability to down-regulate negative emotion and they also had weaker functional connectivity between the amygdala and the mesial prefrontal cortex (mPFC). Both amygdala and the mPFC are key brain structures for composing defensive reactions to threats from the environment, including stressors (Golkar et al., 2014). Drawing on the Maslach and Leiter burnout framework, the researchers also found that the participant's burnout scores interacted with functional connectivity between amygdala, the thalamus, and a minor part of the hypothalamus. The connectivity increased in strength the higher levels of chronic organizational stress participants experienced (Golkar et al., 2014). Although this was a cross-sectional study, the findings are interesting because they indicate that a dysregulation of the emotion and stress processing networks in participants who suffer from chronic organizational stress, prevents a restoration of their internal homeostasis response to negative emotional stress. The struggle to down regulate negative emotions may potentially make individuals who experience chronic organizational stress more susceptible to experience depressive symptoms (Golkar et al., 2014). Although more future research is needed, the findings of this study may facilitate a starting point for a better understanding of the relationship between chronic negative organizational stress and ill health. Perhaps the novel approach applied in the Jebelli et al. (2018) study is a fruitful future opportunity to explore in order to make sure that organizational stress is captured, and not only acute stress.

Further, despite the scarce amount of organizational stress/fMRI/EEG studies, there exists a few studies which look into flow, a state which is characterized by a person being fully absorbed in an activity (Csikzentmihalyi & Csikzentmihalyi, 1988), and flow-proneness as a positive stress (eustress) state (e.g., Barros et al., 2018; Kavous et al., 2019; Ulrich et al., 2014, 2015). For example, Ulrich et al. (2014) found that the higher the subjective experience of flow, the greater the decrease in neural activity in the amygdala. One may speculate that flow and flow proneness as positive stress states contribute to more positive emotions and thus reduced activity in the amygdala (Ulrich et al., 2014). Such studies on flow and flow proneness as positive stress states may give inspiration to the design of future studies interested in exploring positive organizational stress with fMRI or EEG.

IMPLICATIONS FOR STRESS THEORIES AND FUTURE RESEARCH DIRECTIONS

We have so far presented a selection of theories attempting to explain the organizational stress process considering neuroscience perspectives. However, most of the existing studies are conducted with a focus on stress in general, not organizational stress processes. By drawing on organizational neuroscience, future organizational stress research may address several interesting topics and questions. In the following sections, we will present a selection.

First, we highlight the importance of *nonconscious (automatic) processing*, as the brain often responds to stressful events without conscious (controlled) involvement of the mind. As opposed to conscious processes – in which individuals can be aware, are able to control and intentionally initiate and guide – in nonconscious processes individuals are typically not aware, they cannot control, and initiatives are taken unintentionally (Bargh, 1994). Although nonconscious processes are hidden, such implicit and internal influences may play a significant role in shaping appraisals, coping strategies, behaviors, etc. The initial responses following triggering stimuli (e.g., stressors) are according to the dual-process model generally nonconscious, particularly in terms of emotional responses (Levesque et al., 2008), which are likely to be triggered in a stress process (cf. Lazarus & Folkman, 1987; Lovallo, 2016). Processes that are conscious are essential to temper the expression of a nonconscious process (Levesque et al., 2008). Organizational researchers should be aware that there is a distinction between what is perceived by the brain and what the individual is aware of perceiving (Becker et al., 2011). Accordingly, more research on the role of nonconscious processes is needed for a better understanding of organizational stress. More knowledge about automatic processes is useful because they contribute to successful adaptation and self-regulation (Bargh & Williams, 2006). Future research may address questions such as What characterizes nonconscious processes and what are the implications of these processes for organizational stress? What role do conscious and nonconscious brain processes play in determining whether individuals engage in challenge versus hindrance appraisal of stressors?

Interestingly, empirical evidence suggests that individuals who are more aware or mindful are less susceptible to nonconscious processes (Levesque et al., 2008). This may partly explain the beneficial outcomes of mindfulness-based stress-reduction training, which has been shown to increase regional grey matter density in the prefrontal cortex, cerebellum, and hippocampus – the regions of the brain involved in emotional regulation, memory and learning processes, perspective taking, and self-referential processing (McEwen, 2019). Further, studies on the hippocampus have found that it has capacity for plasticity (McEwen & Gianaros, 2010). There is a need for longitudinal studies that determine organizational stress related changes that are independent of pre-existing individual differences in hippocampal volume and function.

Leaders and their employees spend a large amount of time working. In so doing, as described in Chapter 3, they are likely to experience a host of different job stressors. These job stressors may be acute or chronic in nature, have different levels of intensity, or put physical, emotional, and cognitive demands on the workers. Our current understanding of how the brain responds to and may be changed by these different types of 'ordinary' stressors is limited. It is unclear to what extent the brain modulates its functionality and structure in response to chronic job stressors. Combining organizational stress theory and organizational neuroscience, it may be possible to further clarify whether and how various types of job stressors affect the brain in different ways. For example, with new forms of work arrangements such as extensive work in the evening or from home (see Chapter 10), with the possible consequence of decreased recovery, there is a need for additional knowledge on how this may affect the brain (e.g., endocrine balance). Recovery refers to the process of restoring and gaining new resources that have been depleted during work (Sonnentag & Fritz, 2007). Previous research has shown that some individuals find it more difficult than others to recover after stressful situations and that recovery may be considered as a form of prolonged arousal (Brosschot et al., 2005; Meurs & Perrewé, 2011). Thus, other interesting topics for organizational stress research to explore are the potential causes of such sustained arousal and prolonged experiences of stressful work-related events from an organizational neuroscience perspective. For example, according to CATS, the health and well-being of individuals are only threatened by sustained arousal, and extended activation may be the result of an exacerbation of stressful experiences – i.e., preservative cognition – which is revealed in phenomena such as rumination, worry and anticipatory stress (Brosschot et al., 2005). Preservative cognition concerning stressful events are likely to happen partly through unconscious processes (e.g., during sleep) and may help explain prolonged experiences of stressors and subsequent sustained arousal (Meurs & Perrewé, 2011; Pieper & Brosschot, 2005). Organizational neuroscience may be helpful to explore these ideas further and clarify what happens in the brain and to what extent preservative cognition plays an important role in the organizational stress process.

Drawing on the literature on general stress it may also be relevant to clarify how social factors such as social support may benefit brain circuits that are affected by chronic work-related stress and allostatic load (McEwen & Gianaros, 2010). Such an approach would give the opportunity to consider both organizational neuroscience and organizational stress theory (e.g., the job demands-control-support model).

Conclusion

With this chapter we hope to trigger the interest of students, scholars, and practitioners to consider the link between organizational stress and organizational neuroscience. Although there are psychological stress theories that already include ideas from neuroscience (e.g., CATS), we believe there is great potential for a better understanding of the organizational stress process by considering an additional level of analysis, i.e., where individuals are deconstructed to discrete brain processes (Becker et al., 2011). An advantage of applying organizational neuroscience to understand organizational stress processes is that it may facilitate more precise measurement as well as enhance the ability to predict various phenomena related to organizational stress. Still, it should be noted that ethical concerns (i.e., neuro-ethics; privacy, confidentiality, informed consent; inadvertent discovery of potential medical or pathological issues to research participants or their employers) should be considered in the decision of conducting organizational stress research by applying organizational neuroscience methods (Waldman et al., 2019).

3

JOB-RELATED SOURCES OF STRAIN

An important aspect of stress-coping is awareness of the events, issues, and objects (including people) that may function as *stressors* (sources of strain) for individuals. Lazarus and Folkman (1984) have argued that strain occurs when environmental demands or constraints are perceived by a person to exceed his or her resources or capacities. Stressors may be either of chronical nature (e.g., long-lasting duration) or episodic incidents (e.g., particular events).

Determinants of strain can generally be grouped into three major categories: job-specific sources, organizational sources, and individual (personal) sources. In this chapter, we focus on environmental rather than individual (within-person) factors, but this does not imply that the latter are not important. Indeed, there is an extensive literature, especially in social and clinical psychology, that highlights the salience of dispositional traits and states (such as Type A behavior disposition and neuroticism) for the experience of strain, and in Chapter 6, we consider some of these variables as potential moderators of stressor-strain relationships. For the present, however, we concentrate on factors that lie external to the individual and that can impinge upon their experience of workplace-related strain.

Traditionally, researchers have grouped stressors into various categories. To give an overview that covers a range of various categories of sources of strain, we will use the differentiation of six primary work-related stressors developed by Cartwright and Cooper (1997) which is much in line with more recent categorizations (e.g., Sonnentag & Frese, 2012):

1   Factors intrinsic to the job itself
2   Roles in the organization
3   Relationships at work, such as those with supervisors, colleagues, and subordinates
4   Career development issues
5   Organizational factors, including the structure and climate of the organization as well as its culture and political environment
6   The home–work interface

The first five of these categories relate to stressors within the workplace environment, whereas the sixth focuses on the interplay between the job and life off the job. Our intention here is not to provide an exhaustive description of all potential stressors within each category but to highlight some of the critical factors that have been explored in research and to illustrate the relationship between these factors and worker experiences of strain. Each category will be reviewed separately, but it is important to note that they are not necessarily discrete and that people's responses to stressors are part of a dynamic process (see Figure 1.1 in Chapter 1).

Research on job-related stressors has typically built upon theories such as the transactional theory of stress (Lazarus & Folkman, 1984), Karasek's (1979) job demands-control (support) model, the conservation of resources theory (Hobfoll, 1989), the challenge-hindrance framework (Cavanaugh et al., 2000), and the cognitive activation theory of stress (Ursin & Eriksen, 2010). These and other theoretical accounts of the stress-coping process emphasize the importance of thoroughly exploring the nature and scope of environmental factors that have the potential to create strain for individuals in the workplace. Relevant aspects in which they differ are the extent to which they address the role of stressor appraisals in creating strain, if they address stressors as both adaptive and/or maladaptive (O'Brien & Beehr, 2019), as well as if they emphasize stressors (narrow focus) or the total organizational stress process (broad focus). The order of discussion that follows does not imply that, across occupational groups, certain forms of stressors are uniformly more salient than others. Further, in the discussion, we also do not divide the certain forms of stressors into either an adaptive and/or a maladaptive stressor category (e.g., challenge versus hindrance stressors). This is because the influence of stressors on outcomes may depend on how these stressors are appraised by each individual (O'Brien & Beehr, 2019; Webster et al., 2011). It should also be noted that although a stressor is not appraised as being stressful, it may be detrimental to individuals (Webster et al., 2011). For instance, noise, vibration, temperature, or chemical exposure may function as harmful stressors, even though the individual might not appraise them as such (Selye, 1956).

Early research on job stress tended to focus predominantly on aspects of the physical environment, with a prevalence of research on jobs where these factors were likely to have a significant impact upon individuals. During the 1960s, particularly in the wake of research conducted by Kahn et al. (1964), interest shifted somewhat away from physical factors to role stressors, and this emphasis has continued. From the end of the 1990s to the present, however, alternative work arrangements that dilute the boundaries between the spheres of work and nonwork have fueled interest in issues surrounding the nature of the job and job security, new technological advancements that enable knowledge work to be completed almost anywhere, and the balance between job or career demands and family commitments and responsibilities (Bliese et al., 2017). Further, societal changes such as decreased tolerance of sexual misconduct and harassment at work exemplified in the 'MeToo – movement' is likely to spur research into the manifestation and consequences of different forms of destructive and unwanted behaviors at work. We reflect upon some of these trends later in this chapter.

INTRINSIC JOB CHARACTERISTICS

These stressors are associated with the performance of specific tasks that make up an individual's job, sometimes referred to as *task content* factors (Kahn & Byosiere, 1990), as well as work environment and work-scheduling factors. Here we will survey some of the physical demands and environmental stressors that workers may have to contend with and that may influence their levels of strain. The physical demands of work surroundings and the distress caused by noise, vibration, and extremes of temperature will be briefly reviewed first, as they represent some of the earliest forms of stressors that were investigated by organizational psychologists and other researchers in the field. Then we examine workload (both quantitative and qualitative), work hours (including shift work), the effects of technological changes, and exposure to risks and hazards as potential agents of job-related strain. Chapter 6 examines the role of lack of discretion and control as a major predictor of job-related strain.

Noise

Poor working conditions (including excessive temperature or noise) can have a serious detrimental impact on worker physical health and psychological well-being (Cooper, 1987). Although certain kinds of sound (for instance, language and music) enrich people's lives and underpin culture and society, unwanted sound is referred to as *noise*. Exposure to excessive noise (85 decibels and above) on a recurring, prolonged basis can cause hearing loss (Prince et al., 1997) and physical strain (Gan et al., 2016). Exposure to continuous noise operates less as a stressor than in those circumstances where it is unpredictable or unexpected (Szalma & Hancock, 2011).

Noise below hazardous levels (i.e., <85 decibels) also negatively affects workers (Szalma & Hancock, 2011). Several organizations have shifted to open-plan environments compared to traditional offices – e.g., cellular or enclosed offices (Ashkanasy et al., 2014). While open-plan offices have benefits for the organization (Davis et al., 2011), the level of noise is in general higher than in more traditional offices (Venetjoki et al., 2006). Jahncke et al. (2011) investigated the effect of different levels of noise in open-offices on participant's performance, fatigue, and physiological response. In a laboratory experiment using actual recorded office sounds manipulated to be at either low (39 decibel) or high (51 decibel) level, participants who were exposed to a high level of noise performed worse were less motivated and reported higher levels of fatigue than participants working in a more quiet office. The level of noise did not affect participant's endocrinological response (i.e., levels of cortisol and norepinephrine) (Jahncke et al., 2011).

Vibration and Temperature

Along with noise, vibration and temperature are acknowledged as major environmental sources of strain. Vibrations that transfer from physical objects to the whole body adversely affect performance, especially in tasks dependent on visual perception and fine motor control (Conway et al., 2007). Extended vibration also increase fatigue and discomfort (Yung et al., 2017) and prolonged vibration increases the risk of low back pain

(Burström et al., 2015). Unfortunately, the psychological long-term effects of this exposure are not known, and further longitudinal studies are needed to ascertain the full range of vibration effects on psychological well-being.

Temperature is another characteristic of the physical environment that may have a significant impact on workers. Extreme temperatures (hot or cold) can induce physiological responses that might have undesirable effects on both work performance and individual health and well-being (Flouris et al., 2018; Pilcher et al., 2002). Performance of perceptual and motor tasks deteriorates (Jewell, 1998), cognitive performance is impaired (Gaoua et al., 2011), and fatigue increases (Brake & Bates, 2001) in very high temperatures. Given that climate change is predicted to increase the frequency and intensity of thermal stressors, it becomes incumbent on scholars to conduct controlled research that examines the range of effects of extreme temperatures (Kjellstrom et al., 2016). Importantly, intrinsic physical job characteristics such as heat, vibration, and noise are often co-occurring, which necessitates the investigation of possible additive or synergistic effects of these stressors on human performance and well-being (see for instance Lamb & Kwok, 2016).

Workload

Workload refers to 'the amount of work an employee is required to complete in a given amount of time, along with the effort it takes to complete it' (Nixon et al., 2011, p. 9). Given the general definition of the construct, it becomes clear that workload is a multifaceted construct that has been further delineated into different dimensions. A common distinction is between quantitative and qualitative workload (Spector & Jex, 1998). *Quantitative workload* refers to the sheer amount of work required and the time frame in which work must be completed. Thus, a worker may be given a very tight deadline for the completion of a project. *Qualitative workload* refers to 'the mental effort required to complete the tasks' (Nixon et al., 2011, p. 9), where qualitative overload occurs when individuals believe they do not have the skills or capacities to satisfactorily perform job tasks. Quantitative workload has received the most scientific investigation (Bowling et al., 2015). Research has also investigated the effect of perceived and objective workload (Ganster et al., 2001).

Nixon et al. (2011) conducted a meta-analysis of various job stressors (including workload as a general construct) and their relationship with physical strain, measured both as individual physical symptoms (e.g., headache, sleep disturbance, fatigue) and as a composite construct of the aggregated physical symptoms included in the meta-analysis. Workload was positively related to all physical symptoms, with the strongest relationship between workload and fatigue (mean weighted correlation .31). Workload was also positively related to the composite measure of physical symptoms (mean weighted correlation .22), and based on this strength of relationship, emerged as a medium important predictor of physical health compared with the other job stressors (Nixon et al., 2011).

The meta-analysis of Bowling et al. (2015) also included the psychological consequences of perceived workload. In line with the previous meta-analysis by Nixon et al.

(2011), perceived workload positively predicted physical symptoms. Further, perceived workload was significantly positively related to a class of psychological well-being variables (e.g., emotional exhaustion, strain, and depersonalization) and negatively related to affective organizational commitment (Bowling et al., 2015). Thus, research suggests that workload is negatively related to employee well-being and job attitudes.

The meta-analyses are important for the accumulation of knowledge on the physical and psychological consequences of workload. However, there are some limitations worth addressing that reflect the current state of the research on workload. First, the limited number of studies investigating qualitative workload prevents a more fine-grained analysis on the extent to which different dimensions of the workload construct (for example quantitative and qualitative workload) are equally related to workers' health and well-being (Bowling et al., 2015). Second, research on workload often investigates the presence of linear relationships between workload and potential outcome variables. However, the proposal of curvilinear relationships is part of many theoretical models on stress (for an overview see Karanika-Murray, 2010). For example, Shultz et al. (2010) classified employees in three groups based on their perception of their skills to be either insufficient (overload), adequate (matched), or surpassing (underload) to meet the workload demands of their job. Results suggested that while overload and underload were negatively related to health-related outcomes, overload had the worst impact on health-related outcomes.

Qualitative underload, resulting from tedious and understimulating tasks, may lead to boredom stress (Parasuraman & Purohit, 2000). Further, under qualitative underload the individual is not given the opportunity to use acquired skills or to develop full potential ability (Erdogan & Bauer, 2021; Erdogan et al., 2011). One group that may be vulnerable to qualitative underload is young graduates. Underemployed graduates report lower opportunities for using their skills and higher levels of job, career, and life dissatisfaction compared to graduates with a job that matched their level of education (Nabi, 2003).

New technology and the increasing automation of industry can lead to the simplification of work and repetitive jobs that are potentially stressful in terms of workload (Hamborg & Greif, 2015). Although a hectic work pace is stressful, work that is dull, repetitive, and monotonous is equally detrimental to the individual's physical and psychological well-being (Cummings et al., 2016). Lack of stimulation, underutilization of skills, and boredom characterize many blue-collar occupations and may also be dangerous (Cummings et al., 2016; Game, 2007). Workers who feel unchallenged and bored at work are more prone to experience distress and have depressive complaints (van Hooff & van Hooft, 2014).

An important issue to consider in research on workload is the distinction between perceived and actual (or objective) demands (Bowling & Kirkendall, 2012; Ganster et al., 2001). The transactional model of stress-coping emphasizes that the individual's perception of his or her environment is critical for the experience of strain and the activation of coping responses. From this perspective, objectively defined characteristics of the work environment do not necessarily contribute to strain, because these may be perceived as a threat to well-being by one individual but not by another. Research on job design, for instance, has indicated that perceptions of job characteristics may be salient for individuals' reactions but that actual job characteristics are also important to assess (Melamed et al., 1995). From an organizational intervention standpoint, it is relevant to determine whether certain environmental factors are consistently reported by a large proportion of the workforce as being stressful, for such consensus would indicate that the effects of these factors could not be explained by differential perceptions.

From the above overview, it is evident that optimal matching between work demands and individual capabilities is required to prevent strain from developing. This may necessitate greater flexibility in the design of jobs to tailor them more directly to the skills and interests of individual workers. One of the major challenges is to create job designs that promote the achievement of organizational goals, while at the same time providing individuals with the opportunity to engage in satisfying and fulfilling job tasks that do not create unmanageable strain.

Work Hours

The sheer number of hours that a person works can produce strain. Numerous studies have found a significant correlation between the overall number of hours worked and various indices of health and well-being (Sparks et al., 2013; Virtanen et al., 2018; Wong et al., 2019). Individuals who worked excessive hours showed more symptoms of ill health than their counterparts who worked fewer hours. The effect of work hours was particularly associated with health outcomes associated with impaired sleep, fatigue and injury (Goh et al., 2015; Wong et al., 2019). Employees who work more than 50 hours a week or more than 10 hours a day are at greater risk of health problems than employees who work below these levels (Wong et al., 2019).

A recent meta-analysis pointed out that the relationship between working long hours and mental well-being is inconclusive (Ganster et al., 2018). One potential avenue for investigating this relationship further is from the lens of the challenge-hindrance framework. Work hours represent a type of stressor that may change its characteristic from a challenge to a hindrance stressor depending on the overall number of working hours (O'Brien & Beehr, 2019). When the number of work hours is demanding, but not excessive, workers may feel challenged and consequently feel empowered and engaged at work (Kim & Beehr, 2018). However, at a certain point, the number of work hours and its associated workload may become intolerable and overload workers. Hence, in such circumstances, work hours will represent a hindrance stressor that causes mental strain (O'Brien & Beehr, 2019). Research suggest that the work hour stressor is perceived as both a challenge and hindrance stressor (Webster et al., 2011), supporting the duality of the nature of this stressor.

Recent years have witnessed the emergence of an increasing variety of patterns of working hours or weeks, generically referred to as work *schedules*. There are many social and economic reasons for the utilization of alternatives to the typical 9 a.m. to 5 p.m., 40-hour working week, but there can be no doubt that they have significantly affected quite a large proportion of the workforce. Shift work is typically defined as a changing pattern of work hours (although some workers are employed on so-called permanent shifts). In some industries, particularly leisure and hospitality industry, more than 50% are shift workers (McMenamin, 2007) and include one-fifth of workers in industrialized societies (Åkerstedt & Wright, 2009).

A great deal of research has been carried out to determine the effects of shift work on workers' job performance (especially efficiency), work attitudes, and overall psychological and physical well-being. There is now considerable evidence that shift work can lead to a variety of difficulties for shift workers and their families, primarily because of distur-bances in circadian rhythms (the 'body clock') and disruptions to family and social life (Geiger-Brown et al., 2012). In many cases, these effects have been associated with a decline in physical health, satisfaction, and overall subjective well-being (Costa, 2010).

However, problems with shift work are not uniform across all shift work schedules, nor do all individuals experience the same kinds of problems or to the same extent, and further investigations are needed to determine the factors that mediate and moderate the effects of shift work. Shift work tolerance is defined as the ability to adapt to shift work without adverse consequences (Andlauer et al., 1979). A systematic review of research on shift work tolerance revealed a number of individual characteristics that increases toler-ance for work hours that does not conform to the traditional fixed eight hours during the day, five days a week (Saksvik et al., 2011). To name a few, young age, male gender, low score on neuroticisms, and low score on morningness increased shift work tolerance (Saksvik et al., 2011). Factors outside the individual, such as how the working hours are organized, also influence shift work tolerance (Costa, 2003). For instance, it has long been known that fixed shifts are less harmful to employees than rotating shifts, especially backward rotating (Jamal & Baba, 1992). Further, in the regular three-shift system, there seems to be some benefit from changing from a slowly backward-rotating to rapidly forward-rotating shifts (Sallinen & Kecklund, 2010) and allowing for individual flexibility is also related to decreased strain (Viitasalo et al., 2008).

New Technology

The advances of information and communication technology (ICT) have profoundly changed where and when non-manual employees can perform their job. While the rise of ICT may have clear advantages (e.g., facilitating the shift to home-offices in the pre-vention of the pandemic COVID-19), it also poses challenges to work-life boundaries (Bliese et al., 2017). Several studies point to the adverse consequences of ICT on the employee's ability to recover from work, their well-being, and work–life balance (Ďuranová & Ohly, 2015; La Torre et al., 2019; Schlachter et al., 2018). The smartphone is an example of ICT that is often used to access job-mail or job-related information at home. However, the use of smartphones late in the evening may come at a cost as it is related to reduced hours of sleep, and in turn increased feeling of depletion the next day at work and reduced work engagement (Lanaj et al., 2014). Intensive smartphone users seem to be the most vulnerable to the detrimental effects of smartphones on their health (Derks & Bakker, 2014).

The change in working arrangements due to technological innovations has been acknowledged in the literature for a long time (e.g., Nilles, 1975). The prevalence of new work arrangements accelerated because of COVID-19 and may have long-term consequences for how we work in the future. Understanding how these new ways of working will affect employees is important. Currently, the research suggests a mixed and complex picture, pointing to both beneficial and detrimental effects on employees working remotely (Allen et al., 2015). Charalampous et al. (2019) suggested that the field would benefit from operationally defining ICT and applying longitudinal or experimental designs that can examine a range of short-term and long-term consequences of being virtually boundless.

Exposure to Risk and Hazards

Various occupational groups, such as police officers, mineworkers, and soldiers, have increased risk of physical danger. Research suggests that encountering extreme sources of physical hazards affect worker's health. For instance, combat exposure in soldiers is associated with higher levels of mental health problems such as posttraumatic stress disorder, depression, and alcohol problems (Porter et al., 2018). Firefighters who perceived their work as dangerous were more likely to experience an acute stress reaction in response to an emergency situation experienced at work (Prati et al., 2013). Finally, the risk of exposure to certain chemicals, including the inhalation of vapors, dust, and exposure to chemicals that are irritants to the skin, is frequently reported as one of the most harmful stressors among workers in the chemical industry (ILO, 1986).

To summarize this overview of the impact of job-related environmental factors on workers' experience of strain, two overarching issues should be noted. First, as noted earlier, it is important to investigate both objective and subjective work conditions to develop a comprehensive profile of physical stressors in the workplace, as well as to understand workers' reactions to these stressors. Although some research has explored both, the predominant focus has been on subjective perceptions of the work environment, although researchers do not always make clear the distinction between subjective and objective aspects. We address this issue again toward the end of this chapter. Second, it is evident that stressors do not operate in isolation from each other and there can be additive and interactive effects where several stressors are experienced concurrently (see for instance Melamed et al., 2001). Unfortunately, however, and perhaps due to the constraints on conducting multivariable research within organizations, many studies have examined individual stressors (such as those identified above) in isolation, rather than considering their combined impact.

ORGANIZATIONAL ROLES

Roles encompass the behaviors and demands that are associated with the job an individual performs. The importance of role-related strain was first underlined by Kahn et al. (1964), whose early investigations in this area have provided a platform and a framework for most subsequent research on role strain. According to Kahn et al. (1964) dysfunction in roles can occur in two primary ways: role *ambiguity* (lack of clarity about the role) and role *conflict* (competing or conflicting job demands). These two role stressors have been the most frequently investigated sources of job-related strain and are frequently examined by the measure developed by Rizzo et al. (1970).

Role Ambiguity

As defined by Kahn et al. (1964), *role ambiguity* refers to unpredictability of the consequences of one's role performance. Later conceptualizations have extended the definition to include a lack of information needed to perform the role, and the typical measure of this construct assesses both unpredictability of consequences and information deficiency regarding expected role behaviors (Pearce, 1981). Meta-analyses have demonstrated a consistent link between substantial role ambiguity in the job and high levels of psychological strain (Gilboa et al., 2008; Nixon et al., 2011; Schmidt et al., 2014; Tubre & Collins, 2000).

Role Conflict

Similarly, role conflict, which reflects incompatible demands on the person (either within a single role or between multiple roles occupied by the individual), can induce negative emotional reactions due to perceived inability to be effective on the job (Schaubroeck et al., 1989). Meta-analyses have confirmed the detrimental effect of role conflict on both psychological and physiological strain (Gilboa et al., 2008; Schmidt et al., 2014). Typically, however, the association between role conflict and psychological strain is not as strong as that between ambiguity and strain (Gilboa et al., 2008). However, for physical symptoms, the association between the two roles has been found to be equally related (Schmidt et al., 2014), or conflict to be more strongly related than role ambiguity (Nixon et al., 2011). Role conflict and ambiguity also show a similar association with organizational citizenship behavior (Eatough et al., 2011). Both types of role conflict are also related to decreased compliance with safety rules and regulations and reduced participation in safety-related activities which, in turn, increase the probability of work-related accidents (Clarke, 2012).

Role Overload

A third role variable is overload, which refers to the number of different roles a person has to fulfill (see the above discussion on work overload). Not only can role overload lead to excessive demands on an individual's time, but it also may create uncertainty about his or her ability to perform these roles adequately. Along with role ambiguity and conflict, overload has been found to be a major negative correlate of job satisfaction (Eatough et al., 2011; Fried et al., 2008).

One potential explanation for the negative effects of these role variables on employee physical and psychological well-being is that they create uncertainty, which in itself is psychologically uncomfortable and, if persistent and at high levels, can result in emotional disturbance in the individual. Beehr and colleagues (Beehr, 1987; Beehr & Bhagat, 1985) adapted the expectancy theory of motivation to explain the diverse forms of uncertainty that may arise from role stressors. Specifically, role ambiguity, conflict, and overload may be linked with reduced effort-to-performance expectancy (E → P) because they create uncertainty among employees that their efforts will lead to satisfactory job performance, and with performance-to-outcome expectancy (P → O) because employees are unsure of the link between rewards and successful job performance.

Before turning to the next organizational factor, we should note that almost all research on role variables has been based upon self-reports of the amount of ambiguity, conflict, and overload that workers experience. From the transactional perspective, this is entirely appropriate because it focuses on individuals' perceptions of their environment as the critical determinant of psychological strain. However, it would also be valuable to map these perceptions onto more objectively defined work conditions.

WORK RELATIONSHIPS

Both the quality of interpersonal relationships and lack of social support (from others in the workplace) have been examined as potential sources of job-related strain. The literature has assumed that social support may have a main effect on strain, but also function as a moderator of the impact of stressors on individual strain and well-being (Bavik et al., 2020). As we shall discuss in Chapter 6, there is some dispute over the role of social support as a moderator (or buffer). Nevertheless, it is clear that negative interpersonal relations and the absence of support from colleagues and superiors can be a major stressor for many workers (Ilies et al., 2011). Conversely, having social support from others within the organization can directly alleviate psychological strain (Sconfienza et al., 2019). However, there are certain circumstances when social support increases the level of strain. Although the intentions behind the support may be benevolent, social interactions that make the recipient focus on the stressful aspects may in fact decrease psychological and physical health (Beehr et al., 2010).

There are potentially multiple sources of social support inside and outside organizations (Baruch-Feldman et al., 2002). A meta-analysis conducted by Ng and Sorensen (2008) examined the different strength of perceived supervisor support versus perceived co-worker support on different work-related attitudes. While both sources of support were positively related to job satisfaction and affective commitment, support from the supervisor had the greatest impact. Conversely, when leaders are the source of stressors, for instance by causing role conflict, supervisor support is less effective than co-work support in mitigating employee strain (Mayo et al., 2012).

As discussed in the next section, leaders may also induce stressors on their employees. Inconsiderate, nonsupportive or abusive behavior from a supervisor appears to contribute significantly to feelings of job pressure and strain (Harms et al., 2017; Inceoglu et al., 2018; Schyns & Schilling, 2013). A critical issue for research on supervisor support is the optimal level of various kinds of support, including the provision of information and advice, guidance on how to perform the job, and feedback on job performance. Also of interest are differences between individuals in terms of the amount of supervision required. For instance, O'Driscoll and Beehr (2000) found that the extent to which subordinates had a need for clarity moderated the relationship between role stressors and psychological strain. Athletes with a strong need for clarity experienced greater strain in the presence of role ambiguity than athletes with a lower need for clarity (Bray et al., 2005). It is evident that some individuals can tolerate uncertainties in the work environment more readily than do others and that their need for close guidance and supervision may therefore be lower. Moreover, most of the current research in the work domain has not examined the difference between perceived and received social support, and their potential differential influence on psychological strain (Melrose et al., 2015).

Leadership Style

As already mentioned, leadership style is a potential source of strain at work for employees. Being maltreated by a leader is more harmful to workplace attitudes and behavior than being maltreated by a peer (Hershcovis & Barling, 2010). Recent years have witnessed a surge of interest in destructive (Padilla et al., 2007) or 'dark sides' (Judge et al., 2009) of leadership. These forms of undesirable leadership are both prevalent and costly (both economically and on the psychological toll on employees) (Aasland et al., 2010). A meta-analysis by Schyns and Schilling (2013) suggests that destructive leadership (a broad umbrella term of various leadership terms related to destructive leadership) is negatively related to employee well-being and positively related to strain. Specifically, autocratic and authoritarian leadership styles have generally been observed to induce strain among subordinates (Bass & Bass, 2008; Harms et al., 2018; Schaubroeck et al., 2017). On the other hand, employees who have leaders who encourage, inspire, and motivate them experience fewer demands, more resources, and less psychological strain (Fernet et al., 2015) and employees of mindful leaders experience less stress and greater relationships with their leader (Reb et al., 2019).

Reactions to an authoritarian style of leadership vary between individuals. Employees with higher levels of the personality trait neuroticism experience higher levels of psychological strain under authoritarian leaders than their emotional stable peers (De Hoogh & Den Hartog, 2009). Although some people appreciate a clear sense of direction and may prefer not having to make decisions relating to their work, the majority of employees would appear to value having input into (relevant) decision-making processes and some degree of self-determination in their workplace. As illustrated later in our discussion of Karasek's demands-control model of job strain (see Chapter 6), lack of opportunity to exercise some judgmental discretion contributes significantly to psychological strain for most individuals. Nevertheless, the impact of different leadership styles in various work settings and on different occupational groups is certainly an area that requires further exploration.

CAREER DEVELOPMENT

This category of potential stressors includes job insecurity (the threat of unemployment), perceived underpromotion or overpromotion within the organization, and a general sense of lack of achievement of one's goals or ambitions. Before the turn of the century, the concept of career significantly shifted (Hall, 2002; Sullivan & Baruch, 2009), with a wider array of different forms of employment contracts being negotiated (in some cases) or enforced. For many employees, the linear career development path is no longer a feasible, or perhaps even a desired, option. Nevertheless, compared with some of the other factors described above, the relationship between career issues and strain has been less studied empirically.

There is a growing body of evidence that a perceived lack of promotion opportunities and lack of progress in one's career represent primary sources of job and career dissatisfaction (Ng & Feldman, 2014) and hence may function as major stressors for many people. There is also substantial evidence that, despite changes in societal attitudes concerning equal employment opportunities, inequality still persists (Amis et al., 2018; ILO, 2017). Women and minority groups still encounter organizational barriers to their career development, which inevitably will lead to higher levels of psychological strain for these groups of employees. Although many organizations are making efforts to enhance career development opportunities for women and minorities, the persistence of inequality calls for significant progress in this area.

Job Insecurity

One aspect of many people's careers in the current and future employment context is the prospect or threat of job loss due to redundancy. While there are multiple individual predictors of job insecurity (Keim et al., 2014), organizational factors and societal changes are also important predictors (Lee et al., 2018). With the increasing incidence of mergers and downsizing in industries around the world and with attempts to reduce levels of management within organizations, many individuals face the threat of losing their jobs. Organizational changes such as these are potential sources of strain for employees (Dahl, 2011; Sverke et al., 2002). The rate of involuntary unemployment increased considerably in the late 1980s (Latack et al., 1995). After the year 2000, global unemployment has remained high and showed further peaks in response to the 2008–2009 economic crises and the COVID-19 pandemic in 2020 (ILO, 2020; The World Bank, 2020). Further, the predicted changes of the Fourth Industrial Revolution with the introduction of new technologies that entail automation have the possibility to disrupt labor markets (Schwab, 2017). To put it bluntly, in the new millennium job insecurity may be one of the single most salient sources of strain for employees, and its effects will be experienced at all organizational levels.

Latack et al. (1995) noted, 'The impact of job loss is generally detrimental to individuals by virtually any criteria a researcher chooses to examine' (p. 312). In addition to its potential socio-emotional effects on individuals, the threat of job loss is negatively related to employee mental and physical well-being and organizational attitudes such as affective commitment (Jiang & Lavaysse, 2018). Longitudinal studies have the benefits of investigating different causal pathways between job insecurity and relevant outcomes variables. While the literature often assumes a causal direction from job insecurity to outcome variables such as reduced well-being, a reverse relationship in which for instance reduced well-being influences job insecurity (or that there is a reciprocal relationship) is also conceivable (Hellgren & Sverke 2003). An overview of longitudinal studies up to 2015 suggests that job insecurity functions primarily as a predictor of negative outcomes such as impaired health and reduced well-being, not the contrary (De Witte et al., 2016; Vander Elst et al., 2018). Job insecurity seldom occurs in a vacuum but co-occurs with other stressors. Employees experiencing high levels of insecurity together with high levels of job pressure are at particular risk of impaired health outcomes (Strazdins et al., 2004).

The impact of job insecurity and job loss goes beyond the individual victim and extend to employees who maintain their jobs (conceptualized as 'survivor syndrome' in Appelbaum et al., 1997). The survivors' perception of the rationale and execution of downsizing (Hareli & Tzafrir, 2006; Van Dierendonck & Jacobs, 2012), their perception of their own control (Brockner et al., 2004), as well as time passed after the downsizing (Allen et al., 2001) have an impact on how severely survivors are affected by the downsizing. Many firms downsize in successive rounds. It does not seem that surviving one round of downsizing, causes resilience and protects against the next round of downsizing. On the contrary, repeated experiences of downsizing involve more strain for employees (Moore et al., 2004).

Interestingly, the ultimate consequences of job layoffs for organizational productivity and effectiveness are far from clear-cut. Although managers and decision makers tend to subscribe to the view that making the organization 'lean and mean' is essential to maintaining competitiveness in today's economic climate, the evidence is mixed and suggests that downsizing can have both positive and negative influences on the bottom line (Datta et al., 2010; Gandolfi & Hansson, 2011). While downsizing is often implemented to increase organizational performance, Datta et al. (2010) concluded after an extensive review involving a diverse set of organizational performance indicators such as market returns, firm profitability, and other organizational outcomes, that 'downsizing often fails to live up to expectations' (p. 341).

For example, Schmitt et al. (2012) noted that downsizing may impair knowledge retention which result in a loss of organizational 'memory' and sharing of knowledge across departments and organizational levels, loss of tacit knowledge and damage to informal network structures, disruption of routines that have built up over time and that ensure that the organization functions smoothly, and even a decline in personal motivation to engage in knowledge retention and organizational learning. In a study of various industries in Portugal, Neves (2014) observed that leaders in organizations that had downsized, treated submissive employees more harshly (e.g., ridiculed, devalued, and publicly humiliated employees) than leaders in organizations that had not downsized. The authors note that a work context post downsizing may be characterized as uncertain and threatening, and hence targets of abusive behavior will be less likely to speak up against maltreatment in such an environment.

The 21st century has experienced a rise in various non-standard or alternative work arrangements that differ from the fulltime traditional regular employment (Ashford et al., 2007; Spreitzer et al., 2017). The term 'alternative work arrangements' encompasses a range of different work arrangements such as gig worker, contract worker, temporary help agency workers, but also part-time workers (Cappelli & Keller, 2013a, 2013b; Kuhn & Galloway, 2019). Previously, we also briefly discussed new work arrangements related to technological changes that affect the work domain. These work arrangements differ in the type of flexibility they offer; from flexible work arrangements, flexible work schedules, or flexible work sites, although these dimensions are sometimes interdependent (Spreitzer et al., 2017). An important question regarding flexible work arrangement is the extent to which the flexibility is for the advantage of the organization or the worker (Cooper, 2005). For the high-skilled worker who might not fear being superfluous, flexible work tasks and a tailored work-life schedule offered by alternative work arrangements may be beneficial. For the low-skilled worker, however, the threat of job insecurity may have detrimental consequences for physical and psychological well-being (Spreitzer et al., 2017). For some workers, existing research today suggest that alternative work arrangements increase health and role risks (Benach & Muntaner, 2007; Howard, 2017). Thus, future research needs to disentangle what type of alternative work arrangements, under which circumstances, and for what type of workers, as well as the processes behind, alternative work arrangements may increase physical and psychological strain.

In this new century, it is clear that the nature of employment and careers will be dramatically affected by such factors as globalization of the labor market, changes in work arrangements, increasingly sophisticated technologies that will make many current jobs superfluous or even obsolete, and the need for firms and companies to seek new ways of enhancing their competitive edge and to maintain (if not increase) their market share. Research on job stress therefore needs to extend beyond the immediate workplace environment to consider employment as one of the elements that make up individuals' lives. Hence, rather than focusing solely on strain that is manifested on the job, researchers will need to develop more comprehensive perspectives on the dynamic interrelationship between employment, family, and other elements of people's lives. Such research must include consideration of broader economic and social issues surrounding employment and unemployment in an era when job security may become the exception rather than the norm (Bidwell et al., 2013; Kochan et al., 2019; Tran & Sokas, 2017). We will return to this issue in Chapter 10.

Promotion and Career Advancement

Even in situations where individuals may believe that their job is secure, issues related to advancement in one's career or promotion within the organization is a major source of dissatisfaction and psychological strain (Yang et al., 2008). Typically, strain is caused by a *lack of* advancement (or underpromotion), but in some cases the reverse may apply: Individuals feel promoted beyond their capabilities. This may occur, for example, when a person is promoted to the role of supervisor from the 'shop floor' or is given new responsibilities for which he or she has received inadequate preparation or training. Both under and overpromotion can have serious detrimental effects on individual well-being and satisfaction levels.

Related to the above is the issue of career plateauing. Formulations of career development proposed in the 1970s (see, e.g., Osipow, 1973) suggested that career development occurred in stages, one of these being the plateau stage, when individuals experience a leveling off in their career and skill development and their career reaches a point of maintenance where the probability of receiving further promotion is unlikely (Ference et al., 1977). The concept and operationalization of career plateau has developed after its origination, where the dominant focus within the research field had been on either hierarchical plateau (same as the original career plateau) or job content plateau (individuals are not assigned further job responsibilities or perceive their job to be unchallenging) (Yang et al., 2019). While research on the hierarchical plateau in general suggest that individuals' well-being suffers when there is no probability of further advancement, the relationship between job content plateau and well-being is less clear (Yang et al., 2019).

Career mobility is not solely a consequence of employers' decision-making. While traditionally many organizations used a top-down approach to job-redesign, the last decade has shown an interest in a bottom-up approach whereby employees redefine and redesign their tasks, the relational or cognitive boundaries of their job through job crafting (Wrzesniewski & Dutton, 2001). Thus, employees may advance their career by modifying their existing job to improve the fit between their job and their own needs, abilities, and preferences (Demerouti, 2014). Job crafting is related to enhanced well-being for the employee (Tims et al., 2013). However, recent research suggest that an employee's job crafting may have potential personal and interpersonal negative effects such as burnout, higher levels of workload for and conflict with coworkers (Tims et al., 2015, 2021). While job crafting may offer an opportunity for the individual employee to customize their job, it also puts a greater responsibility upon employees to manage their own career within the organization.

ORGANIZATIONAL FACTORS

Psychological strain that may be attributed to organizational factors is often due to the culture and management style adopted within an organization (Dextras-Gauthier et al., 2012). There are, of course, multiple organizational factors that impinge upon organizational members and may generate feelings of strain. All we can do here is highlight some that have been observed in research investigating organizational-level stressors.

Hierarchical, bureaucratic organizational structures may permit little participation by employees in decisions affecting their work. Studies of organizational climate have indicated that the content and nature of communication processes within organizations contribute to employee reactions to their job and the organization as a whole (Parker et al., 2003). For example, Nerstad et al. (2020) found that a work climate that values employee's mastery, development, participation in decision-making, and cooperation, contributes to increase employees' need satisfaction (autonomy, competence, and belongingness), which in turn reduces their experiences of strain and increases their well-being. On the other hand, a work climate that encourages rivalry between employees, normative ability, and is controlling, was found to reduce employees' need satisfaction and in turn enhance their experiences of strain. Also, inadequate communication, cynicism, and negative attributions seem to contribute to employee strain. Lack of participation in the decision-making process, lack of effective consultation and communication, office politics, and no sense of belonging have all been identified as potential organizational stressors. Increased opportunity to participate, on the other hand, has been associated with greater overall job satisfaction, higher levels of affective commitment to the organization, and an increased sense of well-being (Burris et al., 2008; Morrison, 2014; Olafsen et al., 2017).

Research conducted on Karasek's demands-control model supports these suggestions. Karasek's (1979) original prospective study demonstrated that lack of decision latitude and freedom to choose one's work schedule were significant predictors of the risk for coronary heart disease. In an experimental test of the demands-control model, Cendales-Ayala et al. (2017) bus operators participating in a simulation exercise were randomly assigned to either an experimental condition with increased (high demand) or reduced (low demand) number of bus stops to pick up passengers. Bus operators with an increased number of bus stops showed increased levels of strain when they had a low decision latitude compared to bus operators who had more control over their decisions in a demanding situation (Cendales-Ayala et al., 2017).

Finally in this category, organizational politics also have a substantial impact on employee strain (Hochwarter et al., 2020). In a meta-analysis of organizational politics and employee outcomes, Chang et al. (2009) noted a strong relationship between employees' perceptions of a negative political climate within their organization and their experience of psychological strain. Perceptions of organizational politics were indirectly related to both reduced performance through psychological strain and increased turnover intentions through weakened morale (i.e., lower levels of job satisfaction and affective commitment).

Given the large range of organizational factors that have the potential to induce strain in employees, it is hardly surprising that few generalizations are possible. Lack of participation (in decision making), inappropriate levels of formalization of work procedures, lack of adequate communication within the organization, and organizational politics are all potential sources of strain, yet none function universally as stressors. Research needs to focus on the conditions under which these factors create a stressful environment for organizational members, as well as considering differential impacts on various levels and groups of employees.

THE HOME-WORK INTERFACE

Managing the interface between one's job and various roles and responsibilities off the job is another potential source of strain (O'Driscoll, 1996), often referred to as *work/ nonwork conflict* or *work-life conflict* (Frone et al., 1992; Greenhaus & Beutell, 1985), this issue has received considerable attention from researchers in recent years (Bianchi & Milkie, 2010; Eby et al., 2005). Changes in family structures, increased participation by women in the workforce, and technological changes enable job tasks to be performed in a variety of locations and 'after-hours' (Boswell & Olson-Buchanan, 2007). These changes have blurred the boundaries between the job and life off the job for many workers and have created the potential for conflict to occur between job and off-job roles (Hill et al., 1998) but also for more flexibility that may reduce strain (Hill et al., 2010).

One particular conflict in the home-work interface that has been thoroughly examined is work-family conflict. Multiple work and family stressors are roots to work-family conflict (Michel et al., 2011), which consistently has been linked with psychological strain, dissatisfaction and reduced well-being (Amstad et al., 2011; Ford et al., 2007). Recently, the unidirectional relationship assumed between work-family conflict and strain was challenged. Building upon the conservation of resources theory (Hobfoll, 1989) and its notion of loss spirals, Nohe et al. (2015) documented a reciprocal relationship between work–family conflict and strain using meta-analytic path analysis. Thus, while work-family conflict may predict strain, strain is also an antecedent of work-family conflict.

Work-family conflict is commonly defined as 'a form of interrole conflict in which the role pressures from the work and family domains are mutually incompatible in some respect. That is, participation in the work (family) role is made more difficult by virtue of participation in the family (work) role' (Greenhaus & Beutell, 1985, p. 77). Implied in this definition is the existence of a bidirectional relationship where work can interfere with family and family can interfere with work (Frone, 2003). There are two models for the relationships between the two types of conflict and outcomes related to the work or family domain. In the cross-domain model, a conflict where work role interferes with the family role will negatively affect family related outcomes such as family well-being – and vise versa (Ford et al., 2007; Frone et al., 1992). Thus, conflict originating in one domain is the greatest source of strain in the other domain. In the matching-model, the greatest source of strain is experienced in the same domain where the conflict originated (Amstad et al., 2011). Thus, a conflict where work role interferes with the family role is expected to be more strongly related to strain in the work-domain than to strain in the family domain. In a meta-analysis testing these two alternative models, Amstad et al. (2011) found that although both types of conflict were related to strain in both work and family domains, the strongest relationships were observed in the same domain in line with the matching-model. Further, both types of conflict were most strongly related to domain-unspecific outcomes such as general stress experienced.

Empirical work on the home-work interface illustrates that this is a significant source of strain for both women and men but that gender differences may exist. Two primary questions have been explored: (a) Are there gender differences in the amount or extent of work-family conflict experienced? and (b) Are the correlates of work-family conflict different for men versus women? In a meta-analysis that investigated antecedents of work-family (and family-work) conflict, gender played a minor role in predicting experienced conflict (Byron, 2005). Thus, men and women seem to experience equal amount of work-family conflict. While gender may not be a direct source of work-family (and family-work) conflict, men and women may still experience and react differently to antecedents and outcomes of work-family conflict. The support for gender as a moderator of the relationship between antecedents and work-family (family-work) conflict is mixed. Of 14 explored job related antecedents to work-family conflict, gender moderated two relationships (Michel et al., 2011). Men experienced greater work-family conflict with increasing work role ambiguity, but also a greater reduction of work-family conflict with increasing job autonomy, compared to women (Michel et al., 2011). Gender did not moderate the relationship between family related antecedents and family-work conflict. Research on the moderating role of gender on the consequences of work-family conflict is also inconclusive. In the meta-analysis by Kossek and Ozeki (1998) women reported lower life satisfaction in response to work-family conflict than men (although confidence intervals were overlapping), however, in another meta-analysis by Ford et al. (2007) women reported higher family satisfaction in association with job stress than men. Although life and family satisfaction are clearly separate constructs, the opposite valence of the reactions to work-family conflict in these findings suggests that the role of gender in the reactions to work-family conflict is still worth exploring (Kinnunen et al., 2004).

In sum, recent studies do not uniformly confirm the existence of gender differences in the level and direction of inter-role conflict, and some in fact contradict the popular belief that family responsibilities are more likely to intrude upon women's careers and job satisfaction. Nevertheless, it is evident that men and women *do* have different experiences. In particular, despite considerable shifts in societal attitudes and values surrounding gender roles, research indicates that women still shoulder the major responsibility for family and household activities, especially those related to child rearing. As suggested recently by Cheung and Halpern (2010), however, women may have developed more adaptive strategies for coping with these burdens by redefining their work role.

In any event, it is evident that inter-role conflict (in particular between job and family demands) is a major stressor for an increasing number of individuals, especially as economic pressures require people to spend more and more time in paid employment. Recent interest in job-family conflict has focused not just on the sources of this form of strain, but also on strategies attempted at alleviating it, including the use of flextime, on-site child care centers, and other 'family-supportive' organizational programs (Thompson & Prottas, 2006). The effect of these organizational interventions and policies on alleviating work-family conflict is mixed (Kelly et al., 2008). However, employee's perceptions of support and control seem important in reducing levels of work-family conflict (Kelly et al., 2008).

We also need to examine generational differences. Research illustrates that there has been a significant increase in the number of multigenerational families in society, at a time when midlife individuals need to make provision for the onset of retirement and may themselves have health, relationship, and financial issues to contend with (Infurna et al., 2020). One consequence of this trend is a 'sandwich-generation' of employees who shoulder responsibility for the care of both their (typically adolescent or young adult) children and their aging parents (Turgeman-Lupo et al., 2020). Employees with a dual caregiving burden experienced higher levels of depressive symptoms compared with employees without caregiving or employees with only one caregiving role (Turgeman-Lupo et al., 2020).

Conclusion

In this chapter, we have summarized the effects of a variety of sources of work-related strain that have been studied in stress research. This review has not been exhaustive but has highlighted some of the most commonly reported, and most intense, stressors that are experienced by workers. Some of these variables will be discussed further in Chapter 5, which examines factors that contribute to job-related burnout. It is also important to note that although this chapter predominantly has referred to stressors that has maladaptive effects, research also suggest that the experience of some types of stressors may increase resilience (Crane & Searle, 2016) and intrinsic motivation (Kim & Beehr, 2018).

Two further issues need to be recognized when conducting research on potential stressors. First, as noted earlier, frequently stressors are not experienced in isolation, but rather occur in combination. For instance, a worker may simultaneously experience role ambiguity (perhaps due to lack of a clearly specified job description) and other stressors, such as interpersonal conflict with colleagues (over job boundaries) and pressures from a supervisor (concerned about lack of productivity). The combined impact of these stressors needs to be ascertained, not just their individual effects, and the whole (effect) may well be more than the sum of its parts. For example, a challenge stressor may be appraised as a hindrance stressor when encountered simultaneously with other stressors, which in turn may be the tipping point for experiencing strain. For instance, research suggests that different patterns (i.e., unstable or stable) of challenge stressors determine the effect on well-being outcomes (Rosen et al., 2020). Relatedly, another theoretical distinction that also has methodological ramifications is the differentiation between stressors that are short-term or one-off events (episodic stressors) and those that are ongoing (chronic stressors). Research has predominantly focused on chronic stressors at the expense of episodic events (Grebner et al., 2004). Investigating the effect of their co-occurrence on strain is also valuable as life seldom honors you with only one type of stressor. Importantly, there can be an interplay between chronic and episodic stressors, where the experience of chronic stressors affects the reaction to episodic stressors. Research suggests that chronic stressors may act as a background variable that escalates strain when encountering a stressful event (Wirtz et al., 2013). However, research in this area is still nascent. Further research is therefore needed to elucidate the potential interplay between chronic and episodic stressors. To study the interaction of chronic and episodic stressors, one possibility is to use experimental methods such as the inducements of work-related episodic stressors (Wetherell & Carter, 2014) while measuring various levels of chronic job-related stressors. Another possibility is to employ experience-related sampling methods where participants are asked to complete repeated surveys with brief intervals in their daily life during a relatively short study duration (Beal, 2015).

Second, there is continuing debate in the job stress literature about whether stressors should be investigated 'subjectively' or 'objectively' (O'Brien & Beehr, 2019; Spector, 1999). For example, in support of the subjectivity position, appraisal theories (e.g., the transactional model of stress) emphasize that the *perception* of a stimulus or event as threatening is critical for the experience of strain. The majority of stress studies in the occupational literature use self-reports of stressors and hence are based, either explicitly or implicitly, upon the assumption that subjective perceptions are the key to understanding stressor-strain relationships. On the other hand, resource theories (e.g., conservation of resources theory) highlight that major stressors at work are objective and affect workers relatively equally (Hobfoll et al., 2018). Further, stress management interventions, particularly those at the organizational level (see Chapter 8), are typically built upon a belief that certain stressors may transcend individual cognitions and attributions and can therefore be regarded as 'objective'. Again, to put this view simply, stressors may be assessed in some objective manner that is independent of how particular individuals perceive them. As noted earlier, for some stressors (e.g., decibel and working hours), there seem to exist thresholds that when passed increases the risk of strain for many people. Additionally, it is both of theoretical and practical relevance to investigate the convergence between objective and subjective assessments of job-related stressors. Do ratings from observers or other types of external data overlap substantively with self-report measures of stressors? Preliminary findings suggest some degree of convergence (Ganster & Rosen, 2013). However, subduing subjective self-report data with more 'objective' rated data on stressors is not without its own pitfalls (see Semmer et al., 2004 for a thorough assessment and discussion of alternative types of data). Limitations associated with self-report data, particularly when measures of stressors and strains are all based upon self-reports also need to be taken into account (this issue is discussed further in Chapter 9 of this book).

As the nature and forms of jobs are continually changing, it is imperative that job stress researchers explore new kinds of stressors that may result from new and different working conditions. For example, as discussed briefly here, an increasing number of employees are engaged in alternative work arrangements. The types of stressors associated with alternative work arrangements are only just beginning to surface, and the possible longer-term effects of this form of work are yet unknown. Longitudinal investigations are needed to determine the types of stressors and outcomes related to alternative work arrangements. Chapter 4 explores in more detail the potential outcomes, for both individual employees and organizations, of job stressors. Similarly, further research is needed on how individuals adapt and adjust to various job-related stressors and what organizations can do to offset the negative effects of environmental and psychosocial stressors in the workplace. In Chapter 7, we examine theoretical perspectives and empirical findings concerning individual stress-coping strategies, and Chapter 8 discusses stress management interventions at the organizational level. In our view, it is important to emphasize that the responsibility for stress management lies with both individual workers and employers. It is therefore relevant for researchers and practitioners alike to reflect upon the following questions: How can work environments be constructed to minimize negative stressful experiences? How can psychological strain be alleviated when it does occur? How can working environments with sufficient levels of challenges to facilitate psychological growth be co-created?

4

ASSESSING JOB-RELATED STRAINS

In this chapter, we discuss the assessment of strain – that is, the individual's physical, psychological, and behavioral responses to stressors – and we review the large array of measures that have been used to capture workplace strains. As noted in Chapter 1, strain may be conceptualized as a dependent variable (a response to disturbing or threatening stimuli) and may cover a range of manifestations. The variety and scope of strain measures may stem from the fact that the common expression 'being under stress' illustrates that at times virtually any response may be seen as reflecting strain. In addition, because individuals respond in many different ways, a variety of different responses have been treated by researchers as indicators of strain. The aim of this chapter is to examine these strain indicators and to consider the implications of such measures for job stress research. While the bulk of strain indicators represent adverse experiences, there is, however, a rising interest in the possible beneficial consequences of stressors that involves growth and learning. We will briefly discuss this research toward the end.

CLASSIFYING STRAIN

Stress researchers often distinguish between three major categories of possible stress responses or strains: *physiological, psychological*, and *behavioral* (Bliese et al., 2017). Each of the three categories will be discussed in turn. Our aim is to draw attention to the range of measures used, to explore difficulties associated with each of the three categories, and to raise issues that may help to clarify stressor–strain relationships. We begin with an overview of physiological indicators.

Physiological Strain

While self-reports of well-being and health still represent the most prevalent way to operationalize outcome variables (see for instance the review of studies using experience sampling design by Ilies et al., 2016), the last two decades have witnessed a growth in the use of physiological indicators to investigate physiological strain in job stress research. There are multiple reasons for the increased examination of physiological responses to work related stressors. First, the concept of stress has been examined from a wide array of research disciplines, encompassing clinical (e.g., epidemiological), biological, and psychological research traditions. Recently, these perspectives of stress have become more integrated (Cohen et al., 2016). This trend has likely stimulated research on the physiological responses to stressors in the work domain. Second, technological advances, both in the laboratory and in field settings, have made collecting physiological data feasible (Akinola, 2010; Bliese et al., 2017). While measuring physiological data still require, at times, sophisticated technology, the use of such equipment is more budget-friendly than before. Third, ill health caused by stress is costly (Goh et al., 2016). Physiological responses to stressors may be important mechanisms explaining health-related outcome variables such as absenteeism, health-related costs, and ultimately declined productivity warranting a deeper understanding of the physiological mechanisms involved.

Ganster et al. (2013, 2018) have provided reviews of the types and nature of physiological measures used in job stress research. To do so, they build upon the allostatic load model (McEwen, 1998; McEwen & Stellar, 1993; McEwen & Wingfield, 2003) that we will briefly explain. Allostasis is 'a fundamental process through which organisms actively adjust to both predictable and unpredictable events' (McEwen & Wingfield, 2003, p. 2). Although allostasis ensure that the physiological systems adjust in the response to stressors, it also comes with a potential cost to the body (McEwen & Wingfield, 2003). The allostatic load refers to the wear and tear on the body due to prolonged, repeated, or inadequate physiological activation to stressors (McEwen, 1998). The allostatic load model provides an overarching description of the sequential physiological responses to stressors. These responses encompass multiple biological systems (e.g., neuroendocrine and cardiovascular) that interact with each other and that the body naturally advance and recalibrate in a coordinated fashion when encountering threats to its equilibrium. Importantly, while these responses are instigated in order to meet the environmental demands, a prolonged activation or a failure to be turned off when the stressor terminates, can impair health (Ganster & Rosen, 2013).

The allostatic load model distinguishes between three stages of physiological processes with different physiological indicators of strain (see Figure 4.1). The first stage of allostatic load refers to the immediate physiological responses to a stressor. The sympathetic–adrenal–medullary (SAM) axis responds within seconds and the hypothalamic–pituitary–adrenal (HPA) axis within minutes after encountering a stressor (Sapolsky et al., 2000). Cortisol, often labeled 'the stress hormone', is the most common physical indicator reported in job stress research (Ganster et al., 2018). Studies suggest that work stressors are related to physiological indicators of strain such as cortisol and blood pressure (measured as the momentary reaction to stressor) with higher effect detected in studies using controlled laboratory experiment compared to event based sampling in field studies (Ganster & Rosen, 2013; Ganster et al., 2018). One challenge when studying primary allostatic load

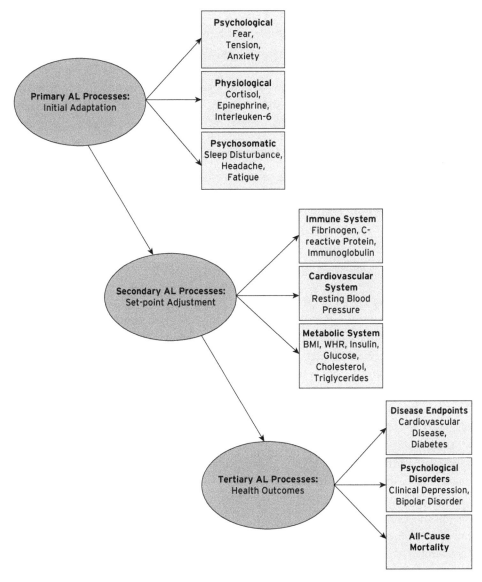

Figure 4.1 Allostatic load model of the stress process. *Note:* AL = allostatic load; BMI = body mass index; WHR = waist-to-hip ratio

Source: Ganster and Rosen (2013).

indicators is the immediacy of the physiological responses to a work stressor. Thus, data collection of these physiological indicators needs to operate in close vicinity to the work-related stressor, an effort that is not without its difficulties.

If the physiological responses in the first stage are malfunctioning or activated over an extended amount of time, this may lead to the second stage of allostatic load. In this stage, biological systems, such as the cardiovascular system, the immune system or the metabolic system, alter their normal operating set points. The second stage in the allo-static load model has accumulated more research than the first stage, perhaps reflecting a less strenuous data collection scheme. Secondary allostatic load is the result of multiple systems that interact in potentially non-linear ways (Juster et al., 2010). This may explain why research solely focusing on one particular regulatory system and its physiological indicators of strain has provided mixed evidence, while research that relies on multiple indicators combined into an index has more consistently found support for the effect of stressors on secondary allostatic load indicators (Ganster & Rosen, 2013). There is still no consensus on which physiological indicators to combine into a multi-system index of biomarkers and how to best calculate the index (Ganster et al., 2018; Mauss et al., 2014). Commonly, physiological indicators of secondary allostatic load include abnormal levels of high density lipoprotein cholesterol, glycosylated hemoglobin, cortisol, norepineph-rine, diastolic and systolic blood pressure, c-reactive protein, interleukin-6, and waist-to-hip ratio (Juster et al., 2010). In more plain language, a person in this stage can over time show, for example, increased blood pressure and disproportionate insulin glucose ratio, have abnormal activation in the immune system, and experience weight gains in the belly area. Approaches to create an allostatic load index range from a simple count of subclinical scores on each indicator to more sophisticated calculations such as k-Means cluster analysis (Juster et al., 2010). More recent approaches involve factor analysis (Wiley et al., 2016), however, not without critique (Crook & Booth, 2017). Albeit, the unresolved questions regarding at what level each physiological indicator signifies health risk and how to best combine the indicators (Mauss et al., 2014), research suggests that the cur-rent operationalizations of secondary allostatic load still serve a value as they are pre-dictive of health outcomes (Juster et al., 2010).

Finally, in the third stage of allostatic load, the body suffers disease endpoints such as cardiovascular disease, clinical depression, or even mortality as a result of the accumu-lated physical toll on the body. The bulk of this research is situated in the epidemiological literature (Ganster & Rosen, 2013). Nevertheless, scholars in the work stress area need to be informed of this line of research given the aversive individual consequences, such as increased probability of sickness and death (Gonzalez-Mulé & Cockburn, 2020), and the organizational economical tolls involved, such as healthcare costs (Ganster et al., 2001) or working days lost (UK Health and Safety Executive, 2020).

A range of disease endpoints have been examined such as cardiovascular diseases, mental disorders, and endocrine disorders (Ganster & Rosen, 2013). A considerable number of meta-analyses have examined work stressors and cardiovascular diseases. In a meta-analysis by Virtanen and Kivimäki (2018), working long hours (≥55 hours a week) increased the risk of both coronary heart disease and stroke, in line with a previous meta-analysis (Virtanen et al., 2012). Many epidemiological studies have been guided by the job-demands-control model (Karasek, 1979) and its extensions (job-demands-resources by Bakker & Demerouti, 2017). People who experience high levels of job strain (defined as high job demands, and low control and support) are also at risk of coronary heart disease (Kivimäki et al., 2011). Job strain has also been related to decreased heart rate variability, an indicator of imbalance in the autonomic nervous system (Jarczok et al., 2013, 2020). In their review of the literature, Ganster and Rosen (2013) conclude that people with high job demands and low control are more likely to suffer from depression. Likewise, people who work excessive overtime hours are at risk of depressive symptoms (Virtanen et al., 2018). A meta-analysis also suggests that stressors at work increased the risk of type 2 diabetes (Kelly & Ismail, 2015). For working long hours, the risk of suffering with type 2 diabetes seems to only hold for people with low socioeconomic status (Kivimäki et al., 2015). To sum up, several job stressors are found to increase the risk of developing serious medical conditions.

While we have emphasized research using objective measurements of biological processes, it is worth mentioning that subjective measurements (i.e., self-report) are valuable tools in understanding the physiological toll experienced by the individual. The studies included in the meta-analysis by Nixon et al. (2011) were solely self-reports of eight different physical symptoms (e.g., head-aches, dizziness, appetite). The nature of these symptoms makes self-reports appropriate and reflects the clinical assessment of such symptoms. All of the work-related stressors were related to physical symptoms with varying strength (Nixon et al., 2011).

The allostatic load model represents a pedagogical mediated model, with stressors as antecedents, the first and second stage of allostatic load functions as mechanisms for the subsequent stage, and the third stage represents the final outcome variables. As noted unanimously, the fine-grain mechanisms are far more complicated, represented by multisystems that interact in complex way. Thus, understanding more precisely what type of physiological response, the intensity, frequency, and duration of that response in interplay with various other physiological responses that over time will result in dysfunction of biological systems, ill health and disease for workers is warranted. Likewise, according to the allostatic load model the type of physiological strain produced by an acute (episodic) stressor is quite different from that produced by stressors that are more ongoing (chronic). Yet, there is a paucity of research in understanding how the role of time plays out, and the exact timeline for when the initial adaptation in the first stage leads to dysregulation in the second stage (Ganster & Rosen, 2013). In Chapter 9, we will briefly address some of the technical and ethical considerations to consider when applying physiological measurement. The conclusions that can be drawn from reviewing physiological responses to job-related stressors suggest that this field represents an intriguing area for future research.

Psychological Strain

Research in the job-stress literature has demonstrated a decided interest in the psychological consequences of stressor exposure. As noted earlier, psychological strains resulting from job stressors are the most commonly studied (Spector & Pindek, 2016). This does not mean that these manifestations of strain are necessarily the primary or the most frequent reactions to work stressors. It more likely reflects the fact that most job stress researchers have a background in psychology and are perhaps more familiar with this type of measurement (Jex & Beehr, 1991). In response to societal trends and shifting work practices, researchers have examined an expanded range of psychological strain variables in the last two decades compared to earlier decades (Bliese et al., 2017).

Research reviews have revealed that, regardless of how they are conceptualized and assessed, psychological strains are strong correlates of work-related stressors (Amstad et al., 2011; Bowling et al., 2015; De Witte et al., 2016; Ford et al., 2014). Two issues are of interest here: (a) whether any patterns can be identified in the number and types of strain measures used in research and (b) the extent of conceptual overlap between these measures (Kahn & Byosiere, 1992). Numerous psychological indicators have been adopted in job-stress research. For example, in the meta-analysis of potential consequences of work-load by Bowling et al. (2015), 17 different measures of strain were used, of which 11 could be classified as psychological strains. Examples of variables included as indexes of psychological strain in the studies were emotional exhaustion, distress, depersonalization, organizational commitment, employee engagement, mental well-being, and life satisfaction. The six other strain measures assessed behavioral and physical health factors. Of the psychological strains, job dissatisfaction was the most investigated psychological strain reported in 97 out of 469 samples. Job satisfaction was also the most investigated outcome variable in a meta-analysis on the outcomes of self-reported organizational constraints (Pindek & Spector, 2016). Given the prominent status of job satisfaction, this raises questions about how best to measure it. Traditionally, both global and multi-faceted measures have been used (Judge et al., 2020).

While we in the first edition of this chapter of strain asked the question 'What about emotions'?, variants of emotional strain is now widely examined (Pindek & Spector, 2016). Given that models of stress are essentially theories about emotional reactions (Lazarus, 1993) and 'stress constitutes an emotional subset referring largely to emotions that are distress related' (Lazarus, 1995, p. 183), the increased explicit attention to emotionally related outcome variables in job stress research is reassuring. Several meta-analyses investigating psychological responses to work-related stressors include emotional reactions such as depression, irritation, anxiety, cynicism, and depersonalization (Ford et al., 2014; Nohe et al., 2015; Schmidt et al., 2014). Further, emotional variables such as exhaustion, emotions, and burnout are increasingly common in stress research (Bliese et al., 2017) reflecting a trend within organization psychology/behavior (Ashkanasy & Dorris, 2017). We will address exhaustion and burnout in more depth in Chapter 5.

Different operationalizations of emotional strain are used in the literature. In the meta-analysis by Chang et al. (2007) that investigated emotional strain and organizational citizenship behaviors (OCB), the studies included operationalized emotional strain predominantly by the 'Work Tension Scale' (House & Rizzo, 1972) or by emotional exhaustion. However, it is important to note that categories of emotional and affective strain may represent heterogeneous indicators, an observation that is also relevant for other types of psychological strain indicators. For example, in the categorization of affective strains by Pindek et al. (2019), indicators included 'negative affect, mood, anger,

anxiety, embarrassment, irritation, affective distress, mental health complaints, rumination, worries, affective well-being, emotional exhaustion, burnout, fatigue, ego
depletion, job satisfaction, and need for recovery' (pp. 8–9). While most of these indicators on face value are related to affect, others are traditionally considered to be attitudinal or mental health indicators. The lack of consistent definitions of constructs
related to affect and emotion is not reserved to organizational stress research, but is
pertinent to much broader research streams (Gooty et al., 2009).

Measurements of emotional strain are predominantly based on self-report that are
assessed cross sectionally. However, self-report may not be the most appropriate measurement to capture various affective constructs of interest (e.g., physiological arousal
involved in emotions), and often employment of experience-sampling methods is
necessary to capture the fluctuating nature of emotional states (Ashkanasy & Dorris,
2017). Despite the increased inclusion of emotional variables as potential indicators of
psychological strain, there is a lack of systematic treatment of the general construct of
affect and emotion within the job stress framework and, more specifically, the role that
emotions play in the stress-coping process.

Different categorizations of psychological strains have been employed in the work
stress literature. In their meta-analysis of the consequences of job insecurity, De Witte
et al. (2016) distinguished between work-related psychological strains and non-specific
general psychological strains, noting that the majority of studies had examined the latter.
In the meta-analysis, 15 studies examined work-related psychological strains, mainly
burn-out and job dissatisfaction and to a lesser degree work engagement, and 32 studies
investigated non-specific, general strain mainly indicated by responses to general health
measures and depression symptoms (De Witte et al., 2016). Thus, in relation to the
stressor job insecurity, research has mainly investigated generic strains, not directly
coupled with the job domain.

A related, yet different, way of conceptualizing psychological strains is by categorizing
the strains in relation to the domain of the stressor. In research on work-family conflict,
conflict is created by work interfering with the family role or the family role interfering
with work (Amstad et al., 2011). The resulting outcome of work-family conflict can be
strain experienced in the work domain such as lowered level of job satisfaction, organizational commitment, and higher levels of burnout. Another group of outcome variables
are related to the family domain, such as lower levels of marital and family satisfaction
(Amstad et al., 2011). This categorization of work-related strain or family-related strain
cut across the general distinction between physiological, psychological, and behavioral
strains as both include behavioral strain such as performance. Yet, this categorization
suits the testing of specific theoretically proposed relationship, were the effects of work
(family) to family (work) interference can either be more pronounced in the same
domain as the origin of the stressor or in the opposite domain. Recent meta-analyses
have found support for the matching of stressor and outcome domain, where work
(family) stressors have a more pronounced effect on work (family) strains than family
(work) strains (Amstad et al., 2011; Nohe et al., 2015).

While the overall categorization of strain into physiological, psychological, and behavioral strain is well accepted, it should still be noted that some constructs do not readily fit into only one of these categories. For example, sleep is an outcome variable related to both physiological, psychological, and behavioral strain. Further, categorizations of strain are sometimes based on the level of interest. For instance, when Bowling et al. (2015) examined the consequences of work load, they distinguished between strains that were relevant for the employee or the organization. While employee well-being such as job satisfaction is closer to the interest of the employee, job performance is of special value for the organization.

Two observations are pertinent at this juncture. First, there seems to be a degree of flexibility and looseness in the way in which the term *psychological strain* has been applied in job stress research. As noted earlier, it would appear that virtually any (negative) reaction to stressors has been interpreted as an indicator of strain – a finding that highlights a lack of conceptual differentiation. To some extent, the conceptual overlap between measures has been accentuated by the predominant reliance solely on self-report techniques. Although these have an important function in the assessment of psychological strain, future research needs to more clearly define the roles of different strain indicators, rather than assuming their functional equivalence.

More importantly, greater attention needs to be given to psychological strain as an interrelated sequence that unfolds dynamically to explain individual well-being in a wider time horizon. In doing so, we can seek theoretical refinement of the relationships between work-related stressors and various short-term and long-term psychological strain variables. For example, what are the potential psychological mechanisms between immediate emotional responses to workplace stressors and long-term exhaustion, burnout, and disengagement? Research questions related to time sequences have measurement implications. Often the same constructs are measured in different time intervals without a theoretical justification for the chosen time interval (Lesener et al., 2019). Researchers need to define the appropriate time lag between the measurement of a specific type of stressor and the chosen psychological strain to capture the relationship (Taris & Kompier, 2014). While appraisal theories will suggest that these relationships may happen rather quickly, conservation of resources theory and its notion of downward spirals will propose a longer time frame for their constructs of interest to manifest themselves (Darr & Johns, 2008).

Behavioral Strain

Behavioral responses to work stressors, especially job performance, are frequently examined (Bliese et al., 2017). In the meta-analysis by Bowling et al. (2015), strains were divided into two broad categories. The first category included those of *significance to the organization* (responses that have a direct impact on organizational functioning, including such behaviors as job performance, turnover, and absenteeism). Of these approximately half were behavioral responses. The second set covered those of *significance to the individual* (employee well-being); however, none were behavioral strains.

Although responses of significance to organizations are not unimportant for the individual, for organizations, these responses may serve as indicators that warrant interventions to combat the negative impact of stressors. Research on more proximal behavioral outcome variables of importance to the individual employee such as alcohol (Liu et al., 2009) and tobacco use (Heikkilä et al., 2012) seems scarce.

Behavioral strain has been examined in a number of different but not mutually exclusive ways. In their nature, overt behavioral responses to stressors are observable to others which permit the use of other-assessed data. Further, behavioral outputs may be accessed through secondary sources such as organizational records of absenteeism and turnover. The use of other sources to measure behavioral outcomes may alleviate concerns of inflated relationships attached to self-reported data (Podsakoff et al., 2012).

Job performance is a multifaceted construct measured in different ways (Viswesvaran & Ones, 2000). In their meta-analysis of the relationship between various work stressors and performance, Gilboa et al. (2008) examined studies that included self-rated performance, supervisor-rated performance, objective ratings, qualitative assessed performance and quantitative assessed performance, and more generic performance (unspecified in the original studies). The majority of studies operationalized performance as self- or supervisor rated (approximately 76% of the studied effect sizes), while objective ratings of performance was only investigated in 8% of the studies. Neither quantitative assessments (7%) nor qualitative assessments of job performance (4%) were frequently made. Interestingly, irrespective of the chosen dimension of performance (either self-rated, supervisory-rated or objective performance), the effect sizes were comparable in size suggesting that self-reported performance is of value in stress-research (Gilboa et al., 2008). However, a limitation in the stressor-performance studies is the use of cross-sectional studies that prevents causal interpretations of the relationships (Gilboa et al., 2008).

OCB is related to job performance in that it may impact organizational results but are more discretionary and contextual (Campbell & Wiernik, 2015). OCB may be directed at other individuals or the organization. In the meta-analysis by Eatough et al. (2011) on the relationship between role stressors and OCB, 16 out of 44 samples collected both types of targets of OCB (individuals and the organization), while a smaller number of samples investigated either individually targeted (eight samples) or organizational (seven samples) targeted OCB. Further, OCB may be rated by either the employee or others (often supervisor-reported). In the meta-analysis by Eatough et al. (2011), an equal number of studies used self-reported OCB compared to supervisor-reported, of which the latter suggested stronger relationships between role stressors and OCB.

Absenteeism is another behavioral strain that is frequently assessed in the work stress literature using both different variants of self-report and organizational records (Darr & Johns, 2008; Jiang & Lavaysse, 2018). Records based, frequency (e.g., number of times absent), and time lost (e.g., total number of days absent) are commonly used as measurement of absenteeism (Darr & Johns, 2008). The various ways of measuring absenteeism did not in general affect the magnitude of effects in the meta-analysis of work stressors and absenteeism by Darr and Johns (2008). However, later scrutiny of the relationship between record based and self-reported absenteeism by Johns and Miraglia (2015) suggests that employees may in fact underreport their absenteeism, a finding of both theoretical and practical importance.

Presenteeism, the apparent opposite of absenteeism, is being physically present in the workplace, but functionally absent (Cooper, 1996), or simply 'attending work while ill' (Johns, 2010, p. 519). However, there is no clear consensus of how presenteeism should be defined. The research on presenteeism has either tended to focus on the behavioral act of showing up for work (mainly European scholars) or the productivity loss involved (mainly US scholars) (Johns, 2010). Naturally, the diverging perspectives have measurement implications. The behavioral perspective on presenteeism has relied on self-report, for example a frequency indicator of attending work while ill (Ruhle et al., 2020). The focus on productivity loss has employed self-report measures, supervisor ratings, but also objective organizational records (Karanika-Murray & Cooper, 2018).

Caution needs to be exercised in the interpretation of the above categories because simply identifying and assessing behavioral responses does not necessarily mean that they were caused by work-related stressors. They may, for instance, be the result of other factors operating in an individual's life, including off-the-job stressors and even dispositional tendencies (see Chapter 6). Second, a shared limitation of studies across multiple types of behavioral indicators of strain is the reliance on cross-sectional designs and that they generally fail to capture the presumed complexity of the stressor–strain relationship (Ford et al., 2014; Taris & Kompier, 2014).

While there are indications that self-reported behavioral data may be valid indicators (Gilboa et al., 2008; Johns & Miraglia, 2015), it seems that too often when collecting behavioral data the approach simply involves asking people to describe their responses, rather than collecting other (perhaps more objective) behavioral observations. However, in comparison with psychological strain, multisource data are more often employed when investigating behavioral strain, a natural consequence of the different observability of psychological and behavioral strain.

There is considerable agreement among reviewers on the state of current research and what has to be done. One frequently addressed limitation is the use of cross-sectional designs. The relationship between potentially stressful events (stressors) and behavior is complex; understanding this relationship entails unraveling the process through which different variables are linked (Jex & Beehr, 1991). Theoretically, physiological or psychological reactions are thought to be intermediate variables between stressor and behavioral strain. At the very least, it is necessary to determine whether a direct relationship can be assumed (e.g., work overload causes counterproductive behavior) or whether the causal pathway between stressors and strains is always mediated by some affective state (e.g., workload causes irritability, which in turn causes counterproductive work behavior). Further, a finer distinction between short-term versus long-term behavioral responses as well as the potential of reversed relationship (i.e., strain → stressor) is seldom addressed in the literature (Taris & Kompier, 2014).

Clearly, there is much to be done to increase our knowledge of the behavioral mani-festations of job-related strain. As with psychological indicators, research on behavioral strain has tended not to differentiate between behavioral responses toward various workplace stressors, and there has also been a proclivity to assume causal mechanisms without explicitly testing their validity. Nevertheless, as we shall see in later chapters, recent research has begun to explore the utility of behavioral measures of strain, along with the extreme manifestation of strain known as burnout (see Chapter 5), and to illustrate their relevance in the investigation of stress processes in organizations.

WHAT ABOUT ASSESSING JOB-RELATED THRIVING?

Research on strain has predominantly focused on the aversive responses to stressors, which is not unexpected, given that definitions of strain emphasize the negative and potential harmful reactions to stressors (Beehr et al., 2000). This tendency represents a common symmetrical research frame that investigates (negative) stressors and their (negative) strains (Lindebaum & Jordan, 2012). However, stress theories such as appraisal theories (e.g., Lazarus & Folkman, 1984), conservation of resources (Hobfoll, 1989), the cognitive activation theory of stress (Ursin & Eriksen, 2010), and the challenge-hindrance stressor framework (LePine et al., 2004) all imply, through different mechanisms, that stressors may not always have derailing consequences, but that they also may lead to job-related growth and thriving.

In recent years, research has documented how some stressors that are demanding, but can be overcome through extra effort or skills (i.e., challenges the individual), may have positive consequences for individuals. Stressors that are perceived challenging may pro-vide the employee with 'opportunities to learn, achieve, and demonstrate the type of competence that tends to get rewarded' (Crawford et al., 2010, p. 836). In support of this, stressors that are appraised as challenges are related to increased feelings of learning at work (Prem et al., 2017). Further, challenging stressors are positively related to psycho-logical empowerment and organization-based self-esteem that function as intrinsic motivational resources which fuel employee engagement and protects against ill-health (Kim & Beehr, 2018). Finally, challenging stressors may bolster the individual by building long-term resilience (Crane & Searle, 2016). Nevertheless, to capture the potential beneficial effects of stress within the framework of challenge (and hindrance) stressors, a reformation of the framework may be needed (Horan et al., 2020).

Given the prevalence of stressors at work, it is of value to further explore their potential to increase employees' growth and learning. While it may be tempting to dichotomize stressors into 'good or bad', research suggests that the mechanisms through which stressors work on outcomes may be conflicting and opposing (Rodell & Judge, 2009; Rosen et al., 2020). Thus, we may question whether long-term conse-quences of certain stressors decisively are negative, or whether they may have positive consequences for the individual? Does a positive relationship between stressors and desirable outcomes depend upon the intensity of the stressor and the appropriate regulation (either physiologically, psychologically, or behaviorally) of the individual?

Given the overwhelmingly negative strains that are documented from stressors (including challenging stressors see for example Mazzola & Disselhorst, 2019), investigating the potential positive consequences of stressors should for now be a purely theoretical journey with practical interventions aimed at increasing certain stressors put on hold until the burden of evidence clearly favor the beneficial effects of such stressors.

Conclusion

Despite the large number of physiological, psychological, and behavioral measures available, researchers have paid only moderate attention to delineating the strain side of dynamic stress relationships. A main reason for this is that 'being under stress' has a wide variety of meanings, and to some extent almost any negative reaction could be considered as 'strain'. To advance our understanding of work-related stress, it is time to consider the dynamical process of strain relationships. One major theme emerging from a review of empirical work in this field is that researchers must consider the appropriateness of the type(s) of strain being measured and the temporal lag between measurements. Thus, researchers should specify which and when strains might be anticipated in different contexts, and how one strain may lead to the cascading effect of other types of strains. This work involves including different types of strain (physiological, psychological, and behavioral) and the development of theories that explain the interconnectedness of the strain process. It is necessary to move from generic categories of strains to more detailed descriptions that identify whether, for example, strains are acute or chronic, their temporal sequence, whether they engage in reciprocal relationships, and whether they reflect general or more specific feelings.

It is not just a question of 'fit' between stressors and strain. There is also the question of the relationship across different types of strain. Research exploring the relationship between different strains may well begin to push us toward considering them in terms of notions like risk factors and whether the experience of one strain may make individuals more vulnerable to other types of strain. For example, what are the long-term consequences of job disengagement? Would having a clearer understanding of this help to clarify its impact on health and well-being and provide a context for considering its role as a likely risk factor, thus enabling researchers to reevaluate the significance of such a measure? As our understanding of the stressor–strain relationship improves, it may be time to consider the role of different strain measures and the utility of thinking of them more in terms of notions like risk, vulnerability, and health, in much the same way as we have applied terms like *chronic* and *episodic* to stressors. This type of research would certainly require a test battery approach involving the careful selection of measures, the use of both psychological and physiological measures, and the use of methods like multilevel structural equation modeling and longitudinal design.

The process between stressors and various types of strains (and their interactions) is complex. Other elements that add further complexity are the situational and personal moderators at different stages of the stress process that impact the relationships.

These are issues we reflect upon in Chapter 6, where we examine moderators of the stressor-strain relationships.

The role of emotions in workplace stress needs more systematic attention from researchers. Two conclusions clearly emerge from a review of the organizational behavior literature: (a) Emotions are fundamental to an understanding of stress, as well as other responses; and (b) our knowledge of their functioning in work settings is still progressing (Ashkanasy & Dorris, 2017). One issue that has been identified is the tendency to aggregate emotions into either positive or negative valence categories, instead of focusing on discrete emotions (Gooty et al., 2009). From a research perspective, this means that 'when we theoretically treat all negative (or positive) discrete emotions as functionally the same, we lose sight of the fact that different processes drive each of them, and that different outcomes can result from them too' (Gooty et al., 2009, p. 835). Identifying the meaning of emotions to individuals, specifying the links between specific emotions and environmental events, and delineating the conditions under which particular emotions function as mediators and/or moderators of stressor-strain relationships are high-priority issues for future investigations of job-related stress.

More research is needed on the conditions under which environmental events are perceived as positive challenges versus negative stressors and when a challenge becomes a stressor. Lepine et al. (2005, 2007) investigated the differential impact of challenge and hindrance stressors on various types of strain. While there is still a lack of consensus on the validity of the challenge-hindrance framework (Mazzola & Disselhorst, 2019), it still offers a theoretical framework for linking certain types of stressors with positive consequences for the individual (O'Brien & Beehr, 2019). For certain stressors, the long-term consequence may be increased learning and growth.

Finally, there is the issue of objective or subjective measurement. This is not simply an issue of replacing one set of measures by another. Strain measures need to be evaluated on their own merits. Although common-method variance may be a problem with self-report measures (Podsakoff et al., 2012), that in itself is not a basis to dismiss all such measures or the relationships they produce. The message that we should take from the objective-subjective debate is that each method comes with its own set of difficulties and that consequently measurement should be taken seriously. Irrespective of the measurement approach, problems will always emerge from measures that are poorly developed or not well understood. Therefore, researchers are faced with two priorities. The first is to focus on issues of measurement exploring scale properties to establish their psychometric properties, what such scales are measuring, and the relationship between different measures. The second priority is to further explore the relationships between objective and subjective measures, their predictive abilities, and the utility of juxtaposing objective and subjective methodologies.

The issues raised in this chapter are no different from those presented in other chapters in this book. They all require that researchers give careful consideration to the context within which job stress encounters take place, particularly the processes that link different components. They also require new and innovative ways of thinking about what is being measured, whether measures capture the essence of the variable under investigation, and the meaning behind the measures. In this way, new directions can be identified, creative measurement strategies can be put in place, and research will make a constructive contribution to the creation and maintenance of healthy work environments.

5

A SPECIAL FORM OF STRAIN
Job-Related Burnout

The phenomenon of burnout was first identified by Bradley (1969) in a paper on probation officers and was further elaborated upon by Freudenberger (1974) from his observations of the extreme psychological strain often experienced by workers in the human service professions, such as nurses, police officers, social workers, and school-teachers. Since that time, and especially after the turn of the century, there has been a huge increase in the number of scientific studies of this extreme and specific manifestation of job-related strain. A search in Web of Science and Google Scholar indicated close to 6,000 scientific studies and over 90,000 publications including books, book chapters, research reports, and non-English-language publications on job burnout over the 50 years since the phenomenon was identified (Schaufeli et al., 2019). Studies were initially conducted primarily among human service professionals but increasingly in other areas of employment as well. Given the widespread attention given to burnout in both academic and applied publications and the popular media, along with the very severe consequences of burnout for individuals and their organizations, we believe that this issue warrants separate consideration from other forms of job-related strain.

Burnout, like other manifestations of strain, is a product of the interaction between environmental factors (demands and resources) and individual perceptions and behaviors (such as coping). As we have outlined earlier in this volume, stress does not reside solely within the environment or within the individual but results from the dynamic interplay that occur between these elements. The same overarching framework needs to be applied when considering the unique variety of strain known as burnout.

In this chapter, therefore, we will examine the concept of burnout, models of burnout development, theories of burnout, various methods for measuring levels of job-related burnout, and some of the major antecedents and consequences of this unique form of job strain. Finally, we will discuss recent developments in our understanding of burnout and consider the dynamic interplay between individual, teams and organization. Chapters 7 and 8 explore strategies for combating strain, including burnout.

Maslach (1993), a foremost contributor to the study of burnout, noted that it 'is now recognized as an important social and individual problem' (p. 19). Over the years, job burnout has remained a critical concern for organizations as substantial empirical evidence shows that job-related burnout carries significant costs for individual well-being and organizational functioning, including personal ill health, absenteeism, turnover, and reduced productivity (Pervez & Halbesleben, 2017).

Ahola and Hakanen (2014) have highlighted some of the health-related consequences of excessive strain and burnout, especially mental disorder and somatic health problems, such as cardiovascular and coronary heart disease, diabetes, common infections, and musculoskeletal disorders (see also Chapter 4 of this book). We will examine some of the specific outcomes of burnout a little later in this chapter. Suffice it to say that, as with strain generally, there is considerable concern over the negative impact that burnout can have on individual employees and organizations.

As mentioned previously, early research on this topic concentrated on employees in the helping occupations, especially health care professionals, and attempted to identify the extent and pervasiveness of burnout in these occupational groups, as well as some of the possible causes of burnout. This line of research has continued, but in the past two decades attention has also been given to nonservice occupations, including managers and supervisors, the military, and various other employee groups.

DEFINITION

Early conceptualizations of burnout, e.g., Freudenberger and Richelson (1980) who described burnout in terms of chronic fatigue, depression, and frustration; incorporated some of the key elements of the burnout phenomenon, but were problematic because they confounded burnout with variables that are normally considered as distinct from, although related to, burnout – especially depression and chronic fatigue. While studies of the overlap between burnout and depression have yielded inconsistent results (Bianchi et al., 2015; Koutsimani et al., 2019), there is considerable evidence that depression should be differentiated from burnout, in that the former refers to a particular psychological condition that could be regarded as a potential outcome of burnout rather than as part of the burnout syndrome itself (Ahola & Hakanen, 2014; Schaufeli, 2017). Similarly, it is important to differentiate burnout from just physical fatigue, as the burnout syndrome encompasses much more than fatigue. The medical condition known as chronic fatigue syndrome (Hobfoll & Shirom, 1993) refers to long-term physical exhaustion characterized by tiredness or lethargy, impairment of one's activities and performance, and a general depletion of energy resources. These features may to some extent be shared with burnout as it is operationalized in the stress literature. However, burnout encompasses emotional as well as physical exhaustion and also cognitive and psychological impairment.

Another early definition of burnout is that of Cherniss (1980), who described it as a process of disengagement in response to job-related stressors. Imbalance between job demands and available resources leads to an emotional response characterized by anxiety, tension, fatigue, and strain (or exhaustion). This response in turn produces changes in the individual's attitudes and behavior, including defensive coping (preoccupation with gratifying one's own needs) and depersonalization (a cynical detachment from clients and their problems).

In the late 1970s and early 1980s, systematic investigations of burnout led to greater communality in definitions. At that time, Christina Maslach and her colleagues (Maslach, 1982; Maslach & Jackson, 1981) conceptualized burnout as having three core components: emotional exhaustion, depersonalization, and (lack of) personal accomplishment. Maslach's classic model of burnout characterizes emotional exhaustion as a depletion of emotional energy and a feeling that one's emotional resources are inadequate to deal with the situation. This emotional exhaustion may also be linked with physical fatigue and cognitive 'weariness'. According to Pervez and Halbesleben (2017), employees who are suffering from exhaustion feel that the effort they put into their job has reached its limit and therefore are no longer able to adapt to their work environment.

A common consequence of emotional exhaustion is a tendency toward *depersonalization*, in which employees feel detached from work and not caring about their job or individuals in the work setting (e.g., clients, customers, or even coworkers) (Leiter, 1993; Leiter & Maslach, 1988). Although this may help to reduce intense emotional arousal, which can interfere with functioning in crisis situations, excessive detachment from others can produce a callous and cynical approach to their welfare (Bianchi et al., 2015). Finally, the third component of burnout in Maslach's formulation is diminished *personal accomplishment*, characterized by a tendency to evaluate one's behavior and performance negatively. As a result, the person experiences feelings of incompetence on the job and an inability to achieve performance goals (Halbesleben & Buckley, 2004).

The above three-component conceptualization is the most widely accepted model of burnout (Pervez & Halbesleben, 2017), partly at least because Maslach and her associates constructed an easy-to-use questionnaire (the Maslach Burnout Inventory [MBI]) to measure the three dimensions of burnout (see the section 'Measurement of Burnout' later in this chapter). While the burnout concept initially referred to individuals doing 'people work' of some kind (Maslach, 1993), the modern definition and measure of burnout have generalized beyond human service occupations. The formulation of burnout introduced in 1996 (Schaufeli et al., 1996) retained the original emotional exhaustion dimension, although it extended the sources of exhaustion beyond problems with people (especially clients). The new characterization substituted *cynicism* for *depersonalization* and *professional efficacy* for *personal accomplishment*. Whereas *depersonalization* refers specifically to relationships with other people, cynicism represents indifference or a 'distant' attitude toward work generally, which may (or may not) include people encountered in the context of the job. As the authors describe it, 'cynicism represents dysfunctional coping … in that [it] reduces the energy available for performing work and for developing creative solutions to the problems work presents' (Leiter & Schaufeli, 1996, p. 231). Like depersonalization, cynicism is positively correlated with emotional exhaustion. Finally, professional efficacy is a similar construct to personal accomplishment but has 'a broader focus, encompassing both social and nonsocial aspects of occupational accomplishments … and explicitly assesses an individual's expectations of continued effectiveness at work' (Leiter & Schaufeli, 1996, p. 232).

There has been some controversy over the inclusion of depersonalization (or cynicism) and reduced personal accomplishment (or professional efficacy) as core components of burnout, with some investigators (Koeske & Koeske, 1989, 1993; R. T. Lee & Ashfort, 1996) suggesting that they may be separate, albeit related, variables. This distinction is important because initially Maslach argued that the term *burnout* should be reserved for human service occupations, where depersonalization in particular may be a prevalent response to excessive demands from clients or patients. However, while exhaustion captures the stress dimension of burnout, it does not on its own sufficiently explain the burnout phenomenon (Pervez & Halbesleben, 2017). Evidence suggests that exhaustion leads to depersonalization across many different occupations (Maslach et al., 2001), whereas reduced efficacy may be a function of either exhaustion or depersonalization (R. T. Lee & Ashforth, 1993).

Other researchers have raised doubts about whether reduced personal accomplishment (or professional efficacy) even constitutes a symptom of burnout (Demerouti et al., 2003; Schaufeli & Taris, 2005). Early on Leiter (1993) proposed that personal accomplishment may be relatively independent of the other two symptoms. Recently, Schaufeli and his coworkers (Schaufeli et al., 2019) have argued that personal accomplishment should not be considered a core symptom of burnout, but rather it constitutes a consequence of burnout. They conceptualize burnout as fatigue characterized by both inability (exhaustion) and unwillingness (mental distancing) to exert effort at work. In addition, burnout is characterized by both cognitive and emotional impairment. Thus, Schaufeli et al. (2019) propose that four dimensions constitute the core of burnout: They provide the following definition of burnout:

> a work-related state of exhaustion that occurs among employees, which is characterized by extreme tiredness, reduced ability to regulate cognitive and emotional processes, and mental distancing. These four core dimensions of burnout are accompanied by depressed mood as well as by non-specific psychological and psychosomatic distress symptoms. (p. 29)

To summarize, the term *burnout* refers to an extreme state of psychological strain and depletion of energy resources arising from prolonged exposure to stressors that exceed the person's resources to cope, initially associated with human services professions, but today acknowledged to occur in other occupational groups. According to the prevailing viewpoint, the major component of burnout is physical and emotional exhaustion, and there has been considerable dispute over the role of Maslach's third dimension, reduced personal accomplishment (or professional efficacy). There seems to be agreement that core characteristics of burnout constitute exhaustion and mental distancing, and recent formulations have included cognitive and emotional impairment as core dimensions. Later in this chapter, we will reflect further on the adequacy of current conceptualizations of burnout. Finally, whereas psychological strain may result from both episodic and chronic stressors, burnout probably develops over an extended time period and, accordingly, tends to be more difficult to eliminate than other forms of job-related strain.

MODELS OF BURNOUT DEVELOPMENT

Along with the variety of definitions, several models of the development of burnout have been proposed. In the main, these models build upon the three-dimensional model of burnout proposed by Maslach and her colleagues, although there has been considerable debate about the centrality of each component and the chain of events in burnout development. Most conceptualizations of the construct refer to burnout as a reaction to chronic or ongoing demands from the job (Hobfoll & Shirom, 2001; Pervez & Halbe- sleben, 2017; Schaufeli et al., 2009) involving the progressive development of emotional exhaustion (and perhaps other responses) as a result of ongoing, and seemingly insur- mountable, job-related problems or demands.

One of the earliest theories about how burnout develops was advanced in 1980 by Cherniss, from research conducted among novice professionals in the fields of mental health, poverty, law, public health nursing, and teaching. Cherniss suggested that aspects of the work environment and characteristics of the individual may both function as sources of strain. Individuals endeavor to cope with these stressors in a variety of ways, some of which may entail negative attitude changes, including reducing work goals, taking less responsibility for work outcomes, becoming less idealistic in one's approach to the job, and becoming detached from clients or the job itself. The limitation of this model is its overinclusiveness. By equating burnout with 'negative attitude changes', it incorporated a wide range of potential variables under the heading of burnout, making burnout indistinguishable from job strain more generally.

Another early theory of how burnout develops is the phase model proposed by Golembiewski and colleagues (Golembiewski & Munzenrider, 1988; Golembiewski et al., 1985). Golembiewski and his colleagues adopted the Maslach three component model of burnout but claimed that the second component in that model, depersonalization, is the aspect that is first experienced in the sequence. They contended that a certain amount of professional detachment is functional when dealing with clients or patients in a pro- fessional manner. However, when role demands and pressures reach a level that goes beyond the individual's coping capacity, this detachment can be transformed into depersonalization as an ineffective coping strategy. As a result, the individual's sense of personal achievement on the job is jeopardized, leading to reduced personal accom- plishment. This in turn leads to the development of emotional exhaustion, as the strain associated with the first two elements surpasses the person's coping ability. Emotional exhaustion, therefore, has the most potency and represents the end stage of burnout development in the Golembiewski model.

Empirically, the Golembiewski phase model has received mixed support. In the perspective initially proposed by Leiter and Maslach (1988) and later modified by Leiter (1991, 1993), they argued, as did Golembiewski, that emotional exhaustion is the critical component in the burnout process. However, these authors contended that emotional exhaustion develops first in that process rather than as the final stage of burnout. The original Leiter and Maslach (1988) model stated that stressors from jobs that have high interpersonal contact with clients or other individuals with significant problems lead to emotional exhaustion on the part of the human service worker. This emotional exhaustion then induces depersonalization as workers attempt to cope or deal with their feelings of exhaustion. Depersonalization is essentially a coping response that is called upon when other forms of coping (e.g., changing the demands from the job) have not succeeded in alleviating the amount of strain experienced. However, as depersonalization occurs, the individual begins to lose a sense of accomplishment on the job because the very act of depersonalizing clients undermines his or her professional values and goals. Put another way, depersonalization mediates the relationship between emotional exhaustion and reduced personal accomplishment. R. T. Lee and Ashforth (1993) conducted a longitudinal investigation that illustrated greater support for the Leiter and Maslach (1988) model.

Studies by Leiter (1992, 1993) based upon structural equation modeling of the burnout process, led to modifications of the original model. Leiter (1993) suggested that the relationship of personal accomplishment with the two other burnout dimensions may be explained better by their shared relationship with other variables, particularly the extent of resources available to the person in the work environment, such as the amount of social support and skill utilization.

Evidence supporting Leiter's revised model was reported by Lee and Ashforth (1996) in a meta-analysis of the correlates of burnout, in which they examined antecedents and consequences in relation to each of the three burnout components. Using the conservation-of-resources theory of job stress developed by Hobfoll and colleagues (Hobfoll, 1989; Hobfoll & Freedy, 1993), which is outlined next, they found that emotional exhaustion and depersonalization were strongly correlated with outcomes such as organizational commitment and turnover intentions, whereas these variables were only weakly related to personal accomplishment. On the other hand, control coping (which is parallel to Lazarus and Folkman's (1984) notion of problem-focused coping (see Chapter 7 of this book) was more closely linked with personal accomplishment than with either exhaustion or depersonalization. They concluded that that exhaustion leads to depersonalization, and that personal accomplishment develops relatively independently of emotional exhaustion and depersonalization, rather than being a consequence of either of the variables. Two longitudinal studies by Taris et al. (2005) also showed that exhaustion led to depersonalization, and that reduced accomplishment only played a minor role.

To summarize, empirical support for the Leiter and Maslach model of burnout development, particularly Leiter's (1993) reformulation of that model, has been obtained, and today it is accepted that emotional exhaustion represents the initial outcome of excessive and chronic job demands and pressures. Depersonalization (or cynicism) would appear to be a response adopted by workers as they endeavor to cope with this exhaustion. Finally, (reduced) personal accomplishment (or professional efficacy) may be regarded as a separate element in the process that can be influenced by emotional exhaustion but is also dependent upon other factors in the work environment, as well as the person's use of coping strategies (especially control coping).

THEORIES OF BURNOUT

Today there are two major theories of burnout. In a review of burnout and well-being, Pervez and Halbesleben (2017) outline these dominant theories. The first is the conservation of resources theory (COR) (Hobfoll, 1989; Hobfoll & Freedy, 1993; Hobfoll & Shirom, 2001) outlined in Chapter 1, and the other is the job demands-resources theory (JD-R) (Demerouti et al., 2001), described as an offshoot of COR theory.

Conservation of Resources Theory

Hobfoll and his colleagues have constructed a general perspective on stress that has particular relevance to burnout in work organizations and has been used as a framework for much empirical research in the field of burnout. Their conservation of resources (COR) theory postulates that individuals have access to four major categories of resources: objects (e.g., a house, a car), conditions (e.g., a steady job), personal characteristics (e.g., self-esteem), and various forms of energy (e.g., money, favors owed by other persons).

The basic tenet of COR theory is that stress occurs when people lose resources, perceive a threat to their resources, or invest in their resources without receiving expected returns on their investments (Pervez & Halbesleben, 2017). Hence, events such as the loss of one's job, impaired health, and breakdown in a personal relationship are serious forms of resource loss. Although these traumatic events sometimes may be compensated by a resource gain (such as finding a better job), in many cases there is a net loss of resources, which produces strain for the individual. Burnout results when resources are continuously lost or threatened (e.g., increased work load or lack of autonomy and support) after significant resource investment at work, producing a downward spiral in energy loss for the individual. In a work situation, some of the major resources available to workers are social support (from their colleagues, supervisors, and others), personal control over their job, involvement in important decision-making processes, and appropriate reward systems (Burke & Richardsen, 2001). Major demands that might bring about resource loss include role ambiguity and conflict, role overload, inadequate resources to perform the job, and unremitting demands from clients or other people in the work environment. Chronic strain or burnout can arise when there is a significant and ongoing draining of one's resources, particularly as individuals strive to meet the above or other demands on their energy. According to Hobfoll and Shirom (2001), burnout results from a process of depletion of energy resources, i.e. 'the erosion of emotional, physical, and cognitive energy in any combination' (p. 66). At the advanced stages of burnout, the person develops a sense of helplessness (to address the situation), hopelessness (for any improvement), and depression.

COR theory is pitched at a more general (and abstract) level than the other models outlined here. Rather than providing a specific model of burnout itself, it focuses on the general conditions under which job-related strain and burnout arise. Nevertheless, it offers a conceptual framework of principles that can underpin other approaches, such as the Leiter and Maslach model and the job demands-resources model (described next). COR theory also highlights the environmental factors that may contribute to burnout development. Before addressing the antecedents and potential consequences of burnout later in this chapter, however, we will examine methods used to assess and measure the extent of burnout experienced by individuals in their workplaces.

The Job Demands-Resources Model

The second theory of burnout is the job demands-resources model (JD-R) (Demerouti et al., 2001). This model assumes that although every occupation may have its own work characteristics, all types of job characteristics can be classified in one of two categories – job demands and job resources (Bakker & Demerouti, 2017; Bakker et al., 2023). It hypothesizes two processes, a health impairment process whereby job demands requiring sustained physical or mental effort may lead to energy depletion, health impairment and burnout, and a motivational process in which job and personal resources foster engagement. Job demands refer to those physical, psychological, social, or organizational aspects of the job that require sustained physical or mental effort and are associated with certain physiological and psychological costs (e.g., exhaustion) (Bakker & Demerouti, 2007). Examples are high work pressure, difficult physical environments, and emotionally demanding interactions with clients. Job resources refer to those physical, psychological, social, or organizational aspects of the job that are functional in achieving work goals, stimulate personal growth and development, and reduce job demands and their associated physiological and psychological costs. Examples include job autonomy, opportunities for development, participation in decision making, feedback, and work social support.

The model predicts that when employees are confronted with high job demands requiring sustained effort, they may adopt performance protection strategies resulting in extra costs (Schaufeli & Bakker, 2004). Active coping as a response may be adaptive in the short run, but over time it may be maladaptive and deplete the individual's energy resources. With the persistence of high demands, employees may be able to maintain target performance, but the compensatory costs over time are manifested in psychological responses, such as fatigue and irritability, and physiological responses, such as increased cortisol levels. Burnout is caused by high job demands that drain the employee's energy and result in mental withdrawal (depersonalization) as an attempt to cope with the resulting exhaustion (Maslach, 1993). Work engagement results from the inherently motivating nature of resources, both job resources and personal resources, defined as aspects of the self that are associated with resilience and refer to the ability to control and impact one's environment successfully (Schaufeli, 2014).

Research has shown that burnout is mainly predicted by high job demands and lack of resources, in contrast to engagement, which is mainly predicted by available job resources (Schaufeli & Bakker, 2004). There is also evidence that job and personal resources may buffer the effects of job demands on burnout (Bakker et al., 2005); a combination of high demands (work overload, emotional and physical demands, work-home interference) and low resources (autonomy, social support, supervisor support, performance feedback) produced the highest levels of exhaustion and cynicism. The JD-R model has figured prominently in burnout research since its introduction in 2001, and studies have provided convincing support for the theory (Bakker & Demerouti, 2017).

MEASUREMENT OF BURNOUT

As with all other constructs, measurement is a critical issue in the study of burnout. Early work in this field was based primarily on observations of human service workers (Freudenberger, 1974), but in the late 1970s efforts were directed toward the development of questionnaires to assess self-reported levels of burnout. While several other measures have been developed, for example the Burnout Index (Pines et al., 1981) and the Oldenburg Burnout Inventory (Demerouti et al., 2003), one questionnaire measure has figured prominently in the research literature: the MBI (Maslach & Jackson, 1981, 1986). By far the most widely employed measure of burnout, it has been estimated that the MBI has been used in 88% of published research on burnout (Boudreau et al., 2015).

Maslach Burnout Inventory

The MBI was initially developed to gauge levels of burnout specifically among human service professionals. The original MBI (MBI-Human Services Survey, MBI-HSS) is a self-report questionnaire containing 22 items, divided into the three subscales described earlier: emotional exhaustion (nine items), depersonalization (five items), and (reduced) personal accomplishment (eight items). Burnout is indicated by a high score on emotional exhaustion and depersonalization, and a low score on personal accomplishment. In the 1981 version of the questionnaire, respondents were asked to report both frequency (*never* to *every day*) and intensity (*very mild* to *very strong*) for each item. However, though some early research studies investigated both frequency and intensity of burnout, typically a high correlation between these indices was obtained, and studies since have assessed the frequency dimension only. The 1986 version of the MBI excluded the intensity dimension (Maslach & Jackson, 1986).

In 1986, the questionnaire was expanded to include a scale designed to measure burnout in educational settings (MBI-Educational Survey, MBI-ES) (Maslach & Jackson, 1986), and in 1996 was revised to include a scale designed to measure burnout in non-service occupations (the MBI-General Survey, MBI-GS) (Schaufeli et al., 1996). The MBI-GS contains 16 items: five assessing emotional exhaustion, five cynicism, and six professional efficacy. The introduction of the MBI-GS was a milestone because it made it possible to assess burnout among all employees, not just employees in the human services, and the enormous growth in scientific studies of burnout in a wide variety of occupations since the turn of the century coincides with its introduction. Leiter and

Schaufeli (1996) initially tested and then replicated the three-dimensional structure of the MBI-GS in several samples of hospital workers and proposed that 'burnout, as measured by the MBI-GS, pertains to any occupation in which people are psychologically engaged in the job' (p. 240). A fourth edition of the MBI manual was published in 2016 and introduced specific versions of the questionnaire for medical staff and students (Maslach et al., 2017).

The MBI has been translated and validated in a large number of countries, and this has facilitated an increase in cross-cultural research on burnout (Halbesleben & Buckley, 2004). Many studies have shown that the psychometric properties of the MBI have remained fairly consistent across language translations, although some differences between countries in terms of the level of burnout has been identified (Garcia et al., 2019; Gilla et al., 2019; Hawrot & Koniewski, 2018; Richardsen & Martinussen, 2005; Tomas et al., 2016). Over the years, all three original versions of the MBI have been tested for their psychometric properties, and the results indicate that the measure is not without some problems. Initial exploratory factor analyses of the three MBI scales tended to support the construct validity of the instrument, as well as its convergent and discriminant validity (Burke & Richardsen, 2001; Cordes & Dougherty, 1993). Numerous confirmatory factor analyses have questioned the factor structure of the MBI and the reliability of particular items in the questionnaire. According to Schaufeli et al. (2019), the shortcomings of the MBI include conceptual, technical, and practical problems.

Serious doubts have been raised about the inclusion of personal accomplishment (professional efficacy) as a core element of burnout on the basis of both conceptual and methodological arguments (Pervez & Halbesleben, 2017). One of the psychometric problems with the MBI is that the questions of the personal accomplishment factor are positively worded, and a low score rather than a high score indicate burnout. Consequently, the personal accomplishment factor seems to behave differently from the other two. For example, the three burnout factors are differentially related to common job demands and organizational outcomes (Halbesleben & Buckley, 2004). Both emotional exhaustion and depersonalization have shown consistent relationships with work demands (e.g., workload, role conflict) and work outcomes (e.g., job satisfaction, organizational commitment), whereas personal accomplishment has shown far less consistent relationships with these factors. In addition, the correlation of personal accomplishment with emotional exhaustion and depersonalization is usually lower than the intercorrelations between those two (Worley et al., 2008).

Other methodological issues were also raised early on in validation studies (Koeske & Koeske, 1993; R. T. Lee & Ashforth, 1996; Schaufeli & van Dierendonck, 1993), suggesting lack of factor independence. Some researchers argued that because personal accomplishment does not seem to form a coherent factor, it should be eliminated and the model of burnout should be respecified to contain only two factors (de Beer & Bianchi, 2019; Kalliath et al., 2000). In their confirmatory factor analysis of the MBI, Kalliath et al. (2000) found that emotional exhaustion was clearly the most robust of the three MBI factors. There were also indications that several emotional exhaustion and depersonalization items did not contribute to factor reliability, so these were removed from the measure. The resulting two-factor instrument showed good reliability and predictive validity, indicated by significant negative correlations with variables such as job satisfaction, organizational commitment, and significant positive correlations with turnover intentions. Based on these and other research findings, it would appear that (reduced) personal accomplishment may not be a 'core component' of burnout (Demerouti et al., 2003; Walkey & Green, 1992), but may be better considered as an outcome of burnout (Schaufeli et al., 2019). In fact, several other measures of burnout have eliminated personal accomplishment as a subfactor, as we shall see later in the chapter.

In summary, the MBI has been the measure of choice for most research on burnout and has exhibited reasonable psychometric properties and predictive validity. Nevertheless, confirmatory analyses have not always generated three coherent factors. Despite being the measure used in close to 90% of research studies, several other measures have been developed to overcome some of the problems with the MBI.

Other Burnout Measures

As an alternative to the MBI, Pines et al. (1981) constructed a 21-item instrument (the Burnout Measure, BM) to tap into burnout, or what they initially labeled as 'tedium'. These items focus predominantly on cognitive and emotional elements, such as feeling worthless, depressed, and rejected. As noted earlier, Pines et al. (1981) contended that burnout and tedium are identical constructs but that whereas tedium may apply to workers in a wide range of situations, burnout results from working with people in situations that are emotionally demanding (Burke & Richardsen, 2001). In contrast to the earlier versions of the MBI, the BM was developed for usage with both human service and nonservice occupations. Schaufeli and van Dierendonck (1993) reported that the Burnout Measure reflects the core dimension of exhaustion. Although the authors of the instrument distinguished conceptually between three kinds of exhaustion (physical, mental, and emotional), in practice a single index of burnout is obtained; hence, the BM can be thought of as a unidimensional measure. According to Pervez and Halbesleben (2017), researchers have also identified statistical problems with how the questions align with the underlying theory. Compared with the MBI, the BM has been used by relatively few studies as an index of burnout levels.

Pervez and Halbesleben (2017) have summarized other self-report questionnaire measures of burnout, which are similar in content to the BM and MBI, but which have not received the same attention in the research literature. These include the Shirom-Melamed Burnout Measure, the Oldenburg Burnout Inventory (OLBI), and Copenhagen Burnout Inventory (CBI). Recently a new measure has been introduced, the Burnout Assessment Tool (BAT) (Schaufeli et al., 2019). All these measures have been developed in response to perceived shortcomings in the MBI. Each will be briefly described here.

The Shirom-Melamed Burnout Measure (Shirom, 2003) is based on Hobfoll's conservation of resources theory, focuses on burnout as a result of depletion of energetic resources, and includes subscales of emotional exhaustion (four items; 'e.g., I feel I am unable to be sensitive to the needs of coworkers and customers'), physical fatigue (six items; e.g., 'I feel physically drained'), and cognitive weariness (four items; 'e.g., I have difficulty concentrating') (Michel et al., 2022). Strengths of the measure is its strong theoretical foundation, its strong psychometric properties, that it is relatively short (14 items), freely available, and Shirom and Melamed (2006) found their measure to be superior to the MBI. The Shirom-Melamed measure of burnout is therefore popular and extensively applied in research and clinical settings. Recent meta-analytical findings have shown that in line with the theoretical predictions, the subscales have strong intercorrelations and the measure has quite high test-retest reliability (even across days and months), which may suggest a more dispositional component of burnout (Michel et al., 2022). Further, job- and personal resources were negatively related to burnout while job demands, and personal vulnerabilities were positively related to burnout as measured by the Shirom-Melamed measure. The results also showed strong associations with motivational covariates (e.g., work engagement) and both job-related and personal outcomes. It should also be noted that older, longer-tenured, and more educated employees reported lower burnout, although the measure was weakly related to gender and unrelated to work hours (Michel et al., 2022). In sum, the use of the Shirom-Melamed burnout measure in both organizational research and practice is supported.

The OLBI (Demerouti et al., 2003) is based on a similar conceptual model to that of the MBI but was developed to overcome the potential wording biases of the MBI. Many researchers have argued that since the items in each of the MBI subscales are worded in the same direction, i.e., emotional exhaustion and depersonalization are worded negatively and personal accomplishment positively, this may result in response biases and affect the clustering of factors in statistical analyses (Bouman et al., 2002; Demerouti & Nachreiner, 1996; R. T. Lee & Ashforth, 1990). However, in a study investigating the convergent validity of four burnout measures it was found that positively phrased items constituted a separate factor which was considered an artifact (Qiao & Schaufeli, 2011). The OLBI have items that have balanced positive and negative wording, and include questions designed to assess not only affective components, but also cognitive and physical components of emotional exhaustion (Bakker et al., 2004). In addition, the OLBI features just two scales, emotional exhaustion and depersonalization, taking out reduced efficacy as a result of the inconsistent findings described earlier. Studies have found that the OLBI demonstrated convergent validity when compared to the MBI (Demerouti et al., 2003, 2010). However, it has not been as widely used in research as other measures.

The CBI includes three scales measuring personal, work-related and client-related burnout (Kristensen et al., 2005) and is essentially a measure of fatigue. Early empirical support for the scale was found in several studies (Borritz et al., 2006; Winwood & Winefield, 2004), and it has been translated and validated for use in over ten countries. Over the past decade an increasing number of studies have used the CBI to assess burnout within human services professions, such as health care, social work and education (Andersen et al., 2010; Brown et al, 2019; Jacobs et al., 2012; Parrello et al., 2019).

While most find support for the factor structure of the CBI, a study comparing the psychometric properties of the MBI, the BM and the CBI concluded that the MBI is a more appropriate instrument for assessing burnout compared to the other two because their inner structure was not as well defined and the subscales were highly correlated (Platsidou & Daniilidou, 2016).

The most recent burnout measure is the Burnout Assessment Tool (BAT) (Schaufeli et al., 2019). The BAT was developed using a combination of a deductive (theoretical) and inductive (empirical) approach, resulting in a new definition of burnout (see earlier in this chapter). Theoretically, burnout is seen as a state of mental exhaustion that manifests itself as both the inability (fatigue) and unwillingness (mental distance) to spend effort at work. Two more symptoms were added based on in-depth interviews with clinicians: emotional and cognitive impairment. The BAT consists of 34 items that measure four core symptoms and two secondary symptoms of burnout. The core symptoms of burnout are: *Exhaustion* (eight items), referring to a severe loss of energy that results in both physical and mental exhaustion; *emotional impairment* (five items), which manifests itself in intense emotional reactions and feeling overwhelmed by one's emotions; *cognitive impairment* (five items), indicated by memory problems, attention and concentration deficits, and poor cognitive performance; and *mental distance* (four items), indicated by a strong reluctance or aversion to work. Secondary symptoms are *psychosomatic complaints* (five items), physical complaints unrelated to physical disorder (e.g., palpitations and chest pain, headaches, muscle pain and getting sick often), and *psychological distress* (six items), non-physical symptoms related to a psychological problem (e.g., sleep problems, worrying, feeling tense, or anxious).

Psychometric analyses carried out in two representative samples of the Flemish and Dutch workforce indicated that the four core symptoms were strongly interrelated, yet could be distinguished (Schaufeli et al., 2019). The authors conclude that the total score of the four core dimensions can be used as an indicator for burnout. Also, based on the analyses, cut-off scores have been calculated and can be used to identify employees at risk or most likely suffering from burnout. Thus, the BAT can be used for individual burnout assessment as well as in organizations for screening those who are at risk. The psychometric research indicated both discriminant and convergent validity with the MBI regarding exhaustion and mental distance (depersonalization). It also adds the measurement of emotional and cognitive impairment, which in a recent review were found to be highly connected to burnout (Deligkaris et al., 2014). The BAT overcomes many of the shortcomings of the MBI, and the psychometric properties are well researched. Only a few studies have used the BAT so far, and time will tell if this questionnaire will take hold in the scientific community.

As is evident from the above discussion, almost all measures of burnout that have been used in empirical research have focused on individuals' own reports of their level of burnout. There has been little effort to develop alternative indexes of burnout, such as reports from other people (e.g., coworkers or supervisors) or observational measures of burnout (Demerouti et al., 2021). Given the oft-cited problem of common-method variance in research based solely on self-report measures, it is perhaps surprising that more attention has not been devoted to the development of corroborative measures. In particular, although burnout may be a subjective individual experience, this experience is associated with certain behavioral manifestations, such as depersonalization (cynicism) or aloofness and reduced cognitive functioning and job performance. We would anticipate, therefore, that these signs of burnout would be observable within the organizational setting and could be reported upon by other organizational members or clients.

CORRELATES OF BURNOUT

In the first edition of this book, we described a number of correlates of burnout grouped into three major categories: individual (or personal), job, and organizational. Many of the stressors that fall in these categories are comparable to those linked with job strain in general (see Chapter 3), although some would appear to be more explicitly associated with burnout. At the time of the first edition we did not differentiate between antecedents and consequences of burnout, given the cross-sectional design of most of the research in this field up until then. Today, however, many longitudinal and metaanalytic studies have made it possible to classify variables more clearly as causes or outcomes. In this edition of the book, we will therefore present correlates of burnout as antecedents and consequences.

Antecedents

Antecedents of burnout are often classified into situational or work-related factors and individual factors (Bakker et al., 2014; Maslach et al., 2001), and we will follow this tradition in our presentation.

Work-Related Factors

Like the more general literature on work stressors (see Chapter 3), research on job characteristics related to burnout has focused particularly on role demands, including role ambiguity, role conflict, and work overload. Numerous studies have demonstrated positive links between each of these variables and burnout, especially emotional exhaustion and depersonalization (Burke & Richardsen, 2001).

As we described earlier in this chapter, the JD-R model of burnout and engagement (Demerouti et al., 2001) assumes that although every occupation may have its own work characteristics, all types of job characteristics can be classified in one of two categories – job demands and job resources (Bakker & Demerouti, 2017). Research has shown that burnout is mainly predicted by job demands and lack of resources, in contrast to engagement which is mainly predicted by available job resources (Schaufeli & Bakker, 2004). In other words, job demands such as high work pressure and conflicting and ambiguous expectations are factors that over time may deplete employees' energy and create a risk for burnout, whereas resources such as the ability to determine one's work methods, work schedules, and even issues such as breaks and vacations would be expected to have an ameliorating impact on burnout. Job resources therefore are thought to buffer the impact of job demands on strain (Bakker & Demerouti, 2017).

Early studies of burnout antecedents focused on people in human service professions and focused on job demands such as case load, shift work, and difficult client interactions. With the introduction of the MBI-GS, the study of burnout mushroomed into a variety of occupations, which may have totally different sets of job demands. The strength of the JD-R model is that while every occupation may have its own specific risk factors associated with job stress, the characteristics of any job can be classified as job demands and job resources. The model therefore constitutes an overarching model that can be applied to a wide range of occupational settings, regardless of the particular demands and resources involved. Nevertheless, there are some aspects of job characteristics that have been particularly associated with burnout.

Several meta-analyses have investigated the role of both job demands and job resources in relation to job burnout. R. T. Lee and Ashforth (1996) conducted a meta-analysis of the correlates of the three dimensions of burnout outlined by Maslach using 61 studies of predominantly human service providers. Their findings indicated that demands (role conflict, workload, role stress, and role ambiguity), were more strongly related to exhaustion and depersonalization than lack of resources (autonomy, supervisor and coworker support, participation, development opportunities). The authors suggest that these results support the conservation of resources explanation of burnout, i.e., individuals may be more sensitive to the demands in the work situation than the resources offered. The correlations between demands and personal accomplishment were much weaker, suggesting that personal accomplishment develops separately from the other two dimensions. The associations of the resource correlates with personal accomplishment were also quite weak.

A more recent meta-analysis by Alarcon (2011) was based on 231 published studies from all types of occupations, not just human services professions. His results confirmed the importance of role ambiguity, role conflict and workload in predicting burnout, particularly exhaustion and cynicism, and also demonstrated stronger relations than in previous meta-analyses. He found that resources, such as control and autonomy, showed weaker relationships with the burnout dimensions than demands, again supporting COR theory that demands will have a greater impact on stress than resources. Another meta-analysis by Nahrgang et al. (2011) investigating the effects of burnout and engagement on safety outcomes, supported these findings. In a sample of 179 studies in four major industries (construction, health care, manufacturing, transportation), they found that job demands in the form of risks and hazards, and complexity were associated with health impairment leading to burnout, whereas job resources such as knowledge, autonomy, and support were found to mitigate burnout. These studies provide convincing evidence for the role of job demands and lack of resources across occupations in the development of job burnout.

Lesener et al. (2019) performed a meta-analysis of longitudinal studies in order to validate the essential assumptions within the JD-R model. They identified 74 studies that fulfilled the inclusion criteria and used a two-stage structural equation modeling to analyze the data. Their results indicated that all the assumptions in the JD-R model were confirmed: job demands predict burnout over time, job resources negatively predict burnout, and positively predict engagement over time. The best model fit was a reciprocal model, in which engagement predicts job resources over time, and burnout predicts job demands and job resources over time. The results are in line with both COR and JD-R theory suggesting that engaged employees may be proactive and increase their job resources and reduce hindrance job demands, so that over time they can optimize their working environment and stay engaged (Bakker & Demerouti, 2007). When job resources are available, people feel energized and able to deal with their work goals, and when people feel self-efficacious, valuable and optimistic, they may create an even more resourceful work environment (Xanthopoulou et al., 2009a). Similarly, employees who experience job strain may perceive and create more job demands over time in a self-undermining process (Bakker & Costa, 2014). Employees experiencing high levels of strain likely communicate poorly, make more mistakes, are less able to manage their emotions, thus adding to the already high job demands and creating a vicious cycle of high job demands and strain.

The influence of organizational factors in the development of burnout has also received considerable attention from researchers. For instance, Schulz et al. (1995) suggested that management processes play a vital role in either creating or alleviating burnout among employees. Recently studies have shown that the company's HR practices are related to employee well-being, especially exhaustion. In a study of over 400 employees and 50 line managers in diverse industries (e.g., technology, finance and insurance, health care), it was found that both promotion opportunities and developing leadership behaviors, characterized by encouraging staff to improve their job-related skills and coaching, was negatively correlated with exhaustion (Marescaux et al., 2019). Another study found that high performance work systems (HPWS), which comprise bundles of HR practices like ability enhancing practices (training and skill development), motivation enhancing practices (high pay, career development and information sharing) and opportunity enhancing practices (employee involvement and teamwork), significantly and negatively affect burnout (Jyoti & Rani, 2019). HPWS facilitate employees to get the essential resources to meet their job demands, which reduce their level of burnout and enhance performance, which again helps in providing sustainable competitive advantage to the organization.

Research in the area of organizational climate has also illustrated the relationship of organizational variables and employee burnout. O'Driscoll and Schubert (1988) found that lack of communication between organizational levels and influence processes used by managers were strongly related to burnout among social workers. Schulz et al. (1995) observed that in organizations possessing a 'clan' culture, characterized by teamwork, participation, and autonomy, employees displayed less burnout because they functioned in favorable work conditions. Similarly, transactional and transformational leadership processes enhanced the development of positive work attitudes by contributing to employee-organization goal congruence, job clarity, and work satisfaction, all of which were linked with reduced burnout. In a study of over 1,000 engineers and technologists, Nerstad et al. (2013) found that a perceived motivational climate influenced burnout. A perceived mastery climate, characterized by co-operation, self-development, and team work, was associated with a decrease in burnout over time, whereas in a perceived performance climate, characterized by competition, ego-involvement, and normative comparison, was associated with an increase in burnout over time.

One organizational variable that consistently has been linked with burnout reduction is social support. In Chapter 6, we will examine some of the potential moderating (buffering) effects of this variable; hence, our comments here will be brief. The impact of support on employees has been debated in the literature. Hobfoll and Freedy's (1993) COR theory suggests that support is a resource that can energize individuals and enable them to deal with stressors in their work environment. However, the extent of influence of support may depend on a variety of other factors, including the individual's willingness (and ability) to harness this resource, as well as the nature of support available. Several researchers have found that different sources of social support are differentially related to different burnout dimensions. For example, Aronsson et al. (2017) found that lack of support from coworkers and supervisors contributed to increased emotional exhaustions and depersonalization. In a meta-analysis of 114 articles on social support and burnout, Halbesleben (2006) found that work sources of social support was more strongly related to emotional exhaustion than to depersonalization and personal accomplishment, while non-work support was more strongly related to depersonalization and personal accomplishment than to exhaustion.

During the recent COVID-19 pandemic, remote and virtual work have become a necessity for many employees. Even before the pandemic, surveys have found increasing numbers of employees working remotely once a week or more (Moss, 2018). Despite findings that remote work and flexible hours offer tangible benefits such as time saved on commuting, lower travel and childcare costs, as well as increased job satisfaction and decreased stress, Kelliher and Anderson (2009) reported that one unexpected risk of adopting flexible work practices is burnout. Using social exchange theory, they suggest that people who are able to work remotely may feel more grateful to their employers and consequently exert additional effort and time in order to return benefit to their employer. It remains to be seen if this unanticipated consequence may constitute a long-term effect of the pandemic.

Individual Factors

Despite researchers' interest in personality, attitudinal, and behavioral (e.g., performance) correlates of burnout, the predominant research focus has been on job-related and organizational factors, particularly because their relationship with burnout may be more directly assessed and because of the more obvious implications for interventions to reduce burnout levels. Individual factors refer to relatively stable individual differences and personality characteristics that may play a role in the development of burnout. Individual factors also include demographic variables.

Demographic variables (such as age and gender) represent examples of variables that have been studied at the individual level. Gender has been investigated frequently as a correlate of burnout, although findings for this variable are mixed. Early results suggested that females may exhibit higher levels of burnout than males, but this may be confounded by the gender composition of the samples investigated (e.g., nurses, social workers). Pines and Kafry (1981) suggested that women experience higher levels of burnout due to greater overload and inter-role conflict, such as between job and family. Later research, however, does not support this argument (Burke & Richardsen, 2001; Maslach et al., 2001; Purvanova & Muros, 2010). Interestingly, there is some evidence that females report higher scores on the emotional exhaustion subscale while males report higher scores on the depersonalization or cynicism subscale of the MBI (Maslach et al., 2001; Purvanova & Muros, 2010; Schaufeli & Buunk, 1996), perhaps suggesting that male employees are more likely than their female counterparts to respond to emotional strain by psychologically separating themselves from their work. Maslach et al. (2001) argue that these results may reflect the confounding of gender with occupation, for example, police officers are more likely to be men while nurses are more likely to be female. However, the meta-analysis by Purvanova and Muros (2010) found no gender differences in male-typed versus female-typed occupations.

Studies have observed a link between age and burnout in that younger employees may be more prone to burnout than older ones (Maslach et al., 2001; Schaufeli & Buunk, 1996), but as with gender, the results need to be interpreted cautiously because older workers who have become burned out may have quit their job for something less strain inducing. Only a few studies in the past ten years have specifically focused on age differences. For example, Marchand et al. (2018) found non-linear relationships between age and emotional exhaustion, while it was linearly related to cynicism and reduced efficacy. Total burnout level reduced with increasing age in men, while women aged between 20–35 and over 55 years showed the highest burnout level. A Finnish study also found higher burnout scores among young and aging women but the association was non-existent in middle age (Ahola et al., 2008). Nevertheless, age differences are of interest, as they may highlight potential mechanisms for preventing or alleviating burnout, as well as pointing to effective coping strategies.

Personality variables have also been explored in relation to burnout, and many of these variables (e.g., hardiness, external locus of control) have been incorporated into the more general stress literature. Personality may influence burnout through the impact of both the perceived and objective nature of the work environment (Alarcon et al., 2009), and we will describe personality as a moderator in the stressor-strain relationships in more detail in Chapter 6. Here we will briefly describe some of the research findings in relation to burnout, recognizing that in addition to situational factors, it is also important to discover which types of people may be at greater risk for experiencing burnout. Schaufeli and Enzmann (1998) reported on over 100 studies on burnout that included personality characteristics. The most frequently studied characteristics were hardiness, external locus of control, Type A behavior, self-esteem, and achievement motivation. Maslach et al. (2001) summarized results from burnout research and described the profile of a stress-prone individual as someone with low levels of hardiness, poor self-esteem, an external locus of control, and an avoidant coping style.

In a meta-analysis of the relationships between personality variables and burnout (Alarcon et al., 2009), the results indicated that personality is consistently related to burnout. The study was based on 114 articles and looked at a wide range of possibly relevant personality variables and burnout. The personality variables included stable higher-order personality traits as reflected in the Five Factor model, i.e., the five broad dimensions of neuroticism or emotional stability, extraversion, conscientiousness, agreeableness, and openness to experience. The study also included a number of lower-order, more malleable personality factors. These were core self-evaluation, consisting of four traits (self-esteem, self-efficacy, emotional stability, and internal locus of control); positive and negative affectivity, defined as the tendency to experience either positive emotional states (happiness, excitement and energy) or negative emotional states (sadness, anxiety, and hostility); dispositional optimism or the tendency to believe only good thing will occur in the future; proactive personality, defined as a person who takes action in any situation; hardiness, defined as perceiving to be in control events and perceiving stressors as challenges; and Type A personality, the extent to which one is hostile, aggressive, and impatient (Alarcon et al., 2009).

The results showed that four of the Big Five personality traits were consistently negatively correlated with all three dimensions of burnout: emotional stability, extraversion, conscientiousness, and agreeableness. Openness to experience was not related to emotional exhaustion and depersonalization, but was positively related to personal accomplishment. Of the other personality factors, self-esteem, self-efficacy, locus of control, positive and negative affectivity, optimism and proactive personality each had a significant relationship with burnout. Alarcon et al. (2009) note that some personality traits yielded stronger relationships with burnout than did others. Emotional stability, positive affectivity, and negative affectivity were more strongly related to emotional exhaustion and depersonalization than other personality traits, possibly because all three of these personality variables and the two burnout dimensions are affective oriented variables. Extraversion, general self-efficacy, and positive affectivity yielded stronger relationships with personal accomplishment than did the other personality traits. The results indicate that stable characteristics as well as more malleable individual differences play a role in the development of burnout.

Another meta-analysis investigating the relationships between the Big Five personality variables and burnout (Swider & Zimmerman, 2010) basically supports the findings of Alarcon et al. (2009). Using 115 empirical studies, Swider and Zimmerman (2010) found that individuals who were higher in neuroticism and lower in extraversion, agreeableness and conscientiousness, scored higher on emotional exhaustion and depersonalization, and scored lower on personal accomplishment. They also found that openness to experience was positively correlated with personal accomplishment, but not related to the other burnout dimensions.

A third category of individual differences that has been explored in burnout research is coping strategies. We will be discussing stress-related coping in more detail in Chapter 7, so we will comment only briefly here on this issue. Of particular relevance is research conducted by Leiter (1990, 1991, 1992) on the relationship between coping patterns and burnout levels. In keeping with the COR perspective (Hobfoll & Freedy, 1993) discussed earlier in this chapter, Leiter conceptualized coping as a resource available to the individual. Specifically, he distinguished between control coping, which equates with Lazarus and Folkman's (1984) problem-focused coping and is reflected by proactive efforts aimed at removing the source(s) of burnout, and escapist coping, which is reflected in avoidance of dealing with these burnout source(s). As predicted, control coping was found to be negatively related to burnout, whereas escapist coping showed a positive association with burnout levels.

Two recent meta-analyses have investigated the role of coping in the development of burnout (H. F. Lee et al., 2016; Shin et al., 2014). In a meta-analysis of 36 studies using the MBI to assess burnout, Shin et al. (2014) found that emotion focused coping (e.g., avoidance, denial, disengagement) was associated with high emotional exhaustion and depersonalization, and with reduced personal accomplishment. Problem-focused coping (e.g., active coping, engagement, planning), along with reappraisal and acceptance, were negatively related to both emotional exhaustion and depersonalization. Seeking social support was associated with lower depersonalization and higher personal accomplishment, but was not significantly related to exhaustion.

The second meta-analysis (H. F. Lee et al., 2016) looked at the effects of coping strategies in reducing nurse burnout and included seven longitudinal studies with randomized controlled trials. Participants in the intervention groups were provided coping strategies such as cognitive-behavior training, stress management, mindfulness-based programs and a team-based support group. All programs included education and practice in problem-focused and emotion-focused coping. The comparison group did not receive interventions. Results indicated that in the intervention groups the feeling of emotional exhaustion decreased over time, whereas in the control group the feeling of emotional exhaustion increased. The trend for depersonalization was similar but the results were not as clear in that the differences between the groups were nonsignificant one year after the intervention. Most of the interventions were effective in increasing personal accomplishment over the first six months. The authors conclude that training and practice of coping strategies can reduce work-related burnout, and the effects can be maintained for up to a year after the intervention. For both emotional exhaustion and depersonalization the reduction was greater in the emotion-focused interventions, whereas for the personal accomplishment the greater improvement was related to problem focused interventions.

Further investigation of the effectiveness of these and other coping strategies is still of interest. In particular, it would be valuable to explore the conditions under which control-oriented coping is more and less effective. For example, would this strategy produce less positive outcomes when demands and pressures are outside the individual's control? Are there limits to the effectiveness of control and other forms of problem-focused coping? These and related issues will be explored in Chapter 6.

Overall, there are clear indications that organizational variables, along with personal and job-related factors, can make a difference in burnout levels experienced by individuals. The cumulative evidence is universal and global, coming from a wide variety of occupations and from a large number of different countries. Employees functioning in organizational cultures and climates that foster collaboration and cohesion, that enable employee participation in decision making, and that acknowledge individuals' efforts (via appropriate reward systems) are less prone to burnout and other stress-related symptoms. It would be simplistic, however, to assume that provision of an environment that enhances these features would totally offset the negative impact of excessive role demands and the emotionally draining effects of continually having to respond to challenging client problems or difficulties with colleagues.

CONSEQUENCES OF BURNOUT

Burnout has been associated with a wide range of negative consequences. The definition of burnout as a syndrome of chronic exhaustion and withdrawal and distancing from work, leads us to expect that burnout would be associated with reduced functioning at work and also with negative attitudes. In addition, studies have shown that employees who demonstrate high levels of burnout report more psychological and physiological health problems (Ahola & Hakanen, 2014; Salvagioni et al., 2017; Shirom, 2010). A systematic review of prospective studies (Salvagioni et al., 2017) showed that burnout was a significant predictor of a number of physical consequences such as prolonged fatigue, musculoskeletal pain, gastrointestinal issues, type 2 diabetes, coronary heart disease, severe injuries and mortality below the age of 45 years. Psychological effects were insomnia, depressive symptoms, use of psychotropic and anti-depressant medication, mental disorders and psychological ill-health symptoms. Similarly, Hakanen and Schaufeli (2012) in their three-wave seven-year prospective study of over 2000 Finnish dentists found that burnout predicted negative emotions and attitudes, performance difficulties and somatic complaints from Time 1 to Time 2, and from Time 2 to Time 3. They also found that burnout was associated with lower life satisfaction over time. Similar findings have been reported in other reviews (Ahola & Hakanen, 2014; Lizano, 2015). In addition, a meta-analysis of burnout and safety outcomes found that burnout predicted accidents and injuries, adverse events such as near misses, safety events and errors, and unsafe behaviors such as the absence of safety citizenship behaviors (Nahrgang et al., 2011).

Much attention has been given to attitudinal variables in the study of burnout, such as job involvement, job satisfaction, and commitment to the organization. Lee and Ashforth (1996) reviewed studies that explored the relationship between Maslach's burnout dimensions and these three work attitudes. Their meta-analysis revealed negative relationships between emotional exhaustion and organizational commitment, and between depersonalization and both satisfaction and commitment. Job involvement, on the other hand, was not significantly linked with any of the three burnout components.

More recent studies have reported substantial relationships between burnout dimensions and job satisfaction (Alarcon, 2011; Yorulmaz et al., 2017), with the inference that high levels of burnout lead to reduced satisfaction with one's job. This inference may not always be warranted, as there is evidence that satisfaction can be a predictor, rather than an outcome, of psychological strain (O'Driscoll et al., 1992). However, in a longitudinal study of burnout and job satisfaction among public welfare workers (Lizano & Barak, 2015), it was found that burnout, especially emotional exhaustion, clearly predicted reduced job satisfaction.

Linkages between organizational commitment and other organizationally relevant variables, such as absenteeism and turnover intentions, have been consistently demonstrated (Alarcon, 2011; Shore et al., 1995); hence, the relationship between commitment and burnout is of considerable interest. However, in their meta-analysis of research conducted between 1982 and 1994, Lee and Ashforth (1996) located just seven empirical studies of this relationship. As previously noted, emotional exhaustion and depersonalization both displayed significant negative correlations with commitment. Alarcon (2011) found 39 studies between 1982 and 2010, and provided convincing evidence in his meta-analysis of negative relationships between emotional exhaustion, depersonalization and reduced personal accomplishment, and organizational commitment. Typically, it has been assumed that burnout is the predictor variable in this relationship. Leiter and Maslach (1988), for example, observed that emotional exhaustion exerted both a direct effect and an indirect effect (via depersonalization) on commitment, although in their study there was no direct contribution of depersonalization to commitment. Although it seems intuitive that burnout can lead to a deterioration of employee commitment to the organization, the possibility that causality may also operate in the opposite direction does not appear to have been given much consideration. Kalliath et al. (1998) argued that high levels of commitment may in fact shield an individual from the impact of stressful working environments, hence leading to a reduction in burnout. Their structural equations analysis demonstrated that this chain of events is a plausible alternative to the burnout → commitment hypothesis.

Finally, consideration needs to be given to burnout's relationship with job performance. Although much has been written about the potential deleterious effects of burnout on individuals' job performance and ultimately organizational productivity, empirical research on this relationship is relatively sparse. According to Pervez and Halbesleben (2017) the results from studies of the relationship between burnout and job performance are counterintuitive. Several researchers have found a negative relationship with exhaustion and job performance (Halbesleben & Bowler, 2007; Halbesleben & Buckley, 2004; Wright & Cropanzano, 2000). In a review by Taris (2006), the results also indicated significant negative relationships between emotional exhaustion and in-role performance, organizational citizenship behavior and customer satisfaction. However, research has shown that burnout has differential effects on performance depending on how performance is operationalized. Garden (1991) noted that it is important to distinguish between perceived and actual job performance when assessing the impact of burnout on employees' behavior. She and others (Keijsers et al., 1995) have found that when participants provided self-reports of performance, burnout and performance were negatively related. However, when compared to their 'objective' performance (either measured by test performance or performance appraisals), burnout was positively related to performance. In other words, employees who are burned out believe they are not performing well, when in fact others observe higher performance levels (Halbesleben & Buckley, 2004). Garden's explanation for this was that individuals suffering from burnout experience decreased self-esteem, which in turn leads them to believe that their performance has declined even when their actual performance may not have altered dramatically. She further speculated that employees may even exert additional effort to maintain their level of performance, despite being burned out. This is worthy of further exploration, along with the differentiation of perceived versus actual performance.

METHODOLOGICAL ISSUES

As with other areas of stress research, it is important to move beyond simple bivariate correlations of specific job factors with burnout. Of a greater interest are the interactive effects of these factors and other variables, including personality and attitudinal variables, as well as coping strategies. The research literature over the past two decades reflects more systematic exploration of these interactive effects. This type of investigation will tease out the complex relationships between aspects of the job and individuals' feelings of being burned out.

Another issue needing more systematic attention in research on burnout (as well as other forms of job-related strain) is the perennial problem of common-method variance. Despite advances in longitudinal studies and meta-analytic evidence, this research typically uses self-report questionnaires that ask respondents for their perceptions of their work environment, including job factors, and at the same time gather self-ratings of burnout levels. Such methodology introduces a potential confounding due to response bias. Hardly any studies have used objective or other-rated measures of burnout levels and various outcome measures. Research using multimethod approaches to data collection would be valuable to ascertain objective relationships between environmental factors on the job and worker burnout levels and (as discussed earlier with respect to behavioral indicators of burnout) to establish the ecological validity of the burnout construct.

Finally, a brief comment on levels of analysis is warranted here. Burnout research typically focuses upon measurement at the individual level. That is, researchers interested in burnout and its correlates gather individuals' perceptions of their environment, along with data on burnout levels in individual workers. However, increasingly burnout is no longer seen as an individual problem, but is recognized as existing at the individual level as well as the organizational level (Pervez & Halbesleben, 2017). These days a lot of work is organized around teams, and burnout at the organizational level can be a shared experience among co-workers and it can be contagious (González-Morales et al., 2012; Halbesleben & Leon, 2014). Halbesleben and Leon (2014) describe the notion of collective burnout as encompassing two perspectives. One is a shared-event approach, in which similar demands and resources in a work environment could lead to similar levels of burnout in that environment. In a longitudinal study, González-Morales et al. (2012) found that employees' shared perceptions of the burnout level of their colleagues could predict individual burnout over and above indicators of demands and resources. The other perspective of collective burnout is built on the processes of emotional contagion, which involves the idea that emotional states can be transmitted from one employee to another. Evidence of burnout contagion was provided in two studies by Bakker and colleagues (Bakker et al., 2005, 2006). While individual-level models of burnout are important, the study of multilevel processes occurring at the organizational level will provide an opportunity to increase our understanding of the burnout phenomenon.

Conclusion

In this chapter, we have explored the phenomenon of burnout as a unique and intense form of job-related strain. Research in this field has mushroomed in the past 20 years, and the topic itself is of immense interest to researchers and practitioners and receives wide media coverage. Over the past two decades sufficient evidence has accrued to enable some conclusions about the nature and occurrence of burnout and its correlates.

However, as should be clear from our discussion in this chapter, there is still no universally accepted definition of burnout, which suggests that further work is needed to reveal the exact nature of this complex phenomenon (Demerouti et al., 2021). A broader perspective on burnout may be needed to recognize the mechanisms by which the experience of burnout can spread throughout a work group or even an organization, ultimately resulting in organization-level or collective burnout. To date, despite evidence indicating that certain work environment factors are conducive to burnout (see our earlier discussion), there has been little research exploring the possibility that burnout may exist in entire work groups or even the organization as a whole. With the statistical methods existing today, it should be possible to design studies and ways to measure burnout at these levels. As became evident many years ago in research on organizational climate (Schneider, 1990), aggregation of individual levels of burnout (gathered from self-report questionnaires) may not be sufficient in itself to draw conclusions about the pervasiveness of burnout within groups or entire organizations. This issue represents an important challenge for future burnout research.

Finally, as also noted in a recent article on new directions in burnout research (Demerouti et al., 2021), there is a need for greater investigation of strategies and interventions to prevent burnout development or to alleviate symptoms of burnout when it does occur. In Chapters 7 and 8, we will discuss various strategies for stress reduction, some of which may be salient to burnout. Two distinguishing features of this syndrome are that it has a long gestation period and that it is resistant to most forms of intervention that are based solely on individual coping efforts. For effective and long-term alleviation of burnout, fundamental changes in job conditions and organizational environments may be required to reduce the exhaustion encountered by individuals and to promote an expectancy that their efforts and performance will be successful and rewarded.

6

MODERATORS OF STRESSOR-STRAIN RELATIONSHIPS

In previous chapters, we have outlined the basic processes involved in the development of job-related strain and burnout and have discussed some of the major sources and outcomes of these experiences. So far, however, we have examined only the direct association between stressors and their potential outcomes and have not discussed other factors that may affect this relationship. In this chapter, we address these potential influences by mainly considering variables that may function as *moderators* of the stressor-strain relationship. However, we will also touch upon *mediation* and *moderated mediation*, given that the stressor-strain relationship is commonly referred to as a process (see Figure 1.1 in Chapter 1).

The effect of a stressor (X) on strain (Y) is moderated by a variable (W) 'if the size, sign, or strength depends on or can be predicted by (W)' (Hayes, 2017, p. 220). Thus, a moderator variable interacts with the stressor in predicting strain (see Figure 6.1). Moderator effects are typically assessed by the interaction between the predictor variable and the moderator in a hierarchical regression, where the predictor and moderator are entered first into the regression equation, followed by the entry of the interaction term (predictor × moderator). This enables the determination of the incremental contribution of the moderator effect once the direct effects have been taken into account.

In contrast to moderator variables, a *mediating* variable is conceptualized as the mechanism through which a predictor variable (X) influences an outcome variable (Y), for example how a stressor (X) influences strain (Y) through coping as a mediator (Hayes, 2017). That is, it provides a link between one variable and another. The mechanism behind the effect of a stressor on strain may be biological, emotional, cognitive, and/or behavioral. The allostatic load model discussed in Chapter 4 is an example of a model that incorporates mediation. For example, the first stage of allostatic load functions as a mediator between the stressor and the second stage of allostatic load. It should also be

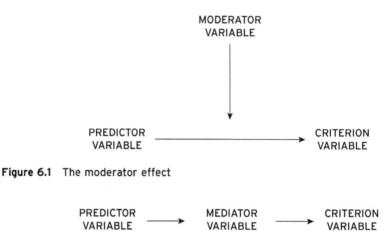

Figure 6.1   The moderator effect

Figure 6.2   The mediator effect

noted that job stressors may function as mediating variables. For example, workers with higher levels of negative affect may perceive higher levels of job stressors, which in turn increases their level of strain compared to workers with lower levels of negative affect. Mediator effects are typically assessed by path analysis using structural equational modeling or ordinary least squares regressions (Hayes et al., 2017) (Figure 6.2).

Moderation and mediation may also be combined into a moderated mediation (or less commonly, mediated moderation). A moderated mediation is when the mediation (i.e., indirect) effect is contingent upon the values of a moderating variable (Edwards & Konold, 2020). For example, in the study by Huyghebaert et al. (2018) the positive relationship between the job stressor workload and exhaustion through sleeping problems was only true for overcommitted workers.

Although mediation and moderated mediation represent interesting and important approaches to exploring various aspects of the stress process, we will mainly focus on moderators of the stressor-strain relationship in this chapter. We have chosen this approach because moderation has been of major emphasis in the stress literature (Bliese et al., 2017). As we noted earlier (see Chapter 1), various kinds of moderator variables have been identified in research on stress processes. For clarity and simplicity, we will group these variables into two categories of factors: (a) dispositional or personality and (b) situational (which in this chapter includes control and social support). An exhaustive review of these topics is beyond the scope of this chapter. The following discussion reviews the relevance of these two categories of moderator variables.

DISPOSITIONAL/PERSONALITY MODERATORS

Dispositional or personality characteristics have been of considerable interest to researchers investigating relationships between job-related stressors (e.g., excessive job demands, role conflict, role ambiguity) and indexes of strain (e.g., psychological strain, job dissatisfaction, and physiological symptoms). In their influential article Bolger and

Zuckerman (1995) suggested that personality may play an important role in affecting (enhancing or inhibiting) the stress process by influencing individuals' *exposure* to stressful events, by affecting their *reactivity* to these events, or by both of these processes. They also discussed how dispositional factors may influence people's choices of coping mechanisms and the effectiveness of coping strategies. Coping strategies and behaviors are reviewed in Chapter 7 and hence will not be covered here.

Figure 6.3 illustrates mediating and moderating linkages between personality variables and outcomes, such as strain. According to the *differential exposure* perspective, personality factors may determine the extent to which individuals are exposed to certain kinds of stressful events or circumstances (Pathway 1 in Figure 6.3), which may then lead to strain (Pathway 3). For example, hostile individuals are prone to experience intense negative affect such as irritation and anger at work. These emotional experiences are likely to influence unfavorable interpersonal perceptions and behavioral patterns that more easily evoke interpersonal conflicts with colleagues and leaders at work, which in turn, may induce greater psychological strain. Although the differential exposure hypothesis is certainly plausible and worthy of investigation, there has been little effort to examine it in studies of job stress. It should also be noted that this model positions stressors, not personality factors, as the mediating variables.

An alternative, and more commonly held, view is the *differential reactivity* perspective, which suggests that certain dispositional variables may moderate the impact of job stressors on individuals' strain. In Figure 6.3, this perspective is reflected in the diagonal arrow (Pathway 2) intersecting the horizontal linkages between stressors and outcomes (Pathway 3). Put simply, this means that the effects of stressors will vary depending on whether an individual is high or low on a specific personality or dispositional attribute. A large variety of personality variables have been studied in the context of the differential reactivity perspective, and these potential moderating effects are discussed in more detail below.

Before turning to specific variables, however, it is important to note that there are several mechanisms by which personality may act as a moderator variable. While a personality trait can be considered a distal factor in the stress process, a personality trait may influence the stress process by affecting more proximal factors such as individuals' appraisals of situations (Schneider, 2004) or coping (Carver & Connor-Smith, 2010). As will be noted in our discussion of coping in Chapter 7, the appraisal of a situation as threatening is a major component of the transactional model of the stress-coping process. Individuals who perceive an event or circumstance as threatening to their physical or

Figure 6.3 The differential exposure and reactivity hypotheses

psychological well-being are more likely to experience negative outcomes. It follows that any factor that influences the appraisal process (e.g., personality trait) is also likely to contribute to stressor outcomes, such as perceived stress, health, and well-being.

Drawing on these general perspectives on the role of personality in stressor-strain relationships, stress researchers have investigated the moderating influence of specific dispositional characteristics. Our intention here is not to discuss all possible dispositions that have been identified empirically but to highlight major findings from this research and to direct attention to their implications for our understanding of organizational stress.

Negative Affectivity/Neuroticism

In an overview of dispositional factors, work-related strain, and health, Semmer and Meier (2009) discussed the concept of vulnerable versus resilient personality, noting that several personality variables may function as vulnerability or resilience factors. Negative affectivity (NA) and neuroticism are traits that may be viewed as components of vulnerability. While stress research has paid much attention to NA, neuroticism and NA show substantial overlap (Watson, 2000) and are both considered to reflect relatively stable predispositions to experience low self-esteem and negative emotional states (Lahey, 2009; Watson & Clark, 1984). There is also evidence that the constructs do not differ substantively in their effects. For instance, results from a meta-analysis investigating the influence of personality dispositions on job satisfaction found that neuroticism and NA had a similar influence on job satisfaction (Bruk-Lee et al., 2009). Hence, we will treat them together below.

NA/neuroticism can take many different (and not always mutually exclusive) roles in the stress process. From early on, NA was proposed to represent an endogenous variable, a source of methodological bias, in the stressor-strain relationship (Watson & Clark, 1984). Watson and his associates argued that NA is generally unrelated to reactivity to stressors and that high-NA individuals uniformly report greater strain (distress) over a range of both stressful and non-stressful situations (Watson & Clark, 1984; Watson & Pennebaker, 1989). There has been considerable debate about whether the effects of NA/neuroticism on strain indeed represent methodological artifacts (Judge et al., 2000) or, in the case that NA/neuroticism has a substantial role (Spector et al., 2000), whether it is best represented as a direct, indirect or moderating role. The debate at the turn of the century sparked numerous research attempts to decipher the complex role of NA/neuroticism in the stress-coping process.

According to Semmer and Meier (2009), persons who are high on NA/neuroticism are more inclined to experience psychological strain and other negative outcomes in their work setting. In the largest meta-analysis yet, neuroticism was indeed the personality trait with the largest (negative) relationship to job satisfaction (Steel et al., 2019). Neuroticism is also related to higher levels of perceived job strain in general (Törnroos et al., 2013). In a meta-analysis of the role of negative affect on numerous job attitudes (e.g., organizational commitment, turnover intentions, and dimensions of burnout), NA consistently showed substantial negative relationships with 'positive' outcome variables (i.e., organizational commitment) and positive relationship with 'negative' outcome variables (i.e., burnout dimensions) (Thoresen et al., 2003). In particular, NA has demonstrated a strong influence on variables related to job stressors (Ng & Sorensen, 2009).

In an influential article, Spector and his colleagues elucidated the ways in which NA might influence stressor-strain relationships. Importantly, these processes may be valid for other individual dispositions. Spector et al. (2000), have outlined six possible processes:

1   The *symptom perception* hypothesis, an explanation favored by Watson and Pennebaker (1989), is that individuals high on NA tend to have a negative 'view of the world.' In a job situation, they tend to perceive (and hence report) the environment as containing a high level of stressors. In other words, according to this view, NA directly influences (the perception of) stressors, rather than the relationship between stressors and strains.

2   An alternative to the above is that high-NA individuals may exhibit a heightened response to stressors because they are more sensitive to the impact of stressors. Given the same environmental conditions, these people will show more strain than their low-NA counterparts. The *hyper-responsivity* mechanism suggests that the effect of NA moderates the effect of stressors on strain.

3   The *differential selection* perspective is that high-NA individuals are more likely to be located in jobs that are 'stressful.' The proposed mechanism behind this perspective is that high-NA may choose jobs that are low in control and high in demand (Törnroos et al., 2013), conditions that research has demonstrated are conducive to strain. Alternatively, individuals displaying high NA are less attractive as applicants for better jobs, potentially caused by their demonstrated lower job performance (Kaplan et al., 2009), and hence that they are less likely to be selected for these positions, but to date, there has been no systematic investigation of this proposition.

4   Another possible explanation is that by their behavior high-NA individuals actually create stressors. Spector et al. (2000) have labeled this the *stress-creation* mechanism. For instance, negative feelings about life, in general, may spill over into a person's verbal and nonverbal behaviors, hence inducing negative reactions from colleagues and leading to a conflictual social environment. This explanation may be especially relevant, therefore, to the effects of social stressors in the workplace. The end result would be similar to that predicted by the symptom perception hypothesis, even though these two predictions posit different mechanisms.

5   *Transitory mood*, which is affected by job conditions, may also have a substantial influence on individuals' reactions to stressors and their experience of strain. This suggests that high levels of stressors trigger workers to feel anxious, upset, or frustrated and that these fluctuations in mood result in their reporting higher strain, as well as elevated levels of NA. From this perspective, NA is an outcome of mood rather than a potential source of strain.

6   Finally, consistent exposure to stressors may itself induce high levels of negativity or exacerbate existing levels of this disposition. This *causality* hypothesis suggests that although NA is typically conceived as a stable trait, job conditions can have an influence on dispositions, including NA.

The proposed processes have received a different amount of research attention in the last two decades, and the research has provided mixed support for the various processes (for examples of research that test several of the processes see for instance Höge & Büssing, 2004; Oliver et al., 2010). Thus, the role of NA in the stress process is by no means simple, and observed relationships of NA with stressors and strains may be explained by various roles of NA. In sum, no single explanation for the effects of NA is likely to encapsulate the full influence of this variable. We will give examples of research that has focused on symptom perception and the hyper-responsivity process of NA/neuroticism given the prominence of these processes in the research field and their overlap with the theoretical construct described at the beginning of the chapter, differential exposure, and differential reactivity, respectively.

In the symptom perception mechanism, NA/neuroticism has an indirect relationship with strain through perceptions of stressors. More specifically, high NA individuals perceive their jobs to be more stressful and thus experience more strain (Oliver et al., 2010; Stoeva et al., 2002). While most studies use self-report to measure all variables, in the study by Falco et al. (2013) of the indirect effect of NA on strain, strain was operationalized as psychophysical strain assessed by an occupational physician and by medically certified sickness absence (collected from the company's database). The results showed that NA was related to increased interpersonal conflict with co-workers (i.e., stressor), which again was related to increased levels of both psychophysical strain and absence. While NA also was related to increased levels of interpersonal conflict with the leader, conflict with the leader did not mediate the relationship between NA and strain. Other lines of research also suggest that the NA → stressor → strain relationship depends on the nature of the stressor and strain variable (Barsky et al., 2004), suggesting that the indirect roles of NA in predicting strain are heterogenous.

NA is also related to strain-producing appraisals beyond the perception of specific stressors. NA is related to increased levels of threat appraisals (i.e., when the demands of the stressor are perceived to outweigh available coping resources) when facing stressors (Schneider, 2004). Threat appraisals are then related to an unfavorable physiological response (Schneider, 2004) and diminished task performance (Schneider et al., 2012). Research also suggests that high-NA individuals may construe aspects of the job that are in general considered as a resource, more unfavorably. Marchand and Vandenberghe (2016) demonstrated that with increasing levels of perceived organizational support, high-NA (but not low-NA) individuals reported to be more emotionally exhausted. While perceived organizational support generally reduced levels of emotional exhaustion, the researchers explain that high-NA individuals experience organizational support as negative and tainted with expectations of more effort (Marchand & Vandenberghe,

2016). Thus, while high-NA individuals show an inclination to perceive negative events as more stressful, they may also have a tendency to perceive positive events as problematic.

Future research investigating the indirect effect of NA/neuroticism on strain would benefit from using more longitudinal research designs and including multiple theoretically grounded mediating variables (i.e., stressors) to compare their relative strength in linking NA/neuroticism with strain. It would also be relevant to increase research efforts on objective assessments of stressors in order to partial out to what extent the objective world (if so exists) is indeed different and harsher for workers with high levels of NA/neuroticism.

The hyper-responsivity process proposes that NA/neuroticism may operate as a moderator of stressor-strain linkages. Accordingly, NA/neuroticism serves to strengthen the correlations between stressors and psychological strain, such that individuals high on NA/neuroticism will exhibit a stronger relationship between stressors and outcomes than their counterparts with low NA/neuroticism. Thus, individuals with high NA/neuroticism show intensified responses to stressors compared to individuals with low NA/neuroticism. The support for the hyper-responsivity process is mixed (Bowling & Jex, 2013). While some research is in line with the process (Kammeyer-Mueller et al., 2009), some find partial support for the process (Fortunato & Harsh, 2006; Oliver et al., 2010), and others have failed to find support (Barsky et al., 2004; Debus et al., 2014; Höge & Büssing, 2004; Näswall et al., 2005), or found the opposite effect (Beehr et al., 2015).

Field studies that employ self-report of stressors and strain have the caveat that the objective level of the stressor (and strain) may differ across participants. While lacking ecological validity, experimental studies where stressors are manipulated assure that the level of intensity of the stressor is equal and allows for a causal interpretation of the effects. In an experimental study, O'Brien et al. (2008) manipulated two types of work stressors; demand (high/low) and control (high/low) to investigate the potential moderator role of NA on the relationship between stressors and strain. As predicted by O'Brien and colleagues, high-NA participants reported more strain in conditions with high demands compared to low-NA participants. Further, high-NA was most susceptible to reduced task satisfaction when they had low control and simultaneously faced high demands in comparison with a situation with high levels of control facing a demanding task. However, NA did not moderate the influence of stressors on performance measures (neither objective nor subjective), giving only partial support for the hyper-responsivity hypothesis.

Further complicating the picture is that different levels of NA/neuroticism may provide either linear or nonlinear effects of stressors on strain. For example, job accountability is suggested to have non-linear effects on strain. While low and high levels of job accountability are related to increased levels of strain, moderate levels of accountability are related to lower levels of strain. However, this non-linear relationship seems to depend upon NA (Hochwarter et al., 2005). While the non-linear relationship between job accountability and strain emerged for low-NA individuals, high-NA individuals displayed a linear pattern. Thus, while increasing levels of job accountability (up to a certain point) for low-NA individuals may reduce strain, increasing levels of job accountability will increase strain for high-NA individuals (Hochwarter et al., 2005).

Currently, there is evidence suggesting that NA/neuroticism is related to strain through aspects of symptom perception (e.g., differential perception of exposure). However, the evidence for a hyper-responsivity (differential reactivity) role of NA/ neuroticism is mixed. Further complicating this debate is the issue of common-method variance (Podsakoff et al., 2012). Because stressors, psychological strain, and NA are all frequently assessed via self-report questionnaires, as addressed above, it is possible that NA serves as a confounding or biasing variable in the relationship between stressors and strain (Judge et al., 2000). Thus, future research should include operationalizations of these constructs beyond self-report when possible. This may involve experimental and quasi-experimental research designs that enable more explicit differentiation between possible processes. When self-report is the only viable way, it has been suggested to choose the type of measurement of NA that shows less conceptual overlap with strain variables (Fortunato, 2004). In addition, it is important to determine which specific stressor-strain relationship is influenced by NA/neuroticism, as it is apparent that not all relationships are affected by this dispositional factor. There is also room for investigating more complex relationships (e.g., Hayes, 2017 discuss for instance serial mediation, moderated moderation, and moderated mediation). In a study by Taylor and Kluemper (2012) neuroticism moderated both the relationship between job stressors and perceived incivility (mediator) and the relationship between perceived incivility and enacted workplace aggression, showing support for moderated mediation. Lastly, the moderating influence of NA on the job stressor – strain relationship may itself be contingent upon other individual characteristics. For instance, while men high on NA showed greater spillover effects of job stress on family life, this was not true for women high on NA (Wang et al., 2011).

Type A Behavior Pattern

Early in the job stress literature, a fashionable topic was the Type A behavior pattern (TABP) as a predictor of strain (and strain-related outcomes). This cluster of characteristics was first identified as a potential contributor to strain-related outcomes by cardiologists Friedman and Rosenman in the 1950s (Rosenman et al., 1964) and since that time has been examined both as a direct predictor of strain and as a moderator in the chain of events between stressors and strain. Type A individuals are characterized as displaying high levels of concentration and alertness, achievement striving (ambitiousness), competitiveness, time urgency, and aggressiveness. Further potential characteristics of this disposition include irritability (when things do not go according to plan), along with hostility and anger toward others who are perceived by the Type A individual as impeding his or her goal achievement (Lee et al., 1993).

Empirical research on TABP has been plagued by controversy, particularly surrounding the measurement of this behavioral disposition. Friedman, Rosenman, and their colleagues

(1964) developed the Structured Interview (SI) to assess Type A tendencies. In a comprehensive review and discussion of the validity of this construct, Ganster et al. (1991) identified three distinct components within the SI but found only one of these elements – hostility toward others – was significantly associated with physiological outcomes. Given the practical inconvenience of conducting lengthy behavioral interviews to assess TABP, several self-report measurements of TABP have been developed. One central problem that emerged when Edwards et al. (2013) conducted an empirical examination of the various self-report measures of TABP was the evidence that different self-report measures assessed different underlying constructs and different underlying dimensions. Instead of trying to measure a global TABP, Edwards et al. (2013) suggested that researchers should measure specific TABP dimensions.

TABP is an interesting dispositional characteristic in stress research in that it may lead to both positive and negative outcomes for the individual. The investigation of distinct dimensions of TABP has revealed that different dimensions, such as Achievement Striving and Impatience/Irritability indeed are related to beneficial and detrimental outcomes for individuals, respectively. While Achievement Striving is related to increased job satisfaction (Day & Jreige, 2002) and engagement (Hallberg et al., 2007), the Impatience/Irritability dimension is related to increased perception of stress and lower life satisfaction (Day & Jreige, 2002) and burnout (Hallberg et al., 2007). More research is needed to ascertain the relative contributions of specific components of the Type A construct.

Turning to the moderator hypothesis, research findings to date have unfortunately been inconsistent in demonstrating that TABP functions as a moderator of stressor-strain relationships. Some research has confirmed this (Day & Jreige, 2002), but other studies have uncovered little support for a moderator effect of this variable (Edwards et al., 1990; Hallberg et al., 2007). One reason for the inconsistency may lie in the different operationalizations of TABP. Theoretically, it is predicted that individuals who are more easily provoked in their work will experience more psychological (and perhaps physical) strain than those exhibiting Type B characteristics. A few recent studies are in line with this proposition. More specifically, employees high in anger (Sliter et al., 2011) or hostility (Zhou et al., 2015) experience more negative affect after experiencing aversive encounters at work. However, there is a paucity of recent research investigating the moderating effect of TABP.

Perhaps even more important is the need for a clearer conceptualization of the role of Type A behavior in the stress process. As noted above, researchers need to clarify the conditions under which positive and negative consequences occur for Type A individuals and whether these consequences apply to all Type A persons or only to certain subgroups, such as those scoring high on anger and hostility. Further empirical work is needed to sort out the relationships between dimensions of TABP, such as the extent to which anger and hostility represent independent constructs or are better fitted under the umbrella of TABP (Semmer & Meier, 2009). After construct validity is established, more research is needed to examine the extent to which TABP has across-the-board negative consequences and to further tease out its effects on a range of psychological and physiological reactions.

Hardiness

The construct labeled as *hardiness* in the 1970s by Kobasa (1979) is a further variable falling under the rubric of vulnerability/resilience factors that have been hypothesized to moderate the effects of environmental stressors on individuals' experience of strain and ill health. Kobasa characterized the 'hardy personality' as one that encompasses high levels of *commitment* or involvement in day-to-day activities, the perception that one has *control* over life events, and a tendency to view unexpected change as a *challenge* rather than a threat to well-being. Maddi (2007) argued that hardiness 'is a pattern of attitudes and skills that provides the courage and strategies to turn stressful circumstances from potential disasters into growth opportunities instead' (p. 61). While some researchers examine the multidimensional construct of hardiness by composing a general measure of hardiness based on the scores of the three facets, others examine the three facets separately.

A meta-analysis of the direct influence of the general measures of hardiness (and other personality variables) on burnout suggested that hardiness was negatively related to burnout (Alarcon et al., 2009). More specifically, hardiness was negatively related to emotional exhaustion and depersonalization, and positively related to personal accomplishment. In fact, hardiness was the personality variable that was most strongly related to the various dimensions of burnout. The results of a meta-analysis by Eschleman et al. (2010) suggested that hardiness and the three facets of hardiness examined separately relate to stressors and strain. More specifically, hardiness, commitment, control, and challenge relate negatively to work-related stressors and physical, psychological, and health-deteriorating behavior (Eschleman et al., 2010). Hardiness emerged as the strongest predictor in most analyses and explained unique variance when the influence of the other predictors was considered. The results of the meta-analysis by Eschleman et al. (2010) showed both conceptual overlap and distinctiveness among the facets of hardiness. Challenge had the least degree of overlap with commitment and control, suggesting that challenge is the most unique component of hardiness. While all the facets of hardiness, in general, were related to stressors and strain, commitment was the predictor that explained the most unique variance in predicting the outcome variables. Importantly, the results suggest that hardiness should be examined at the facet level given that the relationships between hardiness, stressor, and strain may depend upon the conceptualization of the type of hardiness facet and the specific stressor-strain relationship. The exact process behind the relationship between hardiness and stressors and strain is still unclear, suggesting a fertile and important future research ground.

While the results above suggest a direct relationship between hardiness and stressors and strain, as explained above, hardiness is also suggested to buffer against the detrimental effects of stressors. The findings regarding the potential moderating role of hardiness have been mixed (Beehr & Bowling, 2005). However, a recent meta-analytic examination by Eschleman et al. (2010) provided preliminary support for a moderating role of hardiness on the stressor-strain relationship. It should be noted that the relatively few studies included in the examination of the moderating effect (i.e., eight studies) and the heterogeneity of the stressor-strain relationships included in the analysis, limits a precise understanding of the buffering effects of hardiness. Thus, while the hardiness construct at its theoretical core suggests that people with high levels of hardiness withstand the pressure from stressors, there is still a need for research that examines this proposition.

In summary, research suggests a direct influence of hardiness on strain. Although the buffering role of hardiness on the experience of strain has intuitive appeal, to date evidence to support its effects has been somewhat disappointing, partly perhaps because of the different measurement approaches adopted in the research. In their review of hardiness research, Beehr and Bowling (2005) point out that many studies use different operationalizations of the hardiness facets and often rely upon other personality scales that are reframed within the hardiness construct. Furthermore, there are indications that the hardiness construct is too global and that further research should examine the three specific components more closely, especially the commitment component. Specific scales that aim to measure the facets of hardiness have been developed (Bartone, 2007). Thus, future research may examine the potential moderating effect of the three separate facets of hardiness. Further, although this construct would appear to be highly salient to strain reactions in all occupations, most of the research has been on workers in occupations with high levels of stressors such as military personnel (Eschleman et al., 2019).

At this point, there is a lack of substantive evidence that hardiness per se demonstrates a consistent moderating effect on either psychological well-being or physical health. While it is premature to abandon research on the buffering role of hardiness, as reviewed by Beehr and Bowling (2005) there may be multiple other ways that hardiness influences the stress process beyond a moderating role. For instance, people high in hardiness were more likely to find emotionally demanding jobs more attractive than people low in hardiness (Eschleman et al., 2019), suggesting a potential role of self-selection to stressors. A tighter specification of the theoretical construct and a more systematic approach to its measurement and a thorough examination of multiple roles that hardiness may play in the stress process are needed to enhance our understanding of this interesting concept.

Personal Resources

Personal resources 'are aspects of the self that are generally linked to resiliency' (Hobfoll et al., 2003, p. 632) and may help individuals attain their goals (Halbesleben et al., 2014). Conservation of resources theory (COR; Hobfoll, 1989, 2002) and job demands-resources (JD-R) theory (Bakker & Demerouti, 2017) are examples of theories that incorporate the effect of personal resources on the stressor → strain relationship and propose that certain individual characteristics may exert a positive influence on how workers respond to work-related stressors.

Relevant to this chapter, besides the direct effect of personal resources on stressors and strain, personal resources are also proposed to have a moderating effect on the stressor-strain relationship. According to JD-R theory, 'personal resources are expected to buffer the undesirable impact of job demands on strain, and boost the desirable impact of (challenge) job demands on motivation' (Bakker & Demerouti, 2017, p. 275). While the direct effect of personal resources on alleviating the effect of job stressors is commonly found, in general, the buffering effect of personal resources has received mixed support (Sonnentag & Frese, 2012).

To examine the effect of personal resources, researchers have either examined a personal resource independently or in combination with other personal resources where scores from multiple personal resources are aggregated into a composite score or represented by a latent higher-order factor. Because combining personal resources makes it impossible to partial out the separate and discrete effects of a specific personal resource, in our examination of this line of research we will use the personal resource constructs and level of specificity as specified by the researchers. Multiple individual dispositions have been examined within the personal resource framework (Schaufeli & Taris, 2014). Given the scope of this chapter, we will briefly review a limited selection of some of the variables that have been construed as personal resources. More specifically, we will focus on *self-efficacy*, *locus of control*, and *core self-evaluations*. While it is certainly the case that hardiness, as a resilience trait, shares a conceptual overlap with personal resources (Beehr & Bowling, 2005), we decided to keep hardiness in a separate section (above) to reflect the current research trends. As reviewed below, several studies have suggested that self-efficacy, locus of control, and core self-evaluations play a significant role in the stress process.

Self-efficacy

Self-efficacy is 'the belief in one's capabilities to organize and execute the courses of action required to produce given attainments' (Bandura, 1997, p. 3). Self-efficacy has been shown in meta-analyses to relate negatively to both stressors (e.g., work-family conflict in Allen et al., 2012) and strain (e.g., burnout in Shoji et al., 2016). Self-efficacy is also conceived as an antecedent of 'positive' outcomes such as work engagement (Bakker et al., 2008).

Regarding the moderating role of self-efficacy, Jex and Bliese (1999) found that self-efficacy buffered the impact of job stressors and strain. More specifically, workers with high levels of self-efficacy experienced less strain when working long hours or having excessive workloads than workers with low levels of self-efficacy. Likewise, the research by Xanthopoulou et al. (2013) was in line with a buffering effect of self-efficacy as workers with low levels of self-efficacy experienced less engagement when facing emotional demands at work compared to workers with high levels of self-efficacy. Self-efficacy also buffered the negative impact of experienced incivility from co-workers on emotional exhaustion, in such a way that whereas workers with higher levels of self-efficacy were not adversely impacted by others' uncivil behavior, workers with low or average self-efficacy experienced increased emotional strain after uncivil encounters (Rhee et al., 2017). Researchers have also found support for a boosting role of self-efficacy. When workers faced emotional demands or the need to manage their own feelings in their jobs, high levels of self-efficacy were important for work engagement (Xanthopoulou et al., 2013).

Other studies have failed to provide unambiguous support for the buffering effect of self-efficacy. In a study by Panatik et al. (2011) self-efficacy moderated the impact of job demands on psychological strain (but not job satisfaction and turnover intentions), such that workers with lower levels of self-efficacy experienced higher levels of psychological strain when facing job demands. Workers with high levels of self-efficacy did not differ in their levels of psychological strain when facing low vs. high levels of job demands. There is also evidence that personal resources such as self-efficacy, instead of buffering the effects of stressors on strain, in some situations intensify strain. In a study by Toker et al. (2013) workers with high levels of self-efficacy, experiencing either high job demands or low levels of control, had an increase in physiological strain (risk factors associated with diabetes). Thus, high levels of personal resources may backfire in some situations.

The potential negative effects of personal resources may also depend upon the stability of the resources. Personal resources differ between people in their level of fluctuation, in that some may have a rather stable sense of personal resources (being either low or high), while others may experience that their level of personal resources fluctuates. Research by Peng et al. (2015) showed that contrary to their predictions, the relationship between job demands and strain was in fact stronger for workers with *stable* rather than *variable* levels of self-efficacy (Peng et al., 2015). The contradicting results were replicated in their second study, suggesting that the results may not easily be dismissed. The underlying mechanisms behind the potentially detrimental role of personal resources such as self-efficacy are not clearly understood.

Locus of Control

Locus of control (LOC) is another dispositional factor that may play a role in the stress-coping process, although again there has not been a great deal of empirical research recently on the potential moderating influence of this variable on stressor-strain relations. Locus of control differs from perceived control (over the work environment) in that the former refers to a generalized expectancy of having control over life events and hence is a dispositional construct, whereas the latter reflects a person's perception of control in specific circumstances and can vary across situations. Due to these differences in nature and function, our view is that, although the two variables clearly may be interrelated, perceived control should be classified as a situational variable rather than as a personality disposition. (We discuss perceived control in the next section of this chapter.)

Internal locus of control (i.e., the perception that outcomes are contingent upon own behavior) has a direct positive influence on job satisfaction and performance (Judge & Bono, 2001). In a meta-analysis by Ng et al. (2006), locus of control was related to a wide range of work-related outcomes. More specifically, locus of control was positively related to general well-being, such as mental and physical well-being and job-related affective reactions as well as motivation and performance. There was also a negative relationship between locus of control and various job stressors (Ng et al., 2006). Research also suggests that the context-specific work locus of control construct (pertaining to perceiving rewards at work as a consequence of own behavior) is particularly important for job-related outcome variables (Wang et al., 2010).

A review by Hou et al. (2017) examined the buffering role of locus of control on multiple outcomes related to mental and physical health. While in general there was greater support for a buffering role of locus control on the relationship between stressors and mental strain compared to physical health outcomes, most of the reviewed research relied upon self-report outcome measures. The review by Hou et al. (2017) examined health-related outcomes, but locus of control has also been shown to interact with work stressors in predicting work behavior. In a study by Sprung and Jex (2012) individuals with a more external locus of control (i.e., the perception that forces beyond the control of the individual will determine outcomes) reacted with more counterproductive behavior in response to work stressors than individuals with a more internal locus of control. However, in a study by Ito and Brotheridge (2007) locus of control did not moderate the stressor-strain relationship, but instead suggested that workers with an internal locus of control perceived higher levels of stressors in response to change than workers with an external locus of control. The mixed buffering influence of locus of control may be related to weaknesses in how the construct is conceptualized, as the construct may be more appropriately conceived as multidimensional and more fluctuating than previous research has treated it (Galvin et al., 2018).

Core Self-evaluations

Core self-evaluations refer to 'global evaluations individuals make about themselves or their relation to their environment' (Judge et al., 1998, p. 19), and is considered to be a higher-order construct consisting of the facets of self-esteem, locus of control, and emotional stability. In a meta-analysis by Kammeyer-Mueller et al. (2009), core self-evaluations were negatively related to a broad range of stressors and strain. An examination of the specific facets of core-self evaluations, also revealed that whereas all facets were negatively related to stressors, emotional stability (i.e., low neuroticism) had a stronger negative impact on stressors. Core self-evaluations were also negatively related to perceived strain, and in the same vein as with the stressor relationships, all facets were negatively related to perceived strain, with emotional stability emerging with the strongest negative relationship. A review and meta-analysis of the core self-evaluations literature also suggested that core self-evaluations are both negatively related to stressors and trains (Chang et al., 2012). A meta-analysis including several personality variables by Alarcon et al. (2009) suggested that core self-evaluations were negatively related to burnout.

While the direct effect of core self-evaluations on stressors and strain has been established, the support for a moderating role of core self-evaluations is equivocal. While some studies support a buffering role of core self-evaluations (Harris et al., 2009) other studies have not been supportive (Best et al., 2005; Kammeyer-Mueller et al., 2009), overall providing a mixed picture of the moderating role of core self-evaluations. One potential reason for the diverging findings that are discussed in the literature is the conceptualization of core self-evaluations (Chang et al., 2012). For instance, in their assessment of the construct, Johnson et al. (2008) recommended that core self-evaluations should be represented as a multidimensional construct, instead of using summed scale scores, and that other individual dispositions potentially should be included in the construct. Treating core self-evaluations as a multidimensional construct also allows for testing the potential diversified buffering effects of the various subdimensions of core self-evaluations, where some of the subdimensions might have a buffering role related to some job stressors, but not all.

Beyond a Moderating Role of Personal Resources

Research has examined the extent to which personal resources relate directly to job stressors and strain. Workers with high levels of personal resources such as self-efficacy, locus of control, and core-self evaluations, experience fewer job stressors, less strain, and more engagement in their jobs compared to workers with lower levels of these personal resources. As evident from the discussion above, the role of personal resources as a moderator in the stressor-strain relationship is less clear. There may be several explanations for the lack of consistent support for a moderating effect of personal resources. It may be that detecting interaction effects (e.g., moderation) requires large sample sizes, and that previous studies may not have had sufficient statistical power to detect interactions (Shieh, 2009). Another potential explanation may lie in the (missing) theoretical links between the examined variables. De Jonge and Dormann (2006) have argued and also found support for the triple-match principle between job resources, stressors, and strain, suggesting that the likelihood of finding support for a moderating role of job resources increases when there is a conceptual match between the variables. Thus, a job resource is effective in buffering demands and consequently alleviating strain when the resource is relevant to that specific demand (Chrisopoulos et al., 2010). The triple-match principle has mainly been investigated from a job resource perspective, but the same principle would also apply to personal resources. For instance, workers with higher abilities in managing their own emotions would potentially be better equipped to face emotional demands at work and thus experience less emotional exhaustion than workers who are less capable of handling their own emotions. Applying a matching principle would require that researchers specify the exact links between the specific job stressor, personal resource, and strain.

At another level, one might question whether the examination of moderator variables using cross-sectional research designs has deflected attention away from more central issues in job stress research, particularly the exploration of personal resources in the dynamic transactional stress-coping process. In brief, cross-sectional designs may not capture the dynamic interplay between dispositional variables and stress-coping behaviors. Hence, although variables such as those referred to above may have an important buffering effect, their exact role may not be clearly identified in studies that measure stressors and strain at a single time point. Research that examines the dynamic interplay between personal resources, job stressors, and strain is important as a central proposition in COR and JD-R is the existence of gain and loss cycles. The spiraling nature of resources suggests that while acquiring a resource makes gaining additional resources more likely, a loss of a resource often brings about further resource losses. These cycles may be described by different trajectories (Halbesleben et al., 2014) that may depend upon the personal resource examined. Several recent studies are in line with the proposition that people are part of positive gain cycles where resources are accumulated (Reis et al., 2015; Simbula et al., 2011; Xanthopoulou et al., 2009). Incorporating the dynamic nature of gain cycles, Halbesleben and Wheeler (2015) tested and found support for gain cycles using a day-level research design (model tested at the day level with data collected over multiple working days). Understanding the role of specific personal resources and their underlying mechanisms in gain and loss cycles and how these cycles evolve over time represent future possibilities for research.

One example of a mechanism that is involved in gain cycles is job crafting. Job crafting refers to 'the physical and cognitive changes individuals make in the task or relational boundaries of their work' (Wrzesniewski & Dutton, 2001, p. 179). In the JD-R theory, job crafting is proposed as an important mechanism whereby engaged workers will proactively engage in behaviors that increase their resources, which in turn increases work engagement (Bakker & Demerouti, 2017). In a longitudinal study by Vogt et al. (2016) job crafting was related to increased levels of psychological capital (i.e., hope, resilience, self-efficacy, and optimism) and work engagement. However, in this study, work engagement and psychological capital did not predict job crafting, giving only partial support to the JD-R theory. Miraglia et al. (2017) investigated the relationship between self-efficacy and job-crafting as a potential explanatory mechanism for increased job performance. The results showed a positive reciprocal relationship (i.e., variables mutually influencing each other) between self-efficacy and job-crafting where efficacious workers engaged in more job-crafting behavior, which in turn led to higher levels of self-efficacy. Furthermore, job crafting also explained the positive relationship between self-efficacy and performance (Miraglia et al., 2017).

While the findings concerning the moderating effect of personal resources on the stressor-strain relationship are inconsistent, personal resources are also proposed to have indirect effects. For example, whereas the moderating influence of personal resources was not supported in the research by Xanthopoulou et al. (2007), personal resources (i.e., a combination of self-efficacy, organizational-based self-esteem, and optimism) functioned as a partial mediator in the relationship between job resources and work engagement. Thus, people who worked in resourceful environments perceived themselves to be more capable and optimistic, which again was related to higher levels of work engagement. A longitudinal study by Demerouti et al. (2016) found that work-nonwork conflict and facilitation were indirectly related to exhaustion and performance, respectively, through the influence of personal resources. While self-efficacy mediated the relationship between work-nonwork conflict and performance, optimism was the process behind the work-nonwork facilitation and exhaustion relationship (Demerouti et al., 2016), suggesting that these personal resources play different roles. Likewise, in a study by Sonnentag and Spychala (2012) role breadth self-efficacy, defined as an employee's perceived capability to fulfill a broad role (Parker, 1998), functioned as a mediator between the job stressor time pressure and proactive behavior at work. Thus, when facing time pressure at work, employees perceived themselves to be more capable to handle a variety of tasks, which again led them to take personal initiative and charge at work. While personal resources are considered to be relatively stable, the results suggest that they are not immune to changes in response to stressors. Further, the models tested by Xanthopoulou et al. (2007) also supported reversed relationships, suggesting that personal resources may also function as antecedents. Workers high in personal resources perceived higher levels of job resources, which again increased work engagement. In a study of call centers in Italy, the effect of self-efficacy and burnout was partially explained by job demands and job resources (Consiglio et al., 2013). Thus, workers with high self-efficacy perceived more job resources and fewer job demands, which both dampened burnout.

In summary, the evidence above proposes a sound case for multiple roles of personal resources in the job stress process beyond a moderating role. The role of personal resources ranges from antecedents, moderators, mediators, and final outcome variables (Schaufeli & Taris, 2014). A common finding is that personal resources have an impact on the perception of job stressors and strain. The common use of self-report and cross-sectional designs to measure these constructs still poses a threat of common-method bias. We have argued for expanding the researchers' toolkit for examining strain variables (see Chapter 4), and some would also argue that it is possible to assess individual dispositions more 'objectively'. Walker et al. (2017) provided a review of potential biological markers of resiliency that may be useful to expand the measurement of psychological resources. Promising candidates of biological markers are for example heart rate variability, cardiovascular recovery after stress, and cortisol responses (Walker et al., 2017). While it has been proposed that the relationships between NA/neuroticism, stressors, and strain may reflect a methodological artifact, some evidence suggests that this is not reflective of the role of personal resources in the perceptions of job stressors. For instance, while personal resources were related to the perception of job resources, it was not related to the perception of job demands (Xanthopoulou et al., 2007). Thus, in that study people high in personal resources did not perceive lesser job demands than less resourceful people.

One problematic feature of labeling individual traits as personal resources is research showing that these personal resources fail to play a significant role in mitigating the negative effects of stressors (i.e., they do not function as resources) or even more problematic, are associated with detrimental outcomes for the individual (Halbesleben et al., 2014). Thus, while the theoretical conceptualization at its core proposes these traits as mitigating the bad effects of stressors, the empirical evidence is not always aligned with this proposal. Further, the current understanding of these counter-intuitive effects is sparse indicating that there are multiple avenues that are worth exploring. For example, the paradoxical effects of individual traits may depend upon the stressor-strain relationship that is examined (Beehr et al., 2015). The buffering effects of personal resources may be curvilinear such that their buffering role may increase as the level of the personal resource increase up to a certain threshold where the effect either flattens out or reverses. Thus, extremely high levels of 'positive' traits may sometimes be considered a vulnerability when facing stressors. There is also the issue of temporality (Fisher et al., 2019).

Perhaps the moderating effect of certain individual dispositions depends upon the time range between the measurement of the job stressor and the strain variable. It is possible that the buffering role of some individual traits may be operating at the moment, but may not have long-term effects. Theoretically, 'negative' traits, such as neuroticism, may also overlap with other more positive traits, for example, competitiveness, that in certain stressor-strain relationships provide stamina and less strain (Nettle, 2006). Lastly, the moderating effect of personal resources may depend on the level of other variables (i.e., three-way interactions). In a study by Stetz et al. (2006) the mitigating influence of social support on the relationship between job stressors and strain was true for workers with high (but not low) levels of self-efficacy. These possibilities are not exhaustive, and we encourage research that may help provide a nuanced understanding of how individual dispositions impact the stress process. It is also worth noting that while anomalies, such as counterintuitive results, may attract our attention and is worthy of exploration, it is still the case that in many situations personal resources may have a negative impact on stressors and strain.

SITUATIONAL MODERATORS

Among the situational variables that may buffer the impact of stressors (such as work demands, role ambiguity, and role conflict) on the extent of psychological strain experienced by workers, two variables in the work context that have received considerable attention are the degree of autonomy or control that individuals can exert over their work environment and social support both in- and outside the organization.

There are several theoretical frameworks that include control and support as potent moderators of the stressor-strain relationship, and we will briefly outline some of them here. One early influential theory that proposed interacting effects was Karasek's (1979) *job demands-control* model (JDC), also known as the *demands-discretion* model or simply the *decision latitude* model (Fox et al., 1993). The fundamental proposition is that although excessive work demands may clearly be associated with higher levels of psychological strain and even physiological health outcomes, the impact of these demands may be offset by the perception that one has control over important aspects of the work environment. Further, highly challenging or demanding work combined with high control is considered by Karasek to indicate an 'active' job that may have beneficial outcomes for individuals (i.e., reversal effects as proposed by Gonzalez-Mulé & Cockburn, 2017). At the other extreme, jobs that have low demands and low levels of control (e.g., repetitive assembly line work) create strain and are referred to by Karasek as 'passive' jobs.

Much of the early epidemiological research was based on the assumed degree of actual control held by various occupational groups. One criticism of this line of research, however, is that it contains no direct measurement of the amount of control that different occupations may actually exert in their jobs. Thus later, more attention has been given to workers' perceptions of control, supported by research indicating that the extent to which individuals believe they have control, and not objectively assessed control, is a major determinant of their responses (Rau et al., 2010; Spector, 2009).

While JDC incorporated only one situational moderator on the demand (job stressor) → strain relationship, Johnson and Hall (1988) proposed an extension of Karasek's demands-control model of stress to incorporate social support as a moderator of the linkage of job demands and control with strain. According to the job-demands-control-support (JDC-S) model (Karasek & Theorell, 1990), workers are more likely to experience strain when facing high levels of demands, decreasing levels of control and/or support, or an adverse interaction of these variables (e.g., high demands, low control, low support) (Fila et al., 2017). However, if workers experience high levels of control/support when facing high demands, they may show higher levels of learning, satisfaction, and performance. Thus, the JDC-S proposes main effects of each variable on strain and also proposes a Job Demands X Control X Support interaction effect on strain.

The Job Demands- Resource (JD-R) theory is an even more recent theory development that proposes a moderation effect (Bakker & Demerouti, 2017). In contrast to the two other theories, the JD-R proposes multiple job resources, among them control/autonomy and support, to have buffering effects. The earliest JD-R model (Demerouti et al., 2001) proposed main effects of job demands and job resources on strain and engagement, respectively. Further, and relevant to the moderation topic, the latest extension of the JD-R theory included interaction propositions such that job resources (e.g., control and support) can (1) buffer the effect of job demands (i.e., stressors) on strain and (2) particularly have an impact on motivation and engagement when job demands are high. Thus, control and support are especially useful and motivating when most needed (Bakker & Demerouti, 2017).

The three theoretical perspectives are united in that all of them place an emphasis on job demands and either control or support or both, in predicting strain. All three theories include propositions concerning main and interaction effects. A main effect is described by an *additive* hypothesis that proposes that control/support/resources function independently of job stressors to promote well-being and reduce strain; hence, strain would be predicted by a combination of the demands and control/support/resources. This parallels the 'direct effect' described above (see Figure 6.1). On the other hand, the *interactive* hypothesis suggests an interaction of job demands × control/support/resources (depending on the theoretical framework). While this has not always been spelled out, the interaction is typically referred to as the *stress-buffering hypothesis*, which proposes that the relationship between stressors and strains will differ depending on the level of control the person has, the support a person utilizes, or the availability of other job resources.

Researchers have begun to distinguish between the proposed additive (main) effects and the interaction (moderation) effects to see which one is better at explaining strain (Gonzalez-Mulé et al., 2020; Häusser et al., 2010). Because the predictions of the theories resemble each other, research that suggests that demands relate positively to strain or that control lessens strain when facing a job stressor, is consistent with all the theories described above. The theories differ in the specific proposed mechanisms and the extent to which they incorporate the dynamic nature of the variables in the stress process. The theoretical perspectives also differ in the extent to which they are restrictive (one or two moderator variables) or broad in their focus. For more discussion of the theoretical perspectives, see Chapter 1.

PERCEIVED CONTROL OVER THE ENVIRONMENT

As explained earlier, we discuss perceived control as a 'situational' factor because it reflects individuals' perceptions of their specific (work) environments rather than cross-situational dispositional beliefs. In other words, perceived autonomy or control has more to do with environmental characteristics (i.e., whether the situation permits individual control) than with beliefs about control in general (e.g., generalized LOC). Nevertheless, the interplay between specific control perceptions and global control beliefs should not be overlooked (Stiglbauer, 2017).

There is growing consensus among researchers that appropriate levels of control over the environment are important for workers' well-being and even their physical health, and considerable evidence has accumulated to indicate that control (or perceived control) is significantly associated with these outcomes (Crawford et al., 2010; Spector, 2009). However, the critical issue for the present discussion is whether control functions as a moderator of the relationship between job demands (stressors) and individuals' affective and physiological outcomes (strains). Unfortunately, evidence relating to this question is not clear-cut as the literature is replete with mixed findings.

Several findings within the epidemiological literature are in line with the alleviating effect of control on physiological health-related outcomes when experiencing high job demands (Belkic et al., 2004). For instance, in a meta-analysis including over 47,000 people, Nyberg et al. (2013) found that workers with high-strain jobs (defined as high demand and low control) were related to several cardiovascular risk factors (e.g., increased prevalence of diabetes, smoking, and obesity) compared to workers with low strain jobs. Similarly, in a meta-analysis on the relationship between job strain and coronary heart disease involving 13 cohort studies, workers with a high-strain job had a small increased risk of cardiovascular heart disease (Kivimäki et al., 2012). In their review of the literature investigating the primary physiological indicators in the Allocation Load model, Ganster and Rosen (2013) also suggested a buffering effect of control. However, epidemiological studies have received a critique on the way that the buffering effect is examined (De Lange et al., 2003; Gonzalez-Mulé et al., 2020). As described above, it is common that researchers within this tradition create a binary strain variable (strain vs. no strain). Participants who are considered to have jobs with strain have job demands above and job control below the study-specific median, whereas all other participants are considered to have jobs with no strain (see for instance Kivimäki et al., 2012). In the epidemiological tradition, it is also common to make a typology of four categories of jobs based on a median split of scores on demand and control: high strain, low strain, active, or passive (De Lange et al., 2003). While both approaches inevitably lead to a loss of statistical power, they also do not test the interactive effects of demands and control.

Two fairly recent studies from the organizational behavior literature properly tested for and found an interaction effect of job demands and control in predicting physical health and mortality. Interestingly, in both studies by Gonzalez-Mulé and Cockburn (2017, 2020) the interaction effect the researchers found was not a buffering effect, but a reversed effect. More specifically, high job demands under conditions of high job control were related to *decreased* risk of death (34% decrease in the odds of death) compared to low demands and high control (Gonzalez-Mulé & Cockburn, 2017). Likewise, high job demands and high job control were related to *better* physical health, while high demands and low control were unrelated to physical health (Gonzalez-Mulé & Cockburn, 2020). In the same study, job control also showed the theoretically proposed buffering effect on the relationship between demands and mental health. To add further to the complexity, job demands were related to death through divergent pathways. High job demands and low control (or low cognitive ability) were related to an increased likelihood of death via poor mental health, while high job demands and high control were associated with decreased probability of death via better physical health (Gonzalez-Mulé & Cockburn, 2020). Thus, these two studies highlight that the interaction between demands and control may buffer the effect on strain, and also reverse the effect of demands on strain.

Several reviews have suggested that the support for a buffering role of job control in the relationship between demands and strain is weak or inconsistent. In their review of research from 1979 to 1997, Van der Doef and Maes (1999) found mixed support (approximately half the studies were supportive) for the moderating effect of job control on the relationship between demands and psychological well-being. The review also suggested that studies that supported a moderating role of job control were almost exclusively cross-sectional, whereas most longitudinal studies failed to provide support. Further, studies that did indeed find a moderating role of support had a higher degree of conceptual match between demands and control (Van der Doef & Maes, 1999).

De Lange et al. (2003) made a quality assessment of the longitudinal studies that had applied the JDC and JDC-S model, and based on the high-quality studies, examined whether a moderating role of job control (and social support) on the relationship between demands and a range of strain variables was supported. The results indicated modest support for the main effects of job demands and control, however, few studies found support for an interaction effect (De Lange et al., 2003). The few studies that did find an interaction effect often involved self-reported measures of well-being and health.

In a meta-analysis of studies that followed up the period 1998–2007, Häusser et al. (2010) investigated both the main effects and the interaction effects of demands and job control on psychological well-being. The results indicated that the main effects of demands and job control on psychological well-being (general and job-related) received partial support in 57% and full support in 42% of the studies. A large number of sup-portive studies made the researchers conclude that 'the existence of additive effects has been established beyond doubt' (Häusser et al., 2010, p. 29). The support for additive effects was somewhat weaker in studies using longitudinal data, especially concerning job-related well-being. When investigating the interaction effect of job demand and control, only 30% provided partial and 13% full support. The researchers discuss several possible explanations for the inconsistent support for the buffering hypothesis and lend most credibility to the idea that the buffering effect may be more likely when the constructs of job demands and job control match each other. Thus, if the demand is related to workload, control over when and how to conduct the work tasks may be more effective in alleviating the effect of the demand, than if the demand is related to being exposed to others' suffering, which may instead require emotional self-regulation to reduce the pressure of the demand (Häusser et al., 2010). An exploratory analysis supported the distinction between matching, where studies that had matching categories between demand and control to a greater degree found support for an interaction effect than non-matching studies. Other studies that have empirically examined the matching principle have also to a greater degree found support for a moderating effect when demands and job-related resources are matched compared to when they are not (De Jonge & Dormann, 2006).

The most recent investigation of main effects and interactive effects on strain is the meta-analytical test by Gonzalez-Mulé et al. (2020) that involved 77 samples and 140,000 people. Overall, testing the main effects of job demands and control was more consistently associated with strain than when testing the interaction between job demands and control in predicting strain. Job control had a negative main effect on strain. The researchers examined many different boundary conditions, such as strain severity, strain type, demands type, and study design, which potentially could affect the interaction. From all the potential boundary conditions, only the demands type (challenge or hindrance) had an impact on the strength of the interaction model. The interaction effect was significantly stronger for the hindrance demands compared to the challenge demands. For both challenge and hindrance demands' effect on strain, job control had a weak buffering effect. One limitation of the meta-analysis is that the researchers were only able to conduct their analysis on approximately 10% of the located studies that fit their criteria as they were unable to access the raw data/statistics from the remaining studies.

Overall, several reviews and meta-analyses lend more support for the additive (i.e., main effects) compared to the multiplicative (i.e., moderating effect) model. This led Gonzalez-Mulé et al. (2020) to conclude that 'future research drawing from the JDC-S model should have a compelling rationale for employing a multiplicative rather than additive approach' (p. 17). Indeed, several of the reviews have consistently found that job demands and job control have direct influences on strain. These findings have practical implications as well. Generally, the positive correlation between job demands and strain is larger than the negative correlation between job control and strain. Thus, if workers have high levels of job demands, increasing their job control may decrease strain somewhat, but it may not be sufficient to combat the pressure from job demands. These results suggest that organizations need to be conscious of the level of demands that their workers experience, and seek remedies to decrease the burden if the demands are high (Gonzalez-Mulé et al., 2020).

It is still relevant to point out, as Gonzalez-Mulé and his colleagues also do, that there are still avenues worth exploring when it comes to interaction effects. Based on our review the most consistent evidence for a combined role of demands and control on strain comes from the epidemiological literature. While this stream of research has received criticism for its choice of statistical analyses, recent findings suggest that demands and control interact in predicting objective health outcomes. One clear advantage of studies within the epidemiological literature is the use of large sample sizes that gives sufficient statistical power to detect interaction effects. The interaction effects that are discovered in other studies are normally small in size, suggesting that insufficient statistical power may lead to false negative results. Thus, research that involves testing the interaction effect with psychological and behavioral strain outcomes should aim to increase their sample sizes to have sufficient statistical power to avoid potential Type II error (i.e., concluding falsely that there is no interaction effect).

Further, the moderating role of job control on the relationship between job demands and strain also seems to be dependent on the way that job demands are operationalized. In the review by Gonzalez-Mulé et al. (2020), interaction effects, albeit small, were discovered when job demands were differentiated into challenge and hindrance demands, where the latter provided more support for a moderating role of job control. Commonly, research has predominantly examined challenge demands, which may be one potential reason for the lack of consistent results, which led Dawson et al. (2016) to suggest a revision of the JDC-S theory in which the distinction between the types of job demands is included. While in the challenge-hindrance framework stressors have often been predefined and categorized as either challenge or hindrance stressors, suggestions have been made to incorporate workers' *appraisals* of job demands as challenges and/or hindrance stressors (O'Brien & Beehr, 2019). Thus, future research may distinguish more systematically among challenge and hindrance demands, and also include the subjective appraisals of these demands.

Further, researchers have also pointed to the importance of a match between job demands and control if the latter is to buffer the effect of the former (Häusser et al., 2010). Thus, instead of relying on the global buffer hypothesis of job control against any type of job demand, researchers need to make precise evaluations of why job control will be effective against a specific job demand (Daniels & De Jonge, 2010). Preliminary findings suggest that specifying occupational job demands in contrast to generic job demands may not be sufficient in increasing the match (Brough & Biggs, 2015). Researchers could aim to investigate job-specific stressors matched with specific job control and their ability to alleviate the pressure of those stressors. For example, shift work is considered to be a job stressor (see Chapter 2). Perhaps giving workers control and autonomy into when and how these shifts are organized may alleviate strain caused by ill-suited schedules, while giving workers control over their work tasks within the shift may not be sufficient. Further, the matching relationship may itself depend upon workers' personal control beliefs (Stiglbauer, 2017).

Another possibility is the need to model more advanced relationships among the variables. While our review has focused on the relatively simple moderator effect of job control, it is likely that job control is involved in more complex relationships. For example, Brough et al. (2018) investigated a moderated mediation model where job control did not moderate the relationship between demands and outcome variables, but the relationship between demands and coping (mediator), and coping and outcome variables. Thus the positive relationship between emotional demand and engagement through the use of accommodation coping (e.g., effort to change expectations) was stronger with increased levels of job control (Brough et al., 2018). Including mediators in the equation may provide a more nuanced understanding of how job control works.

Although many other situational variables may function as moderators of the impact of job stressors on psychological strain and physical health, because of the substantial interest in and research conducted on JD-C and JDC-S theories we have focused our attention on perceived control. Perceived control has had a prominent status as a moderator in stress research. In fact, to their self-imposed question of a universal moderator in the stressor-strain relationship, Jex and Yankelevich (2008) stated that 'in our opinion the variable that comes closest to fitting in this category is perceived control' (p. 501), although they also pointed out that perceived control might have limited value and be culturally dependent.

Evidence to date shows inconsistent support for the interaction-model. As we have pointed out, there are viable ways forward given that research has not generated definitive conclusions about the moderating influence of the control variable. The lack of unquestionable support of job control as a buffer variable has practical implications for job design in that the negative effects of high-demanding jobs may not be sufficiently alleviated by solely increasing control, but may also require a reduction in demands (Häusser et al., 2010). Given inconsistencies across research findings, however, there is clearly a need for further investigations that include individual, organizational, and perhaps societal factors that may influence the moderating effects of perceived autonomy or control. There is also a need to examine the effects of control in combination with other resources, such as the amount of social support provided by other people within the individual's environment.

EFFECTS OF SOCIAL SUPPORT ON STRESSOR-STRAIN RELATIONSHIPS

The literature on stress in general, including job stress, is replete with studies of the effects that support from others has on an individual's level of well-being and psychological strain. Individuals' stress-coping endeavors (which we discuss in Chapter 7) may be assisted by support from significant others in both their work and off-the-job settings, and there has been considerable research on the moderating functions of social support. In their multi-disciplinary review of the social support literature, Bavik et al. (2020) noted that the findings concerning the effects of social support are still inconclusive given the diverging conceptualizations and operationalizations of social support across disciplines. Further, while research has indicated that social support may mitigate the negative relationship between stressors and strain, other lines of research suggest that social support may exacerbate feelings of strain (Beehr et al., 2010; Gray et al., 2020). In the following discussion, we will examine the various ways and mechanisms by which social support may operate, summarize evidence on the impact of support, and consider potential explanations for research findings.

Social support may exert an influence on stressor-strain relationships in different ways. First, there may be a *main* or *direct* effect, whereby increases in support are directly associated with reduced strain, irrespective of the number or intensity of stressors that the individual encounters. This relationship between support and strain, shown in Figure 6.4, is expressed by a significant zero-order correlation between these variables.

Social support may also function as a mediating variable in the stressor-strain relationship (see Figure 6.5). In this model, stressors (such as role ambiguity, conflict, and overload) may spur individuals to mobilize their support resources, which in turn help to reduce the amount of strain experienced, for instance by providing direct help or emotional care. A variant of the mediating model, depicted in Figure 6.6, occurs when social support affects the experience of the stressor, rather than having a direct effect on strain itself. For instance, support from others may lead individuals to reappraise the intensity of a potential stressor (e.g., the level of insecurity in the job) or the significance of the stressor for their well-being. In this case, the stressor, rather than social support, is the mediating variable.

Finally, as illustrated in Figure 6.7, social support may act as a moderator of the relationship between stressors and strain. In this scenario, having support from others is hypothesized to attenuate the correlation between stressors and strain, primarily because support may help individuals to cope with their job demands and problems. In other words, individuals who receive social support will experience less strain than their counterparts who do not receive support from others because support shields or protects individuals from the potentially harmful consequences of aversive events or circumstances. This is in line with the buffering hypothesis of social support, which may occur instrumentally, by helping workers attend to a problem, or emotionally, by modifying their perception that the stressor is damaging to their well-being.

In summary, the model shown in Figure 6.4 depicts a direct effect of social support on perceptions of strain, whereas Figure 6.7 suggests that support influences the impact of stressors on the individual, rather than having a direct influence on either stressor (Figure 6.6) or the resultant strain (Figure 6.4). In a statistical sense, only Figure 6.7 illustrates a moderating effect of social support. While most moderating effects have been examined within the buffer perspective, it is important to note that social support may also have an enhancing effect on positive outcomes (Buch et al., 2015).

Figure 6.4 Direct relationship between social support and strain

Figure 6.5   Social support as a mediating variable

Figure 6.6   Alternative mediation mechanism

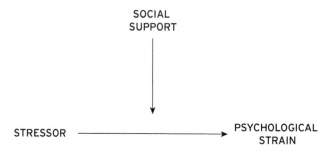

Figure 6.7   Social support as a moderating variable

In an early meta-analysis by Viswesvaran et al. (1999), the researchers examined the various roles (e.g., main, mediating, moderator) that social support may play in work stress. The results suggested that social support plays multiple roles, such as reducing the experienced level of stressors and strain and buffering the effects of stressors on strain. Hence, support for both direct and interaction effects was found. Several reviews and meta-analyses based on the JDC-S have investigated the main effect and/or interaction effects of social support. Overall, the results of the reviews and meta-analyses are in line with a main influence of social support on strain, whereas data on the interaction effect of social support on the relationship between stressor and strain give a mixed picture (De Lange et al., 2003; Gonzalez-Mulé et al., 2020; Häusser et al., 2010; Van der Doef & Maes, 1999). The mixed evidence for an interaction effect may partly be explained by the same factors as discussed in the section on job control (differentiating types of demands, lack of match between variables, statistical power to detect differences, etc). Another methodological reason is the reduced likelihood of confirming the three-way interaction hypothesis (demands, control, and support) that is inherent in the JDC-S theory, but not the JDC theory (Häusser et al., 2010).

While meta-analyses are indispensable for knowledge accumulation, they may require that constructs such as social support are treated as a homogenous variable. Hence, nuances of the proposed diverse effects of various characteristics of social support may be lost. Researchers from multiple disciplines have investigated several different character-istics of social support, such as quality and quantity, utilization, source, content, format, and consistency (Bavik et al., 2020). We will take a closer look at sources and types of support, given their prominence in the work stress literature.

Sources of Support

Research has examined multiple sources of support from both work and non-work domains. Within the work domain, sources of support may originate from entities, such as perceived organizational support, which refers to the belief that the organization values contributions and cares about employees' well-being (Rhoades & Eisenberger, 2002). Sources of job-related support may also come from different levels within the organization, such as supervisors, coworkers, and subordinates. Within the family domain, sources of support may come from the spouse or more generally the family.

An important question is the extent to which the sources have domain-specific effects, or if a source of support in one domain (e.g., work) may also be beneficial in another domain (e.g., family). The meta-analysis by Ford et al. (2007) suggested that sources of support from the work and family domain are, besides being related to satisfaction in their own domain, also related to satisfaction in the other domain. French et al. (2018) examined the relationship between social support and work-family conflict in a meta-analysis. Generally, sources of support within the work domain and within the family domain were negatively related to work-family conflict. Results also indicated a domain-specific effect of support concerning work-to-family conflict, where sources of support from the work (organizational support and supervisor support) reduced work-to-family conflict to a greater extent than did sources of support from the family (general family support and spousal support). There was not a domain-specific effect of support for the family-to-work conflict. Thus, sources from work and family were equally important in mitigating family-to-work conflict. Further, perceived organizational support was often more strongly negatively related to work-family conflict than other support sources from the work such as supervisor and co-worker. However, the different sources of support from the family domain did not relate differently to work-family conflict (French et al., 2018). Because most of the included studies in the meta-analysis were cross-sectional, this limits the possibility to test what role (e.g., antecedent or mediator) the different sources of support play. The meta-analysis involving longitudinal studies by De Lange et al. (2003) did not include different sources of support in their analysis, thus preventing further insight into the temporal dynamics.

Researchers have examined the extent to which different sources of support relate differently to various outcome variables (Baruch-Feldman et al., 2002). In a meta-analysis by Chiaburu and Harrison (2008) co-worker support and leader support were negatively related to role stressor perceptions (e.g., role ambiguity) and withdrawal, and positively related to work attitudes (e.g., job satisfaction) and effectiveness. Support from a co-worker was more strongly related to job involvement, effort reduction, and absenteeism than was support from a leader, suggesting that sources of support matter when predicting different outcome variables. Halbesleben (2006) conducted a meta-analysis of the relationship between social support and burnout. While social support did not differently relate to the three dimensions of burnout (emotional exhaustion, depersonalization, and personal accomplishment), sources of support originating either in the work or non-work sphere demonstrated different relationships with different dimensions of burnout. Work-related support was more strongly related to exhaustion, potentially because of reduced work demands than to depersonalization and personal accomplishment. Non-work sources of support showed the opposite pattern and were more strongly related to depersonalization and personal accomplishment, than exhaustion.

The results above illustrate the advantages of examining different types of sources when investigating relationships within the work stress process. However, reviews that include broader variables such as general strain or job demands, have not found support for differential effects depending on the source of support. While the review by Häusser et al. (2010) points to the differential effect of various sources of support for the additive and interactive effects to occur, the meta-analysis by Gonzalez-Mulé et al. (2020) did not find any differential effects depending on the sources being a co-worker or supervisor when testing additive or interactive effects. While both coworker support and supervisor support were negatively related to strain, their effects on strain did not significantly differ (Gonzalez-Mulé et al., 2020). Thus, the mixed pattern of results suggests that the role of different sources of support is still unresolved. Future research should therefore examine sources of support within specific domains of stressors and strain.

Type of Support Provided

In addition to consideration of the impact of different sources of support, research has also explored the effects of different types of support. Commonly investigators have investigated types of support based on the functions they serve. Whereas instrumental (practical) support concerns among other things, providing knowledge, and defining and executing work tasks, emotional support is to listen, empathize with work and provide encouragement (Mathieu et al., 2019). Researchers have debated whether instrumental and emotional support are independent and distinct, or whether they are better conceived as one type of support given their high intercorrelation (Fenlason & Beehr, 1994). For instance, research by Semmer et al. (2008) showed that people in some contexts may interpret instrumental support as emotional in meaning.

Mathieu et al. (2019) conducted a large meta-analysis to investigate the interrelationship between instrumental and emotional support, as well as the relationship between the two types of support on stressors and strain. The results suggest that instrumental and emotional are strongly related, also when different sources and types of scales were examined. The relationship between instrumental and emotional support seems to be work-dependent, as these support types are more strongly related in occupations with high levels of emotional demands compared to occupations with lower emotional demands. The researchers also examined the interaction of instrumental and emotional support on the relationship between stressors and various outcome variables. Both instrumental and emotional support were negatively related to work stressors of role conflict, role ambiguity, role overload, and work-family conflict. Instrumental support was more strongly related to role conflict and role overload, while emotional support was more strongly related to work-family conflict. Both types of support were also negatively related to physiological and psychological strain, with emotional support having a somewhat stronger average effect. Further, the two types also predicted job attitudes and work behaviors.

Importantly, both buffering effects, as well as reversed effects (exacerbating) of instrumental and emotional support, were also examined in the meta-analysis by Mathieu et al. (2019). The researchers counted the number of studies that were in line with a buffering effect or a reversed effect. Whereas support is typically viewed as having a positive impact on individuals, the concept of reverse effects is that higher levels of support exacerbated, rather than alleviated, the amount of strain experienced by workers. Whereas an interaction effect of instrumental support was found in approximately 60% of the studies, reversed effects (43%) were reported more often than buffering effects (30%). For emotional support, interaction effects were reported in 72% of the studies, a buffering effect was found slightly more often (48%) than a reverse effect (40%). Results also indicated that sources and types of support interacted to predict strain, whereas the effect of emotional and instrumental support from supervisors on average was somewhat higher than that of coworkers. A limitation was that the meta-analysis was conducted on cross-sectional data. The authors therefore examined and found support for many of the same relationships in a follow-up cross-lagged study. However, tests of the interaction effect of types of support on the relationship between emotional demands and strain were mixed. Whereas all interaction effects were in line with a buffering effect of types of support, this effect was only significant for extra-role behavior, but not job satisfaction and organizational commitment (Mathieu et al., 2019).

Overall the meta-analysis by Mathieu et al. (2019) questions the distinctiveness of the two types of support, especially in work contexts with high levels of emotional demands. There were, however, some indications that instrumental and emotional support have some distinct relationships with stressors and strain, suggesting that treating them as distinct may add value. While support for interaction effects is found in many studies, the present research suggests that the types of support may in some instances mitigate and help when encountering stressors, while in other instances actually make the strain worse. A clear understanding of the conditions and processes that affect the direction of the interaction effects is important, as adding a burden to workers encountering stressors should be avoided.

Findings such as these suggest that the impact of social support is neither simple nor unilinear. Though most research has typically examined only the frequency or amount of support provided, the research illustrates that it is important to unravel the multidimensional character of support, to examine both the nature and source(s) of support simultaneously (Boyar et al., 2014). Clearly, a more systematic and extensive exploration of these factors using longitudinal studies is needed in order to generate a complete understanding of the role of this important, yet complex variable.

Unresolved Issues

From this brief overview of research on the role of social support in the stress process, data on the moderating effect of support are inconclusive. Though some studies have obtained evidence of stress buffering, these effects typically have been quite small and of questionable practical importance. More often, social support has displayed a significant direct relationship with lower levels of psychological strain, suggesting that having support is generally beneficial to well-being, irrespective of the stressors encountered.

Having said this, several issues require deeper examination in social support research. First, as noted by several researchers, there needs to be a closer matching between the types of support and the particular stressors encountered by individuals. Not all forms of support are likely to buffer the impact of all stressors. More likely, the effectiveness of support will vary across situations, as well as across individuals (see for instance Stetz et al., 2006). Although some studies have controlled for some individual differences (particularly demographic variables), there has been no systematic effort to determine critical dispositional factors that may themselves moderate the effects of support in stressor-strain relationships. Along with this is a need to examine the importance of support to different individuals, rather than assuming that social support is always relevant to everyone.

A second issue needing resolution is the level of specificity of support. Fenlason and Beehr (1994) found that specific types of support predicted affective outcomes better than more global measures of instrumental and emotional support. Although the latter may be useful in terms of describing and classifying support types, a more detailed investigation of the form and nature of social supports and their utilization is necessary to better understand how and when support functions as a buffer. Future research may also further examine other relationship variables that may affect the moderating role of social support (Nahum-Shani & Bamberger, 2011).

Finally, as examined in the literature, social support may take multiple roles. Future research should aim to include longitudinal data to examine what roles (antecedent, mediator, moderator) best explain social support since a large amount of research is cross-sectional and prevents empirically testing such relationships. Further, research suggests that support should engage in reciprocal relationships with outcome variables, and be part of downward spirals (Sconfienza et al., 2019). Testing of such relationships requires multiple data assessments, and future research may incorporate the different characteristics of support (e.g., source and type) to get a nuanced picture of how support and stress relate over time.

Conclusion

In this chapter, we have focused on two broad categories of potential moderators of the relationship between job stressors and strain indexes, and also touched upon the direct and indirect effects of the variables examined. First, we considered the stress-buffering effects exerted by several personality or dispositional factors. In recent years, there has been an upsurge of interest in personality variables as predictors of employee attitudes, affective reactions, and behaviors, and the field of job stress has mirrored research in other areas. There are multiple studies that suggest a direct effect of individual dispositions and personality traits on both stressors and strain. While some individuals (e.g., workers with high levels of negative affectivity) are more prone to report experiencing stressors and strain, others (e.g., workers with high levels of self-efficacy) are less susceptible to reporting these experiences. However, evidence for the moderating effects of specific dispositions is, at this point anyway, less than conclusive. Of the individual dispositions reviewed here, few if any provided consistent support for a moderation effect, suggesting that further research is needed on the specific circumstances under which they may function in this capacity. Importantly, while we have only briefly touched upon these relationships, individual dispositions and personality traits may also be part of mediation and moderated mediation models.

The second line of research that we have examined focuses on the situational variables of control over the work environment and social support, both of which have received considerable attention in job-related stress research. Important theoretical frameworks that propose both main and interaction (moderating) effects are JDC, JDC-S, and JD-R. Overall, the theories predict that high levels of perceived control (and support for JDC-S and JD-R) will ameliorate the aversive consequences of excessively demanding jobs. While most research findings are in line with direct/additive effects, the support for an interaction effect is mixed. Again, although there has been some support for this perspective, several studies have failed to obtain the predicted demands × control/support interaction. Thus, the interaction hypothesis has been described as 'theoretically viable but empirically elusive' (Brough & Biggs, 2015, p. 146).

In conclusion, we believe that the search for moderators of and mediators in the stressor-strain relationships is important and can yield significant information about the stress process overall. However, the ability to detect moderator effects in organizational research, especially studies conducted in field settings, is constrained by a number of factors. One potential explanation for the lack of significant moderator effects in several of the studies cited in this chapter is the lack of conceptual match between the variables. From existing evidence, it is clear that closer matching between the types of stressors and specific forms of resources is needed to enable appropriate assessment of the buffering effects of those resources. Further, the demonstration of moderation requires the inclusion of individuals (respondents) who exhibit more than just 'average' scores on the criterion variable(s)—that is, people who are experiencing reasonably high levels of strain.[1] Given that individuals with high strain are likely to withdraw from the environment (see Chapter 5 for a discussion of the linkage between strain and withdrawal) or maybe too 'stressed' to contemplate involvement in a research project on job-related strain, it may be difficult to capture these individuals for this type of research. Finally, it is crucial that moderator variables be investigated within a dynamic framework of the stress process, rather than as peripheral issues that may or may not impinge upon stress-coping mechanisms. This means that the focus on moderators must be considered within the context of the dynamic transaction between the individual and the environment over time. This will require theoretical models that integrate moderators more explicitly into the coping process, which we turn into Chapter 7.

---

[1]We wish to thank Ben Schneider for this suggestion.

7

COPING WITH JOB STRESS

Research in the field of stress illustrates the growing belief that coping is a fundamental element in the relationship between stressors and strain (Dewe, 2017; Dewe & Cooper, 2021). Still little is known about how individuals cope with various stressors, the strategies important to coping, and the role of coping in the work stress process. The present chapter draws attention to conceptual (definitional) and methodological (measurement) issues surrounding the study of coping in workplace contexts, points to some of the limitations and concerns about existing coping research and offers some suggestions for future research in this area. Our aim is not to present final solutions to all the problems and dilemmas associated with research on stress coping but more modestly to contribute to the debate on how these difficulties may be approached and resolved.

Although there exist several theoretical approaches to the definition and classification of coping, this chapter, in line with the general stress literature, will draw on the transactional theory of stress perspective and its classification of coping (Bliese et al., 2017; Dewe & Cooper, 2017; Folkman, 2011; Folkman & Moskowitz, 2004; Zhang et al., 2019). In addition, we will discuss a selection of other conceptualizations (i.e., conservation of resources theory and cognitive activation theory of stress) and approaches to coping, including higher order categories of coping (i.e., promotion and prevention-oriented coping), to facilitate a platform of inspiration for future research and practice in the field of coping. Although we have chosen to build our discussion on a certain selection of theoretical frameworks, it does not mean that the definition of coping from other theoretical lenses is irrelevant. On the contrary, other theoretical coping frameworks may be valuable for the reader to consider and we refer the interested reader to the original sources of those particular theories (see for example references to the theories described in Chapter 1). The theoretical frameworks of focus in this chapter are mainly selected based on what has been the major frameworks applied in the organizational stress-coping literature. We have also chosen to focus on the theoretical frameworks that are clearly underlying frameworks of the organizational stress process depicted in Chapter 1. Our hope is that this chapter about stress coping may be helpful to facilitate further understanding of the organizational stress process (see Figure 1.1 in Chapter 1).

COPING THEORIES, DEFINITIONS, AND THE RESEARCH CONTEXT

Like the concept of stress itself, various definitions of coping have been proposed, including coping as a psychoanalytic process; as a personal trait, style, or disposition; as a description of situationally specific strategies; and as a process. Traditional approaches to conceptualizing coping defined it in terms of a relatively stable trait or some enduring behavior or characteristic of the person. The notion that coping is a stable dispositional characteristic is however vigorously debated (Carver & Connor-Smith, 2010). Some empirical evidence suggests that personality only has a modest influence on an individuals preferred coping style, thus coping styles are suggested to only be modestly heritable (Jang et al., 2007). The debate needs to be kept separate from the role of individual differences and their moderating effect on coping. Meta-analytic evidence also shows some gender differences in coping. When compared to men, women have been found to engage in more coping strategies, particularly ruminating about problems, using positive self-talk, and seeking emotional support (Tamres et al., 2002). Also, the empirical evidence suggests that women appraise certain stressors as being more severe than men (Tamres et al., 2002). Although a portion of our stress response is a result of biological heritage (Folkman, 2011), Lazarus (1991) has suggested that the static model implied by a dispositional definition of coping does not fit well with the dynamic, process-oriented nature of coping and tends to overlook the situational context in which coping behaviors occur.

Transaction theory views coping as thoughts and actions that are initiated in response to a specific encounter and that change over time as efforts are reappraised and outcomes are evaluated. This implies a dynamic interaction between the person and the environment, whereby the individual imposes a particular appraisal on the environment, while the environment is also influential in shaping that appraisal (Folkman & Moskowitz, 2004). It also highlights the fact that efforts initiated in relation to a particular encounter will affect subsequent appraisals of the demand and hence further coping efforts. Clearly, if our interest in coping is to capture what individuals actually think and do in any encounter, then definitions and assessments of coping need to express a breadth and range of strategies that reflect the diversity and complexity of coping behaviors (Skinner et al., 2003). Definitions that reflect a static approach (e.g., person-environment fit) are simply not designed to do this or to deal with the empirical issues raised by the process-oriented perspective (Dewe & Cooper, 2017). Using a *transactional perspective*, one can define coping as 'cognitive and behavioural efforts to master, reduce or tolerate the internal or external demands that are created by the stressful transaction' (Folkman, 1984, p. 843). Coping efforts can be conceptually distinguished from the results (success or failure) of these efforts. The three key features of this definition are (a) the emphasis it places on the process in contrast to the more interactional (cause-effect) nature of traditional approaches (Cox, 1987; Edwards, 1988); (b) the positioning of coping in the relationship between the person and the environment (Folkman & Moskowitz, 2004); and (c) the link it provides with other components of the stress process. Central to this definition of coping is the integrating role of cognitive appraisal. Defined in this way, coping is offered as a conceptually distinct variable, capable of assessment independently of stressors and resultant strains (Folkman, 2011; Folkman & Moskowitz, 2004). As a result of ongoing transactions with the environment, individuals are confronted with demands that impinge on their cognitive processes and activate a requirement to cope or adapt. The unit of analysis that captures the transactional nature of stress is appraisal, of which there are two kinds (Folkman & Moskowitz, 2004; Lazarus, 1991). The first is *primary appraisal* – where individuals give meaning and significance to the situation and evaluate what is at stake for them and whether the situation (or events within it) pose a potential or actual threat to their well-being. *Secondary appraisal*, on the other hand, refers to the perceived availability of coping resources for dealing with a stressful encounter. At this stage, coping options are evaluated in terms of available social, personal, economic, and organizational resources and the level of control that individuals perceive they have over the situation. Intense negative emotions characterize these appraisals (Folkman & Moskowitz, 2004).

Coping behaviors are initiated in an emotional environment as a consequence of primary and secondary appraisal (illustrated in Chapter 1). These processes are interdependent, influencing each other and shaping the nature of any encounter (Folkman, 1984). With a successful resolution, positive emotions are expected to dominate while with an unfavorable or unclear resolution, negative emotions are expected to dominate (Folkman & Moskowitz, 2004). In the case of organizational stress, emotions are tied to variables – such as an employee's beliefs systems, personal values, goals, personal resources, environmental events, and goal hierarchies – which will form the appraisals on which each emotion rests (cf. Lazarus, 1999). The presence of positive emotions (e.g., hope, joy, love, forgiveness, gratitude, compassion) in the stress process has been emphasized as 'an exciting new development in the field of coping' (Folkman & Moskowitz, 2004, p. 764). This emphasis derived from what has been referred to as the positive psychology movement – a study of the processes and conditions which facilitate optimal functioning, flourishing and growth of individuals, groups and institutions – and the awareness that positive emotions can occur even in terribly stressful situations (Dewe & Cooper, 2017; Folkman & Moskowitz, 2004; Fredrickson, 2001; Gable & Haidt, 2005; Seligman & Csikszentmihalyi, 2000). Given that psychology is encompassing both the positive and the negative (McNulty & Fincham, 2011), in stressful encounters, positive emotions have been found to co-occur with negative emotions (Dewe & Cooper, 2012; Folkman & Moskowitz, 2004). This means that even in very stressful situations individuals tend to look for positive meaning (or even infuse it) which can lead to positive emotions and an opportunity to rebuild resources that can help sustain coping and facilitate growth (Dewe & Cooper, 2021; Folkman & Moskowitz, 2004; Tugade & Fredrickson, 2007). Future research needs to clarify further the coping processes employees use to develop positive emotions in stressful work-related encounters, as well as to clarify how the co-occurrence of positive and negative emotions may contribute to determine effective coping and thriving versus strain outcomes at work.

A further development of appraisal centered research, which is in line with the theorizing of the transactional theory of stress, has pointed to the relevance of distinguishing between the appraisal of job demands as either challenges or hindrances (O'Brien & Beehr, 2019). *Challenge appraisals* are evident when a stressful situation has the potential for growth, mastery and rewards, while *hindrance appraisals* are evident when stressful encounters are perceived to potentially threaten and thwart development, goal attainment, and personal well-being (Webster et al., 2011). This distinction is relevant because such different appraisals translate into diverging outcomes (Lepine et al., 2005; Podsakoff et al., 2007). Still, the distinction may not always be clear, as employees may appraise the very same job demand as being both challenging and hindering to some extent (Webster et al., 2011). When job demands (stressors) are appraised as both challenges and hindrances they are likely to have maladaptive influence on employees (Webster et al., 2011). In a more recent study, Li, Taris, and Peeters (2020) found that although the presence of high job demands was associated with negative outcomes (e.g., burnout), these maladaptive influences were weaker when employees engaged in challenge appraisal. Although the relevance of challenge and hindrance appraisals have been acknowledged and supported in the literature, more knowledge is needed on how employees cope with challenge and hindrance stressors, particularly over time (Zhang et al., 2019).

Identifying coping behaviors as the processes that link the individual to the environment shifts the focus of research toward developing an understanding of what people actually think, feel, and do in a stressful encounter (Folkman & Moskowitz, 2004). Understanding coping therefore may require researchers to focus on the individual level. As we shall see in Chapter 8, this by no means undermines the importance of investigating organization-level stress management interventions, which may be necessary to deal with certain kinds of stressors, especially those over which individuals can exert little or no control. Nevertheless, even in these interventions, individual appraisals and activities must be taken into account. Still, recent advances in demands-resources theories on organizational stress acknowledge the relevance of taking a multilevel perspective (e.g., individuals nested within their work group and organizational culture) to understand and explore the important coping functions of resources (Dewe, 2017; Holmgreen et al., 2017). This may add an important insight for future research to consider when further exploring the nature and relevance of resources from the lens of coping (Dewe, 2017).

Conservation of resources theory (COR), which we described in Chapter 1, considers that threat and loss can have objective elements and that appraisals are not only individualistic, they can be common, i.e., individuals sharing a culture/biology can jointly experience them (Hobfoll, 2010). This points to the importance of the objective reality and the circumstances in which stressors occur (Hobfoll, 2010; Hobfoll et al., 2018).

A strength of the COR perspective is that it suggests that stressful encounters may be experienced in social groups and that coping can emerge as a combined individual and group effort (Hobfoll et al., 1994). To get around what is referred to as 'rugged individualism' in the field of coping, social/communal aspects of coping should therefore also be considered (Dunahoo et al., 1998; Hobfoll et al., 2003). *Social/communal coping* refers to responses that are influenced by and are in reaction to the context (Folkman & Moskowitz, 2004; Wells et al., 1997). To be invested effectively, individual resources must fit the context (Hobfoll, 2001). When one or more employees perceive a stressor as a common ('our') problem, communal coping based on a social appraisal and a joint collaboration to handle it occurs (Lyons et al., 1998; Zajdel & Helgeson, 2021). The responsibility for dealing with the stressful encounter is shared by two or more individuals in a social unit. The multiaxial coping model that distinguishes coping into pro-social/antisocial and active/passive dimensions has been commonly applied to study communal coping (Folkman & Moskowitz, 2004; Wells et al., 1997). Active, prosocial coping represents communal coping and has been linked to better emotional outcomes (Wells et al., 1997). More recent research indicates that communal coping is associated with better individual coping, reduced psychological distress, better physical health, more collaboration and support, enhanced relationship well-being, and more positive mood after a stressor is shared in dyads (e.g., Van Vleet et al., 2018; Wells et al., 1997; Zajdel & Helgeson, 2020, 2021). Recent research addresses the importance of distinguishing between the two components of communal coping: (1) the shared appraisal of the stressor, and (2) the common collaboration to manage it (Zajdel & Helgeson, 2021). There is a need for more (intervention) studies on communal coping – incorporating both of these dimensions – in the work setting (Dewe & Cooper, 2017; Folkman & Moskowitz, 2004; Zajdel & Helgeson, 2021).

COR proposes four principles: (1) 'resource loss is disproportionately more salient than resource gain'; (2) 'people must invest resources in order to protect against resource loss, recover from losses, and gain resources'; (3) 'resource gain increases in salience in the context of resource loss'; and (4) 'when their resources are outstretched or exhausted, individuals enter a defensive mode to preserve the self that is often aggressive and may become irrational' (Hobfoll et al., 2018, p. 106). When individuals invest resources they are better able of coping more effectively with stressors, and thus the second principle of COR addresses the importance of proactive coping (Hobfoll, 2001). According to COR, both individuals and groups are coping proactively when (a) they strive to gain and preserve their reservoirs of resources, (b) when they engage in action as they experience initial cautionary signs of a stressful encounter, and (c) when they position themselves according to the fit between their resources and the stressful encounter or in another way position their social group, family, or themselves in an advantageous position (Hobfoll, 2001). Employees who have sufficient resources are better able to anticipate potential stressors and act to position themselves and plan for how to handle such future stressful encounters (Aspinwall, 2011; Aspinwall & Taylor, 1997). Those who lack resources have to shield them and therefore are not taking the risk to invest them, or they may simply not have the proper resources (Hobfoll, 2001). The approach to proactive coping in COR is in line with the theorizing of Aspinwall and Taylor (1997) as well as Greenglass (2002) who view proactive coping as a future oriented anticipation or detection of potential stressors which makes it possible to act in advance to either mute stressor impact or prevent it. Contrary to the traditional reactive coping framework (i.e., risk appraisal), in which stressful events are dealt with when they have occurred, proactive coping is more active and positive in its approach by seeing the stimulating and challenging aspects of stressful situations and actively dealing with these beforehand (Greenglass, 2002; Hobfoll, 2001). This means that those who cope proactively do not engage in threat appraisal, rather they engage in challenge appraisal where they focus on demands, risks, and opportunities in the future (Stiglbauer & Batinic, 2015). Coping in these terms becomes goal management and not management of risks (Greenglass, 2002). By being proactive, employees initiate action in advance of potential future stressful encounters and pursue opportunities for growth. When proactively coping, employees need to engage in various behaviors to eliminate, modify, or reduce negative stress. Such behaviors include organizing, planning, setting goals and rehearse cognitively (mental stimulation; Aspinwall & Taylor, 1997). Further, the constant effort of employees to build up their resources that can help them to achieve self-imposed challenging goals and promote their personal growth is critical (Aspinwall, 2011; Koen & Parker, 2020). This means that proactive coping can help to control potential stressors by building resources that can reduce their impact; however it may all depend on the employee's pool of resources (Aspinwall, 2011; Stiglbauer & Batinic, 2015).

Empirical evidence shows that proactive coping is beneficial for individual well-being as it relates to reduced levels of depression, higher levels of engagement, increased positive affect, and overall well-being (Gan et al., 2007; Greenglass & Fiksenbaum, 2009; Greenglass et al., 2006; Stiglbauer & Batinic, 2015). More recently, in a three-wave design study, Koen and Parker (2020) investigated how employees proactively cope with job related insecurities. The findings showed that employees who coped proactively with a stressful situation (i.e., their temporary work contract was close to expiring) did not experience the same amount of uncontrollability and job insecurity as the employees who were coping less proactively. The future of work, which we discuss in Chapter 10, brings along several potential stressful encounters in which research needs to further clarify the role of proactive and communal coping from a resource perspective.

In *cognitive activation theory of stress (CATS)* appraisal is an important component of the stress process because employees develop *expectations* through their appraisal (Meurs & Perrewé, 2011). Appraisals determine whether a certain stimulus is perceived as a work stressor and whether employees believe that it is possible to cope with it (Eriksen, 2017).

While most theories on stress coping are focused on the coping strategies individuals select when they are confronted with stressful encounters (Lazarus & Folkman, 1984; Zhang et al., 2019), CATS is concerned with *the result* of coping strategies, regardless of actions such as problem-focused actions (Eriksen, 2017; Meurs & Perrewé, 2011). According to CATS, coping can only be predictive of employee's arousal, stress, and health with a focus on the result (Eriksen, 2017; Ursin, 1998). In line with Higgins (1997) emphasis on the importance of expectancy for self-regulation, which we will touch upon later in this chapter, CATS draws on expectancy theory of motivation, which suggests that a motivating force for employees is the expectation that certain efforts will lead to valued outcomes (Meurs & Perrewé, 2011). Accordingly, CATS defines coping as positive response outcome expectancies – 'the acquired expectancy that most or all responses lead to a positive result' (Eriksen, 2017, p. 49; Ursin & Eriksen, 2004, 2010). When the brain (see Chapter 2) has stored information about coping success in previous stressful encounters, it produces a positive response outcome expectancy (i.e., coping) (Eriksen & Ursin, 2004). The outcome of this is a reduced level of arousal (Ursin & Eriksen, 2004). When individuals do not experience a relationship between their previous action and subsequent results, the brain stores this information as an expectancy of *helplessness* (Eriksen & Ursin, 2004; Meurs & Perrewé, 2011; Reme et al., 2008). An even more critical form of expectancy, *hopelessness*, develops when employees experience that all their actions lead to devastating results – a negative response outcome expectancy (Eriksen, 2017; Meurs & Perrewé, 2011). Hopelessness (e.g., depression) is considered to be the direct opposite of coping (Ursin & Eriksen, 2004).

Instead of being concerned with the coping strategies in themselves, CATS fronts the importance of the belief in chosen coping strategies (Eriksen, 2017). To exemplify, Ursin, Baade, and Levin (1978) conducted a study on parachutists in the military. The findings suggested that the trainees' beliefs in their ability to perform developed early in the learning phase (Ursin & Eriksen, 2004). Further, trainees' endocrine and vegetative responses to the jump as well as their reported fear was reduced after the first session in a training tower situation. This was long before the trainee's performance had reached a satisfactory level. Interestingly it was the trainees' feelings of being able to perform that mattered, not their performance or the performance feedback they received. In terms of coping, this means that when potentially stressful encounters have been dealt with in a successful manner in the past, such learning will strengthen individuals trust in their own abilities to be successful again. Thus, the concept of *self-efficacy* comes close to being identical to the CATS coping concept', particularly when the expectancy relates to an encounter of high affective value and when it is generalized (Reme et al., 2008, p. 179).

According to CATS measuring coping strategies, coping behaviors or ways of coping, which we will discuss more in the following sections, is troublesome because such strategies and behaviors typically occur under various degrees of arousal and future expectancies (Meurs & Perrewé, 2011; Ursin & Eriksen, 2004). This is important to consider in future research on coping in work settings.

TAXONOMIES OF COPING

Central approaches to the study of coping in work settings have been described as *taxonomic* (Cox, 1987) or *families of coping* (Skinner et al., 2003), where researchers describe and categorize coping behaviors that are broadly applicable to all or most work situations. The most common approach is based on the work of Lazarus and his colleagues (Dewe et al., 2010; Zhang et al., 2019). In the next sections we will present Lazarus and Folkman's (1984) coping categories as well as a selection of other 'additions' to these categories. This further leads to the discussion of higher order coping action types.

The transactional theory of stress has identified two broad categories of coping strategies: *problem focused*, in which attempts are made to deal with the demands of the encounter (e.g., making an action plan), and *emotion focused*, in which attempts are made to deal with the emotional disturbance resulting from those demands (e.g., distracting activities, using alcohol or drugs). These coping strategies are 'used by everyone in virtually every stressful encounter' (Lazarus & Folkman, 1984, p. 157). Empirical evidence suggests that problem focused coping is associated with lower levels of strain, while the opposite is evident for emotion focused coping (e.g., Adriaenssens et al., 2015; Jex et al., 2001).

Although several scholars have found these major strategies to be a good starting point, other strategies have been identified (Dewe & Cooper, 2021; Folkman & Moskowitz, 2004) and reflect additions to overcome the 'major gaps in the original formulation' of coping strategies. The first addition was *meaning-focused coping* – the application of cognitive strategies to search for meaning when a situation is appraised as stressful (Park, 2011). Despite being in the middle of a stressful work encounter, employees may instill this experience with positive meaning helping them to respite, sustain, and restore their resources (Dewe et al., 2010; Folkman & Moskowitz, 2004). In this sense, coping can be thought of as having the potential to also create positive psychological states, which helps employees to deal with stressful experiences at work. In terms of the transactional perspective, this may be linked to the cognitive strategies that employees may apply to reinterpret a stressful encounter at work in a positive way, i.e., positive reappraisal.

The second addition was *social/relation-focused coping*, which refers to the seeking of instrumental and social support (Dewe & Cooper, 2017; Folkman & Moskowitz, 2004). Various approaches exist under this label, and in this chapter we have focused on communal coping and a resource (e.g., social support) approach to coping (see Folkman & Moskowitz, 2004 for a further discussion). In addition to the 'ways of coping' already mentioned, other approaches have been discussed in the stress coping literature. For example, *emotion regulation*, which refers to employees attempt to influence the emotions they have as well as how they are experienced and expressed (Gross, 1998); *religious/ spiritual coping*, which addresses the role of religion and how it is embedded in the entire stress process, influencing appraisal of stressful encounters as well as how individuals respond to such encounters over time (Pargament, 2011; Pargament et al., 2000); *leisure coping (beliefs and strategies)*, which addresses how leisure can help employees cope with stress (Iwasaki et al., 2005; Iwasaki & Mannell, 2000); and more recently *cyberloafing coping*, which refers to employees' voluntary acts to surf non-work-related web sites for nonwork purposes during office hours as an energizing experience, helping employees to feel more healthy (Dewe & Cooper, 2021; Lim & Chen, 2012). We refer the interested reader to other reviews and chapters that cover these important topics more in depth

(Dewe & Cooper, 2017, 2021; Dewe et al., 2010; Folkman, 2011; Folkman & Moskowitz, 2004). Although all of these ways of coping have contributed to the coping framework, no clear consensus has been reached as to how best to classify coping strategies. As Skinner et al. (2003) pointed out, a good taxonomy has yet to be achieved in the continuous search for a structure of coping. Although several alternative proposals have been suggested (Dewe et al., 2010; Skinner et al., 2003), these do not appear to totally satisfy the precision required, to encapsulate the different functions that coping strategies may perform, or to adequately capture the range of potential coping responses. Any schema for classifying coping strategies must take into account not just the focus (e.g., problem vs. emotion) of a particular strategy but also its form (cognitive/behavioral) and the variety of different strategies used (Dewe et al., 2010). Skinner et al. (2003) conducted a comprehensive review of the general coping literature in which they concluded that coping categories such as *emotion- and problem-focused coping* are **not** useful as higher order coping categories because any coping strategy may serve both or potentially many other functions (Dewe et al., 2010; Folkman & Lazarus, 1980; Skinner et al., 2003). Thus, treating the emotion-versus problem-focused coping functions as distinct types of coping may be too simplistic. They should rather be considered as *action types* that can have several functions (Lazarus, 1996; Skinner et al., 2003).

Furthermore, it is also important to not assume that one action type necessarily is better than the other, thus the richness of such coping action types makes the categorization of them a challenging task (Dewe et al., 2010). Several scholars have suggested that we abandon two other commonly applied approaches to coping, i.e., *approach* (efforts to handling a demand) *versus avoidance* (efforts to escaping the stressful situation) (see Carver & Connor-Smith, 2010) and *cognitive* (e.g., adopt a positive perspective on the situation) *versus behavioral* (e.g., taking positive steps to address the problem (Dewe et al., 2010; Skinner et al., 2003). Coping is considered to be much more complex and may be represented by a coping system consisting of 13 higher order categories of coping behaviors (Skinner et al., 2003):

- problem-solving (e.g., instrumental action, planning)
- support seeking (e.g., seeking help or comfort)
- escape (e.g., disengaging, stay away from stressful encounter, denial)
- distraction (e.g., engage in alternative pleasurable activity)
- cognitive restructuring (e.g., active effort to change view of stressful encounter)
- rumination (having intrusive, repetitive and negative cognitions, self-blame, worry)
- helplessness (e.g., inaction, pessimism, giving up)
- social withdrawal (e.g., staying away from others, avoidant attachment)
- emotional regulation (e.g., emotional control, relaxation, emotional expression)
- information-seeking (e.g., attempt to learn more about stressful condition, observation)
- negotiation (e.g., prioritizing, reducing demands)
- opposition (e.g., projection, anger, aggression)
- delegation (e.g., dependency, maladaptive help seeking, self-pity)

Still, uniformity in definitions and categorization of coping strategies does not exist making it impossible to draw firm conclusions (Dewe & Cooper, 2021; Dewe et al., 2010). Furthermore, although research on coping is very much alive in general psychology, so far there only exists one systematic investigation of coping strategies in the organizational stress literature (Zhang et al., 2019).

Extending Previous Coping Research: Promotion and Prevention Focused Coping

By drawing on the work of Skinner et al. (2003), Zhang et al. (2019) conducted the first meta-analysis on coping in the domain of work, where they decided to extend previous coping research by conceptualizing coping within a self-regulation framework. Zhang et al. (2019) draw on the challenge-hindrance framework of stress (Cavanaugh et al., 2000) to argue that the problem versus emotion focused coping categorization does not sufficiently account for the differential influence of challenge and hindrance stressors and appraisals. To rectify this, the authors empirically integrate regulatory focus theory (Higgins, 1997) and transactional theory to propose a new taxonomy of coping action types represented by the self-regulatory motivational systems of prevention and promotion focused coping. These systems address how individuals self-regulate when they experience various stressful situations at work, such as threats of potential losses (e.g., hindrance stressors) or chances for potential growth (e.g., challenge stressors) (Zhang et al., 2019). When employees engage in *prevention focused coping,* they are driven by safety and security needs (e.g., safety of receiving a high performance evaluation or the danger of receiving a poor performance evaluation) to strategically strive for alignment (avoid mismatch) with their ought self, i.e., the attributes that they believe they should possess, which is based on a sense of duty, responsibility and obligation (Gorman et al., 2012; Higgins, 1997; Zhang et al., 2019). Thus, an employee engages in prevention focused coping through behavioral and cognitive efforts which are instigated to avoid mistakes, potential losses (e.g., failed attempts), or letting others down (Brockner et al., 2004; Zhang et al., 2019). When employees engage in *promotion focused coping,* they are driven by growth needs (e.g., pursuing advancement), which motivate them to strategically strive for an alignment with their ideal selves – attributes that they ideally would like to posess – (aspirations, wishes, and hopes; e.g., accomplishing more at work) (Higgins, 1997; Zhang et al., 2019). This helps them increase the opportunity for attaining positive gains (match between current situation and dreams/aspirations). These coping action types are proposed to serve both the function of emotion regulation and problem solving, meaning that both prevention and promotion focused coping can encompass emotion-focused and problem-focused coping strategies (Lazarus & Folkman, 1984; Zhang et al., 2019). For example, when employees deny or suppress the experience of negative emotions when under stress, they apply prevention- and emotion-focused coping (Zhang et al., 2019). When employees engage in reappraisal and construe a stressful work encounter in a positive way to change the emotional impact, promotion and emotion-focused coping strategies are applied to attain positive gains (Zhang et al.,

2019). Promotion- and problem-focused coping strategies are applied when employees use tactics such as making action plans, seeking support, or working harder to achieve goals and enhance their performance (Zhang et al., 2019). Prevention- and problem-focused coping strategies are applied when employees engage in actions such as helping them to fulfil required job duties and avoid errors of commission in their work (Zhang et al., 2019).

The meta-analytical evidence (Zhang et al., 2019), which was based on 156 samples and over 75,000 employees, supported that challenge and hindrance stressors differentially predicted prevention and promotion focused coping. Challenge stressors positively predicted promotion focused coping while hindrance stressors positively predicted prevention focused coping. In turn, prevention and promotion focused coping action types (with the underlying emotion- and problem-focused coping strategies) mediated the relationship between work related stressors and outcomes. Promotion focused coping was *positively* associated with task performance and organizational citizenship behavior (OCB), job attitudes, and employee well-being. Prevention-focused coping was, on the other hand, negatively associated with task performance, OCB, job attitudes, and employee well-being. Although these finding are promising with respect to applying the promotion-prevention coping distinction as higher order action types of the underlying problem-emotion focused coping framework, we believe that it is only a starting point. This interesting approach has the potential for further development that would also encompass the role of other ways of coping, such as meaning-focused coping, social/relational coping, etc. (Folkman & Moskowitz, 2004). Further, anticipatory coping (e.g., proactive coping; Aspinwall, 2011) would be an intriguing next step to explore, as Higgins (1997) original theory emphasizes the importance of regulatory anticipation, a specific form of expectancy. In support of exploring this topic, the transactional theory, COR, CATS, and regulatory focus theory of coping all address the relevance of anticipation to facilitate a better understanding of the stress process. (Aspinwall, 2011; Folkman & Lazarus, 1985; Hobfoll, 1989; Meurs & Perrewé, 2011; Zhang et al., 2019). In research on daily workload anticipation and its influence on well-being, Casper et al. (Casper & Sonnentag, 2020; Casper et al., 2017) found that employees engage in both productive and counterproductive coping when anticipating high job demands in the form of workload. The anticipatory coping strategies were in turn associated with exhaustion and vigor. Still, the research did not clarify how anticipated stressors shape reactions to current stressors and to what extent beliefs about stressors may change over time. DiStasio and Shoss (2020) used COR theory as a foundation to show that when employees anticipated an increase in job demands (i.e., workload), the relationship between the perceived stressor and strain increased. However, when employees anticipated a decrease in job demands, the relationship between the perceived stressor and strain was buffered (see also discussion in Chapter 10). Although the study does not directly discuss coping strategies, these findings depict coping as defined by COR. It would be interesting for future research to clarify the anticipatory coping action types that are operating under such circumstances, and the promotion versus pre-vention focused coping framework may serve as a novel contribution.

Despite the promising contribution of the Zhang et al. (2019) meta-analysis, more comprehensive approaches to understanding coping in the work setting are needed, particularly to facilitate the development of valid promotion and prevention focused coping measures.

THE ROLE OF COPING

The functions of coping in the stress process have also been of considerable interest to job stress researchers, who have endeavored not simply to describe variations in coping responses but also to delineate the conditions under which different coping strategies are used and to assess the effectiveness of such strategies. One of the dilemmas in this type of research is that the relationship between coping and other stress-related constructs is reciprocal. Coping operates as both a cause (an independent variable) and an effect (a dependent variable) of other stress-related constructs (Litt et al., 2011). Similarly, coping responses may function as both mediators and moderators of stressor–strain relationships (Litt et al., 2011). Consequently, researchers have examined, for example, (a) the influ-ence of personality, gender, and race on the use of different coping strategies; (b) stra-tegies used when coping with specific stressful work experiences; (c) the relationship between coping and adaptational outcomes; (d) the effectiveness of coping strategies; and (e) the mediational properties of coping strategies. The basic proposition that environ-mental and personality variables influence the choice of coping strategies has been generally supported in empirical research, but the relationships between coping strategies and outcomes are inconsistent, and moderating effects of coping have not always been demonstrated (Dewe & Cooper, 2017; Litt et al., 2011).

To understand these results, it is important to consider the theoretical role of coping in the stress process. A number of themes emerge. The first is whether coping functions as a mediator or moderator. The transactional model of stress views coping as a mediating variable (Lazarus & Folkman, 1984). Treating coping as mediating the link between stressors and strain entails a different research design from considering it as moderating the stressor-strain relationship.

There is sometimes both theoretical and methodological confusion between coping 'behaviors' and coping 'styles'. Whereas dispositional styles are more likely to moderate linkages between environmental conditions (stressors) and individual reactions (strains), specific behaviors may function as mediators between these variables. For instance, increased job demands may lead to an individual's working harder to achieve required goals, which in turn reduce the strain associated with the initial demands.

Inferential support for this distinction comes from studies that have demonstrated a clear relationship between personality and coping (Carver & Connor-Smith, 2010). Although there are powerful arguments for measuring coping behaviors rather than style or personality variables (Dewe et al., 2010), equally strong arguments can be mounted for considering the relationship between personality and coping (Carver & Connor-Smith,

2010; Dewe & Cooper, 2017). For example, secondary appraisals of what coping resources are available to the person include assessment of dispositional factors such as the person's resilience or hardiness and self-efficacy as possible buffers of the impact of stressors on an individual's well-being (see Chapter 6). Clearly, individual differences may play an important role in both the selection of coping strategies and their effectiveness.

COPING EFFECTIVENESS

Another approach to conceptualizing the functions of coping behaviors is to consider whether they are effective or ineffective in removing stressors or alleviating strain (Dewe & Cooper, 2021; Folkman & Moskowitz, 2004): i.e., to evaluate them on the basis of their outcomes. Effective coping strategies result in outcomes that are favorable for the individual, whereas ineffective strategies may not produce favorable outcomes or, worse, may lead to unfavorable outcomes. In particular, differences between situations and individuals make it impossible to judge a priori whether a coping effort has been successful or unsuccessful. Furthermore, definitions and measures of 'effectiveness' must be based upon the perceptions and goals of the individuals enacting the behaviors rather than developed around so-called objective indexes. For example, both problem-focused and emotion-focused coping may contain both effective and ineffective strategies (Zhang et al., 2019). Studies of coping effectiveness must assess the cognitive processes that individuals engage in when evaluating their coping efforts. How individuals themselves define effectiveness is an issue that has yet to be explored and raises the interesting questions of effectiveness for whom and at what cost, in addition to consideration of the best methodology to tease out such distinctions.

An alternative approach to judging coping effectiveness is to examine the notion of goodness of fit (Dewe & Cooper, 2017; Dewe et al., 2010; Folkman & Moskowitz, 2004). Using this approach, the focus shifts to considering the fit between situational appraisals and coping. The greater the misfit between how a situation is appraised and a coping response, the greater the probability that coping will not be effective. This approach requires measures of both appraisal and coping (Folkman & Moskowitz, 2004), and perhaps for this reason it has received less attention in settings involving work stress.

Researchers focusing on coping effectiveness should carefully consider (a) the context within which coping is being judged, particularly the level of control individuals have over the situation; (b) the outcome that is being used as the criterion variable, given that different outcomes are associated with different coping strategies; (c) the role of individual differences in the selection of a coping strategy; (d) the nature of the situation and the demands it places on the individual, together with how such demands are appraised; (e) the impact of confounding between coping and outcomes; (f) the merits of longitudinal versus cross-sectional research design, including issues like the episodic or chronic nature of demands and short-term versus long-term effects; and, finally, (g) whether contradictory findings concerning coping effectiveness are due to the difficulties inherent in self-report measures of coping rather than to the nature of the coping strategy being judged (Carver & Connor-Smith, 2010; Dewe & Cooper, 2017; Dewe et al., 2010;

Folkman & Moskowitz, 2004). It is difficult to understand the meaning of fit without knowledge about the particular context and the role played by individual differences (Folkman & Moskowitz, 2004). This underlines the complexity of understanding what it means to cope effectively (Dewe & Cooper, 2017; Dewe et al., 2010), which future research needs to clarify (Dewe & Cooper, 2021).

METHODOLOGICAL APPROACHES AND MEASUREMENT

Coping can operate both as a dependent or an independent variable, thus researchers must be mindful about their methodological choices regarding research design. Coping research should therefore address both the effects of appraisal and strain on coping and the effects of coping on appraisal and strain (Harris, 1991; Litt et al., 2011).

The research methods employed to generate measures of coping are of some concern. There has been debate over the merits of using deductive or inductive methods for constructing coping instruments. Coping measures have been constructed both deductively – that is, from existing literature and research on coping – and inductively, by examining, describing, and developing coping items based on strategies that individuals report using (Dewe et al., 2010; Folkman & Moskowitz, 2004; Skinner et al., 2003). The major advantage of the inductive method is that it makes no assumptions about how individuals might respond and does not prescribe the range or type of response that individuals may engage in during a stressful encounter (O'Driscoll & Cooper, 1994). Coping measures constructed inductively are based on what individuals actually think and do and therefore expose meaning rather than impose it (Dewe et al., 2010; Skinner et al., 2003). However, it is this very feature – the classification of such information into meaningful and reliable self-report categories – that may also be its greatest weakness. Such classification may prove to be impossible without losing the very richness of the data, the dynamic nature of the coping process (Litt et al., 2011), and perhaps the very advantage of using the inductive approach in the first place.

Difficulties when constructing coping measures are not limited just to identifying and classifying coping strategies. A number of reviews (e.g., Dewe et al., 2010; Folkman & Moskowitz, 2004; Skinner et al., 2003) have drawn attention to a range of other issues that confront researchers wishing to measure coping. These include (a) whether measures should focus on how individuals cope with stress in general or on assessing coping with specific encounters; (b) whether the response category should ask individuals to rate how frequently they used a particular strategy or whether to obtain ratings of coping effec- tiveness; and (c) whether self-report rating scales are the most appropriate vehicle for measuring how people actually cope. Researchers may also consider whether a combi- nation of qualitative and quantitative measures should be used, or whether coping is best tested indirectly, asking no direct questions about coping at all but capturing how people cope by having them describe the nature of stressful encounters and their responses within those situations (Dewe & Cooper, 2021; Dewe et al., 2010; Folkman & Moskowitz, 2004).

The above issues raise two significant questions. First, are coping strategies best determined deductively (from existing research and the literature on coping) or inductively (from individuals' own accounts of what they have done to manage stressors in their work environment)? If researchers rely on the former, how can they ensure that the coping responses identified through the literature actually reflect the experiences and responses of the population under investigation? On the other hand, if inductive procedures are favored, how should questions be framed to elicit valid accounts of individuals' actual responses to various environmental demands, bearing in mind the constraints of social desirability and selective recall of behaviors? As stated by Folkman and Moskowitz (2004, p. 751), 'the measurement of coping is probably as much art as it is science'. It is important to choose the approach of conceptualizing and measuring coping that is most aligned with the research question at hand. Potentially the best approach may sometimes be to address the research question from several approaches. For example, a narrative approach – where the participants would be asked to tell a story about a stressful situation, what they were thinking and what they did as the situation developed – could be applied as a baseline for defining a range of stressors to explore further with a quantitative measure (Dewe et al., 2010; Folkman & Moskowitz, 2004).

To overcome the well-known challenges with retrospective reports of coping, approaches such as daily and momentary assessments of coping (e.g., experience sampling methods; see Chapter 9) could contribute to clarify how coping ebbs and flows in monthly, weekly, daily and momentary events (Litt et al., 2011). This is particularly relevant because in order to advance coping assessment and measurement it is important to better understand the trajectories of coping as well as the context in which coping occurs as it facilitates meaning to the understanding of coping (Dewe & Cooper, 2017; Litt et al., 2011).

Researchers wishing to investigate coping with work stress may also need to consider alternative qualitative methods that capture the richness and idiographic nature of the process in order to overcome some of the structural limitations imposed by self-report quantitative measures. Examples of other alternative approaches to studying coping include critical-incident analysis (Bacharach & Bamberger, 2007; Caldas et al., 2020; Monnier et al., 2002), the use of open-ended/idiographic questioning (Haynes et al., 2009), and a combination of qualitative and quantitative approaches (Dewe & Cooper, 2021; Mazzola, Walker, et al., 2011). Use of multimethod approaches would enable simultaneous exploration of the extent of use of various coping strategies, as well as the meaning and relevance of those strategies for the individual under study, thereby producing a more complete understanding of the stressor-coping-strain process. The antagonism between qualitative and quantitative approaches will need to be overcome, and the challenge will be to achieve precision in measurement while at the same time considering how best to capture the richness and complexity of the stress coping process (Folkman & Moskowitz, 2004; Mazzola, Schonfeld, et al., 2011; Mazzola, Walker, et al., 2011).

When measuring coping behaviors by getting individuals to describe a potentially stressful encounter, it is as important to understand the 'event' as it is to acknowledge the distinction between coping behaviors and style. Conversely, a specific event may not necessarily involve an individual's full coping repertoire (Dewe et al., 2010), and what is gained in terms of specificity may be lost in terms of breadth, so researchers must decide clearly what they want to measure – style or behavior.

What emerges from the debate surrounding coping measurement is the question of whether traditional methodologies have provided an adequate basis for exploring and understanding the coping process (Dewe & Cooper, 2021; Litt et al., 2011; Mazzola, Schonfeld, et al., 2011). A growing body of opinion and research suggests that greater use of qualitative methods will enhance our understanding of coping. On the other hand, as researchers use self-report measures – the traditional approach to measuring coping – it becomes possible to identify an array of measurement issues that will continue to impede our understanding of coping and our ability to adequately assess the efficacy of this approach to the measurement of coping. The issue is not abandoning one approach in favor of another. A balance of quantitative and qualitative approaches may provide the conceptual richness and generalization that coping researchers are seeking.

Conclusion

There is no doubt that the intensity of the debate surrounding coping as a field of study reflects its fundamental importance to our understanding of the stress process. The research literature is dominated by the issues of how coping should best be defined, measured, and how coping strategies should be classified. Even when the primary aim has been to explore the broader context within which coping takes place, measurement issues have dominated and influenced results. To ensure that coping measures provide comprehensive information on the coping process, an integrated analysis of coping is required that captures the reality of those experiencing stressful events at work. This can be achieved only by considering various methods that capture the richness of the process and the idiographic nature of the experience.

How coping with job-related stress will be investigated in the future will be decided by how well the strengths of all methods can be integrated into research designs. The importance of coping and how it should best be measured is too important an issue to allow the debate to degenerate into mutual antagonism and distrust between advocates of alternative methodologies. Research on coping and the appraisal process represents the most likely means of enhancing our understanding of the stress process and for fulfilling our obligations to those whose working lives we research. We should not allow it to be obstructed by arguments about the superiority of one conceptual or method- ological approach over another.

8

ORGANIZATIONAL INTERVENTIONS

As was mentioned earlier in this volume, the human and financial costs of job-related strain can be substantial (Campbell Quick & Henderson, 2016; Hassard et al., 2018). However, despite widespread acknowledgment of the detrimental impact of stress on individuals and organizations, the amount of attention given by employers to understanding the causes (sources) of work-related strain and to alleviating stressful work conditions is relatively small compared with other areas, such as maintaining effective equipment and balancing financial budgets. Each year, organizations invest considerable sums of money in stress management programs (predominantly stress management training), but often there is an incomplete understanding of the sources of strain to be confronted and of the effectiveness of stress management approaches in dealing with these particular stressors.

For some time now, stress researchers have commented on the seeming haphazardness of stress management within organizational settings and the lack of congruence between workplace practices and theoretical and empirical work in this field (Biron et al., 2012). Along with personnel selection and employee training, this would appear to be another area where there is a gap between theory and practice in the domain of organizational behavior. Many reasons can be proffered for the divergence between scientific research on stress management and organizational practices. Predominant among these are (a) managers' perceptions and beliefs about the impact of the work environment on levels of employee strain and general well-being (Mackay et al., 2012), (b) their beliefs about who is responsible for managing individual employees' levels of strain, and (c) the costs associated with making organization-level changes compared with those related to teaching individuals to cope more effectively (Biron et al., 2012; Cooper & Cartwright, 1994). These three factors are linked, and together they promote a climate where stress management is viewed either as the responsibility of individual employees or as best tackled by the provision of stress management training that will enhance individuals' capability to manage their own levels of strain, without requiring substantial changes in jobs or the work environment itself.

Building upon the models of stress outlined in Chapter 1, the present chapter begins with an outline of a conceptual framework for understanding stress management interventions. Chapter 7 focused on coping behaviors (strategies) at the individual level; here we will describe examples of interventions that have been carried out either at the level of the specific job or at the broader organizational level. Organizational interventions may be defined as planned, behavioral, theory-based actions to change the way work is organized, designed, and managed in order to improve the health and well-being of participants (Nielsen, 2013; Nielsen & Noblet, 2018). Research on the effectiveness of these interventions will be reviewed, along with some of the major problems associated with conducting good research in this area and guidelines for evaluating interventions. The chapter concludes with a discussion of practical recommendations for implementing stress management interventions within organizations.

For simplicity, we will not differentiate here between interventions that are designed to offset the effects of strain in general and those that target burnout (discussed in Chapter 5) specifically. It is important to acknowledge, however, that the type of strain indicator (whether general strain, burnout, or some other specific symptom of strain) is critical to consider when implementing an organizational intervention.

A CONCEPTUAL FRAMEWORK FOR STRESS MANAGEMENT INTERVENTIONS

Efforts to combat job-related strain have been conceptualized in a number of different ways (see Table 8.1). These approaches can be differentiated by the level at which an intervention occurs (primary, secondary, or tertiary), the scope of the intervention activity, its target, and the assumptions underlying each intervention. The conceptualization presented in Table 8.1 is from the public health literature (Tetrick & Winslow, 2015), and although the approaches are not mutually exclusive, to some extent each is distinct, and the choice of approach has considerable implications for individuals and the organization as a whole.

A distinction is frequently drawn between the levels at which stress management interventions operate. *Primary interventions* are based on the assumption that the most effective way to combat strain is to eliminate or at least reduce the sources of strain (i.e., stressors) in the work environment, hence alleviating the pressures placed upon individual employees. This type of intervention is the most proactive and preventative approach to stress management and has been reported as generally being effective when implemented systematically, incorporating both individual-level and organizational-level interventions, and as a result of a careful assessment of specific stressors (Lamontagne et al., 2007; Tetrick & Winslow, 2015). Considered from the perspective of the person-environment fit model of stress (Dewe & Cooper, 2017), the focus of primary interventions is on modifying or adapting the physical or social-political environment to meet the needs of workers.

Recent reviews have illustrated a range of primary preventions that might be implemented to reduce workplace stressors, including structural changes in the organization, job redesign, and changes in social systems within the organization (DeChant et al., 2019; Lamontagne et al., 2007; Ruotsalainen et al., 2015; Tetrick & Winslow, 2015). The

Table 8.1 Proposed framework for evaluation of stress management interventions

	Primary interventions	Secondary interventions	Tertiary interventions
Scope	Preventative/ proactive - reduce the number and/or intensity of stressors	Preventative/ reactive - modify individuals' responses to stressors	Treatment - Minimize the damaging consequences of stressors by helping individuals cope more effectively with these consequences
Target	All employees and/ or the organization	Individual	Individual
Underlying assumption	Most effective approach to stress management is to remove stressors	May not be able to remove/reduce stressors, so best to focus on individuals' reactions to these stressors	Focus is on 'treatment' of problems once they have occurred
Examples	Job redesign; role restructuring; organizational restructuring	Conflict management training; coping skills training; fitness programs for employees at risk; 'wellness' programs	Employee assistance programs; counseling

following represent illustrations of the types of intervention that would be classified under this heading:

- Reorganization of lines of authority
- Restructuring of organizational units
- Changes in decision-making processes, such as increased employee participation in relevant decisions
- Redesign of job tasks, such as increasing employee autonomy and control over job functions and work schedules
- Improved communication and team building
- Working conditions, redesign of the physical work environment
- Changes in job roles
- Provision of a more supportive climate, including more constructive feedback on job performance
- Establishment of a more equitable system of reward distribution

A key component of many of the strategies listed above is the provision of greater individual control over the work environment. As discussed in Chapter 6, although empirical findings on the moderating (buffering) effects of employee control on the stressor-strain relationship are not totally conclusive, there is substantial evidence that increased personal control is directly linked with higher levels of employee satisfaction and well-being (Egan et al., 2007).

In contrast to primary interventions, *secondary interventions* focus on stress management training to alleviate the impact that environmental stressors exert on workers, rather than making changes to work conditions or the organizational environment. Secondary interventions represent the most common form of intervention used by organizations to deal with problems of stress management (Ruotsalainen et al., 2008). They are targeted at individual rather than organizational changes, and they aim primarily to increase individuals' awareness of their levels of strain and to enhance their personal coping strategies. Examples of techniques employed under this banner include cognitive restructuring, meditation, relaxation training, biofeedback, time management, coping classes, anger management, and conflict resolution strategies. A large number of organizations have also introduced health promotion activities (often referred to as 'wellness' programs) for their employees (Burke & Richardsen, 2014; Parks & Steelman, 2008). Secondary interventions may be either proactive (preventative) or reactive. For example, training individuals in conflict resolution skills may help to prevent the onset or development of interpersonal conflict between themselves and their colleagues. On the other hand, utilization of this training after such conflict has already surfaced illustrates a reactive approach to this particular stressor.

Stress management training has been found to be useful for some forms of stressors (Richardson & Rothstein, 2008), although its long-term effectiveness and its impact on organizational outcomes (such as strain-related absenteeism, accidents, and performance) have not been consistently demonstrated (Noblet & Lamontagne, 2006). One considerable advantage of this approach over the primary interventions described above is that it can typically be implemented quickly and may cause little disruption to existing work patterns (Murphy, 1995). Furthermore, skills training and increasing employee awareness of strain may play an important role in extending workers' psychosocial resources and in helping people deal with stressors that cannot be changed and hence have to be 'lived with.' These strategies may also function to strengthen a person's general resilience and resistance to stressors.

Despite these benefits, secondary interventions essentially reflect 'damage limitation,' often addressing the outcomes rather than the sources of strain that may be inherent in an organization's structure, culture, or climate. Hence, their exclusive use raises several concerns about ethics and control. For instance, the aim of training workers to cope more effectively means that often stress management training is not designed to eliminate or modify stressors in the workplace (Glazer, 2011). When stressors are systemic or structural (such as continuing excessive workload), individual coping behaviors may be insufficient, and job redesign or role restructuring may be required to alleviate the strain experienced and to prevent the development of burnout.

An even more fundamental issue is that use of stress management training without thorough exploration of the specific sources of strain may entail a shift of responsibility from management to individual workers. The practice of focusing on individual employees while ignoring the influence of stressful work environments reflects a tendency to attribute the causes of strain to individual employees' own behaviors and to view the responsibility for stress management as resting with workers themselves (Noblet & Lamontagne, 2006). However, individual symptoms of stress are often manifestations of organizational-level problems rather than personal failures to cope, and failing to address these conditions is in conflict with the occupational health and safety legislation that exist in many industrialized countries.

The *tertiary* level of stress management intervention is concerned with the rehabilitation of individuals who have suffered ill health or reduced well-being as a result of strain in the workplace. Interventions at this level are based on a 'treatment' rather than a preventative philosophy and are best illustrated by employee assistance programs (EAPs). These programs typically encompass some form of counseling to help employees deal with workplace stressors that cannot be changed structurally, as well as examining any potential spillover between work stressors and life off the job (e.g., marital and family difficulties). EAP programs also involve procedures that identify and respond to personal issues that may be interfering with work performance.

EAPs are characterized by a range of services (Joseph et al., 2018) and are most often provided by external consultants, as one major issue with respect to EAPs is confidentiality and the protection of individual privacy. Although the financial benefits (to the organization) of EAPs have been scrutinized, there is still little agreement on how best to evaluate this type of intervention (Hsu et al., 2020). It is sometimes difficult to reconcile the economic benefits to the organization with a more social therapeutic approach that emphasizes the impact of counseling on individual well-being.

Nevertheless, there is evidence suggesting that counseling services are effective in many cases in improving the psychological well-being of employees, as well as having benefits for the organization as a whole. For example, Joseph et al. (2018) reviewed studies examining the impact of EAPs, mostly from North America, and found significant postcounseling improvements in employee levels of functioning both at work and in their personal lives. Overall, the studies indicated improvements in personal health, decrease in depressive symptoms, and reduced presenteeism and absenteeism. As for organizational outcomes, a positive impact on performance was found. Thus, utilizing EAPs enhanced both individual and organizational outcomes (Joseph et al., 2018).

Finally, as with secondary interventions, the introduction of an EAP or some other tertiary intervention may be beneficial to employees and may be viewed by managers as cost-effective, yet still may not confront workplace stressors themselves, in which case the benefits may be short-lived. Organizational stress researchers continue to assert that most stress management interventions fall short because they offer a partial solution and place the onus on the individual to change his or her coping mechanisms, rather than acknowledging and modifying structural variables (at the job or organizational level). Though considerable emphasis is given to secondary and tertiary level interventions, primary strategies that encompass actual reduction in stressors at the organizational level are comparatively rare.

RESEARCH ON STRESS MANAGEMENT INTERVENTIONS

Despite recognition that levels of employee strain and the costs to organizations of job-related strain may be increasing significantly, the number of published studies assessing *organizational* interventions is disproportionately small compared to individual-level interventions (Biron et al., 2012; Tetrick & Winslow, 2015). In the first major review of stress management interventions, Newman and Beehr (1979) concluded that there was a lack of systematic evaluation of effectiveness and that only six of the 52 studies they reviewed entailed any direct empirical evaluation of organizational inter-vention effectiveness. Ivancevich et al. (1990) found only four evaluations where organization-level interventions had been targeted. More recent reviews of efforts to reduce exposure to psychosocial risks and promote health and well-being at work have shown similar results in the evaluation of organizational interventions (Lamontagne et al., 2007; Richardson & Rothstein, 2008; Tetrick & Winslow, 2015). For example, in a meta-analysis of occupational stress management intervention programs between 1977 and 2007, Richardson and Rothstein (2008) found that only five of 55 interventions included components that were considered primary intervention strategies. In a review and meta-analysis of interventions to reduce physician burnout, West et al. (2016) found only three of 15 randomized controlled studies involving structural interventions within the work environment.

While it seems that organizational interventions can produce some reduction in workplace stress, the results are often inconsistent and modest (Biron et al., 2012). A review of 55 workplace-based organizational interventions and their effects on mental health among healthcare workers conducted by Gray et al. (2019) included mental health measures such as burnout, stress and depression. A variety of research designs was used, including quasi-experimental, randomized trial, longitudinal and cross-sectional surveys, and qualitative methods. Only 25 studies found improvements in their measure of mental health, seventeen found insignificant or partial improvement, and a few studies found improvement in the short term that was not sustained in the long term. Ten studies found no improvement or a decline in their measure of mental health. The authors concluded that there is still limited evidence on how to promote mental health and well-being among employees, and that the studies show the complexity of imple-menting organizational interventions in the workplace.

Several studies have investigated interventions designed to increase levels of employee control or autonomy, for example, decision-making authority, which has already been highlighted here as an important issue in stress management. In a systematic review of organizational-level interventions aimed at increasing employee control conducted between 1981 and 2006, Egan et al. (2007) found 18 studies, 12 of which used a control or comparison group, but no randomized trials. Most of these studies found some evidence of health benefits when employee control improved. For instance, Bond and Bunce (2001) conducted a participative action research intervention among civil servants, observing that increased discretion and choice in their work led to improved mental health, sickness absence rates, and self-rated performance at one-year follow-up. These results were confirmed in a review of 10 randomized control trials and before and after studies (Joyce et al., 2010), which concluded that flexible working arrangements that increase worker control and choice are likely to have a positive effect on health outcomes. Similarly, a systematic review of task restructuring interventions (Bambra et al., 2007), found that interventions focusing on work group autonomy and associated with decreased demands and increased control, resulted in an improved psychosocial work environment and were linked with limited improvements in employee mental health. The implication of these findings is that interventions designed to increase worker control over important aspects of the work environment may have a significant impact on reducing psychological strain due to work-related stressors.

INTERVENTION PROCESS

In an overview of organizational interventions for stress and well-being, Biron et al. (2012) concluded that there is insufficient evidence for firm conclusions on the effectiveness of organizational-level interventions to prevent stress and improve well-being. One reason is that the research designs used are too varied or not considered as sufficiently strong. Many researchers have also argued that interventions often fail, not because of their content or design, but because contextual and process factors that may determine the success or failure of their implementation are often omitted in evaluation studies (Biron, 2012; Nielsen & Randall, 2013; Nytrø et al., 2000; Saksvik et al., 2002). In other words, it is important to understand not only *if* the intervention worked, but also *why* it worked or did not work.

Process evaluation is not a new term and has been used to refer to the study of the reasons why an intervention program succeeds or fails (Linnan & Steckler, 2002). These authors proposed a model for program evaluation that included context (the social, political, and economic environment); reach (proportion of target audience that participates); dose delivered (amount of intended units of each intervention delivered); dose received (extent of participant engagement); fidelity (extent to which the intervention was delivered as planned); recruitment (procedures used to approach and attract participants); and implementation (the extent to which the intervention has been implemented and received by the intended audience).

Other definitions of the term process are broader, referring to intervention development and how the intervention was implemented in addition to effectiveness in preventing work-related illness (Goldenhar et al., 2001). Nytrø et al. (2000) defined it as the evaluation of individual, collective or management perceptions and actions in implementing the intervention and their influence on the overall result of the intervention.

Potential obstacles to intervention implementation have been identified as the inability to learn from failure and motivate participants; lack of participation at all levels and differences in organizational perception; lack of insight into tacit and informal organizational behavior; ambiguity of roles and responsibilities, especially for middle management; and competing projects and reorganization (Saksvik et al., 2002).

When looking at the evidence from studies of organizational interventions to date, surprisingly few studies have considered why and how organizational-level stress interventions succeed or fail, and how they produce their effects on workers and organizations. Karanika-Murray et al. (2016) concluded that intervention evaluation has progressed from a sole focus on evaluating changes in criterion outcomes to acknowledging the importance of paying attention to the implementation process. They promote identifying process variables that can act as moderators or mediators of any effects of the intervention on observed change, and considering how process and outcome evaluations can work together.

Process-related factors also include management support, employee participation and commitment, the social climate, the cultural maturity, level of ownership and readiness for change, and understanding of the social meanings and relational implications of job change initiatives (Sorensen & Holman, 2014). One study investigated how employee participation and perceptions of line managers' support during a participatory organizational intervention related to well-being over time (Tafvelin et al., 2019). The study used a four-wave panel design consisting of 159 hospital workers. Results showed that perceived line manager support in the initiation and active phase was related to employee participation in the active phase, and that participation in the initiation and active phase was related to well-being at follow-up 24 months later.

Studies of organizational interventions in Sweden and Denmark have investigated whether participatory intervention approaches can improve the efficiency and effectiveness of organizational interventions. Results indicated that participation and changes in work procedures concerning teamwork were significantly associated with post-intervention autonomy, social support and well-being (Nielsen & Randall, 2012). Also, employees' participation in the design and use of the intervention tool predicted better integration of organizational and employee objectives after 12 months, which in turn predicted increased job satisfaction and decreased discomfort at 24 months (Schwarz et al., 2017). Another study of eleven intervention projects in Denmark (Nielsen et al., 2007) included process measures of information about the project, participation in interventions, degree of influence on the project and perception of intervention quality. The results indicated that participants' perceived influence on the content of interventions was directly related to higher participation, and positive appraisals of the intervention activities fully mediated the relationships between exposure to the intervention and changes in working conditions, behavioral stress and job satisfaction. When employees are given the chance to influence interventions, then organizational interventions are more likely to succeed. When employees participate in efforts to explicitly manage psychosocial work environment issues, there are positive intervention outcomes in the form of strain reduction and employee well-being.

As noted earlier, removal or reduction of stressors is the most direct way to reduce stress since it deals with the source. There is mounting evidence that job redesign interventions (especially those that increase employee control and autonomy), adoption of more consultative or participative management styles, encouraging employee participation in the development and implementation of interventions, developing interventions that address the specific psychosocial risks in a particular workplace, and use of both process and outcome measures can all increase the chance of organizational interventions to enhance employee well-being and alleviate work-related strain. Though these approaches may entail greater immediate costs for the organization and require higher commitment and effort from management, research suggests that these will be offset by long-term benefits not only for individual employees but also for the organization as a whole. From a managerial standpoint, it may be more convenient to focus stress management interventions on individual perceptions and behaviors than on organizational or job redesign. Programs such as stress management training and EAPs may be viewed as less costly and more readily implemented than long-term restructuring or major changes in work practices and procedures and may also serve to keep management from accepting greater responsibility for excessive strain experienced by their employees.

PROBLEMS IN EVALUATING INTERVENTION EFFECTIVENESS

A number of difficulties associated with the evaluation of organizational health interventions have already been alluded to. Of particular concern is the fact that the considerable knowledge accumulated over the past decades of the antecedents of work-related health and well-being has not been translated into interventions that greatly improve the health and well-being of employees (Nielsen et al., 2010). Results from previous research show that the effectiveness of organizational interventions on measures of health and well-being is often modest, suggesting that commonly used evaluation frameworks have limitations, and are failing to explain how and why context factors may influence intervention implementation and outcomes (Nielsen, 2013). As Biron and Karanika-Murray (2014) observed, researchers 'have mainly focused on understanding *if*, rather than *how*, *when*, and *why*, interventions are effective in reducing the negative consequences of stress at work' (p. 86).

Several critiques of evaluation methodology and practice have been published in recent years, and our intention is not to reiterate all of the criticisms raised by these reviewers. Instead, we focus on a few critical issues relating to the evaluation of organizational health interventions within work settings. A primary concern is the validity of findings obtained from an evaluation. Several recent overviews of theory and methodology in the evaluation of organizational stress and well-being interventions (Biron & Karanika-Murray, 2014; Nielsen et al., 2022; Nielsen, Nielsen, et al., 2017, Roodbari et al.,

2020) address some of the factors affecting the validity of such interventions. We will differentiate between three types of validity issues: (a) internal validity, (b) construct validity, and (c) external validity.

Internal Validity

Internal validity is an indicator of the extent to which a cause-and-effect relationship between working conditions and its outcome is well-founded (Nielsen, Nielsen, et al., 2017). For a long time, the gold standard of evaluating interventions has been the randomized controlled trials (RCT). The RCT approach involves randomly assigning individuals to either an intervention group or a control group in such a way that there are no differences between groups at baseline, and then comparing outcomes in the two groups after the intervention and at follow-up some time later. Any statistical differences in the outcomes of the intervention group and the control group are then assumed to be the result of the intervention. In this approach, the context is conceptualized as confounding variables that need to be held constant, and it also views the participants as passive recipients of interventions (Nielsen, 2013; Nielsen, Nielsen, et al., 2017). However, the model has been found to have limitations in organizational intervention research as both individual psychological factors and the social context have been found to influence intervention effectiveness.

The RCT approach is often incompatible with organizational realities in that the required stability for evaluating the effects of an intervention is difficult in organizations that are constantly changing (Biron et al., 2012). Also, researchers may not be able to employ a research design that includes control groups, either because it is simply not possible to randomly assign workers to an experimental or control group, or because the organization is unwilling to permit such allocations. In addition, ethical considerations associated with withholding an intervention from certain members of the organization, even for a limited time period, may call into question the justification for assigning some study participants to a control group. There are also risks of contamination in the RCT approach (Nielsen, Nielsen, et al., 2017). When changes are introduced they are likely to affect all employees in a department, and therefore in recent studies of organizational interventions cluster randomization has been introduced, in which the organizational intervention targets an entire organizational unit or department.

Threats to internal validity of the RCT approach also include intervening factors (e.g., historical events occurring between pre-intervention and post-intervention measures of an outcome variable, changes within respondents that occur solely due to the passage of time, and employees' own personal characteristics, such as hardiness) which may influence the outcomes of an intervention program, and are frequently not assessed or taken into account when evaluating such programs (Beehr & O'Hara, 1987). Another obstacle to intervention implementation and success are competing projects and reorganization (Saksvik et al., 2002). The intervention process itself; lack of participation at all levels of the organizations; different perceptions of the importance of changes that need to be made; lack of insight into tacit and informal organizational behavior; ambiguity of roles

and responsibilities, especially for middle management; and failure to motivate participants; are other examples of challenges to internal validity of organizational interventions (Nielsen & Abildgaard, 2013; Nielsen, Nielsen, et al., 2017; Nytrø et al., 2000).

Recently, an opposing paradigm – that of realist evaluation of organizational interventions has gained impact (Biron & Karanika-Murray, 2014; Nielsen & Abildgaard, 2013;
Nielsen & Miraglia, 2017; Pawson, 2013; Roodbari et al., 2020). Nielsen, Nielsen, et al.
(2017) describe the realist framework as follows:

> Realist evaluation seeks to answer the questions of what works for whom in which
> circumstances through studying what the *mechanisms* of an intervention are
> (what makes an intervention work?) and the *context* in which these may be
> triggered (what are the conditions in which an intervention is effective?) and how
> these mechanisms bring about certain *outcomes* (which improvements in working
> conditions and in employee health and well-being can be observed?). (p. 41)

Nielsen, Nielsen, et al. (2017) further argue that realist evaluation may offer an
opportunity to develop an integrated context, process, and outcome evaluation framework, and providing a way to conduct rigorous, theory-based analyses of what works for
whom in which circumstances, while also ensuring internal and external validity.
Questions about the process are important in order to understand which mechanisms
bring about changes in employee health and well-being. Realistic evaluation requires
ongoing measurements among all stakeholders, for example, brief monthly questionnaires about the extent to which line managers support the intervention, whether the
process is participatory, and whether intervention activities are aligned with the organizational structures and goals (Nielsen, 2017). A realist review of organizational intervention studies in 28 journal articles concluded that knowledge about the complex
interactions between contexts, mechanisms and outcomes in intervention studies is
rather embryonic (Roodbart et al., 2020). Research needs to move beyond simple before
and after measurements of intended outcomes, and include measurements of process and
implementation on an ongoing basis. Once the mechanisms have been identified it may
be possible to identify which mechanisms may work in other organizational settings.

Construct Validity

The issue of construct validity is, of course, relevant to all research in that valid measurement of constructs is a prerequisite for generalizable conclusions. In the case of
organizational health interventions, construct validation relates to the assessment of
psychosocial risk, the assessment of outcomes (psychological strain in particular), and the
intervention strategy (is it actually directed at reducing psychological strain and
increasing well-being?). A critical question for many stress management interventions is
whether the indicators that are being assessed truly reflect the work demands and strain
experienced by recipient of the intervention. Standardized questionnaires have been the
method of choice for assessing strain and work-related issues both pre-intervention and

post-intervention. While some aspects of the work environment may be shared by many occupations, some are specific to certain occupations and specific workplaces, and standardized screening questionnaires may therefore fail to identify the crucial issues in a particular workplace or context. In contrast, screening with items tailored to intervention contexts may capture the participants' cognitive appraisal and the local context, and thus help to identify appropriate initiatives for that particular workplace (Nielsen et al., 2014; Vignoli et al., 2017).

Some studies have used a mixed methods (qualitative and quantitative) approach to conducting such screening. Qualitative interviews have established context specific job demands, which afterwards were included in a questionnaire used for screening and assessing outcomes. In one study, the job demands identified did indeed relate to employee stress reactions in the form of emotional exhaustion, and the intervention had a positive impact on well-being moderated by social support (Vignoli et al., 2017). In another study focusing on development of a tailored questionnaire to measure employees' appraisals of their working conditions (Nielsen et al., 2014), a similar mixed methods approach was taken. Based on interviews the researchers developed a tailored questionnaire that was then compared to the annual standardized attitude survey used by the company. Participants indicated that the tailored questionnaire highlighted issues previously ignored, and that it was easier to develop detailed action plans to improve employee health and well-being because of the specificity to their particular work context. The authors concluded that tailored questionnaires may be appropriate for use in organizational intervention research and more broadly, that evaluations of organizational interventions need to be contextually grounded (Nielsen et al., 2014).

External Validity

Along with the above forms of validity, a further critical issue for stress researchers is whether an intervention implemented in one setting and time period will also be effective in another context or under other circumstances. Although a particular organization may be interested solely in reducing levels of strain among its own members, for consultants and researchers generalization beyond the immediate setting is an important criterion for assessing the validity of stress management interventions.

Beehr and O'Hara (1987) examined three major threats to the external validity of stress management interventions. The first of these is what they referred to as *subject-by-treatment* interaction, which occurs when an intervention is effective with one group of participants but not with others. For instance, a stress management program may reduce levels of strain among certain occupational groups (e.g., professionals) but have no impact, or even have a deleterious effect, on other groups (e.g., office workers). This issue requires researchers to examine the context and personal characteristics of participants in an intervention to determine whether any of these variables might operate as a moderator of the relationship between the intervention and criterion variables.

A second threat described by Beehr and O'Hara is a *treatment-by-setting* interaction, in which the intervention works well in one environment but not in another. This can occur even within a single organization. For example, the culture and climate of one unit or department may be highly conducive to the introduction of a participative decision-making intervention, whereas another section of the same organization may perceive the intervention as less important and therefore not implement the changes (Albertsen et al., 2014). The intervention may also be viewed by participants as an unwanted intrusion upon their (already heavy) role responsibilities.

Finally in this category, a *history-by-treatment* interaction suggests that an intervention may be effective at some time periods but not at others. Using the above illustration, participative decision-making schemes are effective only when there is adequate time for preparation and involvement of employees. At peak periods, when role demands are high or deadlines loom large, less rather than more participation in decisions (at least in certain areas) may be desired by employees. Involvement in an intervention under these circumstances may become a stressor itself rather than a mechanism for stress reduction.

A final difficulty identified early on has been that of gaining entry into organizations to study organizational health interventions (Murphy, 1988). Often upper-level managers are wary of researchers investigating changes within their organization, particularly if those changes have political and/or legal ramifications. As noted earlier, employers and management tend to favor an individual-oriented approach to stress management and are frequently resistant to approaches that entail structural change by way of either job or organizational redesign. However, national legislation in many countries impose legal requirements to assess the working environment at regular intervals, and interventions to address any issues concerning psychosocial risks must be implemented in the entire organization (Nielsen, Nielsen, et al., 2017; Nielsen et al., 2010). This creates opportunities for organizational change researchers to gain access to organizations and their employees to conduct of systematic research on the effects of organizational interventions.

GUIDELINES FOR EVALUATION RESEARCH

The above discussion illustrates that, as with other evaluations in organizational settings (such as assessment of the impact of training on the job performance of personnel), considerable difficulties may arise in the evaluation of organization-level stress management interventions. Many of these difficulties stem from the challenges of conducting randomized control studies in organizations, limited focus on context and process variables, different perceptions of psychosocial risks, inability to collect data at appropriate time periods (e.g., follow-up assessments), lack of management support for evaluation of organizational change programs, and practical problems associated with carrying out the research. It is clear that evaluation research can be fraught with complexities that are not typically confronted by researchers in other areas of organizational behavior.

Nevertheless, strategies for conducting such research are available and have in fact been used, although admittedly in a small proportion of studies. In the first edition of this volume, we focused on RCTs or quasi-experimental studies and time series designs. As the field has developed to include contextual and process factors in addition to target outcomes, we will here outline some procedures and designs that have recently been recommended for intervention process evaluation.

As we have alluded to already, in many cases the use of fully experimental designs involving independent experimental and control groups (as in RCTs) may simply not be possible, and some variant of quasi-experimental design has been the most feasible approach, e.g., the use of a non-equivalent control groups. For example, a stress intervention program may be devised for delivery within an organization that has separate units or departments, in which the personnel are not identical in terms of their jobs, the structure of the departments, or perhaps even their qualifications and experience. Quasi-experimental designs have the inherent problem that differences between the two groups may be attributable to factors other than the intervention. Therefore, it has become more common to use cluster randomization in which whole departments become the unit of evaluation. Measuring process variables in addition to outcomes at various stages may enable researchers to conclude that the intervention was effective in reducing strain as well as which mechanisms were crucial for its effects.

Nielsen and Abildgaard (2013) presented a research-based framework for the evaluation of both process and effect. Rather than focusing on evaluating change from pre-intervention to post-intervention, their framework is directed at the process aspects of change, specifically how organizational interventions must be adapted to the routines and contextual conditions within the organization. Drawing on process organization theory, the suggested framework 'focuses on documenting specific processes initiated by intervention programs and on how organizational actors and processes interact with the intervention activities to influence intervention outcomes' (p. 280). There are four interlinked categories in their proposed framework:

- Mechanisms to bring about change, defined as the organizational actors who may drive and influence the intervention process, e.g., employees, line and senior managers, researchers, HR consultants.
- The mental models of those actors, including cognitive schemata of the organization, working conditions, and the purpose and outcomes of the intervention.
- The contextual factors surrounding the intervention activities, both discrete and overall (omnibus) context.
- The intervention design and processes, divided into several phases: Initiation, screening, action planning, implementation and effect evaluation.

The last category is divided into the phases commonly observed in organizational interventions, but contrary to traditional frameworks, each of these phases is seen as the outcome of the previous phase (Nielsen & Abildgaard, 2013). For example, procedures for screening are the result of planning in the initiation phase, the outcomes of action planning depend on the quality of screening, and implementation depends on the level of detail in the action plans. The authors believe that it is important to evaluate the different phases separately in order to understand the mechanisms through which progress is made from one phase to the next. The model also assumes a stepwise participatory process in which major organizational actors are involved in each phase of the intervention process. The proposed framework is presented in Figure 8.1.

The stepwise participatory approach to organizational occupational health interventions has been accepted as a strategy to manage the psychosocial environment in many European countries (Nielsen, 2017), however, the process raises some challenges for designing, implementing and evaluating interventions. The realist evaluation perspective assumes that interventions do not have an effect in and of themselves, it is the activation of various mechanisms (e.g., collective efficacy, transformational leadership) that makes the intervention work (Abildgaard et al., 2020). Thus, realist evaluation may provide answers to the question of 'what works for whom in which circumstances' by identifying the mechanisms that make an intervention work and the contextual factors needed to trigger these mechanisms (Biron, 2012; Nielsen, 2017; Nielsen, Nielsen, et al., 2017).

Biron and Karanika-Murray (2014) noted that there is a need to develop theoretical foundations of organizational interventions to increase our understanding of what drives change, how to prepare for change, and the possible mechanisms of change. The use of a mixed methods (qualitative and quantitative) approach to conducting screening for identifying potential context-dependent demands and resources in the workplace makes it

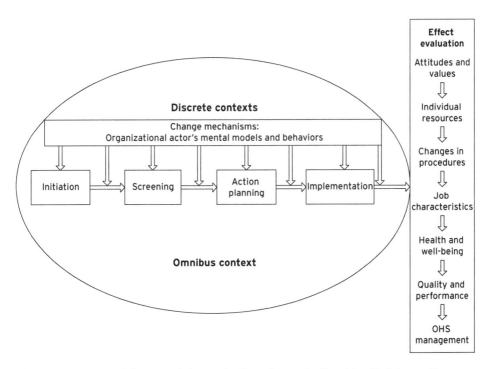

Figure 8.1   Proposed framework for evaluation of organizational health interventions

possible to create context-specific interventions (Abildgaard et al., 2016; Nielsen et al., 2017; Vignoli et al., 2017). Qualitative (most often interviews) and quantitative (most often questionnaire data) methods are both established tools that may be used to evaluate intervention processes as well as outcomes. So far, few studies have used this approach; a review of organizational interventions for improved well-being among health care workers found only four studies that used mixed methods, mostly consisting of longitudinal surveys and focus groups (Gray et al., 2019). Studies using the mixed methods approach have concluded that qualitative process data has the potential to tie together meaning, context, and narratives of the intervention and the organization, whereas quantitative data has the potential to represent a sample of individuals' opinions in a cost-effective manner (Abildgaard et al., 2016; Nielsen, Randall, et al., 2017). In a systematic literature review of intervention studies using quantitative measures, either on their own or combined with qualitative process evaluation, Nielsen et al. (2022) found that there was little consensus of what to evaluate and when. The studies demonstrated that established evaluation frameworks were rarely used and not all of the components of the evaluation framework were included. Acknowledging the need to employ comprehensive frameworks in order to ensure systematic and comparable process evaluation, the authors propose an integrated process evaluation framework, which outlines which dimensions need to be measured during pre-intervention, during the intervention, in the implementation phase and at follow-up (see Nielsen et al., 2022 for more details). Integrating analysis of qualitative and quantitative data may enable researchers to identify contextual factors that interact with the intervention experience and outcomes, and directly explain the quantitative results that would not have been possible in a purely quantitative quasi-experimental study. The studies also demonstrate the complex nature of participatory organizational intervention and demonstrate how one can use a realist framework to study the effects of interventions.

As discussed in some detail in Chapter 4, one final methodological issue that needs to be considered is the use of multiple indicators of strain. Irrespective of whether the research design is experimental, quasi-experimental, or process-oriented, selection of appropriate measures of strain is vital to ensure that the outcomes of stress management interventions are indeed strain related and that method bias does not overshadow the true effects of an intervention. Most research has relied predominantly on self-report measures of psychological strain, which reflect just one element of the constellation of strain characteristics. Stronger conclusions about the impact of interventions can be drawn if evaluations extend beyond the measurement of psychological strain to include behavioral, physical, and even physiological indexes of the strain construct. Although more difficult to carry out, multi-measure assessments of strain will provide a more comprehensive account of the effects of stress management interventions on individual employees and the organization.

GUIDELINES FOR IMPLEMENTING SMIS

To conclude this chapter on organizational interventions, we consider how best to implement such efforts, along with some practical issues that impinge upon the effectiveness of stress management programs. As has already been noted, several factors place constraints on the types of programs that might be introduced within an organization and on how stress management is carried out. The concern is to ensure that strategies used are effective in terms of outcomes and have a high benefits-to-costs ratio. The need to understand what works for whom in which circumstances is important from both a research and a policy perspective (Nielsen & Noblet, 2018; Nielsen et al., 2022). Current European, North American, and Australian national standards for ensuring employee health incorporate a number of key aspects recommended by researchers. As mentioned, organizational interventions often employ a problem-solving approach that typically consists of five phases: Preparation, screening (identification of problem areas), action planning, implementation of action plans, and evaluation (Nielsen, Randall, et al., 2010).

The preparation phase is important as it allows the organization to become familiar with the method employed. If external consultants are employed, this phase gives an opportunity to learn about the organizational structure and culture. Many intervention methods recommend the establishment of a steering group (Nielsen, Randall, et al., 2010). Studies have shown that a mixed representation of human resources, health and safety, senior management and union representatives was ideal for moving the process along. The steering group should monitor the progress and implementation and plan the evaluation of the intervention program, and is therefore important for the intervention's success. Another important aspect of preparing the intervention is to ensure the employees' readiness for change. In order for employees to be motivated to actively participate in intervention activities, they need to perceive the current situation as being unhealthy and be convinced that change is necessary and beneficial (Nielsen & Noblet, 2018). It is important to prepare employees for change and develop their capabilities in participating in the intervention. All of this requires the development of a communication strategy to support the intervention, in which the method is explained and tasks and roles clearly defined. One could also consider identifying champions of the project, people who are trusted within the organization and who can be effective drivers of change.

Screening involves identifying problem areas and prioritizing which problem to focus on changing. First, one needs to begin by ascertaining existing levels of strain among members of the organization. This can be done systematically using questionnaires, interviews of selected employees, and other means to determine the relative levels of strain experienced. Coupled with this is the need to identify relevant stressors in the workplace. The method most often used to identify problems are standardized questionnaires, i.e., pre-existing questionnaires that identify a broad range of psychosocial risks. Standardized measures may cover a wide variety of common workplace stressors, such as those described in Chapter 3 of this volume. However, they often do not reveal specific stressors that may exist in the local context and therefore the focus of the intervention may not address the most relevant problems in that particular workplace, which could be one explanation for outcomes indicating little improvement in working conditions and well-being (Biron et al., 2010). Many researchers have advocated the use of the mixed methods approach to conduct screening for developing and implementing organizational interventions that are tailored to the local context (Egan & Bond, 2015; Vignoli et al., 2017), and claim that the approach is useful in stress intervention research as well as to organizations in prioritizing their intervention activities.

The target of interventions is the next major consideration required. Action planning is a phase of activity that focuses on the development and implementation of initiatives to improve the psychosocial work environment and employee health and well-being. Choosing problem areas and actions can be done in different ways, but an important aspect is employee participation (Nielsen & Randall, 2012). Research has shown that in organizations where management has been the sole drivers in developing action plans, the impact of the intervention was limited (Nielsen & Noblet, 2018). The participation in open action planning workshops and focus groups for prioritizing actions seems to be associated with higher agreement with the action plans and higher engagement in the intervention (Ipsen et al., 2015), as well as a sense of community because participants get to know each other better (Saksvik et al., 2015).

According to Biron and Karanika-Murray (2014), an action plan is only as good as its implementation. Essential elements of well-implemented interventions are ongoing monitoring of the implementation process; having specific, achievable, and measurable goals; allocation of roles and responsibilities; and clear communication plans. Nielsen and Noblet (2018) note that senior management play an important role in getting action plans implemented through championing the intervention and providing resources. The real drivers of change are often middle managers and line managers who are involved in the daily running of the intervention and active engagement with intervention participants (Nielsen & Noblet, 2018). In organizations where health and well-being management is successfully integrated into performance management, middle managers and line managers more easily support the process and involve employees in the integration.

Effect evaluation of organizational intervention may encompass various outcomes such as those outlined in Figure 8.1. These include both organizational outcomes (e.g., changes in job characteristics and procedures, quality of products and performance and financial gains) and individual outcomes such as attitudes and values, strain reduction, and increased health and well-being. Our focus in this volume is on reducing organizational stress, and a number of indicators of strain and their measurement have been described in Chapter 3. In addition, there are three elements of the process that should be evaluated: the intervention process itself (who is involved, action plans developed), hindering and facilitating factors in the context, and the mental models of the participants (what did they think of the intervention, changes in attitudes) (Nielsen & Abildgaard, 2013). Nielsen and Noblet (2018) recommend that an integrated process and effect evaluation of these elements should take place at each phase of the organizational intervention. According to Abildgaard (2018), this approach requires following scientific methodological principles and applying practical craftsmanship for collecting data in a concrete setting. Future research following the process-oriented approach to organizational interventions will hopefully ensure that they achieve their intended outcomes and increase our knowledge of how to reduce organizational stress and create psychologically healthy workplaces.

Conclusion

Earlier in this chapter, we described three levels of intervention (primary, secondary, and tertiary) to deal with strain and its consequences. From the research and other information presented here, it is clear that the large majority of interventions concentrate on strain *management* rather than strain *prevention*. This emphasis is associated with the complexity of implementing organizational interventions, making the training of individuals to cope with workplace strain the most viable approach. Many managers focus attention on the enhancement of individual coping skills and strategies rather than addressing the actual sources of strain, whether these are located in job roles or organizational processes. This is not to undermine the importance of individual coping strategies in the stress-coping process (see Chapter 7), but simply to acknowledge that at times individual efforts may not be sufficient to ameliorate the impact of stressors, and a more direct approach may be needed. As commented by Nielsen and Miraglia (2017), the crux of successful interventions is accurate identification of the sources of strain (i.e., the stressors), along with the implementation of stressor-specific interventions.

If we consider stress from a transactional perspective, some practical implications emerge. First, the transactional approach provides an integrated framework for understanding the complexities of the stress-coping process. For stress management programs, this means that the emphasis must be on the relationship between the individual and the environment; hence, these programs must be designed to capture the processes that link individuals and their environments. Individuals' interpretations of events and their coping resources (both personal and within the organizational context) are key design factors. Little can be gained from stress management programs that provide individuals with a wider range of coping skills and opportunities but fail to recognize that these are of little use if appropriate environmental resources and supports are not available (Nielsen, Nielsen, et al., 2017).

The importance of increasing the involvement of workers themselves in designing workplace interventions has been highlighted by many researchers and practitioners. For example, the review by Nielsen (2013) illustrates the critical role of employee participation in stress management processes for the effectiveness of organizational efforts to address strain-related issues. A key factor in the development of more systematic (and hence more effective) organizational interventions is also the extent of commitment from all layers of the organization — employers, management, unions, and employees — to alleviating the impact of stressors. This may require more open communication and a dismantling of organizational norms and expectations that promote, rather than help to reduce, strain among employees: for instance, norms that encourage individuals to work excessively long hours and to take work home with them or that create feelings of guilt about arriving at and leaving work 'on time'. The commitment to address stress issues will stem from a supportive organizational climate, one that recognizes that strain is inherent in the workplace and that the experience of strain by workers is not a sign of personal weakness or incompetence.

As we will outline in Chapter 10, new forms of employment contracts and relations may blur the boundaries between workers' job responsibilities and their off-the-job (home) life, creating another form of strain due to conflict between the two domains (Spreitzer et al., 2017). For example, the rapid development of new computer technologies has led to considerable changes in job conditions for many workers. An increasing number of individuals are now employed on a contractual (rather than 'permanent') basis and perform their job responsibilities from home or other non-office settings. Although the psychosocial effects of these changes have been given some consideration, there is a dearth of empirical evidence on their long-term implications for individuals and their families. More systematic exploration of the interplay between job and off-job conditions and experiences is essential for the development of work conditions that do not create another form of stressor for workers.

In conclusion, organizational interventions to remove stressors or at least reduce their impact will be more effective if a number of steps are carried out. These include (a) identification of context factors that may be functioning as potential sources of strain; (b) thorough assessment of the levels of strain experienced by employees, including a range of strain indicators; (c) implementation of interventions that aim to resolve or prevent the problem(s) rather than simply dealing with the symptoms; and (d) use of integrated evaluation criteria that examine a variety of specific processes and outcomes, not just an aggregate improvement in overall well-being. The challenge is to persuade employers and managers of the long-term benefits of this approach to stress management, both for their employees and for the organization as a whole.

9

METHODOLOGICAL ISSUES IN JOB STRESS RESEARCH

Previous chapters have illustrated the variety of research designs, methods, and measures that have been used in organizational stress research to date. A fundamental question is whether current methodologies satisfactorily assess the complex and dynamic nature of the organizational stress process. Here we consider some critical issues in the debate over appropriate methodologies and examine arguments that have been proposed for broadening the approach taken in job stress research to include a greater range of assessment procedures and to adopt convergent methodologies.

While highly-ranked journals in other areas of psychology have almost abandoned the use of cross-sectional designs, this type of research design is frequently published within organizational stress and in top ranked journals within occupational health psychology (Spector & Pindek, 2016). The cross-sectional design is not without merit (Spector, 2019), and in the current chapter, we will also give a brief introduction to other types of research designs and align these designs with current methodological issues in organizational stress research. More specifically, we will address issues related to quantitative self-report methods and a few associated types of analyses, time interval issues in the measurement process, causal relationships, objective measurement, and the use of qualitative and mixed methods. The aim of this chapter is not to provide an in-depth analysis of theoretical nor analytical aspects, but to give an overview of some of the current methodological issues in the organizational stress literature.

QUANTITATIVE MEASUREMENT ISSUES

Cause and Effect

One of the central aims of research is to understand the causal relationship between variables. Does variable A cause or predict variable B? Or in the interest of this book, for example, does the work stressor workload cause physiological strain in workers?

Knowledge about causal relationship provides the foundation to design effective interventions that target causes of stress and thus, alleviate the negative consequences of stress in organizations.

According to Cook and Campbell (1979), the fulfillment of three conditions is necessary in order to infer a causal relationship between variables; (1) establishment of covariation between two variables (e.g., independent and dependent variable), (2) the independent variable must precede the dependent variable, and (3) alternative explanations for the assumed cause-and-effect relationship are ruled out. While there are multiple research designs that can meet the first two conditions, randomized experiments are regarded by many as the only research design that fulfills the third condition and thus the gold standard for establishing causal relationships. We analyzed the prevalence of experimental designs in *Journal of Occupational Health Psychology* (JOHP) and *Work & Stress* (WS) from 2011 to 2021 using text mining methodology (Truyens & Van Eecke, 2014).[1] In total, experimental designs were used in 10% of all articles. In the analysis by Chen et al. (2012), 7% of the articles in the same journals included experimental design studies in the time period 2000–2010, suggesting a slight increase in the last decade. *JOHP* had more articles including experimental designs (13% in total) and also a higher number of randomized experiments (8%), compared to *WS* (3%) from 2011 to 2021. *WS* has published a similar number of articles including experimental designs each year. Articles including an experimental design increased from 2016 in *JOHP* with a peak in 2019, likely caused by a special issue devoted to 'Interventions in Occupational Health Psychology' that often employ an experimental design.

In a randomized experiment the independent variable is deliberately manipulated in that some workers are, for example, given a high workload while other workers are given a normal workload. The crucial aspect is that the assignment into high or normal workload is *random*. The random assignment of treatment increases the probability that workers in the two groups are similar to each other on average (Shadish et al., 2002). Hence, any observed difference in strain between the two groups of workers (high workload or normal workload) is then most likely caused by their difference in workload, not by alternative causes such as differences in personality, intelligence, or health as these differences most likely are randomly distributed in the two groups. Quasi-experimental designs share many of the same features as randomized experiments in that researchers may manipulate the independent variable and apply control groups. However, the crucial distinction is that quasi-experimental designs do not have random

---

[1]Using text mining techniques, we identified relevant experimental articles from the total body of published articles in *WS* and *JOHP* (excluding editorials, call for papers, etc.) for 2011–2021 using search words such as «experiment», «quasi-experiment», «random», «intervention» etc. Based on this sample, we then manually examined and coded each identified article according to their use of experimental design and the type of experimental design (random vs. quasi-experimental). We then calculated the percentage of articles that included an experimental design, and the type of experimental design, across journals, and in each specific journal. We are indebted to Dr Heidi Karlsen at BI Norwegian Business School for running the analysis.

assignment, so that workers may self-select into groups or that the researchers decide who gets the treatment (Shadish et al., 2002). The lack of randomized assignment of treatment in quasi-experiments comes with the cost that alternative explanations for the causal relationship are harder to rule out. Perhaps workers high in ambition, intelligence, and stamina are more likely to sign up for a higher workload, and these factors may pose an alternative explanation for the assumed effect of workload on strain.

To optimize control over alternative explanations, researchers often conduct experiments in a laboratory where they have control over extraneous factors. However, the artificial setting of the laboratory reduces the possibility of generalizing findings to real-life organizational settings. Field experiments provide the opportunity of investigating assumed causal relationships in their natural occurring setting (Eden, 2017), albeit with less experimental control. An analysis of the use of experimental method in JOHP and WS suggest that field experiments are commonly used to study causal factors related to stress (Chen et al., 2012).

Using experimental research design to investigate stressor-strain relationship warrants ethical considerations. Exposing workers to stressors that might cause physical or psychological harm will often be judged to violate the ethical guideline to not inflict harm on research participants. One ethical possibility of addressing stressor–strain relationships is to design interventions that are designed to prevent or alleviate stressors (Eden, 2017). Researchers may then assess the effect of a stressor on a strain indicator by comparing workers given the intervention (i.e., experimental group) with workers not given the intervention (i.e., control group). For example, in the randomized experiment by Leger et al. (2021) workers in the intervention group were given increased supervisory support whereas workers in the control group received the supervisory support level they always had received. Workers with increased supervisory support reported lower levels of negative affect reactivity compared to workers with normal levels of supervisory support. While the experiment by Leger et al. (2021) provides evidence of a successful intervention, it also sheds light on the causal relationship between supervisory support and strain. If an intervention is deemed stress alleviating, workers in the control group should subsequently be given the intervention.

Experience Sampling Method

Experience sampling method (ESM) is a broad term that refers to methods that provides 'a representative sampling of immediate experiences in one's natural environment' (Beal, 2015, p. 384), and often includes event-sampling studies and diary studies. In studies of organizational stress, workers are typically asked to respond to survey items multiple times a day and/or over consecutive days. Thus, ESM studies involve intense periodic assessments of workers involving brief intervals between assessment and with relatively short overall study duration. According to Beal (2015), ESM research is characterized by the goal of capturing a range of immediate experiences in their natural environment. One benefit of the ESM design is the reduced threat of retrospective memory bias. In self-report studies with weekly or monthly intervals between assessments, respondents are asked to aggregate their states and experiences and as such, are more likely to be influenced by other factors than the immediate experience.

Wheeler and Reis (1991) distinguished among three types of measurement methods often used within ESM-research. *Interval-contingent recording* refers to data collection at predetermined, regular intervals. Within stress research, workers may for instance report levels of strain in the morning, the intensity of work stressors during the day, and levels of strain in the evening. *Signal-contingent recording* refers to data collection practices where the workers are signaled by the researcher (e.g., via mail or app) and asked to respond to the survey. These signals can be delivered at fixed or random intervals, or a combination. The third type is referred to as *event-contingent recording* where workers are asked to provide their response following a specific predefined event. For instance, workers may be asked to respond to a survey every time they encounter a conflict with a colleague or a near-accident at work. In event-contingent recording, the specific event must be clearly defined for the respondents. The respondents may include a short description of the event in the survey to increase the probability that respondents indeed answered to the specified events of interest. The last few years have witnessed a host of different apps and technological devices that may ease the use of ESM designs for researchers.

There are several advantages and disadvantages to ESM designs, of which we will discuss only a few (interested readers are referred to Gabriel et al., 2019; Sonnentag et al., 2012). One of the strengths of ESM in comparison with longitudinal studies that traditionally span over much longer time intervals is the possibility of testing short-term stress processes. Stress theories in the psychological tradition (see Chapter 1) highlight the role of appraisals of stressors and coping abilities in understanding strain. Because appraisal processes occur rapidly and may be fluctuating, an ESM design with brief intervals between assessments of stressors, appraisals and strain, is appropriate. Furthermore, workers' level of stressors and strain vary day-to-day. During a day or a work week a worker can experience an episodic encounter of a heated argument and conflict with their colleague on a Tuesday and a deadline that is pressing at the end of the week. The worker's appraisals of stress and coping ability may vary accordingly, resulting in higher reported strain on Tuesday and at the end of the week.

Importantly, ESM designs also allow researchers to investigate temporal dynamics of the stress process. For example, does the intensity of strain change during a workday, a work week or after a weekend? As part of one of the research questions in an ESM study by Hülsheger (2016), workers responded to fatigue-related items in a survey four times a day during a full week. The results suggested that fatigue, across individuals and days, showed a U-shaped pattern, with an initial reduction and then increasing toward the evening. Researchers interested in trajectories across time may further investigate if trajectories related to stressors and strain show the same patterns for all or depend upon individual and situational factors. Thus, ESM allows testing within-persons variability as well as between-persons variability in these short-term processes.

While ESM opens up for testing theoretical predictions regarding within-persons variability and temporal dynamics, there are also some caveats. One measurement issue worth considering is the potential fatigue of the respondents when using frequent measurement points with multiple items. There is no easy fix to this problem, as trimming the survey items might impact the validity of the constructs of interest. Another current problem is to calculate the statistical power and sufficient sample size to detect real effects, as there are few guidelines to adhere to (Gabriel et al., 2019). Nevertheless, ESM research opens up for exciting new possibilities in both testing and advancing stress theories.

Longitudinal Research Design

There is still a lack of consensus on what constitutes a longitudinal study. One of the discussion points addresses the sufficient number of observations required to be called a longitudinal study. According to the definition by Ployhart and Vandenberg (2010) longitudinal research is 'research emphasizing the study of change and containing at minimum three repeated observations (although more than three is better) on at least one of the substantive constructs of interest' (p. 97). Thus, according to this definition, longitudinal studies are appropriate when we seek to understand either how constructs change over time and how one construct influence change in another construct (Ployhart & Vandenberg, 2010). Others, such as Wang et al. (2017), regard Ployhart and Vandenberg's definition as overly narrow and restrictive as the definition excludes prospective designs that still may provide insights into causal processes and change. Likewise, the editorial of WS also argued for the use of at least two observations for one of the constructs in the study when addressing intra-individual change (Taris et al., 2021).

While most would adhere to 'the more, the better', in a realistic world this is not always possible. It is more important to align the number of observations with the given research question/hypothesis and consider the methodological limitation of the chosen design. For example, with the use of two waves of observation, change always needs to be considered linear and further, would limit the possibility of disentangling measurement error from the true change (Singer & Willett, 2003). The use of three or more observations over time of the same constructs allows more complex investigations of the stress process that develops over time, as is suggested by theoretical models (Frese & Zapf, 1988). Given that most longitudinal studies in occupational stress studies are limited to two observations (Ford et al., 2014), there is a great opportunity to empirically investigate and expand our knowledge on the temporal dynamics of the stress process.

Longitudinal studies also allow for testing of *reciprocal effects*. That is where strain at one time point can predict stressors at a later time point, controlling for stressor levels at the first measurement time point (Ford et al., 2014). For example, an employee suffering from early experiences of burnout, may, as a result, experience limited or no improvement in the working conditions, which may facilitate a perceived increase of stressors. This means that such reciprocal effects occur when individuals' strain levels contribute to an increase in stressors over time. Unfortunately, there is limited empirically based guidance to what may be appropriate time frames for reverse causation effects (reciprocal effects) to develop as well as how they may change over time (Ford et al., 2014). A meta-analysis (Guthier et al., 2020) of 48 longitudinal studies on the stressor–strain relationship (stressor-effect) and the reverse causal strain–stressor relationship (strain-effect), found support for reciprocal effects between stressors and strain (i.e., burnout), where the *strain-effect* was larger compared to the stressor-effect. Further, the strain-effect was reduced (moderated) by job resources (support and control). When investigating the reciprocal effects of the three burnout dimensions, a reciprocal relationship was only found for emotional exhaustion, depersonalization/cynicism, and stressors, although depersonalization/cynicism was not directly related to stressors at another time point. The authors advised researchers to increase the range of time intervals employed as well as the frequency of stressor assessments, to enhance the understanding of the reciprocal effect of strain on stressors. The importance of analyzing other moderating variables of strain effects was also emphasized (Guthier et al., 2020), and others have emphasized the potential of also exploring mediating variables in stressor-strain relationships (e.g., Rubino et al., 2009). Specifically, where the reciprocal effects of strain on stressors may not necessarily only occur directly, strain-effects may have a reciprocal effect on potential mediating variables, such as employee motivation (autonomous or controlled).

Time Interval Issues/Temporal Aspects of the Stress Process

The temporal process of stress, that is, how stressors affect physiological and psychological strain over time, may unfold within the range of milliseconds to a lifespan. Thus, the effect of stressors may occur synchronous or have various lagged effects across different types of strain (Ford et al., 2014). Likewise, interventions aimed at mitigating the negative effects of stress may be expected to work almost immediately or not kick in before several months or years have passed. Given this wide time range, it becomes paramount that researchers define the appropriate time interval to assess the effects of stressors on diverse types of strains or the effect of interventions in mitigating strain. Unfortunately, there are few detailed theoretical propositions regarding time frame and few general empirical guidelines to adhere to when deciding the appropriate time interval for data collection (Tetrick, 2017). As a consequence, time lags are 'determined more by convenience or tradition than by theory or careful research' (Cole & Maxwell, 2003, p. 563). The consequence of inaccurate time lags between data observations is that true relationships are underestimated or, in worst case, not detected (Scholz, 2019).

How can these matters be solved? There is a general need to refine theories to give a more precise indication of how processes unfold over time (Kelloway & Francis, 2012; Mitchell & James, 2001; Ployhart & Vandenberg, 2010). Frese and Zapf (1988) proposed an overall framework of how effects of stress may play out over time that may inspire theoretical developments of temporal issues within work stress. Several theories within the stress literature include a temporal dimension and some of these temporal aspects have been empirically tested. For example, of theoretical (and practical) interest is the question of whether the effects of stressors on strain accumulate or if workers adapt to stressors resulting in reduced strain over time. Currently, there is support for both scenarios. The meta-analysis of cross-lagged studies by Ford et al. (2014) provided support for the proposed accumulated effect of stressors on strain over time, and the adjustment reaction to stress has also been supported by longitudinal studies (Matthews et al., 2014; Ritter et al., 2016). Clearly, our understanding of the dynamical stress process as it unfolds over time is worth exploring in future studies.

There are other temporal aspects in stress theories worth examining. For example, COR theory suggests that resource gain and loss spirals over time gain in magnitude and momentum and are distinct in their form and pace (Hobfoll et al., 2018). While research within the COR theory have explored the role of time in these spirals, there is still a lack of precise theoretical temporal frameworks that can inform researchers about the expected latency between each iteration in the spirals. For example, an increasing gain in momentum might suggest that researchers need to decrease the time intervals between data observations at the end of the assumed spiral to fully capture the dynamic development of the spirals.

There are also methodological considerations to the time interval issues. Taris and Kompier (2014) have suggested that researchers need to be explicit about the theoretical reason for choosing a specific time lag when describing their research design. If the theoretical foundation is lacking, Taris and Kompier (2014) advice researchers to increase the number of measurement points with relative shorter time latencies between measurement points. Dormann and Griffin (2015) also suggested that time lags between measurement points are generally too long, and that researchers would benefit from estimating the optimal time lags in their studies. Meta-analyses on the lagged effects of stressors and strain (e.g., Ford et al., 2014; Sonnentag & Frese, 2012), have reached different conclusions regarding the appropriate time span to capture lagged effects. While Ford et al. (2014) advocate for a three year span, Sonnentag and Frese (2012) suggest a shorter time span of one year to capture effects of stressors on strain. Future research should investigate the various temporal effects of stressors that surely depend upon the type, intensity, and duration of the stressor and the various types of strain, and should use a sufficiently large sample (N> 800) to have sufficient statistical power to capture the oftentimes small effects (Ford et al., 2014).

Multilevel Modeling

Multilevel modeling methods (e.g., Bliese et al., 2007; Bliese & Jex, 2002; Gulseren & Kelloway, 2019; Raudenbush & Bryk, 2002) and related software (e.g., HLM, Mplus, R) are intriguing in that they facilitate the opportunity to explicitly account for the nested nature of the data. Data collected in the field of organizational stress are commonly nested, which means that employees can be embedded within a particular social group, such as nested within direct leaders/immediate work groups/departments, which again are nested within organizations (Bliese & Jex, 2002). Such data belong at different levels of analysis and require using analytical techniques (e.g., multilevel structural equation modeling) to model the embedded structures. In line with a levels perspective (Kozlowski & Klein, 2000), the *individual* is often referred to as the lowest level of analysis (Level 1; within the groups), and the *leader/immediate work group* are examples of the next highest level (Level 2; primary social groups); however, the designated level depends on the research design (Bliese & Jex, 2002; Kath et al., 2016). Although we emphasize two levels of nesting here, it is sometimes meaningful to estimate models with more than two levels of analysis (see for example Snijders & Bosker, 1999). Multilevel modeling can also be applied for data that is measured repeatedly (e.g., ESM data of daily recovery experiences), i.e., multiple observations that are nested within individuals (see for example Bliese & Ployhart, 2002; Singer & Willett, 2003).

Multilevel analysis may be relevant in addressing various research questions related to for instance process hypotheses (e.g., multilevel mediation), moderation hypotheses predicting an effect of Level 2 variables on Level 1 variable relationships, as well as testing hypotheses predicting more complex multilevel models of mediated moderation or moderated mediation (Tetrick, 2017). Previous multilevel research has addressed research questions including, for example, how group-level variables may explain differences in individual stressor-strain reactions and individual coping, how stressors play a role in understanding work team functioning, and how team burnout emerges (e.g., Jex & Bliese, 1999; Kamphuis et al., 2021; Razinskas & Hoegl, 2019; Urien et al., 2021). Based on a review of the multilevel stressor literature, Razinskas and Hoegl (2019) presented a multilevel framework suggesting that individual-level stressors (e.g., workload, relation-ships at work, work-home interface) influence team performance-relevant outcomes (e.g., teamwork behaviors) in team members through two alternative mechanisms – strain-based processes (e.g., burnout) or behavior-based processes (e.g., motivation). Team-level stressors' (e.g., team workload, team role ambiguity, team climate) influence on team performance (e.g., team effectiveness, team innovation) was indicated to happen through either identity-based processes (e.g., team cohesion) or information-based processes (e.g., team communication). In turn, team level identity-based processes (e.g., team identifica-tion) affected lower-level effects of stressors either by moderation or indirectly by acti-vating individual-level moderators (e.g., perceptions of in and out groups). This framework clearly illustrates the relevance of multilevel approaches to better understand what is going on across different levels of analysis.

The review also revealed that research investigating antecedents of stressors at both individual and team levels was scarce, illustrating the need for further multilevel research to identify such antecedents from a multilevel perspective. Another relevant topic for future multilevel stressor-outcomes research is to consider the role of homogeneity versus heterogeneity in individual/collective perceptions of stressors (Razinskas & Hoegl, 2019). This brings us to the next section where we present the potential value of person-based methods, which facilitate investigation of the role and formation of subgroups.

THE PERSON-BASED ANALYTICAL APPROACH

Spicer (1997) and others (e.g., Tetrick, 2017; Wang et al., 2013) have drawn a distinction between variable-based and person-based methods in research on stress. Variable-based designs formulate research questions around a set of constructs that reflect certain aspects of how individuals function, but they tend to reduce the dynamics of the stress process 'to patterns of empirical relationships [between variables] which can be accommodated in multivariate statistical analyses' (Spicer, 1997, p. 168). For example, in predicting outcomes using the challenge-hindrance stressor framework (Cavanaugh et al., 2000; LePine, 2022), researchers typically investigate the influence of challenge and hindrance stressors on certain strain and/or well-being outcomes. Variable-based methods may be limited when the research question concerns how subgroups differ from each other or whether the participants are from qualitatively different subgroups (Leiter & Maslach, 2016; Wang et al., 2013). For such research questions, person-centered analytical approaches, such as latent class analysis (LCA) and latent profile analysis (LPA), are especially helpful because they provide the possibility of grouping individuals into categories (subgroups) based on observed categorical variables (i.e., LCA) or continuous variables (i.e., LPA; Spurk et al., 2020; Wang et al., 2013). Person-based analytical methods position individual characteristics and/or environmental attributes as the central focus of analysis 'to study configurations or patterns of psychological characteristics that a group of people share in common' (Wang et al., 2013, p. 350). Thus, the main goal of this person-centered approach is to identify latent profiles (groups/classes) of individuals based on certain variables (e.g., work-family conflict and work-family enrichment), to investigate patterns of covariation among the variables and then study differences between these profiles/groups on outcomes such as strain and well-being (Spurk et al., 2020). This can also be done in the form of a longitudinal person-centered approach (Fan et al., 2019; Nagin et al., 2018).

Methodologies using this approach can yield certain advantages over traditional variable-centered approaches, including the opportunity to test population heterogeneity and homogeneity. They are also suitable for comparing theories from various perspectives, and they have practical value in terms of being more interpretable and reliable when it comes to group classification results (Wang et al., 2013). The need for variable-based research when investigating work-related stress is, however, not disputed. Rather, variable-based methods, which have been fundamental to much research on work stress, may be complimented by person-centered research to further explore the dynamics of the job stress process in subgroups and over time. To exemplify, drawing on the JD-R framework (Bakker & Demerouti, 2007, 2017), Fan et al. (2019) applied a person-centered methodological approach to identify profiles of job demands and job resources over time to predict changes in employee well-being over a time period of 18 months. The findings suggested five profiles of job demands and job resources: *high strain/low hours, high strain/low hours/shift work, high strain/long hours, active (high demands, high control),* and *lower strain (lower demands, high control).* Workers in the lower strain profile reported decreased psychological distress, emotional exhaustion, and work-family conflict, and increased job satisfaction over time. On the other hand, the employees in the high strain profile and the active profile indicated worse experiences on the same outcomes. It is interesting that the study was able to present a more nuanced understanding of how demands and resources co-occur as well as the implications of these co-occurrences for changes in strain and well-being outcomes.

Another example is the study conducted by Leiter and Maslach (2016), in which they used person-centered analysis to investigate two large datasets (Studies 1 and 2) of individuals in order to identify profiles along the burnout – engagement continuum (measured with the MBI; see Chapter 5 about burnout). Studying latent burnout profiles is relevant because it may identify various groups (profiles) of burnout and may facilitate knowledge on early warning signs (e.g., negative scores on only one burnout dimension) of burnout. From the analysis five profiles emerged: *Burnout* (group of individuals scoring high on all three dimensions of burnout), *Engagement* (group of individuals scoring low on all three burnout dimensions), *Overextended* (group of individuals scoring high on exhaustion only), *Disengaged* (group of individuals scoring high on cynicism only; in Study 2 high on both cynicism and exhaustion), and *Ineffective* (group of individuals scoring high on inefficacy only). These profiles were also found to have distinct relationships with different organizational variables (i.e., workload, resources, social context, and satisfaction), suggesting a requirement of more unique intervention strategies (Leiter & Maslach, 2016). An interesting finding was that exhaustion alone (Overextended profile) does not seem to be a sufficient condition for burnout given that the Burnout profile did indicate more negative outcome experiences (workload etc.). Also, the Ineffective profile was shown to represent a large proportion of both study samples, which points to the importance of giving this group more attention in future research.

Another interesting approach to person-centered analytical methods is the focus on profiles of daily experiences based on ESM data. To illustrate, in a study of full-time employees, Chawla et al. (2020) found five profiles of daily recovery experiences (i.e., *plugged in, controlled non-mastery recovering, moderately unplugged, non-mastery recovering, unplugged*) which were differently related to within-person antecedents (e.g., job demands) and outcomes (e.g., sleep quality, emotional exhaustion). Also, the profiles were dynamic in that most participants were classified in more than one profile during a week, and the researchers found that it was the job demands, not job resources that seemed to determine profile membership. This novel approach could potentially enlighten future research to include measures of daily, weekly, or monthly coping with stressors.

In sum, for a growing number of researchers, person-based methods offer a number of advantages for understanding constellations of variables that may be useful to enhance definitions of situational characteristics and offer meaningful measures of contextual attributes (Tetrick, 2017). However, we believe that it may be important to replicate the findings indicated in such studies and also explore other relevant antecedents and outcomes than the ones addressed so far. Studies such as the ones conducted by Fan et al. (2019), Leiter and Maslach (2016), as well as Chawla et al. (2020) found support for profiles found in the occupational groups and contexts that they investigated. However, future studies would have to clarify if the same profiles are evident in other occupational groups, contexts, and situations, and it is also relevant to clarify how profile members change their profile membership over time using latent transition analysis (Kam et al., 2016). Another relevant thought for future research on stressors to consider is that person-based methods may clarify the inconsistent findings (LePine, 2022) typically found between challenge/hindrance stressors and various outcomes.

OBJECTIVE MEASUREMENT ISSUES

As reviewed in Chapter 4, the accumulated work suggests that stressors are linked with numerous physical indicators of deteriorated health in line with the allostatic load model. Nevertheless, there is room for improvement in the research concerning physiological measurements. One concern raised by Ganster et al. (2018) is the construct validity of physiological indicators. Accordingly, '…researchers must determine which AL [allostatic load] process their research question is representing; identify appropriate physiological markers for that specific process; and lastly, establish when, in what manner, and how many times to assess the physiological marker of interest, given that specific process' (Ganster et al., 2018, p. 271). A challenge in the measurement of physiological responses to stressors is that the same response may represent different constructs depending on its measurement (Ganster et al., 2018). Rather than assessing certain types of strain simply because they fall into recognized categories or have been examined in previous studies of job stress, researchers should give as much thought to selection of an appropriate strain index as they have to identifying the nature and characteristics of the stressors themselves. In short, careful consideration should be given to the specific reactions (strains) that would be anticipated in response to specific stressors. Related to the discussion regarding time interval issues, researchers also need to consider the specific timing and duration of the physiological markers that is needed to capture the physiological process as it unfolds (Akinola et al., 2019).

The technological advances in physiological measures provide ample opportunities for using noninvasive equipment that is suited for measuring physiological indicators of stress in the workplace (Akinola et al., 2019). For example, Baethge et al. (2020) investigated heart rate variability trajectories during workdays, and found different types of trajectories depending on the level of co-worker support. While the inclusion of measurement of physiological data in research can elucidate how stressors encountered at work can increase the wear and tear on the body, Akinola (2010) discusses conceptual, technical, and ethical considerations worthy of exploration when using physiological measurement.

1   Inconsistencies between self-report and physiological responses. Inclusion of physiological indicators may pose challenges in how to interpret contradictory findings relying on subjective versus objective data.
2   The same physiological indicator may represent different psychological states and constructs. This decreases the ability to infer from physiological measures to psychological concepts.
3   Knowledge and training in using physiological measures. The rapid development of such measures may entail collaboration between researchers with different backgrounds, giving ample opportunity of integrating research findings from different fields.

4   Ethical considerations. The use of knowledge that accumulates from investigating physiological responses should be helpful to the members of the organization and not used against them.

Other forms of objective measurement, for example EEG and fMRI have already been discussed briefly in Chapter 2. We refer the interested reader to the special issue on organizational neuroscience published in Organizational Research Methods in 2019 to get a deeper insight to various neuroscientific methods and techniques which may be applied in job stress research (Murray & Antonakis, 2019).

QUALITATIVE METHODOLOGICAL ISSUES

The majority of studies on organizational stress have applied a quantitative approach despite the fact that such studies are not without limitations (Mazzola et al., 2011). One limitation of quantitative research is that due to the structured and pre-defined instruments used to collect data, quantitative researchers may end up ignoring what respondents experience as the most important stressors and strains or how they cope with stressors (Keenan & Newton, 1985; Schonfeld & Chang, 2017). Qualitative data may be particularly helpful to discover important aspects concerning stressors, stress, strain, and coping, which were not initially thought of by the researcher. Thus, qualitative research adds depth to quantitative results by facilitating a more detailed and perhaps previously overlooked understanding of individual experiences at work (Mazzola et al., 2011; Schonfeld & Mazzola, 2013). Qualitative organizational stress research may also facilitate theory development, hypothesis generation, and understanding of quantitative findings that are difficult to interpret, provide a basis for item development for quantitative studies, discovering additional stressors and/or coping strategies, provide rich descriptions of work environments, as well as facilitate an understanding of why interventions succeed or fail (Schonfeld & Chang, 2017; Schonfeld & Mazzola, 2013).

Qualitative research embraces several methods which commonly collect vocalizations and text instead of numbers, and the data is typically analyzed in the form of expressed experiences (e.g., of stressors and or strains) and natural language in the form of words (Greene et al., 1989; Levitt et al., 2018; Spector & Pindek, 2016). Through an iterative process of inferences, identifying patterns which are tied to instances of a phenomenon (e.g., stress), these patterns help to inform a sense of the whole phenomenon (Levitt et al., 2018; ; Schonfeld & Mazzola, 2013).

Compared to quantitative data, qualitative data sets are usually drawn from fewer participants. Such data facilitate detailed, rich, and highly contextualized descriptions from each respondent to explore specific stories or settings in which experiences appear and to explore processes and how events unfold over time (e.g., retrospective event history). Rather than requiring that the finding should hold across all contexts or instead of verifying hypotheses, they engender open-ended discovery (Levitt et al., 2018; Spector & Pindek, 2016).

In the organizational stress literature, qualitative methods are appealing due to their applicability to both identify and discover stressors (Schonfeld & Farrell, 2010; Schonfeld & Mazzola, 2013). In their review of qualitative studies about organizational stress, Mazzola et al. (2011) found that stressors experienced at work were reported more commonly than stressors in other role areas. Further, workplace stress was found to occur almost daily, and the most common stressor appeared to be *interpersonal conflict* with various sources (colleagues, customers, leaders, followers, students, and patients). There were also important differences in experiences of stressors as a result of nationality, occupation, and gender. For example, women more commonly reported stressors related to interpersonal events compared to men, and employees in individualist cultures seemed more likely to experience lack of autonomy and work overload compared to employees in collectivist cultures (China and India), who were found to experience more of organizational constraints and stressors related to evaluation and recognition. The review also found that level of experience (i.e., being early in the career versus later with gained experience) may matter in terms of employees' experiences of different stressors (e.g., work-home balance versus administrative problems). Reactions to stressors in terms of anger and annoyance were more typical in English speaking countries, while in China, tension and anxiety were more likely reactions. In terms of frequently reported coping strategies, social support (e.g., talking with someone), problem-focused coping (e.g., dealing with the situation), and emotion focused coping (e.g., ignoring the stressor, wishful thinking) were frequently mentioned, although which ones were more effective was not explored. While these qualitative findings correspond to some extent with those of quantitative research, they do add more depth, understanding, and ideas for future research. For example, given that organizational stress in qualitative studies has been found to occur almost daily, ESM studies may further explore the stressors that occur in a given time frame (a day, week, month, year), interactions between various stressors (at work and other areas), experienced strains, and how stressors are managed in employee's daily life (Mazzola et al., 2011). Also, there may be variations in findings according to occupational groups. In another study, Schonfeld and Mazzola (2015) explored this further, and conducted a qualitative study involving 54 self-employed entrepreneurs from various solo businesses to identify stressful incidents, coping strategies, and emotional strain that the participants experienced. The study is interesting because self-employed employees, which is an occupational group not often investigated, may be more prone to stress and subsequent strain, particularly at times of downturns in the economy or during crisis situations such as the COVID-19 pandemic. Although the finding indicated that this occupational group experienced many of the same stressors (e.g., interpersonal conflict and constraints) as those commonly reported in other studies, the respondents described greater *income or job threat* compared to employees who are organizationally employed (Mazzola et al., 2011). The self-employed workers also experienced strains such as apprehension/anxiety, frustration, and anger, which have been frequently reported by organizational employees (Schonfeld & Mazzola, 2015). In terms of coping with stressors, the study indicated that the participants seemed to rely on various sources, including themselves (mainly problem-focused coping), others helping the participants (e.g., supportive colleagues), as well as a novel coping strategy in the form of humanitarian behavior (i.e., doing good). These study findings may be relevant also for other occupational groups such as contracted work or gig work which we will discuss more in Chapter 10. What the self-employed workers have in common with contract workers is that they typically lack human resource departments which facilitate stress management programs that can help protect the self-employed from detrimental negative stress-related outcomes.

What is perhaps not so clear from qualitative research on organizational stress so far is the role of positive stress, what characterizes the experience of stressors as challenging or hindering, and how such experiences may fluctuate. Given the role of cognition and perception in the stress process and the potential role of cognitive-emotional factors underlying and influencing the stress process over time, qualitative research may add more in-depth knowledge than what is possible to accomplish with quantitative research. We encourage future research to investigate these aspects further.

MIXED METHODS APPROACHES

It is important to recognize that as the complexity of theoretical models increases, the measurement of certain aspects of those models may require the use of qualitative methods (Mazzola et al., 2011), or at the very least a combination of methods. Inferring the process of the individual's interpretation – a requirement frequently imposed by quantitative methods – in place of capturing the meaning from the person making it, fails to facilitate any understanding of those contextual issues fundamental to making meaningful progress toward an understanding of the stress process. Again, the need is for a more balanced approach that recognizes the usefulness of data generated by different methods (Spector & Pindek, 2016).

Quantitative and qualitative approaches both represent legitimate methodologies for work stress research. They should not be considered mutually exclusive (Morley & Luthans, 1984). Many issues need to be explored when considering the type of method to be employed, and sole reliance on a single method may result in an inability to explore certain dimensions of the stress experience (Mazzola et al., 2011). Combining quantitative and qualitative methods can be beneficial in many ways. For example, qualitative data may help to elaborate on the findings of initial quantitative data, as well as be helpful in the initial process of developing quantitative measures. The strength of such a mixed method approach is that the strengths of one method may offset what may be considered a weakness of the other (Mazzola et al., 2011). Employing both data collection approaches to study the organizational stress process, engenders the opportunity to approach stress related phenomena from different perspectives and in novel ways to facilitate a more complete picture (Schonfeld & Chang, 2017). One example of a mixed methods approach to study stress is the study on e-mail as a source of stress (Barley et al., 2011). The authors elegantly combined quantitative (i.e., communication logs and survey) and qualitative (i.e., in-depth interviews) data to explore the contradiction that technological communications may be experienced as negative stress in individuals' lives, at the same time as it facilitates flexibility and autonomy because it opens up for the opportunity to communicate at anytime from anywhere. The findings suggested that e-mail serves as a cultural symbol of overload, where more time used to handle e-mails created a greater sense of experiencing overload. In fact, e-mail was the only communication medium the informants blamed for the stress they experienced, thus it appeared to represent some kind of scapegoat for their overload. Further, the informants experienced a greater ability to cope the more e-mails they managed to process (often after work hours or in weekends). Therefore, overload (spending time on handling e-mail) seemed to be a combined product of the time spent on handling e-mails, felt anxieties (i.e., loss of control described in terms of two anxieties: *fear of failing* and *fear of missing important information*), social norms of responsiveness (e.g., strong cultural expectations about not leaving senders waiting), as well as non-controllable patterns of communication activities. Having a backlog of e-mail messages seemed to play an important role in engendering an experience of overload, particularly in circumstances of working across time zones and teleconferences. These novel insights were the result of the combined quantitative and qualitative methodological approaches. There has been significant technological developments since this study was conducted and we believe that future research could be inspired to explore the role of digital communication/media in organizational stress research from a mixed methods approach. For example, it may be relevant to further explore how mobile e-mail contributes to feelings of overload and/or feelings of achieving greater control (Barley et al., 2011). Also, one might explore under what circumstances such stressors (communication media) are appraised as hindering, challenging, and/or threatening to employees, and in turn what consequences they may have. There is a potential contradiction in that e-mails/communication media may facilitate an experience of flexibility and at the same time create negative stress, which suggests that it is a form of challenge stressor. A mixed methods approach could explore the potential ambivalent nature of such a challenge stressor, including its consequences (Widmer et al., 2012). In another interesting mixed methods study, Mazzola et al. (2011) investigated stressors and strains in graduate assistants. They combined qualitative critical incident questions (i.e., stress incident record, i.e., an open-ended measure of stressful events) with quantitative scales (measuring interpersonal conflict, organizational constraints, workload, and physical symptoms) to achieve a more complete insight to stressors and strain. The results of the study illustrate the relevance of combining qualitative and quantitative methods finding that the informants who reported a stressor qualitatively (e.g., interpersonal conflict) indicated a higher frequency of the stressor measured quantitatively. Also, those informants who had reported a stressful event qualitatively were found to experience more physical symptoms which were measured quantitatively.

Although there is not a single 'best way' of conducting research on job stress, we suggest that research on this important topic needs to move beyond the mere identification of different components in the stress process to more in-depth exploration of that process itself, especially the dynamic interplay between those components. Just as we have illustrated in the study examples presented above, there is an urgent need to consider how best to investigate the process and to use all the tools at our disposal to conduct meaningful research on stress in the workplace. Furthermore, if progress is to be made, future research must endeavor to close the gap between methodologies by (a) identifying common pathways along which research should now be directed and (b) reviewing whether current measurement practices actually reflect what we are trying to measure.

WHERE DO WE GO FROM HERE?

The ability of conventional methods to adequately unravel the stress process has been intensely debated, and the case for exploring alternative methods is gathering momentum. If understanding the stress process is best advanced by exploring individual meanings and appraisals, then researchers must consider methods that capture the richness of the process and the idiographic nature of the experience. This logic does not mean that one methodology should be replaced by another, nor does it mean that one methodology should be regarded as subordinate to another. Nevertheless, as a first step, several 'midrange' proposals can be advanced. A midrange strategy identifies ways in which conventional measurement practices can be reconsidered. At the same time, it explores how alternative methods can provide a framework for redeveloping current measurement practices. Two types of approach can be identified. The first can be described as the measurement refinement approach. This approach, though accepting the difficulties inherent in conventional self-report measures, claims that research can still benefit from examining how such measures can be refined to ensure a precision in measurement that continues to reflect our understanding of the different elements of the stress-coping process.

The second approach focuses on process issues and is linked closely with qualitative methodologies. This approach points to the complexity of the stress process and the fact that conventional measures may be too imprecise to capture this complexity. Measurement practices, if they are to contribute to our understanding of the stress process, should be free of the structural limitations imposed by traditional conventions. Only in this way can the essence of the stressful experience be truly examined.

These two approaches are not mutually exclusive. Qualitative techniques may represent the primary method of analysis when exploring the subtlety and richness of the stress-coping process. On the other hand, when the focus is on refining measures (which we turn to below), qualitative and quantitative techniques may best be used in combination to capture the reality of the situation and individuals' coping behaviors. Several steps can be taken to facilitate this convergence. These include, for example, (a) reviewing the nature and type of items to be measured; (b) determining the appropriateness of different response categories; (c) examining the way in which response scales are scored – that is, reconsidering the traditional linear additive model; and (d) evaluating the specificity of the stressor–strain relationship under consideration.

There is also a need to adopt methods of research and analytical approaches that are congruent with the theoretical platform upon which the research is based in the first place. Conventional methods of data collection, analysis, and interpretation may limit our ability to validly assess the dynamics of the stress-coping process. We do not advocate simply replacing these techniques with others; rather, we advocate questioning the directions in which current methods might take us and asking what alternative methods might offer. A combination of qualitative and quantitative methods may enable investigators to develop research strategies that benefit from the strengths of both types of approach and that provide more insight into the stress-coping process.

Refining Measures of Stressors, Strains, and Coping

Self-report measures of perceived work stressors (such as role ambiguity, conflict, and overload) have long been available, and psychometric evaluation of these measures suggests high construct validity and continuing usage. Paradoxically, however, the accessibility of such measures to some extent has diverted attention from the fact 'that the explanatory potential of such measures must lie in developing a better understanding of the constructs themselves' (Dewe, 2000, p. 14). Further, measures applied in quantitative variable-based research (e.g., surveys) where responses are collected to test empirical relationships between variables (e.g., stressors and strain), may be predictable a priori because of the semantics of the measurement items (Arnulf et al., 2014). Yet if researchers were to consider whose reality is being measured, perhaps the discussion would extend beyond the psychometric properties of such measures to a more systematic appraisal of the events that significantly impinge on the well-being of individuals: that is, how workers themselves describe the demands of their working lives and how these demands can best be identified. An illustration is provided by items that have traditionally been used to assess variables such as work overload and role conflict. Measures of these variables typically include items such as 'There is too much work to do in the time available', 'No matter how hard I work there always seems to be as much work at the end of the day as there was at the beginning', and 'Conflicting demands make it very difficult to get the work done'. However, empirical studies of these variables only infrequently have explored whether these sorts of events or pressures are ones that research participants themselves would identify as actual demands in their particular work setting. We need to consider, therefore, whether concern over the reliability of measures has taken precedence over their relevance to individuals' lives. Use of qualitative approaches (such as critical-incident interviewing) may assist in the development of taxonomies of work-related stressors that reflect the reality of those whose working lives are being investigated and comparison of these stressors with those most often studied in job stress research.

There is a tendency in job stress research to make inferences about individuals' experiences that may not be justified on the basis of the variables that are actually measured. Similarly, critical dimensions of those experiences are often left unassessed, such as the frequency of the experience, its intensity, its duration, and its ambivalence.

To obtain more comprehensive, and hence more valid, depictions of stressors in the workplace context, researchers may have to move beyond simplistic measurement practices to ones that incorporate the critical dimensions of workplace experiences. As noted above, these issues are not unfamiliar to job stress researchers, but to date relatively little attention appears to have been given to them in empirical studies of job-related stressors.

One potential reason for the absence of more complex assessments of stressors is confusion over what to do with the information once it is obtained. Again, using the above illustration, how should frequency, intensity, duration, and ambivalent responses be combined to derive an estimate of the overall extent of demand or pressure exerted by a particular stressor? For instance, should these responses be added (summative model) or multiplied (multiplicative model) in generating an overall demand score for each person, should each be treated as a separate response dimension, or would it be more appropriate to investigate subgroups (profiles) and their various experiences? Questions such as these continue to confound researchers searching for the most appropriate and relevant measures of workplace stressors.

A further issue to consider is whether assessments of stressors should focus on perceptions of the same or similar work stressors across occupational groups and organizational contexts or on occupation- or organization-specific stressors. The first approach enables comparison across groups and settings and therefore enhances the generalization of research findings. On the other hand, assessing stressors that are directly salient within the specific context being investigated, provides a more ecologically valid account of the demands and pressures actually experienced within that context and may better describe the effects of different work environments, as well as assisting with the development of targeted interventions to alleviate job-related strain and enhance employee thriving.

From a methodological standpoint, another issue of concern is the meaning of different stressors to individuals and whether some types of stressors are more salient or important than others. Typically, research on job-related stressors has used a linear additive model of stressors, combining them (or computing a mean score) to represent the total (or average) amount of stressors being experienced. This total or mean stressor score is then used as a predictor of strain. For instance, it is not uncommon in studies of stressors to combine responses representing various stressors into single indexes labeled 'hindrance stressors' and 'challenge stressors' (e.g., Cavanaugh et al., 2000; LePine, 2022). Even within the separate variables, items that represent separate (albeit related) aspects of the stressor are combined. Such an approach simplifies further statistical analyses by reducing a potentially large array of stressors into more useable and convenient 'bundles', perhaps even a single combined category. However, considerable information about individual stressors is lost when this procedure is adopted because total or mean scores give no indication of the patterns of responses that make up a 'score'. In fact, use of a total or mean score may divert attention from the different ways in which that score can be achieved and the different patterns of responses that individuals may exhibit. This approach may lead to the erroneous conclusion that individuals who manifest the same score have a common experience of the stressor, when in fact their experiences may vary considerably, as indicated by qualitative studies (Mazzola, et al. 2011).

Some scholars may argue that quantitative self-ratings represent the best way to capture the character and essence of demanding events. As we noted earlier, however, qualitative methodologies expose meaning rather than impose it, and they make no a priori assumptions about the nature of the data collected. Researchers need to show how a methodology generates knowledge or moves the field forward in ways that other methods do not. In essence, the requirement is to get researchers to consider what various methods have to offer and not to overstate the contribution of any single methodology.

Job stress researchers are certainly not unfamiliar with qualitative techniques (Barley et al., 2011; Mazzola et al., 2011; Schonfeld & Mazzola, 2015). But from use of different methods (e.g., critical-incident technique, structured interviews, open-ended questions), the general conclusion appears to be that the potential of such approaches needs to be further explored (Spector & Pindek, 2016). Other researchers have combined qualitative and quantitative methods (e.g., Barley et al., 2011; Mazzola et al., 2011). The motivation for this sort of research has been to develop a familiarity with the goals, assumptions, and standards of qualitative methods, as well as to acknowledge that they offer valuable insights into the stress-coping process that may not be obtainable via other research strategies.

Conclusion

Several important themes concerning research strategies and methodologies have been discussed in this chapter. Process issues cannot be easily separated from measure refinement, simply because sound measures are the cornerstone of any attempt to understand stress coping. The fundamental question concerns how the process might be most effectively studied. Given the dynamic nature of stress-coping processes, longitudinal data collection would appear to represent an effective research strategy because it provides the opportunity to clarify causal relationships that are otherwise indeterminable through cross-sectional analysis (Kahn & Byosiere, 1992). Whether longitudinal research is best operationalized through quantitative or qualitative techniques is still part of the current debate, but the inclusion of techniques such as qualitative time diaries and multiple measurement procedures would certainly expand the scope of research investigations and generate a richer understanding of stress process.

This chapter has been concerned with how empirical research on the organizational stress process is conducted, and it has raised some issues relating to measurement (of stressors, strains, and coping behaviors), levels of analysis, analytical approaches, and the design of stress-coping studies. As we have noted, a critical concern is to ensure that research in this field makes progress toward an understanding of the contextual richness of the stress-coping process. To achieve this understanding, it is important for researchers to confront two primary questions: 'Whose reality is being assessed?' and

'Do our measures and related analytical approaches actually focus on the key components of stress processes?' Here we have examined some of the major issues that surround these questions and have suggested that multiple approaches to the assessment of stress are required to enable the construction of comprehensive theories and models of stress. In the final chapter, we turn attention to some elements of work and employment relationships, highlighting the potential effects that new kinds of work arrangements may exert on individuals' lives and the consequences for their experience of stress and their overall well-being.

10

THE CHANGING NATURE OF WORK

Implications for Stress Research

In this book, we have outlined and discussed critical features of the stress-coping process as it manifests itself in work organizations. Specifically, throughout the book, we have applied various stress-related theoretical frameworks to examine the nature of stress in the workplace, some of the more salient sources of stress (*stressors*), along with individuals' responses or experiences (*strains*, including burnout; *thriving*), and possible outcomes of strain and thriving, such as absenteeism and turnover within the organization, performance, and the overall diminution or enhancement of personal well-being. We have also reviewed potential moderators or buffers and mediators of stressor-strain/stressor-thriving relationships. Finally, we have considered how job-related strain might be counteracted at both the individual level (personal coping) and the organizational level (stress management interventions).

Throughout the previous chapters, we have emphasized methodological issues surrounding research on job stress and have provided illustrations of well-conducted studies, as well as pointing to some of the limitations inherent in stress research. Clearly, knowledge about stress-coping processes and how to alleviate strain is fundamentally dependent upon the quality of research that is carried out. As we have illustrated, however, there is considerable room for enhancing the design and execution of workplace stress research; hopefully, the issues raised in this volume and the examples discussed will contribute to critical thinking and debate, as well as sharpening the focus of research in this arena. In this final chapter, our intention is twofold: first, to draw together the threads of information, knowledge, and suggestions that have been outlined in previous chapters in light of the changing nature of work and new work arrangements; and second, to advance some reflections and recommendations about directions for future research on job stress.

In addition to other factors that have been referred to as sources of work-related strain, a further issue that is highly relevant for stress research, and that numerous commentators have reflected upon in recent years, is the changing nature of work and careers that we constantly embark upon. The past half century has seen enormous changes in the nature of society, and of the workplace in particular. Also, the COVID-19 pandemic has contributed to accelerate a transition from the regular bureaucratic employment model of organizing work – defined as work which is executed on a fixed schedule under the organizations' control and at its' place of business – to organizing work based on flexible work and task allocation, as well as flexible and alternative work arrangements (Bal & Izak, 2020; Kalleberg et al., 2000; Norgate & Cooper, 2020; Spreitzer et al., 2017). We must consider the implications of these developments for the experience of strain as well as thriving. The general thrust of these changes has been summarized by Cascio and Montealegre (2016, p. 350), who depicted the new environment as 'a new kind of world', and by Spreitzer, Cameron, and Garrett (2017, p. 493), who referred to it as the 'new world of work' which 'will require much more from (workers) than work ever has and may even take everything they've got' (Ashford et al., 2018, p. 24). Some of the implications of the transition to alternative ways of working and the increased working from home (WFH) situation are still unknown. In this chapter, we will draw upon what we know so far and what may be important issues for future research.

Several environmental, economic, political, sociocultural, and global health-related forces can be identified as shaping the way in which work arrangements (and hence jobs) are being restructured. A major reason for the emergence of new forms of working is the rapid development and implementation of new technologies (Cascio & Montealegre, 2016). These new technologies have revolutionized ways of working, as well as the structure and functioning of organizations themselves. Although computerization and digital transformation has affected the world of work for almost three decades, and some of the dramatic changes witnessed in the 1990s were already beginning to surface in the previous decade, the exponential rate of technological change observed more recently (Cascio & Montealegre, 2016; Vargas Llave et al., 2020) has, we would argue, outstripped efforts to develop sociotechnical perspectives that integrate human needs and values into the management of jobs and organizations. In short, we suggest that work today is driven predominantly by the technological imperative rather than by holistic perspectives that also take account of personal, social, and cultural issues within societies.

There is also the dual issue of unemployment and underemployment, generated by economic and structural transitions within societies. Increased rates of unemployment have been recorded since the 1980s in many societies and continues today. From a base level of 188 million unemployed in 2019, the International Labour Organization (ILO, 2020a) has estimated a rise in global unemployment of approximately 5.3 million to 24.7 million. Although such estimates may be uncertain, global unemployment is expected to rise (ILO, 2020a). Underemployment is a form of time-related employment situation (e.g., seasonal, casual), in which people are employed for a limited time although they are willing or need to work more. This situation is often inadequate economically and preventing people from generating sufficient income (Dooley, 2003; ILO, 2012).

When coupled with the introduction and development of new technologies that require less human input to achieve the same level of work output, the flow-on effects may continue to be considerable. Simultaneously, for many workers who have retained their jobs, the actual amount of work time available has declined and is estimated to continue to decline among millions of employees across the globe (ILO, 2020d). Also, the scope of work has diminished as technology has assumed increasing responsibility, control, and monitoring over employees and their outputs (Cascio & Montealegre, 2016).

In the new world of work, more and more organizations buy many of the skills they need on a contract basis from either individuals working at home and linked to the company by computers and mobile devices (teleworking) or by individuals hired on short-term contracts to do specific jobs or carry out specific projects (Spreitzer et al., 2017). In this way, companies are able to maintain the flexibility they need to cope with rapidly changing organizational realities (Cooper & Lu, 2019). All the trends are in the direction of the 'contingent workforce' or contract working, which clearly influences the employment relationship between individuals and organizations. Accordingly, compared to the traditional job with 'normal' work hours and co-located spaces, it is more and more common that employees are virtually connected to a physical workspace often with temporary contracts (Ashford et al., 2018; Fisher & Connelly, 2016; Spreitzer et al., 2017). These forms of *underemployment* have been found to be both pervasive and significant in their impact on the psychosocial well-being of individual employees (Cascio & Montealegre, 2016; Dooley, 2003).

As a result of the forces described above, three major types of change within organizations have been observed over the past decades – mergers, acquisitions, and downsizing. Organizational stress theory (e.g., transactional theory of stress) has to some extent been applied to investigate their impact on stress coping and well-being (Rafferty & Griffin, 2006). Together, they represent efforts on the part of organizations worldwide to improve their chances of survival in a competitive global environment and to increase their productivity (and hence profitability). The impacts of mergers and acquisitions are sometimes considered together (Finkelstein & Cooper, 2021), in particular their effect on the number of workers employed and the social and psychological outcomes of organizational restructuring. Bereavement in itself is considered to be a universally stressful life event, and a merger or acquisition can be a form of organizational bereavement. However, at the same time that employees may be dealing with feelings of loss, they have to cope with the uncertainty associated with major organizational change. Support for leaders during such organizational change has been found to be important, because employees then experience less psychological uncertainty (Rafferty & Griffin, 2006). Downsizing of organizations is another specific organizational change which has resulted in heavy job losses in many occupational sectors and hence a substantial increase in the amount of psychological strain due to job insecurity and unemployment (Foster et al., 2019; ILO, 2020a). Employees in positions that traditionally have been considered quite stable and secure, such as managerial-level jobs, more commonly experience the uncertainty and strain associated with either actual loss of their position (and career!) or at least the possibility of redundancy.

The COVID-19 crisis has led to challenges for most organizations due to the upended economies. The pandemic has sparked a considerable reduction in activity or closure of numerous businesses, particularly in the aviation, tourism, hospitality, sports, and entertainment industries, in order to reduce the spread of the virus (ILO, 2020d; Kniffin et al., 2021). As a result of governmental decisions and recommendations around the world, many employees have been forced to work from home, in temporary or partial unemployment (ILO, 2020e). In countries where employees are lacking unemployment benefits or income support, there is a risk of both increased poverty and inequalities (ILO, 2020e; Kniffin et al., 2021). The resulting unemployment, layoffs and economic inequality are expected to have more far-reaching impacts on employee stress, health, and well-being than in 'normal times' (Bapuji et al., 2020; ILO, 2020d; Kniffin et al., 2021; McKee-Ryan et al., 2005; Paul & Moser, 2009).

ALTERNATIVE FORMS OF WORK ARRANGEMENTS

As a result of the internal and external forces impinging upon organizations, several new forms of employment relationships have emerged. The outcomes of these new relationships, especially for individuals directly affected by them, are extensively researched to achieve a broader understanding. Still, the fast pacing changing nature of work, paves the way for several unanswered questions and a need for new and evidence-based knowledge. One of the key agendas for future stress research will be to explore these effects more systematically and to generate viable suggestions for counteracting the potential negative impact that the changing nature of work exerts on individuals and their families, as well as on employing organizations. Here we will highlight some of the more evident, and perhaps more influential, changes in organization–worker relationships that have surfaced over the past 30 years or so. First, we briefly review the nature of these changes; then we discuss their likely implications for the health and well-being of individuals and society as a whole.

In addition to restructuring of the workforce, another reaction from many organizations to the changed economic climate has been to move toward a two-tiered workforce of *traditional* (or *standard/core*) and *alternative work arrangement (or contingent)* employees (Mas & Pallais, 2020; Spreitzer et al., 2017). The traditional employee works full-time, is not self-employed, has a work schedule which cannot be changed regularly, does not have on-call work or irregular shifts, works from home less than once per week, and has a regular employment relationship (Mas & Pallais, 2020). Based on data from the 2014, 43% of jobs have been found to be traditional when workers with part-time employment are included (Mas & Pallais, 2020). However, fewer permanent or 'standard' positions are required by organizations to fulfil their goals and objectives. Instead, many tasks, particularly those requiring specific technical skills but perhaps less knowledge of the organization as a whole, are commonly outsourced to individuals or groups who may complete work on contract for several organizations or on platforms, rather than being employed by a single entity (Spreitzer et al., 2017).

These workers are typically referred to as 'contingent' employees because their relationship with the organization depends on the availability of tasks that they have the expertise to complete. Alternative work arrangements refer to non-traditional jobs, such as contract work, temporary and agency work, and on-call work (Mas & Pallais, 2020; Spreitzer et al., 2017) and have developed in response to the demand for more flexibility in fast changing environments as well as the intent to reduce labor costs (Fisher & Connelly, 2017; Vahle-Hinz, 2016). The prevalence of non-standard workers in OECD countries has been reported to be 40% of the total employment (OECD, 2020).

The COVID-19 pandemic practically forced most workers who could work from home to work from home, in order to reduce the potential spread of the virus. This contributed to blur the distinction between traditional work arrangements and alternative work arrangements for several occupational groups (Barrero et al., 2020; Gajendran & Harrison, 2007). A research report based on data collected from 15,000 Americans over time showed that the participants were more efficient while WFH during the pandemic, compared to what they were before (Barrero et al., 2020). The researchers forecasted a persistent shift to WFH with a potential boost in productivity of 2.4%. Although WFH may come with productivity or other benefits, potential costs in terms of health and well-being need to be evaluated.

Emerging as a response to an increasingly digitized economy, a relatively new and growing category of alternative, contracted work, so-called gig work (or crowdwork, eLancing, digital work) represents several flexibility dimensions (Connelly et al., 2021; Norgate & Cooper, 2020; Spreitzer et al., 2017). Gig workers typically provide their services/products directly to the market and may have contracts with several organizations (Ashford et al., 2018), hence having flexible employment relationships. Gig work (e.g., aspirational or digital platform labour) may provide independence, flexibility, and variety in terms of tasks, but it is also uncertain and unpredictable, and it is not clear how these workers should be developed in a sustainable and ethical way (Connelly et al., 2021; Kost et al., 2020). Despite the thrill of experiencing the variety and autonomy which naturally comes with gig work, successes are more uncertain and workers are left alone to initiate and maintain finances, job security, learning, and training (Ashford et al., 2018). For some, these potential stressors may be perceived as energizing and challenging, boosting personal resources, and subsequent thriving (Ashford et al., 2018). For others, the very same stressors may be perceived as hindering, draining their resources, and triggering so-called gig work strain (e.g., worry, anxiety, and sleeplessness) (Ashford et al., 2018; Vahle-Hinz, 2016). The understanding of how these workers move from gig work strain to thriving is unclear. An important task for future research is to clarify how gig workers can attain and maintain the necessary personal and social resources to sustain thriving in the new world of work. As Kost and colleagues (2020) propose, we need to move away from employer-centric human resource management (HRM) practices to new forms of network-based and self-organized HRM practices. In the next section, we discuss the potential consequences of alternative work arrangements and their implications for stress.

POTENTIAL CONSEQUENCES OF ALTERNATIVE WORK ARRANGEMENTS

The shifts and changes in employment patterns and practices highlighted above may have far-reaching consequences, not just in terms of how organizations function but also on the lives of individual workers and their families. It could be anticipated, therefore, that some of the stressors discussed in Chapter 3 and the strains discussed in Chapter 4 may be experienced more strongly and by a greater proportion of the workforce than has previously been observed. For instance, one significant consequence of employment contracts is that individuals working under these arrangements become totally responsible for managing their own career development and advancement (Kost et al., 2020), rather than this being (at least partially) the organization's responsibility. Hall and Moss (1998) initially referred to this type of career progression as the *protean career* in that individuals must personally 'seek out opportunities to develop, practice, and exploit their knowledge, skills and abilities' (Murphy & Jackson, 1999, p. 350), whereas previously many of these opportunities would have been provided for them by their employing organization. This increased responsibility for professional development can produce considerable ambiguity and insecurity, and hence strain, for persons who have received no training or coaching in this area and who previously depended substantially on organizational support for advancing their professional careers. However, on the positive side, it may also potentially produce ways to grow and learn, and hence thriving, for persons who actively appraise such stressors as inherent challenges and opportunities (Ashford et al., 2018).

Employee expectations about job/career security have also, of necessity, shifted. Individuals must focus less on employment security over a long term within a single organization, or even a single occupation, and concentrate more on their 'employability' (Fugate et al., 2004), which relies heavily on both flexibility (in terms of job or career preference) and versatility (of skills and knowledge). Arthur and Rousseau (1996) called this the *boundaryless career* because it is not bounded by development and advancement within a particular organizational context. A similar notion is that expounded by Handy (1994) of the *portfolio career*: 'The portfolio is a collection of different bits and pieces of work for different clients. The word "job" now means a client' (p. 175). Theoretical approaches on boundaryless careers diverge with respect to how they consider either the costs/challenges or gains/opportunities of boundaryless (or portfolio) career transitions (Guan et al., 2019). For some individuals, crossing a variety of different types of boundaries (e.g., hierarchical, relational, organizational), may be seen as positive opportunities to explore and build a career based on personal preferences, as well as to develop new career resources, identities and social networks (Arthur & Rousseau, 1996; Guan et al., 2019; Ibarra, 1999). For other individuals, particularly those who have been employed by, and have invested themselves in, a single organization for a long time, this shift in both attitudes and capabilities can be extremely threatening. Career transitions may create shocking events, for example, family-related problems, which may drain individuals' resources and energy and diminish their health and well-being (Guan et al.,

2019; Halbesleben & Buckley, 2004; Morgeson et al., 2015). From a stress perspective, what seems to matter when it comes to boundaryless careers is whether individuals voluntarily or involuntarily move careers (Guan et al., 2019). Workers who are involuntarily pushed into career transitions (typically workers with lower social status or skills) may be particularly vulnerable to experience reduced mental health and increased strain (e.g., high levels of burnout, depression and anxiety) (Currie et al., 2006; Fouad & Bynner, 2008). A qualitative study of 40 artists in the Netherlands showed that artists who were forced to career transitions because of stressors such as insufficient income from their arts practice, experienced grief, stress, and a loss of identity (Hennekam & Bennett, 2015). Employment changes that are voluntary, on the other hand, have been positively associated with job satisfaction. More research is needed on the extent of psychological strain (and potential thriving) as well as on effective strategies for managing transitions from a career progression based on the expectation of lifetime employment (whether within a single organization or in a single career path) to one that requires flexibility and versatility, and where change is the norm.

A related phenomenon is that of career *plateauing*, which occurs when individuals are unable to advance further within their organization (Yang et al., 2019). Increasingly, both managerial and other employees within organizations are encountering constraints on their career progression, and there has been an erosion of the traditional expectation of a (linear) hierarchical career path that is traversed over a long time period. Plateauing can have serious detrimental effects on individuals who have been socialized to perceive upward advancement as the hallmark of career success and personal achievement. The challenge for many organizations is to identify and implement alternative reward structures for high achievers. Organizational researchers and practitioners have examined other alternatives, including multi-directional career paths, such as lateral (or sideways) career development, in which workers navigate their own career and success (Baruch, 2004; Sullivan & Baruch, 2009), but as yet none of these alternatives has been clearly demonstrated to carry the same reward value as hierarchical career progression. Still, alternative career movements such as job enrichment (revitalizing employees interest in their work by replacing their current work with work which enables them to have greater autonomy) and temporary career movement (participating in project teams or taking short term job assignments), have become popular because careers then involve lifelong learning with alternative ways of realizing career success (De Vos et al., 2008).

Even for individuals who remain within the same organizational setting or continue to develop their career incrementally within the same occupation, there have been sizable shifts in role responsibilities as organizations have changed their modi operandi to meet the demands of the current economic environment and to remain competitive. These role shifts have been particularly significant for middle leaders (Foster et al., 2019), in that there has been a considerable reduction in the numbers of workers employed in that role. Further, those who have retained middle-leadership status have been required to make significant modifications to their way of operating. Due to downsizing and a general flattening of organizational structures, in many organizations the need for supervisory personnel has declined considerably, and the nature of supervision has been radically altered (Foster et al., 2019). Although employees are considered to experience greater job related stress levels compared to their leaders, there is consistent evidence that levels of work-related stress for leaders have increased. This group of employees often experiences as much, or even more, strain than other occupational categories (Barling & Cloutier, 2017; Harms et al., 2017), as well as having to confront the uncertainty of potential job loss (Foster et al., 2019). Job stress researchers need to re-examine the notion of organizational roles in light of these changes and to assess the likely impact of such role shifts on employees' affective experiences at work. As noted earlier, researchers should also adopt perspectives that endeavour to develop alternative approaches to the design of workplace roles and contexts, ones that contribute positively to individual well-being rather than creating strain and perhaps leading to burnout. To date, stress research has been more reactive (to existing conditions) than proactive in this respect.

Being a leader in today's workforce, which includes internal and external workers, regular employees and contract or gig workers, may be challenging. There may be uncertainty as to who is responsible for these workers (Kost et al., 2020), and who is responsible for their health and well-being (Ashford et al., 2018). Currently there are few organizations which lead their entire workforce (internal and external workers) based on a more holistic approach encompassing various types of capabilities and workers (Altman et al., 2021). Organizations and their leaders may benefit from a focus on so-called *workforce ecosystems*, a structure of interdependent actors both from within the organization and beyond, where all actors work to achieve both collective and individual goals (Altman et al., 2021). Workforce ecosystems may equip organizations and their leaders with more effective and efficient collaboration among workers, thereby enabling novel approaches to what work is possible in the organization. Rethinking management practices around employees and non-employees toward a holistic approach of workforce ecosystems may contribute to the design of more proactive workplace roles and contexts that facilitate thriving and well-being. Future organizational stress research may reveal the benefits of workforce ecosystems or other forms of structures.

One other change in the way in which organizations function is the increasing reliance on and utilization of 'virtual teams' (Mak & Kozlowski, 2019), where group members do not actually interact face to face, but communicate via computers and other technologies. From an organizational perspective, virtual teams have opened up new possibilities for teamwork that are unimpeded by time and space constraints. However, difficulties in creating trust, collaboration and communication-, isolation, low levels of media richness, and high levels of social distance between members, pose new, and special challenges for virtual teamwork. These are also challenges for individual employees in developing their interpersonal relations skills (Dulebohn & Hoch, 2017), because virtually connected work limits both emotional and social cues (Connelly & Turel, 2016; Lindebaum et al., 2018). Our knowledge about the unique job-related and non-job related stressors that arise from working in virtual teams is still limited (Gaudisio et al., 2017; Konradt et al., 2003). The long-term effects of remote work and the expansion of virtual teamwork forced upon many workers, especially during a global pandemic, pose questions regarding how experiences of stress and strain best can be communicated, coped with, and regulated in such unique settings (Kniffin et al., 2021). Although remote work may involve positive outcomes (e.g., flexibility, work-life balance, improved team performance, cost reduction, sales increase, acceleration of decision processes) for both the organization and its employees (Connelly & Turel, 2016; Liao, 2017), it is important to establish potential negative outcomes.

One such negative aspect is referred to as *technostress* – a negative psychological state concerning the application of or a perceived threat to apply new technology, which typically results in experiences of skepticism, feelings of ineffectiveness, anxiety, and mental fatigue (Salanova et al., 2007, 2013). According to Salanova and colleagues (2013), technostress encompasses two psychological experiences, *technostrain* (inefficacy, fatigue, anxiety and skepticism) and *technoaddiction* (excessive application of ICT with feelings of fatigue and anxiety). Technostress has been associated with several maladaptive outcomes such as anxiety, fatigue, perceived increased levels of time pressure and mental load, irritability and insomnia, reduction in work-life balance, job satisfaction, commitment, and productivity (e.g., Porter & Kakabadse, 2006; Salanova et al., 2013; Tarafdar et al., 2007). Potential techno-stressors (Gaudisio et al., 2017) are application notifications, chats, and e-mails, which are prevalent in most work environments, and increasingly so in the current increased WFH situation. Empirical evidence has shown that several factors (or stressors) may contribute to experiences of technostress, including constant connectivity (techno invasion), communication information technology overload (receiving information from several channels simultaneously), fatigue and discomfort evolving from multitasking engendered by ICTs, lack of support during implementation, testing, and application of ICT adopted by the organization, and task interruptions due to ongoing communication streams (Brivio et al., 2018; Gaudisio et al., 2017; Porter & Kakabadse, 2006; Ragu-Nathan et al., 2008; Tarafdar et al., 2007).

When employees lack necessary coping resources, the experience of such technostressors are likely to engender technostress and subsequent strain (e.g., Zoom fatigue, burnout etc.). For example, drawing on the transactional theory of stress (Lazarus & Folkman, 1984), Gaudisio et al. (2017) collected data from a large government-related organization in the USA and found that techno-invasion and techno-overload are stressors which predict work family conflict and distress. In turn, work family conflict and distress were found to partly determine the choice of adaptive or maladaptive coping strategies, which in turn contributed to either reduced (adaptive coping strategies) or increased (maladaptive coping strategies) strain (work exhaustion) among employees. In another study on how people apply communication devices to construct their availability to others and manage their work life, Barley et al. (2011) found that the participants perceived e-mail as a symbol of overload. The inbox represented a continuous reminder of how overloaded the participants were. The constant anxiety for not being on top of things with respect to responding to emails, resulted in longer workdays, e-mailing in the evening, in the morning (from home), or on weekends, mainly to accomplish control. The more time employees used on e-mails the more they felt overloaded (Barley et al., 2011). Two additional e-mail stressors have been identified, high quantity and poor-quality workplace e-mails (Brown et al., 2014). In a cross-sectional study of academic and administrative employees at a University in Australia, these stressors were related to stress appraisals (e-mail overload and e-mail uncertainty) and in turn with strain (emotional exhaustion).

The experience of techno-stressors may depend on the way the stressors are appraised by individuals (O'Brien & Beehr, 2019; Webster et al., 2011). In turn, the extent to which individuals engage in challenge or hindrance appraisal (Webster et al., 2011) may contribute to determine subsequent coping strategies. Further, leaders may play a vital role in terms of forming socio-emotional bonds with their employees to alleviate and manage negative forms of stress and strain in their workforce, both at the team and individual level (Harms et al., 2017; Liao, 2017).

Finally, to round off this discussion of job-related stressors in the 21st century, whether they be newly emerging or simply more pronounced, we also need to consider the impact of new forms of employment relationships and work organization on individuals' lives off the job. Each of the changes identified above has the potential to significantly influence workers' family lives, relationships with spouses/partners and children, leisure activities, and what is often referred to as 'home-work' balance. In the work-life balance literature, balance has been defined in different ways, and recently the concept of work-nonwork balance has been proposed to recognize that an experience of balance also includes nonwork roles besides family (for a review and discussion see Casper et al., 2018). This is important given that balance also is considered to be relevant for non-parent or single parent employees (Casper et al., 2018). With increasing numbers of people WFH or having other alternative employment relationships, we anticipate that it will become increasingly difficult for individuals to separate their job/career from their lives off the job; hence, there will be a further blurring of boundaries between these two domains. Technological innovations are already making it possible for people to be 'at work' virtually anytime, anywhere. Although these innovations certainly create flexibility and may even enhance productivity at both an individual and organizational level, less attention has been given to their possible negative impacts on individuals' lives more generally.

As noted earlier, we are increasingly becoming a technologically driven society, and there is a distinct danger that sociocultural values will be subordinated to technological and economic imperatives. Although many organizations have implemented family-friendly initiatives, such as flextime and provision of childcare facilities, less attention has been devoted to the more fundamental issue of how employment contracts and the very structure of work itself affect individual and family well-being. For instance, what does 'home-work' balance mean when workers spend their working days WFH with various gigs? Many years ago, Kanter (1977) debunked the myth of separate (job and family) worlds, yet by and large job stress research has continued to assess stressors and strains in the workplace separately from other life domains and has ignored the inherent interplay between various life domains, including work. We suggest that stress researchers need to adopt a more holistic perspective, moving away from examination of work-related stressors and stress management in isolation from other (e.g., family) contexts to a model where work experiences (both positive and negative) are considered along with family and other domains (e.g., nonwork) as part of a gestalt. Recent studies of interdomain (especially job-family) spillover represent an example of a research paradigm that endeavors to identify the stress-coping process from a more holistic perspective. This is even more prevailing during a global crisis (COVID-19) where WFH suddenly has become the 'new' normal for many workers (ILO, 2020). Many of the workers who worked from home to secure physical distancing live in households with children below 12 years and reported that it was challenging to balance their work with childcare responsibilities and hence securing home-work balance (Eurofound, 2020).

The balance issue is also likely to be particularly prevalent for employees in the so-called *sandwich generation*, which refers to individuals who have a dual caregiving responsibility for both their children and parents either in the same home or across multiple homes. In western countries at approximately 8%–28% of the workforce constitute sandwich generation caregivers and these numbers are expected to grow in the future (Boyczuk & Fletcher, 2016; Daatland et al., 2010). Sandwich generation workers have been found to be particularly vulnerable in terms of experiencing reduced well-being including for example depression, poor health, anxiety symptoms, negative stress, and mental fatigue (e.g., Boyczuk & Fletcher, 2016; Hammer & Neal, 2008; Turgeman-Lupo et al., 2020). Several important questions remain underexplored: How does a forced WFH situation, affect sandwich generation workers? How do they experience the forced WFH situation or a WFH situation in general, and what implications does it have for their health and well-being? How do alternative work arrangements influence sandwich generation workers experiences of stress, strain or thriving? What characterizes their coping strategies? What characterizes sandwich generation thriving in general (or during a global crisis)? What roles do organizations, leaders, and colleagues play with respect to helping sandwich generation caregivers during crisis and in general?

Finally, while the roles of women and men have become more similar over time (Galinsky et al., 2009), by and large women still perform the bulk of household chores and shoulder primary responsibility for child rearing and other family activities (Neilson & Stanfors, 2014; Shockley et al., 2017). Although evidence that women report more job → family conflict than men is mixed (e.g., Byron, 2005; Eby et al., 2005; Shockley et al., 2017), there is no doubt that women are more often confronted by demands from both occupational and family domains that may be experienced as conflictual.

There has also been a considerable rise in the proportion of dual-income households, where both partners/spouses are in paid employment. The emphasis of research has been on the types and extent of job-family conflict that partners report, their respective levels of both job and family (or marital) satisfaction and functioning, and the level of psychological strain experienced by each person (Eby et al., 2005; Shockley et al., 2017). Research on dual-career couples has also focused on two forms of 'stress contagion', the first occurring when the strain experienced by an individual in one domain (such as employment) spills over into the other (family), and the second ('crossover'), where one partner's strain gets transmitted to the other partner (Bakker & Demerouti, 2012; Westman, 2001). The latter occurs especially when there is substantial job → family conflict for one individual in the relationship.

Due to the downturn in the economy of many countries and the accompanying shifts in employment relationships discussed earlier, many couples have been forced into the dual-earner situation, where having both partners employed is not necessarily a (career) choice but a financial necessity. Frequently, one or even both individuals are employed in short-term, perhaps even part-time, contracts that hold little if any prospect for career advancement. The stressors encountered under these circumstances, and therefore the kinds of strain or thriving experienced, are likely to differ considerably from those confronted by dual-career couples. To date, however, research has not systematically compared and contrasted these markedly different situations. Along with our previous recommendation of more 'integrated' empirical studies of job stress, we suggest that the job-family interface is important in stress research and that various employment and family circumstances need to be more carefully differentiated. In this way, studies of the stress-coping process can better describe the types of stressors and strains, as well as examining implications for stress management at both the individual (or couple) level and the organizational level.

A range of future research topics has been proposed in the area of job-family balance (e.g., Ashford et al., 2018; Casper et al., 2018; Kniffin et al., 2021; Shockley et al., 2017). First, because jobs are becoming more contingent and based on short-term contracts (alternative work arrangements), hence intrinsically more insecure, what is the impact of these changes on the interface between work and the family? Second, as more and more women pursue careers and not just jobs, what will be the impact of this on work culture and on home life, and what strategies do couples adopt to manage work and family? Third, how does the behavior of one partner influence the other partner's experience of job-family balance? Fourth, if the two-earner family encourages flexible working arrangements, how effective are they when considering the broader family context? Are some flexible working arrangements more successful than others, or does there have to be a match between family circumstances and the particular arrangement (e.g., compressed work week, teleworking, gig work)? Accordingly, do spillover issues take a new form or are they the same across alternative work arrangements and cultures? Fifth, as jobs become more insecure and individuals are increasingly WFH and are expected to work longer and more unsocial hours, what will the impact of these hours and WFH be on personal health, on the family, on other nonwork roles besides the family, and on productivity? Sixth, will changing gender patterns of employment and consequent shifts in home-work balance continue to encourage the emergence of virtual organizations, and, if so, what will be the consequences for the health and well-being of individuals, their families, and nonwork roles and relationships? Finally, in light of the COVID-19 crisis and potential future similar crises that require forced WFH, how are working parents, particularly those who are responsible for children, affected by a forced WFH situation? What implications may such a situation have for their work-home balance, health, well-being, and to what extent does such a work arrangement facilitate for continued even division of labor among men and women?

AGENDAS FOR JOB STRESS RESEARCH

The issues and phenomena that we have surveyed above pose major challenges for job stress researchers. To conclude this chapter, we suggest some directions for future research in this field. These suggestions are not intended to be exhaustive, nor are they presented in any specific order of importance. However, they do highlight some key issues that we believe need to be attended to for research to continue to make a meaningful contribution to theories about the stress-coping process, as well as for the application of empirically based knowledge to the management of stress in the workplace.

Consistent with arguments we have outlined earlier in this volume (see, e.g., Chapters 3 and 4), our first suggestion is that there needs to be more explicit focus on the *context* in which stress coping occurs. Currently, there is a tendency to regards the strains or thriving that individuals experience as being the same, irrespective of the setting in which they arise and of the stressors that the person is confronted with. For example, frequently used indexes of strain include variables such as general depression, anxiety, and tension (Kahn & Byosiere, 1992), and popular instruments for assessing psychological strain, such as the General Health Questionnaire (Goldberg, 1972), tap generic indicators of strain (including items such as 'felt constantly under strain', 'lost confidence in myself', and 'felt I couldn't overcome my problems'), without locating these experiences within any specific context. Combined with the tendency to use cross-sectional designs that depend almost exclusively on self-report measures (of both stressors and strains), concentration on these generic variables and measures means that researchers are unable to differentiate between the forms of strain that arise in the workplace, the family/nonwork environment, or some other setting. Consequently, only limited knowledge has been acquired about various manifestations of strain and the possibility that the kind of strain experienced in one environment may differ from that experienced in another.

Second, and following from the above recommendation, it may be advantageous for stress-coping research to adopt a holistic perspective that takes into account the totality of an individual's life space rather than simply assessing one domain in isolation from others. This becomes particular important given the many alternative work arrangements that represent the 'new normal' for several occupational groups (Kniffin et al., 2021; Spreitzer et al., 2017). For instance, despite acknowledgment of the dynamic interplay between various life domains, there has been a tendency for researchers interested in job stress to study only what happens in the work setting and to ignore other areas (such as family/ nonwork domain). Hence, though a particular study might uncover statistically significant relationships between (for example) workplace stressors, such as techno-overload, time pressure, role ambiguity or conflict, and psychological (or other forms of) strain, we cannot be certain that these are the only, or even the primary, determinants of strain for the individuals under investigation. It may be that family pressures or personal relationship problems are major predictors of an individual's affective reactions at the time of measurement. Furthermore, personal (dispositional) characteristics may also be contributing to the nature and extent of strain experienced. Resources may also play a role. The work-home resources model proposes that both personal (e.g., self-efficacy, optimism) and contextual (e.g., social support, autonomy) resources are likely to play an important role with respect to the work-home interface (Ten Brummelhuis & Bakker, 2012). With sufficient resources, individuals may be more likely to cope with difficult situations either at work, at home or both, and subsequently collect new resources (Aw et al., 2021). Sufficient resources may facilitate an overall global work-family/nonwork balance and thriving (cf. Casper et al., 2018). The extended JD-R theory (see Chapter 1; Bakker et al., 2023; Demerouti & Bakker, 2022) is an example of a theoretical model which may be helpful for future research in addressing the role of and interplay between various life domains (e.g., personal, home, organization, job) to better understand the organizational stress processes. In sum, implementing one or more of the perspectives on stress coping presented in this book requires a joint approach that incorporates contextual factors and dispositional variables and examines the total set of stressors impinging upon a person.

Third, stress researchers may also want to consider the role of employee's *future anticipations* of stressors for their experiences of strain and/or thriving (Casper et al., 2017; DiStasio & Shoss, 2020). DiStasio and Shoss (2020) elegantly showed how anticipated changes in workload might influence how current experienced workload influences strain even before a change takes place. In a sample of employees engaged in project work, the authors found that when employees anticipated a workload decrease, they anticipated a future opportunity to recover from current workload. However, an anticipated increase in workload was viewed as a threat of losing valuable resources (DiStasio & Shoss, 2020). These findings suggest that employees may be better able to cope with stressors in general if they can see a future positive change (reduction) of the current stressor/s. We believe that this is relevant for future research to explore further.

Future research may also clarify how employees from various occupational groups (e.g., who experience more or less frequent change in stressors) may differ in how they cope with changes in stressors. COR theory does not propose how contextual factors may impinge on perceptions of future resource loss or potential for recovery (DiStasio & Shoss, 2020). This brings us to the model we presented in Chapter 1, suggesting that it may be beneficial for future stress research to draw on several stress related theoretical frameworks in an integrative way, to facilitate a clearer and perhaps better understanding of the stress phenomena (cf. O'Brien & Beehr, 2019). For example, CATS proposes that the extent to which a stressor will be experienced as stressful or not is dependent on the situational setting as well as previous learning. Thus, previous learning may play an important role in employee's anticipations of future resource loss or potential for recovery (Eriksen, 2017). Our point is that by using COR (Hobfoll, 1989) and CATS (Ursin & Eriksen, 2004, 2010) theories in an integrative way, we may increase our understanding of actual and/or anticipated stressors and strains.

Another important aspect to consider is the stress-related beliefs system – *stress mindset* – of employees engaged in both traditional and alternative work arrangements because it is capable of shaping their stress response (Crum et al., 2017). Stress mindset may be conceptualized as two stress related beliefs systems that operate on a continuum. On one hand, individuals may believe that stress is beneficial—a 'stress-is-enhancing mindset'—for various consequences (Crum et al., 2013). On the other hand, individuals may believe that stress has negative consequences—a 'stress-is-debilitating mindset'—such as impaired growth and well-being (Crum et al., 2013, 2017). When compared with a stress-is-debilitating mindset, a stress-is-enhancing mindset has been associated with more adaptive physiological responses (e.g., moderate cortisol reactivity), as well as approach-oriented behavioral responses (e.g., more receptive to feedback) in stressful situations (Crum et al., 2013). Casper et al. (2017) conducted a five day daily diary study about the role of employees' stress mindset on the anticipation phase of the stress process among employees from various organizations. The findings showed that employees who held a stress-is-enhancing mindset engaged in more approach oriented coping efforts when they anticipated a high workload. In turn, such coping efforts positively predicted task performance and vigor. Employees with a stress-is-debilitating mindset made less approach-oriented coping efforts during a workday. These findings illustrate that challenge and hindrance appraisals may depend on individuals' particular stress mindset. We see great potential in further exploring the role of stress mindset in the stressor-strain/thriving relationship (O'Brien & Beehr, 2019), as well as investigating the role of stress mindsets in interpersonal relationships at work (Ben-Avi et al., 2018).

A fourth recommendation, also discussed earlier in this chapter, is that job stress research could be more 'proactive' in its approach. The typical stress study examines predictors (stressors) and outcomes (strain responses) after they have occurred. This is necessary for us to establish putative cause–effect relationships between stressors and strains as they unfold in the workplace. Although this line of research is important, we suggest that it would also be valuable now to move beyond these post hoc approaches. Specifically, we advocate the use of research designs that examine theoretically driven stress management systems (at both the individual and organizational level) that may yield positive benefits for workers, their employing organizations, and ultimately society as a whole. In short, we believe it is time to become more innovative, 'experimental', and forward looking in our approaches to research on stress management, rather than continuing solely with 'after-the-fact' investigations that simply attempt to replicate previous findings concerning the predictors of workplace strain.

Fifth, and emerging from our discussion of the impact of new technologies and changing employment conditions, more needs to be done to counteract the detrimental effects of strain induced by the new organizational realities. For example, given that alternative work arrangements are becoming more common, several organizations aim to save costs by reducing their office space (Engelen et al., 2019; Spreitzer et al., 2017). A growing number of organizations adopt activity-based work (ABW) environments (Hoendervanger et al., 2019; Wohlers & Hertel, 2017), in which employees do not have permanent workstations, but instead share an office space which offers various types of non-assigned work settings (Hoendervanger et al., 2019). These settings are supposed to be applied for various types of activities, depending on the respective tasks (Engelen et al., 2019). ABW environments have been found to predict positive outcomes such as performance, collaboration, satisfaction with the work situation, and perceived control (Engelen et al., 2019; Hoendervanger et al., 2019). However, the implications of ABW environments for stress, health, and well-being are still unclear (Engelen et al., 2019).

An ongoing discussion in the academic literature, as well as public policy and mass media concerns the number of work hours and the potential benefits of shortening the workweek or workdays (e.g., Chokshi, 2020; Ganster et al., 2018; Laker & Roulet, 2019). Although the benefits of employment for mental health and well-being have been emphasized, we know less about how much or little paid work is needed to obtain such benefits (Kamerāde et al., 2019). Kamerāde et al. (2019) conducted a study among 156,734 respondents from U.K. who were either unemployed, economically inactive (i.e., on sick leave, maternity leave etc), or employed. The findings showed no evidence that a standard workweek of 36–40 hours enhanced employee health and well-being. However, the results indicated that the standard full-time workweek may be shortened by a day without having a detrimental influence on employee's health and well-being. It is possible that a shorter workweek may induce thriving and prevent experiences of strain. However, a shortened workweek may also induce even more strain because of less time to get the work done, or because a shorter workweek does not necessarily meet the needs of all employees (Wadsworth & Facer, 2016). More research is needed on compressed workweek schedules for employees working in alternative work arrangements.

Due to the 'always on' nature of work, another important topic for future research is the role of overwork or excessive availability for work (Cooper & Lu, 2019). Excessive availability for work can manifest itself in several ways, such as teleworking, long working hours (including nonreported and reported overtime work), leavism (e.g., taking work on holiday and/or home when it could not be completed in paid working hours), and sickness presenteeism (see Chapter 4). All of these topics need more research attention from an organizational stress perspective (Cooper & Lu, 2019).

To a large extent, these realities are driven by economic and technological forces, and less importance has been attached to personal, social, and societal outcomes, including disruption of individuals' personal and family lives. Although there have been some investigations of (individual) coping mechanisms and (organizational) stress management interventions (see Chapters 7 and 8), generally speaking much less is known about how to effectively combat the kinds of strain brought about by the massive organizational transformations that have been occurring in the past decade and currently in times of a pandemic. This is important as every indication suggests that such transformations will become increasingly pervasive in the foreseeable future. We endorse the view, also expressed by various other commentators (Lamontagne et al., 2007; Tetrick & Winslow, 2015), that the development, implementation, and evaluation of effective stress management mechanisms, at both individual and organizational levels, represent a critical agenda item for job stress researchers over the next years.

SOME IMPLICATIONS FOR METHODOLOGY

In addition to the above general issues concerning the nature of future job stress research, some specific recommendations about methodological refinements are appropriate at this juncture. Other chapters in this volume have addressed some of the critical issues concerning the design and execution of research on job stress (see especially Chapter 9), so we will not repeat these issues in detail here. Rather, the following discussion focuses on four additional areas that we believe should be considered.

Earlier, we discussed the need to expand our perspectives on the nature of job-related strain to encompass a broader range of strains and to differentiate between types of strain that may be experienced in various contexts. To achieve this objective, it is necessary for researchers to examine a greater range of affective reactions in their research designs and to assess the specific strains, as well as their future anticipation, that are experienced in reaction to particular stressors. At a very simple level, we need to ask, for example, whether stressors such as role ambiguity and conflict induce the same kinds of strain as other stressors, such as work overload and time pressure. We also need to know when, to what extent, and under what circumstances (challenge) stressors lead to positive outcomes such as employee thriving. Similarly, is the strain or thriving experienced in response to workplace stressors the same kind of strain/thriving as that encountered in other environments (e.g., the family) or as a result of interdomain (e.g., job-family) conflict? As yet, these questions have been given scant research attention, so there has been little attempt to specify the nature of strain or thriving that is created by different stressors.

Allied with the above notion is the need to move away from total reliance on self-reports of stressors and strains. Gathering data on individuals' perceptions of the environment and their affective reactions is clearly important and yields valuable information on subjective interpretations of life experiences. However, to generate knowledge that can be used to develop effective stress management interventions, we must tap sources of data that complement (and supplement) self-reports, including physical reactions (e.g., recordings of physiological processes) and behavioral responses (including those perceived by significant others). Furthermore, as we have suggested in Chapter 8, although psychology may be the study of individual behavior, it is important to move beyond the study of individual coping to analysis of stress management at the organizational and occupational levels. Only then will we be able to determine whether certain organizational and workplace conditions create strain (or thriving) for people, irrespective of their (different) subjective responses. Put another way, stress researchers have a unique opportunity to assist with the construction of 'healthy organizations' (Burke & Richardsen, 2019) that contribute to individual well-being rather than inducing or exacerbating levels of strain.

A third recommendation is that there needs to be greater triangulation of research methodologies or perspectives to enhance our ability to obtain comprehensive and generalizable findings. Typically, job stress research falls into one of two camps: deductive (based on a priori hypotheses) and inductive (exploratory), and these approaches tend to be mutually exclusive. Deductive research is normally carried out using structured questionnaires or interview schedules, and the data are subjected to statistical analysis (e.g., multiple regression, structural equation modeling) of predictor and criterion variables. Such research is useful for testing hypotheses concerning relationships between known entities. Inductive research, on the other hand, tends to use more open-ended interview questions and is usually designed to 'discover' entities or to explore particular areas of interest in depth.

We suggest that a convergence of methodologies would substantially advance our knowledge of the stress-coping process and would provide a more detailed account of stressor–strain relationships than is possible using either methodology alone. Deductive and inductive methods both have advantages and limitations, and each generates information that is not readily obtainable using the other approach. Although it may not always be practical or feasible to combine these approaches, we recommend that a convergent strategy be adopted wherever possible.

Finally, by its very nature, the term *stress* conveys a negative connotation of workplace experiences and life in organizations. On the other hand, we also need to acknowledge the benefits of working, the advantages that accrue to individuals in paid employment, and the positive contributions that jobs and careers make to individuals' overall well-being (Blustein, 2008; Danna & Griffin, 1999). Again, it is time for organizational research to more explicitly adopt a broader perspective that incorporates the variety of experiences – both positive and negative – that individuals encounter in their jobs and to develop research designs that capture the depth and richness of those experiences, rather than focusing simplistically on relationships among a limited subset of variables.

Ultimately, the value of job stress research will be judged by its contribution to the enhancement of individual well-being and thriving, as well as organizational productivity and effectiveness. The responsibility rests with researchers themselves to ensure that their empirical studies provide 'added value' to the expanding body of knowledge about stress-coping processes and interventions. Work can create strain and lead to ill health and reduced well-being (Cooper & Lu, 2019; Dewe & Cooper, 2017), which incur economic costs and productivity losses for organizations (Hassard et al., 2018). The onus rests with stress researchers to conduct research that contributes to the development of more 'healthy' working environments (in the fullest sense of that expression), and that enables individuals and organizations to alleviate the negative effects of stressors when they cannot avoid them altogether.

The challenge is there for stress researchers to strive toward having a significant practical input into the health and well-being of individuals, organizations, and ultimately the societies in which they live and function. We believe, and hope, that the issues and recommendations presented in this volume contribute to the ongoing development and enhancement of research in this important field of investigation.

REFERENCES

Aasland, M. S., Skogstad, A., Notelaers, G., Nielsen, M. B., & Einarsen, S. (2010). The prevalence of destructive leadership behaviour. *British Journal of Management, 21*(2), 438–452.

Abildgaard, J. S. (2018). Tricks of the trade: Practical advice from the PIPPI project for evaluating organizational interventions. In K. Nielsen & A. Noblet (Eds.), *Organizational interventions for health and well-being* (pp. 144–166). Routledge.

Abildgaard, J. S., Nielsen, K., Wåhlin-Jacobsen, C. D., Maltesen, T., Christensen, K. B., & Holtermann, A. (2020). 'Same, but different': A mixed-methods realist evaluation of a cluster-randomized controlled participatory organizational intervention. *Human Relations, 73*(10), 1339–1365.

Abildgaard, J. S., Saksvik, P. Ø., & Nielsen, K. (2016). How to measure the intervention process? An assessment of qualitative and quantitative approaches to data collection in the process evaluation of organizational interventions. *Frontiers in Psychology, 7*, 10. https://doi.org/10.3389/fpsyg.2016.01380

Adriaenssens, J., De Gucht, V., & Maes, S. (2015). Association of goal orientation with work engagement and burnout in emergency nurses. *Journal of Occupational Health, 57*, 151–160.

Ahola, K., & Hakanen, J. (2014). Burnout and health. In M. P. Leiter, A. B. Bakker, & C. Maslach (Eds.), *Burnout at work: A psychological perspective* (pp. 10–31). Psychology Press.

Ahola, K., Honkonen, T., Virtanen, M., Aromaa, A., & Lönnqvist, J. (2008). Burnout in relation to age in the adult working population. *Journal of Occupational Health, 50*, 362–365.

Åkerstedt, T., & Wright, K. P. (2009). Sleep loss and fatigue in shift work and shift work disorder. *Sleep Medicine Clinics, 4*(2), 257–271.

Akinola, M. (2010). Measuring the pulse of an organization: Integrating physiological measures into the organizational scholar's toolbox. *Research in Organizational Behavior, 30*, 203–223.

Akinola, M., Kapadia, C., Lu, J. G., & Mason, M. F. (2019). Incorporating physiology into creativity research and practice: The effects of bodily stress responses on creativity in organizations. *Academy of Management Perspectives, 33*(2), 163–184.

Alarcon, G. M. (2011). A meta-analysis of burnout with job demands, resources, and attitudes. *Journal of Vocational Behavior, 79*(2), 549–562. https://doi.org/10.1016/j.jvb.2011.03.007

Alarcon, G. M., Eschleman, K. J., & Bowling, N. A. (2009). Relationships between personality variables and burnout: A meta-analysis. *Work & Stress, 23*(3), 244–263. https://doi.org/10.1080/02678370903282600

Albertsen, K., Garde, A. H., Nabe-Nielsen, K., Hansen, Å. M., Lund, H., & Hvid, H. (2014). Work-life balance among shift workers: Results from an intervention study about self-rostering. *International Archives of Occupational and Environmental Health, 87*(3), 265–274. https://doi.org/10.1007/s00420-013-0857-x

Allen, T. D., Freeman, D. M., Russell, J. E., Reizenstein, R. C., & Rentz, J. O. (2001). Survivor reactions to organizational downsizing: Does time ease the pain? *Journal of Occupational and Organizational Psychology, 74*(2), 145–164.

Allen, T. D., Golden, T. D., & Shockley, K. M. (2015). How effective is telecommuting? Assessing the status of our scientific findings. *Psychological Science in the Public Interest, 16*(2), 40–68.

Allen, T. D., Johnson, R. C., Saboe, K. N., Cho, E., Dumani, S., & Evans, S. (2012). Dispositional variables and work–family conflict: A meta-analysis. *Journal of Vocational Behavior, 80*(1), 17–26.

Allen, A. P., Kennedy, P. J., Dockray, S., Cryan, J. F., Dinan, T. G., & Clarke, G. (2017). The Trier social stress test: Principles and practice. *Neurobiological Stress, 6*, 113–126. https://doi.org/10.1016%2Fj.ynstr.2016.11.001

Altman, E. J., Kiron, D., Schwartz, J., & Jones, R. (2021). *The future of work is through workforce ecosystems.* MIT Sloan Management Review. https://sloanreview.mit.edu/article/the-future-of-work-is-through-workforce-ecosystems/amp

Amis, J. M., Munir, K. A., Lawrence, T. B., Hirsch, P., & McGahan, A. (2018). Inequality, institutions and organizations. *Organization Studies, 39*(9), 1131–1152.

Amstad, F. T., Meier, L. L., Fasel, U., Elfering, A., & Semmer, N. K. (2011). A meta-analysis of work–family conflict and various outcomes with a special emphasis on cross-domain versus matching-domain relations. *Journal of Occupational Health Psychology, 16*(2), 151–169.

Andersen, I., Borritz, M., Christensen, K. B., & Diderichsen, F. (2010). Changing job-related burnout after intervention-a quasi-experimental study in six human service organizations. *Journal of Occupational and Environmental Medicine, 52*(3), 318–323. https://doi.org/10.1097/JOM.0b013e3181d1cd87

Andlauer, P., Reinberg, A., Fourré, L., Battle, W., & Duverneuil, G. (1979). Amplitude of the oral temperature circadian rhythm and the tolerance to shift-work. *Journal de physiologie, 75*(5), 507–512.

Appelbaum, S. H., Delage, C., Labib, N., & Gault, G. (1997). The survivor syndrome: Aftermath of downsizing. *Career Development International, 2*, 278–286.

Arnetz, B. B. (2005). Subjective indicators as gauge for improving organizational well-being: An attempt to apply the cognitive activation theory to organizations. *Psychoneurodocrinology, 30*, 1022–1026. https://doi.org/10.1016/j.psyneuen.2005.03.016

Arnsten, A. F. (2009). Stress signaling pathways that impair prefrontal cortex structure and function. *Nature Reviews Neuroscience, 10*(6), 410–422.

Arnulf, J. K., Larsen, K. R., Martinsen, Ø. L., & Bong, C. H. (2014). Predicting survey responses: How and why semantics shape survey statistics on organizational behavior. *PlosOne, 9*(9), 1–13. https://doi.org/10.1371/journal.pone.0106361

Aronsson, G., Theorell, T., Grape, T., Hammarström, A., Hogstedt, C., Marteinsdottir, I., … Hall, C. (2017). A systematic review including meta-analysis of work environment and burnout symptoms. *BMC Public Health, 17*(1), 264. https://doi.org/10.1186/s12889-017-4153-7

Arthur, M. B., & Rousseau, D. M. (1996). *The boundaryless career: A new employment principle for a new organizational era*. Oxford University Press.

Ashford, S. J., Caza, B. B., & Reid, E. M. (2018). From surviving to thriving in the gig economy: A research agenda for individuals in the new world of work. *Research in Organizational Behavior, 38*, 23–41. https://doi.org/10.1016/j.riob.2018.11.001

Ashford, S. J., George, E., & Blatt, R. (2007). 2 old assumptions, new work: The opportunities and challenges of research on nonstandard employment. *Academy of Management Annals, 1*(1), 65–117.

Ashkanasy, N. M., Ayoko, O. B., & Jehn, K. A. (2014). Understanding the physical environment of work and employee behavior: An affective events perspective. *Journal of Organizational Behavior, 35*(8), 1169–1184.

Ashkanasy, N. M., & Dorris, A. D. (2017). Emotions in the workplace. *Annual Review of Organizational Psychology and Organizational Behavior, 4*, 67–90.

Aspinwall, L. G. (2011). Future-oriented thinking, proactive coping, and the management of potential threats to health and well-being. In S. Folkman (Ed.), *The Oxford handbook of stress, health, and coping* (pp. 1–52). Oxford University Press.

Aspinwall, L. G., & Taylor, S. (1997). A stitch in time: Self regulation and pro-active coping. *Psychological Bulletin, 121*, 417–436.

Aw, S. S. Y., Ilies, R., Li, X., Bakker, A. B., & Liu, X.-Y. (2021). Work related helping and family functioning: A work-home resources perspective. *Journal of Occupational and Organizational Psychology, 94*, 55–79. https://doi.org/10.1111/joop.12331

Bacharach, S. B., & Bamberger, P. A. (2007). 9/11 and New York City firefighters' post hoc unit support and control climates: A context theory of the consequences of involvement in traumatic work-related events. *Academy of Management Journal, 50*(4), 849–868.

Baethge, A., Vahle-Hinz, T., & Rigotti, T. (2020). Coworker support and its relationship to allostasis during a workday: A diary study on trajectories of heart rate variability during work. *Journal of Applied Psychology, 105*(5), 506.

Bakker, A. B., & Costa, P. L. (2014). Chronic job burnout and daily functioning: A theoretical analysis. *Burnout Research, 1*(3), 112–119. https://doi.org/10.1016/j.burn.2014.04.003

Bakker, A. B., & Demerouti, E. (2007). The job demands–resources model: State of the art. *Journal of Managerial Psychology 22*, 309–328.

Bakker, A. B., & Demerouti, E. (2012). The spillover–crossover model. In J. G. Grzywacz & E. Demerouti (Eds.), *New frontiers in work and family research* (pp. 54–70). Psychology Press.

Bakker, A. B., & Demerouti, E. (2017). Job demands-resources theory: Taking stock and looking forward. *Journal of Occupational Health Psychology, 22*(3), 273–285. https://doi.org/10.1037/ocp0000056

Bakker, A. B., Demerouti, E., & Euwema, M. C. (2005). Job resources buffer the impact of job demands on burnout. *Journal of Occupational Health Psychology, 10*(2), 170–180. https://doi.org/10.1037/1076-8998.10.2.170. http://search.ebscohost.com/login.aspx?direct=true&db=psyh&AN=2005-03471-007&loginpage=Login.asp&site=ehost-live

Bakker, A. B., Demerouti, E., & Sanz-Vergel, A. I. (2014). Burnout and work engagement: The JD-R approach. In F. P. Morgeson (Ed.), *Annual review of organizational psychology and organizational behavior (Vol. 1*, pp. 389–411).

Bakker, A. B., Demerouti, E., & Sanz-Vergel, A. (2023). Job demands-resources theory: Ten years later. *Annual Review of Organizational Psychology and Organizational Behavior, 10*(13.1–13.29). https://doi.org/10.1146/annurev-orgpsych-120920-053933

Bakker, A. B., Demerouti, E., & Verbeke, W. (2004). Using the job demands-resources model to predict burnout and performance. *Human Resource Management, 43*(1), 83–104.

Bakker, A. B., Le Blanc, P. M., & Schaufeli, W. B. (2005). Burnout contagion among nurses at intensive care units. *Journal of Advanced Nursing, 51,* 276–287.

Bakker, A. B., Schaufeli, W. B., Leiter, M. P., & Taris, T. W. (2008). Work engagement: An emerging concept in occupational health psychology. *Work & Stress, 22*(3), 187–200.

Bakker, A. B., van Emmerik, H., & Euwema, M. C. (2006). Crossover of burnout and engagement in work teams. *Work and Occupations, 33*(4), 464–489. https://doi.org/10.1177/0730888406291310

Bal, P. M., & Izak, M. (2020). Paradigms of flexibility: A systematic review of research on workplace flexibility. *European Management Review,* 1–14. https://doi.org/10.1111/emre.12423

Bambra, C., Egan, M., Thomas, S., Petticrew, M., & Whitehead, M. (2007). The psychosocial and health effects of workplace reorganisation. 2. A systematic review of task restructuring interventions. *Journal of Epidemiology and Community Health, 61*(12), 1028–1037. https://doi.org/10.1136/jech.2006.054999

Bandura, A. (1997). *Self-efficacy: The exercise of control.* Freeman.

Bank, T. W. (2020). *Unemployment, total (% of total labor force) (modeled ILO estimate).*

Bapuji, H., Ertug, G., & Shaw, J. D. (2020). Organizations and societal economic inequality: A review and way forward. *Academy of Management Annals, 14*(1), 60–91.

Bargh, J. A. (1994). The four horsemen of automaticity: Awareness, efficiency, intention and control in social cognition. In R. S. Wyer & T. K. Srull (Eds.), *Handbook of social cognition* (2nd ed., pp. 1–40). Erlbaum.

Bargh, J. A., & Williams, E. L. (2006). The automaticity of social life. *Current Directions in Psychological Science, 15,* 1–4.

Barley, S. R., Meyerson, D. E., & Grodal, S. (2011). E-mail as a source and symbol of stress. *Organizational Science, 22*(4), 887–906. https://doi.org/10.1287/orsc.1100.0573

Barley, S., Meyerson, D., & Grodal, S. (2011). E-mail as a source and symbol of stress. *Organization Science, 22*(4), 887–906. https://www.researchgate.net/deref/http%3A%2F%2Fdx.doi.org%2F10.2307%2F20868902

Barling, J., & Cloutier, A. (2017). Leaders' mental health at work: Empirical, methodological, and policy directions. *Journal of Occupational Health Psychology, 22*(3), 394–406.

Barrero, J. M., Bloom, N., & Davis, S. J. (December 10, 2020). *Why working from home will stick.* https://ssrn.com/abstract=3741644

Barros, M. F. D. S., Araújo-Moreira, F. M., Trevelin, L. C., & Radel, R. (2018). Flow experience and the mobilization of attentional resources. *Cognitive, Affective, & Behavioral Neuroscience, 18*(4), 810–823. https://doi.org/10.3758/s13415-018-0606-4

Barsky, A., Thoresen, C. J., Warren, C. R., & Kaplan, S. A. (2004). Modeling negative affectivity and job stress: A contingency-based approach. *Journal of Organizational Behavior: The International Journal of Industrial, Occupational and Organizational Psychology and Behavior, 25*(8), 915–936.

Bartone, P. T. (2007). Test-retest reliability of the dispositional resilience scale-15, a brief hardiness scale. *Psychological Reports*, *101*(3), 943–944.

Baruch, Y. (2004). Transforming careers: From linear to multidirectional career paths – Organizational and individual perspectives. *Career Development International*, *9*(1), 58–73. https://doi.org/10.1108/13620430410518147

Baruch-Feldman, C., Brondolo, E., Ben-Dayan, D., & Schwartz, J. (2002). Sources of social support and burnout, job satisfaction, and productivity. *Journal of Occupational Health Psychology*, *7*(1), 84–93.

Bass, B. M., & Bass, R. (2008). *The Bass handbook of leadership: Theory, research, and managerial applications*. The Free Press.

Bavik, Y. L., Shaw, J. D., & Wang, X.-H. (2020). Social support: Multi-disciplinary review, synthesis, and future agenda. *Academy of Management Annals*, *14*, 726–758.

Beal, D. J. (2015). ESM 2.0: State of the art and future potential of experience sampling methods in organizational research. *Annual Review of Organizational Psychology and Organizational Behavior*, *2*(1), 383–407.

Becker, W. J., Cropanzano, R., & Sanfey, A. G. (2011). Organizational neuroscience: Taking organizational theory inside the neural black box. *Journal of Management*, *37*(4), 933–961. https://doi.org/10.1177/0149206311398955

Beehr, T. (1987). The themes of social-psychological stress in work organizations: From roles to goals. In A. W. Riley & S. J. Zaccaro (Eds.), *Occupational stress and organizational effectiveness* (pp. 71–101). Praeger.

Beehr, T. A. (1998). An organizational psychology meta-model of occupational stress. In C. Cooper (Ed.), *Theories of organizational stress* (pp. 6–27). Oxford University Press.

Beehr, T., & Bhagat, R. (1985). Introduction to human stress and cognition in organizations. In T. A. Beehr & R. S. Bhagat (Eds.), *Human stress and cognition in organizations: An integrated perspective* (pp. 3–19). John Wiley.

Beehr, T., & Bowling, N. (2005). Hardy personality, stress, and health. In C. L. Cooper (Ed.), *Handbook of stress medicine and health* (pp. 193–211). CRC Press.

Beehr, T. A., Bowling, N. A., & Bennett, M. M. (2010). Occupational stress and failures of social support: When helping hurts. *Journal of Occupational Health Psychology*, *15*(1), 45–59.

Beehr, T. A., & Franz, T. (1987). The current debate about the meaning of job stress. *Journal of Organizational Behavior Management*, *8*, 5–18.

Beehr, T. A., Jex, S. M., Stacy, B. A., & Murray, M. A. (2000). Work stressors and coworker support as predictors of individual strain and job performance. *Journal of Organizational Behavior*, *21*(4), 391–405.

Beehr, T. A., & O'Hara, K. (1987). Methodological designs for evaluation of occupational stress interventions. In S. Kasl & C. Cooper (Eds.), *Stress and health: Issues in research methodology* (pp. 79–112). John Wiley.

Beehr, T. A., Ragsdale, J. M., & Kochert, J. F. (2015). Effects of initial resources on the development of strains during a stressful training situation: Some counterintuitive results. *Journal of Organizational Behavior*, *36*(4), 467–490.

de Beer, L. T., & Bianchi, R. (2019). Confirmatory factor analysis of the Maslach Burnout Inventory a Bayesian structural equation modeling approach. *European Journal of Psychological Assessment*, *35*(2), 217–224. https://doi.org/10.1027/1015-5759/a000392

Belkic, K. L., Landsbergis, P. A., Schnall, P. L., & Baker, D. (2004). Is job strain a major source of cardiovascular disease risk? *Scandinavian Journal of Work, Environment & Health, 30*(2), 85–128.

Ben-Avi, N., Toker, S., & Heller, D. (2018). «If stress is good for me, it's probablygood for you too»: Stress mindset and judgement of others' strain. *Journal of Experimental Social Psychology, 74*, 98–110. https://doi.org/10.1016/j.jesp.2017.09.002

Benach, J., & Muntaner, C. (2007). Precarious employment and health: Developing a research agenda. *Journal of Epidemiology & Community Health, 61*(4), 276–277.

Best, R. G., Stapleton, L. M., & Downey, R. G. (2005). Core self-evaluations and job burnout: The test of alternative models. *Journal of Occupational Health Psychology, 10*(4), 441–451.

Bianchi, S. M., & Milkie, M. A. (2010). Work and family research in the first decade of the 21st century. *Journal of Marriage and Family, 72*(3), 705–725.

Bianchi, R., Schonfeld, I. S., & Laurent, E. (2015). Burnout–depression overlap: A review. *Clinical Psychology Review, 36*, 28–41. https://doi.org/10.1016/j.cpr.2015.01.004

Bidwell, M., Briscoe, F., Fernandez-Mateo, I., & Sterling, A. (2013). The employment relationship and inequality: How and why changes in employment practices are reshaping rewards in organizations. *Academy of Management Annals, 7*(1), 61–121.

Biron, C. (2012). What works, for whom, in which context? Researching organizational stress and well-being using realistic evaluation principles. In C. Biron, M. karanika-Murray, & C. L. Cooper (Eds.), *Improving organizational interventions for stress and well-being* (pp. 163–183). Routledge.

Biron, C., Gatrell, C., & Cooper, C. L. (2010). Autopsy of a failure: Evaluating process and contextual issues in an organizational-level work stress intervention. *International Journal of Stress Management, 17*(2), 135–158. https://doi.org/10.1037/a0018772

Biron, C., & Karanika-Murray, M. (2014). Process evaluation for organizational stress and well-being interventions: Implications for theory, method, and practice. *International Journal of Stress Management, 21*(1), 85–111. https://doi.org/10.1037/a0033227

Biron, C., Karanika-Murray, M., & Cooper, C. L. (2012). Organizational interventions for stress and well-being – an overview. In C. Biron, M. Karanika-Murray, & C. L. Cooper (Eds.), *Improving organizational interventions for stress and well-being. Addressing process and context* (pp. 1–17). Routledge.

Bliese, P. D., Chan, D., & Ployhart, R. E. (2007). Multilevel methods: Future directions in measurement, longitudinal analyses, and nonnormal outcomes. *Organizational Research Methods, 10*(4), 551–563. https://doi.org/10.1177/1094428107301102

Bliese, P. D., Edwards, J. R., & Sonnentag, S. (2017). Stress and well-being at work: A century of empirical trends reflecting theoretical and societal influences. *Journal of Applied Psychology, 102*(3), 389–402. https://doi.org/10.1037/apl0000109

Bliese, P. D., & Jex, S. M. (2002). Incorporating a multilevel perspective into occupational stress research: Theoretical, methodological, and practical implications. *Journal of Occupational Health Psychology, 7*(3), 265–276. https://doi.org/10.1037//1076-8998.7.3.265

Bliese, P. D., & Ployhart, R. E. (2002). Growth modeling using random coefficient models: Model building, testing, and illustration. *Organizational Research Methods, 5*(4), 362–387.

Blustein, D. L. (2008). The role of work in psychological health and well-being: A conceptual, historical, and public policy perspective. *American Psychologist, 63*(4), 228–240. https://doi.org/10.1037/0003-066X.63.4.228

Bolger, N., & Zuckerman, A. (1995). A framework for studying personality in the stress process. *Journal of Personality and Social Psychology, 69*(5), 890–902.

Bond, F. W., & Bunce, D. (2001). Job control mediates change in a work reorganization intervention for stress reduction. *Journal of Occupational Health Psychology, 6*(4), 290–302. https://doi.org/10.1037/1076-8998.6.4.290

Borritz, M., Rugulies, R., Bjorner, J. B., Villadsen, E., Mikkelsen, O. A., & Kristensen, T. S. (2006). Burnout among employees in human service work: Design and baseline findings of the PUMA study. *Scandinavian Journal of Public Health, 34*(1), 49–58.

Boswell, W. R., & Olson-Buchanan, J. B. (2007). The use of communication technologies after hours: The role of work attitudes and work-life conflict. *Journal of Management, 33*(4), 592–610.

Boudreau, R. A., Boudreau, W. F., & Mauthe-Kaddura, A. J. (2015). From 57 for 57: A bibliography of burnout citations. In *Paper presented at the 17th conference of the European association of work and organizational psychology (EAWOP), Oslo, Norway.*

Bouman, A. H., te Brake, H., & Hoogstraten, J. (2002). Significant effects due to rephrasing the Maslach Burnout Inventory's personal accomplishment items. *Pschological Reports, 91*, 84–93.

Bowling, N. A., Alarcon, G. M., Bragg, C. B., & Hartman, M. J. (2015). A meta-analytic examination of the potential correlates and consequences of workload. *Work & Stress, 29*(2), 95–113.

Bowling, N. A., & Jex, S. M. (2013). The role of personality in occupational stress: A review and future research agenda. In N. D. Christiansen & R. A. Tett (Eds.), *Handbook of personality at work* (pp. 692–717). Routledge.

Bowling, N. A., & Kirkendall, C. (2012). Workload: A review of causes, consequences, and potential interventions. *Contemporary Occupational Health Psychology: Global Perspectives on Research and Practice, 2*, 221–238.

Boyar, S. L., Campbell, N. S., Mosley Jr, D. C., & Carson, C. M. (2014). Development of a work/family social support measure. *Journal of Managerial Psychology, 29*(7), 901–920.

Boyczuk, A. M., & Fletcher, P. C. (2016). The ebbs and flows: Stresses of sandwich generation caregivers. *Journal of Adult Development, 23*(1), 51–61. https://doi.org/10.1007/s10804-015-9221-6

Bradley, H. (1969). Community-based treatment for young adult offenders. *Crime and Delinquency, 15*, 359–370.

Brake, D., & Bates, G. (2001). Fatigue in industrial workers under thermal stress on extended shift lengths. *Occupational Medicine, 51*(7), 456–463.

Bray, S. R., Beauchamp, M. R., Eys, M. A., & Carron, A. V. (2005). Does the need for role clarity moderate the relationship between role ambiguity and athlete satisfaction? *Journal of Applied Sport Psychology, 17*(4), 306–318.

Brief, A. P., & George, J. M. (1991). Psychological stress and the workplace: A brief comment on Lazarus' outlook. *Journal of Social Behavior and Personality, 6*, 15–20.

Britt, T. W., Shuffler, M. L., Pegram, R. L., Xoxakos, P., Rosopa, P. J., Hirsh, E., & Jackson, W. (2021). Job demands and resources among healthcare professionals during virus pandemics: A review and examination of fluctuations in mental health strain during COVID-19. *Applied Psychology: An International Review, 70*(1), 120–149. https://doi.org/10.1111/apps.12304

Brivio, E., Gaudisio, F., Vergine, I., Mirizzi, C. R., Reina, C., Stellari, A., & Galimberti, C. (2018). Preventing technostress through positive technology. *Frontiers in Psychology, 9*, 1–5. https://doi.org/10.3389/fpsyg.2018.02569

Brockner, J., Higgins, E. T., & Low, M. B. (2004). Regulatory focus theory and the entrepreneurial process. *Journal of Business Venturing, 19*, 203–220. https://doi.org/10.1016/S0883-9026(03)00007-7

Brockner, J., Spreitzer, G., Mishra, A., Hochwarter, W., Pepper, L., & Weinberg, J. (2004). Perceived control as an antidote to the negative effects of layoffs on survivors' organizational commitment and job performance. *Administrative Science Quarterly, 49*(1), 76–100.

Brosschot, J. F., Pieper, S., & Thayer, J. F. (2005). Expanding stress theory: Prolonged activation and perseverative cognition. *Psychoneuroendocrinology, 30*(10), 1043–1049. https://doi.org/10.1016/j.psyneuen.2005.04.008

Brough, P., & Biggs, A. (2015). Job demands× job control interaction effects: Do occupation-specific job demands increase their occurrence? *Stress and Health, 31*(2), 138–149.

Brough, P., Drummond, S., & Biggs, A. (2018). Job support, coping, and control: Assessment of simultaneous impacts within the occupational stress process. *Journal of Occupational Health Psychology, 23*(2), 188–197.

Brown, R. B., Duck, J., & Jimmieson, N. (2014). E-mail in the workplace: The role of stress appraisals and normative response pressure in relationship between e-mail stressors and employee strain. *International Journal of Stress Management, 21*(4), 325–347. https://doi.org/10.1037/a0037464

Brown, A. R., Walters, J. E., & Jones, A. E. (2019). Pathways to retention: Job satisfaction, burnout, & organizational commitment among social workers. *Journal of Evidence-Based Social Work, 16*(6), 577–594. https://doi.org/10.1080/26408066.2019.1658006

Bruk-Lee, V., Khoury, H. A., Nixon, A. E., Goh, A., & Spector, P. E. (2009). Replicating and extending past personality/job satisfaction meta-analyses. *Human Performance, 22*(2), 156–189.

Buch, R., Dysvik, A., Kuvaas, B., & Nerstad, C. G. (2015). It takes three to tango: Exploring the interplay among training intensity, job autonomy, and supervisor support in predicting knowledge sharing. *Human Resource Management, 54*(4), 623–635.

Burke, R. J., & Richardsen, A. M. (2001). Psychological burnout in organizations: Research and intervention. In R. T. Golembiewski (Ed.), *Handbook of organizational behavior* (Second edition, revised and expanded). Marcel Dekker.

Burke, R. J., & Richardsen, A. M. (Eds.). (2014). *Corporate wellness programs: Linking employee and organizational health*. Edward Elgar.

Burke, R. J., & Richardsen, A. M. (2019). *Creating psychologically healthy workplaces*. Edward Elgar.

Burris, E. R., Detert, J. R., & Chiaburu, D. S. (2008). Quitting before leaving: The mediating effects of psychological attachment and detachment on voice. *Journal of Applied Psychology, 93*(4), 912–922.

Burström, L., Nilsson, T., & Wahlström, J. (2015). Whole-body vibration and the risk of low back pain and sciatica: A systematic review and meta-analysis. *International Archives of Occupational and Environmental Health, 88*(4), 403–418.

Butler, M. J. R., O'Broin, H. L. R., Lee, N., & Senior, C. (2016). How organizational neuroscience can deepen understanding of managerial decision-making: A review of the recent literature and future directions. *International Journal of Management Reviews, 18,* 542–559. https://doi.org/10.1111/ijmr.12071

Byron, K. (2005). A meta-analytic review of work-family conflict and its antecedents. *Journal of Vocational Behavior, 67*(2), 169–198. https://doi.org/10.1016/j.jvb.2004.08.009

Caldas, M. P., Ostermeier, K., & Cooper, D. (2020). When helping hurts: COVID-19 critical incident involvement and resource depletion in health care workers. *Journal of Applied Psychology, 106*(1), 29–47. https://doi.org/10.1037/apl0000850

Camerer, C., Loewenstein, G., & Prelec, D. (2005). Neuroeconomics: How neuroscience can inform economics. *Journal of Economic Literature, 43*(1), 9–64.

Campbell Quick, J., & Henderson, D. F. (2016). Occupational stress: Preventing suffering, enhancing wellbeing. *International Journal of Environmental Research and Public Health, 13,* 1–11. https://doi.org/10.3390/ijerph13050459

Campbell, J. P., & Wiernik, B. M. (2015). The modeling and assessment of work performance. *Annual Review of Organizational Psychology and Organizational Behavior, 2*(1), 47–74. https://doi.org/10.1146/annurev-orgpsych-032414-111427

Cannon, W. (1935). Stresses and strain of homeostasis. *American Journal of Medical Science, 189*(1), 1–14.

Cappelli, P. H., & Keller, J. R. (2013a). Classifying work in the new economy. *Academy of Management Review, 38*(4), 575–596.

Cappelli, P. H., & Keller, J. R. (2013b). A study of the extent and potential causes of alternative employment arrangements. *ILR Review, 66*(4), 874–901.

Cartwright, S., & Cooper, C. L. (1997). *Managing workplace stress.* SAGE.

Carver, C. S., & Connor-Smith, J. (2010). Personality and coping. *Annual Review of Psychology, 61,* 679–704. https://doi.org/10.1146/annurev.psych.093008.100352

Cascio, W. F., & Montealegre, R. (2016). How technology is changing work and organizations. *Annual Review of Organizational Psychology and Organizational Behavior, 3,* 349–375. https://doi.org/10.1146/annurev-orgpsych-041015-062352

Casper, A., & Sonnentag, S. (2020). Feeling exhausted or vigorous in anticipation of high workload? The role of worry and planning during the evening. *Journal of Occupational and Organizational Psychology, 93,* 215–242. https://doi.org/10.1111/joop.12290

Casper, A., Sonnentag, S., & Tremmel, S. (2017). Mindset matters: The role of employees' stress mindset for day-specific reactions to workload anticipation. *European Journal of Work and Organizational Psychology, 26*(6), 798–810. https://doi.org/10.1080/1359432X.2017.1374947

Casper, W. J., Vaziri, H., Wayne, J. H., DeHauw, S., & Greenhaus, J. (2018). The jingle-jangle of work-nonwork balance: A conceptual meta-analytic review of its meaning and measurement. *Journal of Applied Psychology, 103*(2), 182–214. https://doi.org/10.1037/apl0000259

Cavanaugh, M. A., Boswell, W. R., Roehling, M. V., & Boudreau, J. W. (2000). An empirical examination of self-reported work stress among U.S. managers. *Journal of Applied Psychology, 85*(1), 65–74. https://doi.org/10.1037/0021-9010.85.1.65

Cendales-Ayala, B., Useche, S. A., Gómez-Ortiz, V., & Bocarejo, J. P. (2017). Bus operators' responses to job strain: An experimental test of the job demand–control model. *Journal of Occupational Health Psychology, 22*(4), 518–527.

Cerqueira, J. J., Mailliet, F., Almeida, O. F., Jay, T. M., & Sousa, N. (2007). The prefrontal cortex as a key target of the maladaptive response to stress. *Journal of Neuroscience, 27*(11), 2781–2787.

Chang, C.-H., Ferris, D. L., Johnson, R. E., Rosen, C. C., & Tan, J. A. (2012). Core self-evaluations: A review and evaluation of the literature. *Journal of Management, 38*(1), 81–128.

Chang, C.-H., Johnson, R. E., & Yang, L.-Q. (2007). Emotional strain and organizational citizenship behaviours: A meta-analysis and review. *Work & Stress, 21*(4), 312–332.

Chang, C.-H., Rosen, C. C., & Levy, P. E. (2009). The relationship between perceptions of organizational politics and employee attitudes, strain, and behavior: A meta-analytic examination. *Academy of Management Journal, 52*(4), 779–801.

Charalampous, M., Grant, C. A., Tramontano, C., & Michailidis, E. (2019). Systematically reviewing remote e-workers' well-being at work: A multidimensional approach. *European Journal of Work and Organizational Psychology, 28*(1), 51–73.

Chawla, N., MacGowan, R. L., Gabriel, A. S., & Podsakoff, N. P. (2020). Unplugging or staying connected? Examining the nature, antecedents, and consequences of profiles of daily recovery experiences. *Journal of Applied Psychology, 105*(1), 19–39. https://doi.org/10.1037/apl0000423

Chen, P. Y., Cigularov, K. P., & Menger, L. M. (2012). Experimental and quasi-experimental designs in occupational health psychology. In R. R. Sinclair, M. Wang, & L. E. Tetrick (Eds.), *Research methods in occupational health psychology: Measurement, design, and data analysis*. Routledge.

Cherniss, C. (1980). *Professional burnout in human service organizations*. Praeger.

Cheung, F. M., & Halpern, D. F. (2010). Women at the top: Powerful leaders define success as work + family in a culture of gender. *American Psychologist, 65*(3), 182–193.

Chiaburu, D. S., & Harrison, D. A. (2008). Do peers make the place? Conceptual synthesis and meta-analysis of coworker effects on perceptions, attitudes, OCBs, and performance. *Journal of Applied Psychology, 93*(5), 1082–1103.

Chokshi, N. (3 December 2020). What if you had a four-day week? Why don't you? *The New York Times*. https://www.nytimes.com/2019/11/08/business/four-day-work-week.html

Chrisopoulos, S., Dollard, M. F., Winefield, A. H., & Dormann, C. (2010). Increasing the probability of finding an interaction in work stress research: A two-wave longitudinal test of the triple-match principle. *Journal of Occupational and Organizational Psychology, 83*(1), 17–37.

Christian, P., & Lolas, F. (1985). The stress concept as a problem for a theoretical pathology. *Social Science and Medicine, 2*, 363–365.

Clarke, S. (2012). The effect of challenge and hindrance stressors on safety behavior and safety outcomes: A meta-analysis. *Journal of Occupational Health Psychology, 17*(4), 387–397.

Cohen, S., Gianaros, P. J., & Manuck, S. B. (2016). A stage model of stress and disease. *Perspectives on Psychological Science, 11*(4), 456–463. https://doi.org/10.1177/1745691616646305

Cole, D. A., & Maxwell, S. E. (2003). Testing mediational models with longitudinal data: Questions and tips in the use of structural equation modeling. *Journal of Abnormal Psychology, 112*(4), 558–577.

Connelly, C. E., Fieseler, C., Cerne, M., & Giessner, S. R. (2021). Working in the digitized economy: HRM theory & practice. *Human Resource Management Review, 31*. https://doi.org/10.1016/j.hrmr.2020.100762

Connelly, C. E., & Turel, O. (2016). Effects of team emotional authenticity on virtual team. *Frontiers in Psychology, 7,* 1–13, Article 1336. https://doi.org/10.3389%2Ffpsyg.2016.01336

Conrad, C. D. (2011). *The handbook of stress: Neuropsychological effects on the brain* (C. D. Conrad, Ed. Vol. 9). John Wiley & Sons.

Consiglio, C., Borgogni, L., Alessandri, G., & Schaufeli, W. B. (2013). Does self-efficacy matter for burnout and sickness absenteeism? The mediating role of demands and resources at the individual and team levels. *Work & Stress, 27*(1), 22–42.

Conway, G., Szalma, J., & Hancock, P. (2007). A quantitative meta-analytic examination of whole-body vibration effects on human performance. *Ergonomics, 50*(2), 228–245.

Cook, T. D., & Campbell, D. T. (1979). *Quasi-experimentation: Design and analysis issues for field settings.* Houghton Mifflin.

Cooper, C. L. (1987). The experience and management of stress: Job and organizational determinants. In A. W. Riley & S. J. Zaccaro (Eds.), *Occupational stress and organizational effectiveness* (pp. 53–69). Praeger.

Cooper, C. (1996). Hot under the collar. *Times Higher Education Supplement, 21*(June), 12–16.

Cooper, C. L. (2005). The future of work: Careers, stress and well-being. *Career Development International, 10*(5), 396–399. https://doi.org/10.1108/13620430510615319

Cooper, C. L., & Cartwright, S. (1994). Healthy mind; healthy organizations – A proactive approach to occupational stress. *Human Relations, 47,* 455–469.

Cooper, C. L., & Lu, L. (2019). Excessive availability for work: Good or bad? Charting underlying motivations and searching for game-changers. *Human Resource Management Review, 29.* https://doi.org/10.1016/j.hrmr.2019.01.003

Cooper, C., & Smith, M. (1985). *Job stress and blue collar work.* John Wiley.

Cordes, C. L., & Dougherty, T. W. (1993). A review and integration of research on job burnout. *Academy of Management Review, 18,* 621–656.

Costa, G. (2003). Factors influencing health of workers and tolerance to shift work. *Theoretical Issues in Ergonomics Science, 4*(3–4), 263–288.

Costa, G. (2010). Shift work and health: Current problems and preventive actions. *Safety and Health at Work, 1*(2), 112–123.

Cox, T. (1985). *Stress* (2nd ed.). Macmillan.

Cox, T. (1987). Stress, coping and problem solving. *Work and Stress, 1,* 5–14.

Cox, T. (1990). The recognition and measurement of stress: Conceptual and methodological issues. In N. Corlett & J. Wilson (Eds.), *Evaluation of human work*. Taylor & Francis.

Coyne, J., & Gottlieb, B. (1996). The mismeasure of coping by checklist. *Journal of Personality, 64*, 959–991.

Crane, M. F., & Searle, B. J. (2016). Building resilience through exposure to stressors: The effects of challenges versus hindrances. *Journal of Occupational Health Psychology, 21*(4), 468–479.

Crawford, E. R., Lepine, J. A., & Rich, B. L. (2010). Linking job demands and resources to employee engagement and burnout: A theoretical extension and meta-analytic test. *Journal of Applied Psychology, 95*(5), 834–848.

Crook, Z., & Booth, T. (2017). Considering the appropriateness of the factor analytic operationalization of allostatic load. *Psychosomatic Medicine, 79*(1), 117–119.

Crum, A. J., Akinola, M., Martin, A., & Fath, S. (2017). The role of stress mindset in shaping cognitive, emotional, and physiological responses to challenging and threatening stress. *Anxiety, Stress and Coping, 30*(4), 379–395. https://www.tandfonline.com/action/showCitFormats?doi=10.1080/10615806.2016.1275585

Crum, A. J., Salovey, P., & Achor, S. (2013). Rethinking stress: The role of mindsets in determining the stress response. *Journal of Personality and Social Psychology, 104*(4), 716–733.

Csikzentmihalyi, M., & Csikzentmihalyi, I. S. (1988). *Optimal experience: Psychological studies of flow in consciousness*. Cambridge University Press.

Cummings, M. L., Gao, F., & Thornburg, K. M. (2016). Boredom in the workplace: A new look at an old problem. *Human Factors, 58*(2), 279–300.

Currie, G., Tempest, S., & Starkey, K. (2006). New careers for old? Organizational and individual responses to changing boundaries. *International Journal of Human Resource Management, 17*(4), 755–774.

Daatland, S. O., Veenstra, M., & Lima, I. A. (2010). Norwegian sandwiches. *European Journal of Ageing, 7*(4), 271–281. https://doi.org/10.1007/s10433-010-0163-3

Dahl, M. S. (2011). Organizational change and employee stress. *Management Science, 57*(2), 240–256.

Daniels, K., & De Jonge, J. (2010). Match making and match breaking: The nature of match within and around job design. *Journal of Occupational and Organizational Psychology, 83*(1), 1–16.

Danna, K., & Griffin, R. W. (1999). Health and well-being in the workplace: A review and synthesis of the literature. *Journal of Management, 25*(3), 357–384.

Darr, W., & Johns, G. (2008). Work strain, health, and absenteeism: A meta-analysis. *Journal of Occupational Health Psychology, 13*(4), 293–318.

Datta, D. K., Guthrie, J. P., Basuil, D., & Pandey, A. (2010). Causes and effects of employee downsizing: A review and synthesis. *Journal of Management, 36*(1), 281–348.

Davis, M. C., Leach, D. J., & Clegg, C. W. (2011). The physical environment of the office: Contemporary and emerging issues. In G. P. Hodgkinson & J. K. Ford (Eds.), *International review of industrial and organizational psychology* (Vol. 26, pp. 193–237). Wiley Blackwell.

Dawson, K. M., O'Brien, K. E., & Beehr, T. A. (2016). The role of hindrance stressors in the job demand–control–support model of occupational stress: A proposed theory revision. *Journal of Organizational Behavior, 37*(3), 397–415.

Day, A. L., & Jreige, S. (2002). Examining Type A behavior pattern to explain the relationship between job stressors and psychosocial outcomes. *Journal of Occupational Health Psychology, 7*(2), 109–120.

De Hoogh, A. H., & Den Hartog, D. N. (2009). Neuroticism and locus of control as moderators of the relationships of charismatic and autocratic leadership with burnout. *Journal of Applied Psychology, 94*(4), 1058–1067.

De Jonge, J., & Dormann, C. (2006). Stressors, resources, and strain at work: A longitudinal test of the triple-match principle. *Journal of Applied Psychology, 91*(6), 1359.

De Vos, A., Dewettinck, K., & Buyens, D. (2008). To move or not to move? The relationship between career management and preferred career moves. *Employee Relations, 30*(2), 156–175. https://doi.org/10.1108/01425450810843348

De Witte, H., Pienaar, J., & De Cuyper, N. (2016). Review of 30 years of longitudinal studies on the association between job insecurity and health and well-being: Is there causal evidence? *Australian Psychologist, 51*(1), 18–31.

Debus, M. E., König, C. J., & Kleinmann, M. (2014). The building blocks of job insecurity: The impact of environmental and person-related variables on job insecurity perceptions. *Journal of Occupational and Organizational Psychology, 87*(2), 329–351.

DeChant, P. F., Acs, A., Rhee, K. B., Boulanger, T. S., Snowdon, J. L., Tutty, M. A., & Thomas Craig, K. J. (2019). Effect of organization-directed workplace interventions on physician burnout: A systematic review. *Mayo Clinic Proceedings: Innovations, Quality & Outcomes, 3*(4), 384–408. https://doi.org/10.1016/j.mayocpiqo.2019.07.006

Dedovic, K., Renwick, R., Mahani, N. K., & Engert, V. (2005). The Montreal imaging stress task: Using functional imaging to investigate the effects of perceiving and processing psychosocial stress in the human brain. *Journal of Psychiatry & Neuroscience, 30*(5), 319–325.

Deligkaris, P., Panagopoulou, E., Montgomery, A. J., & Masoura, E. (2014). Job burnout and cognitive functioning: A systematic review. *Work & Stress, 28*(2), 107–123. https://doi.org/10.1080/02678373.2014.909545

Demerouti, E. (2014). Design your own job through job crafting. *European Psychologist, 19*, 237–247.

Demerouti, E., & Bakker, A. B. (2011). The job demands-resources model: Challenges for future research. *SA Journal of Industrial Psychology, 37*, 1–9.

Demerouti, E., & Bakker, A. B. (2022). Job demands-resources theory in times of crises: New propositions. *Organizational Psychology Review.* https://doi.org/10.1177/20413866221135022

Demerouti, E., Bakker, A. B., Nachreiner, F., & Schaufeli, W. B. (June, 2001). The job demands-resources model of burnout. *Journal of Applied Psychology, 86*(3), 499–512. <Go to ISI>://000170878300012

Demerouti, E., Bakker, A. B., Peeters, M. C. W., & Breevaart, K. (2021). New directions in burnout research. *European Journal of Work and Organizational Psychology*, 1–6. https://doi.org/10.1080/1359432X.2021.1979962

Demerouti, E., Bakker, A. B., Vardakou, I., & Kantas, A. (2003). The convergent validity of two burnout instruments: A multitrait-multimethod analysis. *European Journal of Psychological Assessment, 19*(1), 12–23.

Demerouti, E., Mostert, K., & Bakker, A. B. (2010). Burnout and work engagement: A thorough investigation of the independency of both constructs. *Journal of Occupational Health Psychology, 15*(3), 209–222. https://doi.org/10.1037/a0019408

Demerouti, E., & Nachreiner, F. (1996). Reliability and validity of the Maslach burnout inventory; A critical approach. *Zeitschrift für Arbeitswissenschaft, 52*, 82–89.

Demerouti, E., Sanz-Vergel, A. I., Petrou, P., & van den Heuvel, M. (2016). How work–self conflict/facilitation influences exhaustion and task performance: A three-wave study on the role of personal resources. *Journal of Occupational Health Psychology, 21*(4), 391–402.

Derks, D., & Bakker, A. B. (2014). Smartphone use, work–home interference, and burnout: A diary study on the role of recovery. *Applied Psychology, 63*(3), 411–440.

Dewe, P. J. (1991). Primary appraisal, secondary appraisal and coping: Their role in stressful work encounters. *Journal of Occupational Psychology, 64*, 331–351.

Dewe, P. (2000). Measures of coping with stress at work: A review and critique. In P. Dewe, M. Leiter, & T. Cox (Eds.), *Coping, health and organizations* (pp. 3–28). Taylor & Francis.

Dewe, P. J. (2017). Demand, resources, and their relationship with coping: Developments, issues, and future directions. In C. L. Cooper & J. C. Quick (Eds.), *The handbook of stress and health: A guide to research and practice* (pp. 427–442). John Wiley & Sons. https://doi.org/10.1002/9781118993811.ch26

Dewe, P. J., & Cooper, C. (2012). *Well-being and work: Towards a balanced agenda*. Palgrave Macmillan.

Dewe, P. J., & Cooper, C. L. (2017). *Work stress and coping: Forces of change and challenges.* SAGE.

Dewe, P., & Cooper, C. L. (2021). *Work and stress: A research overview*. Routledge.

Dewe, P. J., Cox, T., & Ferguson, E. (1993). Individual strategies for coping with stress and work: A review. *Work and Stress, 7*, 5–15.

Dewe, P. J., O'Driscoll, M. P., & Cooper, C. L. (2010). *Coping with work stress: A review and critique*. Wiley-Blackwell.

Dextras-Gauthier, J., Marchand, A., & Haines III, V. (2012). Organizational culture, work organization conditions, and mental health: A proposed integration. *International Journal of Stress Management, 19*(2), 81–104.

DiStasio, M. J., & Shoss, M. K. (2020). Looking forward: How anticipated workload change influences present workload-emotional strain relationship. *Journal of Occupational Health Psychology, 25*(6), 401–409. https://doi.org/10.1037/ocp0000261

DiStaso, M. J., & Shoss, M. (2020). Looking forward: How anticipated workload change influences the present workload-emotional strain relationship. *Journal of Occupational Health Psychology, 25*(6), 401–409. https://doi.org/10.1037/ocp0000261

Dooley, D. (2003). Unemployment, underemployment, and mental health: Conceptualizing employment status as a continuum. *American Journal of Community Psychology, 32*(1/2), 9–20.

Dormann, C., & Griffin, M. A. (2015). Optimal time lags in panel studies. *Psychological Methods, 20*(4), 489.

Dulebohn, J. H., & Hoch, J. E. (2017). Virtual teams in organizations. *Human Resource Management Review, 27*, 569–574. https://doi.org/10.1016/j.hrmr.2016.12.004

Dunahoo, C. L., Hobfoll, S. E., Monnier, J., Hulsizer, M. R., & Johnson, R. (1998). There's more than rugged individualism in coping. Part 1: Even the lone ranger had tonto. *Anxiety, Stress & Coping, 11*(2), 137–165. https://doi.org/10.1080/10615809808248309

Ďuranová, L., & Ohly, S. (2015). *Persistent work-related technology use, recovery and well-being processes: Focus on supplemental work after hours.* Springer.

Eatough, E. M., Chang, C.-H., Miloslavic, S. A., & Johnson, R. E. (2011). Relationships of role stressors with organizational citizenship behavior: A meta-analysis. *Journal of Applied Psychology, 96*(3), 619–632.

Eby, L. T., Casper, W. J., Lockwood, A., Bordeaux, C., & Brinley, A. (2005). Work and family research in IO/OB: Content analysis and review of the literature (1980-2002). *Journal of Vocational Behavior, 66*(1), 124–197. https://doi.org/10.1016/j.jvb.2003.11.003

Eddy, P., Heckenberg, R., Wertheim, E. H., Kent, S., & Wright, B. J. (2016). A systematic review and meta-analysis of the effort-reward imbalance model of workplace stress with indicators of immune function. *Journal of Psychosomatic Research, 91*, 1–8. https://doi.org/10.1016/j.jpsychores.2016.10.003

Eddy, P., Wertheim, E. H., Kingsley, M., & Wright, B. J. (2017). Associations between the effort-reward imbalance model of workplace stress and indices of cardiovascular health: A systematic review and meta-analysis. *Neuroscience and Biobehavioral Reviews, 83*, 252–266. https://doi.org/10.1016/j.neubiorev.2017.10.025

Eden, D. (2017). Field experiments in organizations. *Annual Review of Organizational Psychology and Organizational Behavior, 4*, 91–122.

Edwards, J. R. (1988). The determinants and consequences of coping with stress. In C. L. Cooper & R. Payne (Eds.), *Causes, coping and consequences of stress and work* (pp. 233–263). John Wiley.

Edwards, J. R., Baglioni, A. J., & Cooper, C. L. (2013). Examining the relationships among self- report measures of the type A behavior pattern: The effects of dimensionality, measurement error, and differences in underlying constructs. In C. L. Cooper (Ed.), *From stress to wellbeing volume 1: The theory and research on occupational stress and wellbeing* (pp. 407–437). Springer.

Edwards, J. R., Baglioni Jr, A., & Cooper, C. L. (1990). Stress, type-A, coping, and psychological and physical symptoms: A multi-sample test of alternative models. *Human Relations, 43*, 919–956.

Edwards, J. R., & Cooper, C. L. (2013). The person-environment fit approach to stress: Recurring problems and some suggested solutions. In C. L. Cooper (Ed.), *From stress to wellbeing* (Vol. 1, pp. 91–108). Palgrave Macmillan. https://doi.org/10.1057/9781137310651_5

Edwards, K. D., & Konold, T. R. (2020). Moderated mediation analysis: A review and application to school climate research. *Practical Assessment, Research, and Evaluation, 25*(1), 1–17.

Egan, M., Bambra, C., Thomas, S., Petticrew, M., Whitehead, M., & Thomson, H. (2007). The psychosocial and health effects of workplace reorganisation. 1. A systematic review of organisational-level interventions that aim to increase employee control. *Journal of*

Epidemiology and Community Health, 61(11), 945. https://doi.org/10.1136/jech.2006.054965

Egan, M., & Bond, L. (2015). The 'best available evidence' could be better: Evidence from systematic reviews of organizational interventions. In M. Karanika-Murray & C. Biron (Eds.), *Derailed organizational interventions for stress and well-being: Confessions of failure and solutions for success* (pp. 245–251). Springer.

Engelen, L., Chau, J., Young, S., Mackey, M., Jeyapalan, D., & Bauman, A. (2019). Is activity-based working impacting health, work performance and perceptions? A systematic review. *Building Research & Information, 47*(4), 468–479. https://doi.org/10.1080/09613218.2018.1440958

Erdogan, B., & Bauer, T. N. (2021). Overqualification at work: A review and synthesis of the literature. *Annual Review of Organizational Psychology and Organizational Behavior, 8.* https://doi.org/10.1146/annurev-orgpsych-012420-055831

Erdogan, B., Bauer, T. N., Peiro, J. M., & Truxillo, D. M. (2011). Overqualified employees: Making the best of a potentially bad situation for individuals and organizations. *Industrial and Organizational Psychology, 4*(2), 215–232.

Eriksen, H. R. (2017). The cognitive activation theory of stress (CATS) in occupational health. In A. M. Rossi, J. A. Meurs, & P. L. Perrewé (Eds.), *Stress and quality of working life: Conceptualizing and assessing stress* (pp. 41–64). Information Age Publishing.

Eriksen, H. R., & Ursin, H. (2004). Subjective health complaints, sensitization, and sustained cognitive activation (stress). *Journal of Psychosomatic Research, 56,* 445–448.

Eschleman, K. J., Bowling, N. A., & Alarcon, G. M. (2010). A meta-analytic examination of hardiness. *International Journal of Stress Management, 17*(4), 277–307.

Eschleman, K. J., Mast, D., Coppler, Q., & Nelson, J. (2019). Organizational factors related to attracting job seekers higher in hardiness. *International Journal of Selection and Assessment, 27*(2), 169–179.

Eurofound. (April, 2020). *Living, working and COVID-19: First findings.*

Executive, U. H. a. S. (2020). *Work-related stress, anxiety or depression statistics in Great Britain, 2020.* https://www.hse.gov.uk/statistics/

Falco, A., Girardi, D., Marcuzzo, G., De Carlo, A., & Bartolucci, G. (2013). Work stress and negative affectivity: A multi-method study. *Occupational Medicine, 63*(5), 341–347.

Fan, W., Moen, P., Kelly, E. L., Hammer, L. B., & Berkman, L. F. (2019). Job strain, time strain, and well-being: A longitudinal, person-centered approach in two industries. *Journal of Vocational Behavior, 110,* 102–116. https://doi.org/10.1016/j.jvb.2018.10.017

Fenlason, K. J., & Beehr, T. A. (1994). Social support and occupational stress: Effects of talking to others. *Journal of Organizational Behavior, 15*(2), 157–175.

Ference, T. P., Stoner, J. A., & Warren, E. K. (1977). Managing the career plateau. *Academy of Management Review, 2*(4), 602–612.

Fernet, C., Trépanier, S.-G., Austin, S., Gagné, M., & Forest, J. (2015). Transformational leadership and optimal functioning at work: On the mediating role of employees' perceived job characteristics and motivation. *Work & Stress, 29*(1), 11–31.

Fila, M. J., Purl, J., & Griffeth, R. W. (2017). Job demands, control and support: Meta-analyzing moderator effects of gender, nationality, and occupation. *Human Resource Management Review, 27*(1), 39–60. https://doi.org/10.1016/j.hrmr.2016.09.004

Finkelstein, S., & Cooper, C. L. (2021). *Advances in mergers & acquisitions*. Emerald Publishing.

Fisher, S. L., & Connelly, C. E. (2016). Lower cost or just lower value? Modeling the organizational costs and benefits of contingent work. *Academy of Management Discoveries, 3*(2), 165–186. https://doi.org/10.5465/amd.2015.0119

Fisher, S. L., & Connelly, C. E. (2017). Lower cost or just lower value? Modeling the organizational costs and benefits of contingent work. *Academy of Management Discoveries, 3*(2), 165–186.

Fisher, D. M., Ragsdale, J. M., & Fisher, E. C. (2019). The importance of definitional and temporal issues in the study of resilience. *Applied Psychology, 68*(4), 583–620.

Flouris, A. D., Dinas, P. C., Ioannou, L. G., Nybo, L., Havenith, G., Kenny, G. P., & Kjellstrom, T. (2018). Workers' health and productivity under occupational heat strain: A systematic review and meta-analysis. *The Lancet Planetary Health, 2*(12), e521–e531.

Folkman, S. (1984). Personal control and stress and coping processes: A theoretical analysis. *Journal of Personality and Social Psychology, 46*, 839–852.

Folkman, S. (1997). Positive psychological states and coping with severe stress. *Anxiety, Stress & Coping, 45*, 1207–1221.

Folkman, S. (2011). Stress, health, and coping: Synthesis, commentary, and future directions. In S. Folkman (Ed.), *The Oxford handbook of stress, health, and coping* (pp. 453–462). Oxford University Press. https://doi.org/10.1093/oxfordhb/9780195375343.013.0022

Folkman, S., & Lazarus, R. S. (1980). An analysis of coping in a middle aged community sample. *Journal of Health and Social Behavior, 21*, 219–231.

Folkman, S., & Lazarus, R. S. (1985). If it changes it must be a process: Study of emotion and coping during three stages of a college examination. *Journal of Personality and Social Psychology, 48*, 150–170. https://doi.org/10.1037/0022-3514.48.1.150

Folkman, S., Lazarus, R. S., Gruen, R. J., & DeLongis, A. (1986). Appraisal, coping, health status, and psychological symptoms. *Journal of Personality and Social Psychology, 50*(3), 571–579.

Folkman, S., & Moskowitz, J. T. (2004). Coping: Pitfalls and promise. *Annual Review of Psychology, 55*, 745–774. https://doi.org/10.1146/annurev.psych.55.090902.141456

Ford, M. T., Heinen, B. A., & Langkamer, K. L. (2007). Work and family satisfaction and conflict: A meta-analysis of cross-domain relations. *Journal of Applied Psychology, 92*(1), 57–80.

Ford, M. T., Matthews, R. A., Wooldridge, J. D., Mishra, V., Kakar, U. M., & Strahan, S. R. (2014). How do occupational stressor-strain effects vary with time? A review and meta-analysis of the relevance of time lags in longitudinal studies. *Work & Stress, 28*(1), 9–30. https://doi.org/10.1080/02678373.2013.877096

Fortunato, V. J. (2004). A comparison of the construct validity of three measures of negative affectivity. *Educational and Psychological Measurement, 64*(2), 271–289.

Fortunato, V. J., & Harsh, J. (2006). Stress and sleep quality: The moderating role of negative affectivity. *Personality and Individual Differences, 41*(5), 825–836.

Foster, W. M., Hassard, J. S., Morris, J., & Cox, J. W. (2019). The changing nature of managerial work: The effects of corporate restructuring on management jobs and careers. *Human Relations, 72*(3), 473–504. https://doi.org/10.1177/0018726719828439

Fouad, N. A., & Bynner, J. (2008). Work transitions. *American Psychologist, 63*(4), 241–251.

Fredrickson, B. (2001). The role of positive emotions in positive psychology. *American Psychologist, 56*(3), 218–226.

French, J., Caplan, R., & Van Harrison, R. (1982). *The mechanisms of job stress and strain.* John Wiley.

French, K. A., Dumani, S., Allen, T. D., & Shockley, K. M. (2018). A meta-analysis of work–family conflict and social support. *Psychological Bulletin, 144*(3), 284.

Frese, M., & Zapf, D. (1988). Methodological issues in the study of work stress: Objective vs subjective measurement of work stress and the question of longitudinal studies. In C. L. Cooper & R. Payne (Eds.), *Causes, coping and consequences of stress at work* (pp. 375–411). Wiley.

Freudenberger, H. J. (1974). Staff burnout. *Journal of Social Issues, 30*, 159–164.

Freudenberger, H. J., & Richelson, G. (1980). *Burn-out: The high cost of high achievement.* Anchor Press.

Fried, Y., Shirom, A., Gilboa, S., & Cooper, C. L. (2008). The mediating effects of job satisfaction and propensity to leave on role stress-job performance relationships: Combining meta-analysis and structural equation modeling. *International Journal of Stress Management, 15*(4), 305–328.

Frone, M. R. (2003). Work-family balance. In J. Cambell Quick & L. E. Tetrick (Eds.), *Handbook of occupational health psychology* (pp. 143–162). American Psychological Association.

Frone, M. R., Russell, M., & Cooper, M. L. (1992). Antecedents and outcomes of work-family conflict: Testing a model of the work-family interface. *Journal of Applied Psychology, 77*(1), 65–78.

Fugate, M., Kinicki, A. J., & Ashforth, B. E. (2004). Employability: A psycho-social construct, its dimensions, and applications. *Journal of Vocational Behavior, 65*, 14–38.

Fuster, J. (2015). *The prefrontal cortex.* Academic Press.

Gable, S. L., & Haidt, J. (2005). What (and why) is positive psychology? *Review of General Psychology, 9*(2), 103–110. 10.1037/1089-2680.9.2.103. http://search.ebscohost.com/login.aspx?direct=true&db=pdh&AN=gpr92103&loginpage=Login.asp&site=ehost-live

Gabriel, A. S., Podsakoff, N. P., Beal, D. J., Scott, B. A., Sonnentag, S., Trougakos, J. P., & Butts, M. M. (2019). Experience sampling methods: A discussion of critical trends and considerations for scholarly advancement. *Organizational Research Methods, 22*(4), 969–1006.

Gajendran, R. S., & Harrison, D. A. (2007). The good, the bad, and the unknown about telecommuting: Meta-analysis of psychological mediators and individual consequences. *Journal of Applied Psychology, 92*(6), 1524–1541.

Galinsky, E., Aumann, K., & Bond, J. T. (2009). *Times are changing: Gender and generation at work and at home.* http://familiesandwork.org/site/research/reports/Times_Are_Changing.pdf

Galvin, B. M., Randel, A. E., Collins, B. J., & Johnson, R. E. (2018). Changing the focus of locus (of control): A targeted review of the locus of control literature and agenda for future research. *Journal of Organizational Behavior, 39*(7), 820–833.

Game, A. M. (2007). Workplace boredom coping: Health, safety, and HR implications. *Personnel Review, 36*(5), 701–721. https://doi.org/10.1108/00483480710774007

Gandolfi, F., & Hansson, M. (2011). Causes and consequences of downsizing: Towards an integrative framework. *Journal of Management & Organization, 17*(4), 498–521.

Gan, W. Q., Moline, J., Kim, H., & Mannino, D. M. (2016). Exposure to loud noise, bilateral high-frequency hearing loss and coronary heart disease. *Occupational and Environmental Medicine, 73*(1), 34–41.

Ganster, D. C., Crain, T. L., & Brossoit, R. M. (2018). Physiological measurement in the organizational sciences: A review and recommendations for future use. *Annual Review of Organizational Psychology and Organizational Behavior, 5*, 267–293.

Ganster, D. C., Fox, M. L., & Dwyer, D. J. (2001). Explaining employees' health care costs: A prospective examination of stressful job demands, personal control, and physiological reactivity. *Journal of Applied Psychology, 86*(5), 954–964.

Ganster, D. C., & Rosen, C. C. (2013). Work stress and employee health: A multidisciplinary review. *Journal of Management, 39*(5), 1085–1122.

Ganster, D. C., Rosen, C. C., & Fisher, G. G. (2018). Long working hours and well-being: What we know, what we do not know, and what we need to know. *Journal of Business and Psychology, 33*(1), 25–39. https://link.springer.com/article/10.1007/s10869-016-9478-1

Ganster, D. C., Schaubroeck, J., Sime, W. E., & Mayes, B. T. (1991). The nomological validity of the Type A personality among employed adults. *Journal of Applied Psychology, 76*(1), 143–168.

Gan, E., Yang, M., Zhou, Y., & Zhang, Y. (2007). The two-factor structure of future-oriented coping and its mediating role in student engagement. *Personality and Individual Differences, 43*, 851–863.

Gaoua, N., Racinais, S., Grantham, J., & El Massioui, F. (2011). Alterations in cognitive performance during passive hyperthermia are task dependent. *International Journal of Hyperthermia, 27*(1), 1–9.

Garcia, R. G., Sangregorio, M. A., & Sanchez, M. L. L. (2019). Factorial validity of the Maslach Burnout inventory-human services survey (MBI-HSS) in a sample of Spanish social workers. *Journal of Social Service Research, 45*(2), 207–219. https://doi.org/10.1080/01488376.2018.1480549

Garden, A. M. (1991). Relationship between burnout and performance. *Journal of Applied Psychology, 69*, 615–622.

Gaudisio, F., Turel, O., & Galimberti, C. (2017). The mediating roles of strain facets and coping strategies in translating techno-stressors into adverse job outcomes. *Computers in Human Behavior, 69*, 189–196. https://doi.org/10.1016/j.chb.2016.12.041

Geiger-Brown, J. M., Lee, C. J., & Trinkoff, A. M. (2012). The role of work schedules in occupational health and safety. In R. Gatchel & I. Schultz (Eds.), *Handbook of occupational health and wellness* (pp. 297–322). Springer. https://doi.org/10.1007/978-1-4614-4839-6_14

Gianaros, P. J., Jennings, J. R., Sheu, L. K., Greer, P. J., Kuller, L. H., & Matthews, K. A. (2007). Prospective reports of chronic life stress predict decreased grey matter volume in the hippocampus. *Neuroimage, 35*(2), 795–803.

Gilboa, S., Shirom, A., Fried, Y., & Cooper, C. (2008). A meta-analysis of work demand stressors and job performance: Examining main and moderating effects. *Personnel Psychology, 61*(2), 227–271.

Gilla, M. A., Gimenez, S. B., Moran, V. E., & Olaz, F. O. (2019). Adaptation and validation of the Maslach Burnout inventory in Argentinian mental health professionals. *Liberabit-Revista De Psicologia, 25*(2), 179–193. https://doi.org/10.24265/liberabit.2019.v25n2.04

Glazer, S. (2011). A new vision for the journal. *International Journal of Stress Management, 18*(1), 1–4. https://doi.org/10.1037/a0022307

Godoy, L. D., Rossignoli, M. T., Delfino-Pereira, P., Garcia-Cairasco, N., & de Lima Umeoka, E. H. (2018). A comprehensive overview on stress neurobiology: Basic concepts and clinical implications. *Frontiers in Behavioral Neuroscience, 12*(127). https://doi.org/10.3389/fnbeh.2018.00127

Goh, J., Pfeffer, J., & Zenios, S. A. (2016). The relationship between workplace stressors and mortality and health costs in the United States. *Management Science, 62*(2), 608–628.

Goh, J., Pfeffer, J., Zenios, S. A., & Rajpal, S. (2015). Workplace stressors & health outcomes: Health policy for the workplace. *Behavioral Science & Policy, 1*(1), 43–52.

Goldberg, D. (1972). *The detection of psychiatric illness by questionnaire.* Oxford University Press.

Goldenhar, L. M., LaMontagne, A. D., Katz, T., Heaney, C., & Landsbergis, P. (2001). The intervention research process in occupational safety and health: An overview from the National Occupational Research Agenda Intervention Effectiveness Research Team. *Journal of Occupational and Environmental Medicine, 43*(7), 616–622. https://journals.lww.com/joem/Fulltext/2001/07000/The_Intervention_Research_Process_in_Occupational.8.aspx

Golembiewski, R. T., & Munzenrider, R. F. (1988). *Phases of Burnout: Developments in concepts and applications.* Praeger.

Golembiewski, R. T., Munzenrider, R., & Stevenson, J. (1985). *Stress in organizations.* Praeger.

Golkar, A., Johansson, E., Kasahara, M., Osika, W., Perski, A., & Savic, I. (2014). The influence of work-related chronic stress on the regulation of emotion and on functional connectivity in the brain. *Plos One, 9*(9), e104550. https://doi.org/10.1371%2Fjournal.pone.0104550

González-Morales, M. G., Peiró, J. M., Rodríguez, I., & Bliese, P. D. (2012). Perceived collective burnout: A multilevel explanation of burnout. *Anxiety, Stress, & Coping, 25*(1), 43–61. https://doi.org/10.1080/10615806.2010.542808

Gonzalez-Mulé, E., & Cockburn, B. S. (2020). This job is (literally) killing me: A moderated-mediated model linking work characteristics to mortality. *Journal of Applied Psychology, 106*(1), 140–151.

Gonzalez-Mulé, E., Kim, M. M., & Ryu, J. W. (2020). A meta-analytic test of multiplicative and additive models of job demands, resources, and stress. *Journal of Applied Psychology, 106*(9), 1490–1529.

Gonzalez-Mulé, E., & Cockburn, B. (2017). Worked to death: The relationships of job demands and job control with mortality. *Personnel Psychology, 70*(1), 73–112.

Goodell, H., Wolf, S., & Rogers, F. B. (1986). Historical perspective. In S. Wolf & A. J. Finestone (Eds.), *Occupational stress, health and performance at work.* PSG Inc.

Gooty, J., Gavin, M., & Ashkanasy, N. M. (2009). Emotions research in OB: The challenges that lie ahead. *Journal of Organizational Behavior: The International Journal of Industrial, Occupational and Organizational Psychology and Behavior, 30*(6), 833–838.

Gorman, C. A., Meriac, J. P., Oversteet, B. L., Apodaca, S., McIntyre, A. L., Park, P., & Godbey, J. N. (2012). A meta-analysis of the regulation focus nomological network: Work-related antecedents and consequences. *Journal of Vocational Behavior, 80*, 160–172. https://doi.org/10.1016/j.jvb.2011.07.005

Gray, J. D., Rubin, T. G., Hunter, R. G., & McEwen, B. S. (2014). Hippocampal gene expression changes underlying stress sensitization and recovery. *Molecular Psychiatry, 19*(11), 1171–1178.

Gray, P., Senabe, S., Naicker, N., Kgalamono, S., Yassi, A., & Spiegel, J. M. (2019). Workplace-based organizational interventions promoting mental health and happiness among healthcare workers: A realist review. *International Journal of Environmental Research and Public Health, 16*(22), 22. https://doi.org/10.3390/ijerph16224396

Gray, C. E., Spector, P. E., Lacey, K. N., Young, B. G., Jacobsen, S. T., & Taylor, M. R. (2020). Helping may be harming: Unintended negative consequences of providing social support. *Work & Stress, 34*(4), 359–385.

Grebner, S., Elfering, A., Semmer, N. K., Kaiser-Probst, C., & Schlapbach, M.-L. (2004). Stressful situations at work and in private life among young workers: An event sampling approach. *Social Indicators Research, 67*(1–2), 11–49.

Greene, J. C., Caracelli, V. J., & Graham, W. F. (1989). Toward a conceptual framework for mixed-methodevaluation designs. *Educational Evaluation and Policy Analysis, 11*, 255–274.

Greenglass, E. R. (2002). Proactive coping and quality of life management. In E. Frydenberg (Ed.), *Beyond coping: Meeting goals, visions, and challenges* (pp. 37–62). Oxford University Press.

Greenglass, E. R., & Fiksenbaum, L. (2009). Proactive coping, positive affect, and well-being. *European Psychologist, 14*, 29–39.

Greenglass, E. R., Fiksenbaum, L., & Eaton, J. (2006). The relationship between coping, social support, functional disability and depression in the elderly. *Anxiety, Stress & Coping: An International Journal, 19*, 15–31.

Greenhaus, J. H., & Beutell, N. J. (1985). Sources of conflict between work and family roles. *Academy of Management Review, 10*(1), 76–88.

Gross, J. J. (1998). The emerging field of emotion regulation: An integrative review. *Review of General Psychology, 2*(3), 271–299. https://doi.org/10.1037%2F1089-2680.2.3.271

Guan, Y., Arthur, M. B., Khapova, S. N., Hall, R. J., & Lord, R. G. (2019). Career boundarylessness and career success: A review, integration and guide to future research. *Journal of Vocational Behavior, 110*, 390–402. https://doi.org/10.1016/j.jvb.2018.05.013

Gulseren, D. B., & Kelloway, E. K. (2019). Multilevel analyses. In P. Brough (Ed.), *Advanced research methods for applied psychology: Design, analysis and reporting* (pp. 259–270). Routledge.

Guthier, C., Dormann, C., & Voelkle, M. C. (2020). Reciprocal effects between job stressors and burnout: A continuous time meta-analysis of longitudinal studies. *Psychological Bulletin, 146*(12), 1146–1173. https://doi.org/10.1037/bul0000304

Hakanen, J. J., & Schaufeli, W. B. (2012). Do burnout and work engagement predict depressive symptoms and life satisfaction? A three-wave seven-year prospective study. *Journal of Affective Disorders*, *141*(2–3), 415–424. https://doi.org/10.1016/j.jad.2012.02.043

Halbesleben, J. R. B. (2006). Sources of social support and burnout: A meta-analytic test of the conservation of resources model. *Journal of Applied Psychology*, *91*(5), 1134–1145. https://doi.org/10.1037/0021-9010.91.5.1134

Halbesleben, J. R. B. (2007). Emotional exhaustion and job performance: The mediating role of motivation. *Journal of Applied Psychology*, *92*, 93–106.

Halbesleben, J. R. B., & Bowler, W. M. (2007). Emotional exhaustion and job performance: The mediating role of motivation. *Journal of Applied Psychology*, *92*(1), 93–106. https://doi.org/10.1037/0021-9010.92.1.93

Halbesleben, J. R. B., & Buckley, M. R. (2004). Burnout in organizational life. *Journal of Management*, *30*(6), 859–879.

Halbesleben, J. R. B., & Leon, M. R. (2014). Multilevel models of burnout. Separating group level and individual level effects in burnout research. In M. P. Leiter, A. B. Bakker, & C. Maslach (Eds.), *Burnout at work: A psychological perspective* (pp. 122–144). Psychology Press.

Halbesleben, J. R. B., Neveu, J. P., Paustian-Underdahl, S. C., & Westman, M. (2014). Getting to the «COR»: Understanding the role of resources in conservation of resources theory. *Journal of Management*, *40*(5), 1334–1364. https://doi.org/10.1177/0149206314527130

Halbesleben, J. R., & Wheeler, A. R. (2015). To invest or not? The role of coworker support and trust in daily reciprocal gain spirals of helping behavior. *Journal of Management*, *41*(6), 1628–1650.

Hall, D. T. (2002). *Careers in and out of organizations*. SAGE.

Hallberg, U. E., Johansson, G., & Schaufeli, W. B. (2007). Type A behavior and work situation: Associations with burnout and work engagement. *Scandinavian Journal of Psychology*, *48*(2), 135–142.

Hall, D., & Moss, J. (1998). The new protean career contract: Helping organizations and employees adapt. *Organizational Dynamics*, *26*(3), 22–36.

Hamborg, K.-C., & Greif, S. (2015). New technologies and stress. In C. L. Cooper, J. C. Quick, & M. J. Shabracq (Eds.), *International handbook of work and health psychology* (3rd ed., pp. 221–250). John Wiley & Sons.

Hammer, L. B., & Neal, M. B. (2008). Working sandwiched-generation care- givers: Prevalence, characteristics, and outcomes. *The Psychologist- Manager Journal*, *11*(1), 93–112. https://doi.org/10.1080/10887150801967324

Handy, C. (1994). *The empty raincoat: Making sense of the future*. Hutchinson.

Hareli, S., & Tzafrir, S. S. (2006). The role of causal attributions in survivors' emotional reactions to downsizing. *Human Resource Development Review*, *5*(4), 400–421.

Harms, P. D., Credé, M., Tynan, M. C., Leon, M., & Jeung, W. (2017). Leadership and stress: A meta-analytic review. *The Leadership Quarterly*, *28*(1), 178–194. http://dx.doi.org/10.1016/j.leaqua.2016.10.006

Harms, P. D., Wood, D., Landay, K., Lester, P. B., & Lester, G. V. (2018). Autocratic leaders and authoritarian followers revisited: A review and agenda for the future. *The Leadership Quarterly*, *29*(1), 105–122.

Harris, J. R. (1991). The utility of the transactional approach for occupational stress research. *Journal of Social Behaviour and Personality*, *6*, 21–29.

Harris, K. J., Harvey, P., & Kacmar, K. M. (2009). Do social stressors impact everyone equally? An examination of the moderating impact of core self-evaluations. *Journal of Business and Psychology*, *24*(2), 153–164.

Harris, A., Ursin, H., Murison, R., & Eriksen, H. R. (2007). Coffee, stress and cortisol in nursing staff. *Psychoneuroendocrinology*, *32*, 322–330.

Hassard, J., Teoh, K. R. H., Visockaite, G., Dewe, P., & Cox, T. (2018). The cost of work-related stress to society: A systematic review. *Journal of Occupational Health Psychology*, *23*(1), 1–17. https://doi.org/10.1037/ocp0000069

Häusser, J. A., Mojzisch, A., Niesel, M., & Schulz-Hardt, S. (2010). Ten years on: A review of recent research on the job demand-control (—support) model and psychological well-being. *Work & Stress*, *24*(1), 1–35.

Hawrot, A., & Koniewski, M. (2018). Factor structure of the Maslach Burnout inventory-educators survey in a polish-speaking sample. *Journal of Career Assessment*, *26*(3), 515–530. https://doi.org/10.1177/1069072717714545

Hayes, A. F. (2017). *Introduction to mediation, moderation, and conditional process analysis: A regression-based approach* (2nd ed.). Guilford Publications.

Hayes, A. F., Montoya, A. K., & Rockwood, N. J. (2017). The analysis of mechanisms and their contingencies: PROCESS versus structural equation modeling. *Australasian Marketing Journal (AMJ)*, *25*(1), 76–81. https://doi.org/10.1016/j.ausmj.2017.02.001

Haynes, S. N., Mumma, G. H., & Pinson, C. (2009). Idiographic assessment: Conceptual and psychometric foundations of individualized behavioral assessment. *Clinical Psychology Review*, *29*(2), 179–191. https://doi.org/10.1016/j.cpr.2008.12.003

Heikkilä, K., Nyberg, S. T., Fransson, E. I., Alfredsson, L., De Bacquer, D., Bjorner, J. B., Bonenfant, S., Borritz, M., Burr, H., & Clays, E. (2012). Job strain and tobacco smoking: An individual-participant data meta-analysis of 166 130 adults in 15 European studies. *PloS One*, *7*(7), e35463.

Hellgren, J., & Sverke, M. (2003). Does job insecurity lead to impaired well-being or vice versa? Estimation of cross-lagged effects using latent variable modelling. *Journal of Organizational Behavior: The International Journal of Industrial, Occupational and Organizational Psychology and Behavior*, *24*(2), 215–236.

Hennekam, S., & Bennett, D. (2015). Involuntary career transition and identity within the artist population. *Personnel Review*, *45*(6), 1114–1131. https://doi.org/10.1108/PR-01-2015-0020

Hershcovis, M. S., & Barling, J. (2010). Towards a multi-foci approach to workplace aggression: A meta-analytic review of outcomes from different perpetrators. *Journal of Organizational Behavior*, *31*(1), 24–44.

Higgins, E. T. (1997). Beyond pleasure and pain. *American Psychologist*, *52*(12), 1280–1300.

Hill, E. J., Erickson, J. J., Holmes, E. K., & Ferris, M. (2010). Workplace flexibility, work hours, and work-life conflict: Finding an extra day or two. *Journal of Family Psychology*, *24*(3), 349–358.

Hill, E. J., Miller, B. C., Weiner, S. P., & Colihan, J. (1998). Influences of the virtual office on aspects of work and work/life balance. *Personnel Psychology*, *51*(3), 667–683.

Hobfoll, S. E. (1989, March). Conservation of resources – A new attempt at conceptualizing stress. *American Psychologist, 44*(3), 513–524. <Go to ISI>://A1989T593500003

Hobfoll, S. E. (2001). The influence of culture, community, and the nested-self in the stress process: Advancing conservation of resources theory. *Applied Psychology: An International Review, 50*(3), 337–421.

Hobfoll, S. E. (2002). Social and psychological resources and adaptation. *Review of General Psychology, 6*(4), 307–324.

Hobfoll, S. E. (2010). Conservation of resources theory: Its implications for stress, health, and resilience. In S. Folkman (Ed.), *The Oxford handbook of stress, health, and coping* (pp. 1–38). Oxford University Press.

Hobfoll, S. E., Dunahoo, C. L., Ben-Porath, Y., & Monnier, J. (1994). Gender and coping: The dual-axis model of coping. *American Journal of Community Psychology, 22*, 49–82.

Hobfoll, S. E., & Freedy, J. (1993). Conservation of resources: A general stress theory applied to burnout. In W. Schaufeli, C. Maslach, & T. Marek (Eds.), *Professional burnout: Recent developments in theory and research* (pp. 115–129). Taylor & Francis.

Hobfoll, S. E., Geller, P., & Dunahoo, C. L. (2003). Women's coping: Communal versus individualistic orientation. In M. J. Schabracq, J. A. M. Winnubst, & C. L. Cooper (Eds.), *The handbook of work and health psychology* (pp. 237–257). John Wiley & Sons.

Hobfoll, S. E., Halbesleben, J., Nevu, J. P., & Westman, M. (2018). Conservation of resources in the organizational context: The reality of resources and their consequences. *Annual Review of Organizational Psychology and Organizational Behavior, 5*, 103–128. https://doi.org/10.1146/annurev-orgpsych-032117-104640

Hobfoll, S. E., Johnson, R. J., Ennis, N., & Jackson, A. P. (2003). Resource loss, resource gain, and emotional outcomes among inner city women. *Journal of Personality and Social Psychology, 84*(3), 632–643.

Hobfoll, S. E., & Shirom, A. (1993). Stress and burnout in the workplace. Conservation of resources. In R. Golembiewski (Ed.), *Handbook of organizational behavior* (pp. 41–60). Marcel Dekker.

Hobfoll, S. E., & Shirom, A. (2001). Conservation of resources theory: Applications to stress and management in the workplace. In R. T. Golembiewski (Ed.), *Handbook of organizational behavior* (Second edition, revised and expanded) (2nd ed., pp. 57–80). Marcel Dekker.

Hochwarter, W. A., Perrewé, P. L., Hall, A. T., & Ferris, G. R. (2005). Negative affectivity as a moderator of the form and magnitude of the relationship between felt accountability and job tension. *Journal of Organizational Behavior: The International Journal of Industrial, Occupational and Organizational Psychology and Behavior, 26*(5), 517–534.

Hochwarter, W. A., Rosen, C. C., Jordan, S. L., Ferris, G. R., Ejaz, A., & Maher, L. P. (2020). Perceptions of organizational politics research: Past, present, and future. *Journal of Management*, 0149206319898506.

Hoendervanger, J. G., Van Yperen, N. W., Mobach, M. P., & Albers, C. J. (2019). Perceived fit in activity-based work environments and its impact on satisfaction and performance. *Journal of Environmental Psychology, 65*. https://doi.org/10.1016/j.jenvp.2019.101339

Höge, T., & Büssing, A. (2004). The impact of sense of coherence and negative affectivity on the work stressor-strain relationship. *Journal of Occupational Health Psychology, 9*(3), 195–205.

Holmes, T. H., & Rahe, R. H. (1967). The social readjustment rating scale. *Journal of Psychosomatic Research*, *11*, 213–218. https://doi.org/10.1016/0022-3999(67)90010-4

Holmgreen, L., Tirone, V., Gerhart, J., & Hobfoll, S. E. (2017). Conservation of resources theory: Resource caravans and passageways in health contexts. In C. L. Cooper & J. C. Quick (Eds.), *The handbook of stress and health: A guide to research and practice* (pp. 443–457). John Wiley & Sons. https://doi.org/10.1002/9781118993811.ch27

Holroyd, K. A., & Lazarus, R. S. (1982). Stress, coping and somatic adaptation. In L. Goldberger & S. Breznitz (Eds.), *Handbook of stress: Theoretical and clinical aspects* (pp. 21–35). Free Press.

Hölzel, B. K., Carmody, J., Evans, K. C., Hoge, E. A., Dusek, J. A., Morgan, L., Pitman, R. K., & Lazar, S. W. (2010). Stress reduction correlates with structural changes in the amygdala. *Social Cognitive and Affective Neuroscience*, *5*(1), 11–17.

van Hooff, M. L., & van Hooft, E. A. (2014). Boredom at work: Proximal and distal consequences of affective work-related boredom. *Journal of Occupational Health Psychology*, *19*(3), 348–359.

Horan, K. A., Nakahara, W. H., DiStaso, M. J., & Jex, S. M. (2020). A review of the challenge-hindrance stress model: Recent advances, expanded paradigms, and recommendations for future research. *Frontiers in Psychology*, *11*, 1–12. https://doi.org/10.3389/fpsyg.2020.560346

Hou, N., Doerr, Aaker, J., Johnson, B. A., & Chen, P. Y. (2017). Locus of control. In C. L. Cooper & J. Cambell Quick (Eds.), *The handbook of stress and health: A guide to research and practice* (1st ed., pp. 283–298). John Wiley & Sons, Ltd.

House, R. J., & Rizzo, J. R. (1972). Role conflict and ambiguity as critical variables in a model of organizational behavior. *Organizational Behavior and Human Performance*, *7*(3), 467–505.

Howard, J. (2017). Nonstandard work arrangements and worker health and safety. *American Journal of Industrial Medicine*, *60*(1), 1–10.

Hsu, Y.-C., Wang, C.-W., & Lan, J.-B. (2020). Evaluating the performance of employee assistance programs (EAP): A checklist developed from a large sample of public agencies. *Asia Pacific Journal of Management*, *37*(3), 935–955. https://doi.org/10.1007/s10490-019-09659-z

Hülsheger, U. R. (2016). From dawn till dusk: Shedding light on the recovery process by investigating daily change patterns in fatigue. *Journal of Applied Psychology*, *101*(6), 905.

Huyghebaert, T., Gillet, N., Beltou, N., Tellier, F., & Fouquereau, E. (2018). Effects of workload on teachers' functioning: A moderated mediation model including sleeping problems and overcommitment. *Stress and Health*, *34*(5), 601–611.

Ibarra, H. (1999). Provisional selves: Experimenting with image and identity in professional adaptation. *Administrative Science Quarterly*, *44*, 764–791.

Ilies, R., Aw, S. S., & Lim, V. K. (2016). A naturalistic multilevel framework for studying transient and chronic effects of psychosocial work stressors on employee health and well-being. *Applied Psychology*, *65*(2), 223–258.

Ilies, R., Johnson, M. D., Judge, T. A., & Keeney, J. (2011). A within-individual study of interpersonal conflict as a work stressor: Dispositional and situational moderators. *Journal of Organizational Behavior*, *32*(1), 44–64.

ILO. (18 March 2020). *COVID-19 and the world of work: Impact and policy responses.* https://www.ilo.org/wcmsp5/groups/public/---dgreports/---dcomm/documents/briefingnote/wcms_738753.pdf

ILO. (1986). *Psychosocial factors at work: Recognition and control.* Report of the Joint ILO/WHO Committee on occupational health. Ninth Session, 1984. I. L. Office.

ILO. (2012). *Towards the right to work: A guidebook for designing innovative public employment programmes.* International Labour Organization. https://www.ilo.org/wcmsp5/groups/public/—ed_emp/documents/publication/wcms_559273.pdf

ILO. (2017). *The gender gap in employment: What's holding women back?, 2020.* https://www.ilo.org/infostories/en-GB/Stories/Employment/barriers-women#intro

ILO. (2020b). *ILO Monitor: COVID-19 and the world of work* (5th ed.).

ILO. (2020c). *Teleworking during the COVID-19 pandemic and beyond: A practical guide.*

ILO. (16 September 2020d). *Social protection spotlight—Unemployment protection in the COVID-19 crisis: Country responses and policy considerations.* https://www.ilo.org/wcmsp5/groups/public/—ed_protect/—soc_sec/documents/publication/wcms_754741.pdf

ILO. (24 April 2020). *Restructuring for recovery and resilience in response to the COVID-19 crisis.* https://www.ilo.org/wcmsp5/groups/public/—ed_emp/—emp_ent/documents/publication/wcms_742725.pdf

Inceoglu, I., Thomas, G., Chu, C., Plans, D., & Gerbasi, A. (2018). Leadership behavior and employee well-being: An integrated review and a future research agenda. *The Leadership Quarterly, 29*(1), 179–202.

Infurna, F. J., Gerstorf, D., & Lachman, M. E. (2020). Midlife in the 2020s: Opportunities and challenges. *American Psychologist, 75*(4), 470–485.

Ipsen, C., Gish, L., & Poulsen, S. (2015). Organizational-level interventions in small and medium-sized enterprises: Enabling and inhibiting factors in the PoWRS program. *Safety Science, 71*, 264–274. https://doi.org/10.1016/j.ssci.2014.07.017

Ito, J. K., & Brotheridge, C. M. (2007). Exploring the predictors and consequences of job insecurity's components. *Journal of Managerial Psychology, 22*(1), 40–64. https://doi.org/10.1108/02683940710721938

Ivancevich, J. M., Matteson, M. T., Freedman, S., & Phillips, J. (1990). Worksite stress management interventions. *American Psychologist, 45*, 252–261.

Iwasaki, Y., MacKay, K., & Mactavish, J. B. (2005). Gender-based analysis of coping with stress among professional managers: Leisure coping and non-leisure coping. *Journal of Leisure Research, 37*, 1–28.

Iwasaki, Y., & Mannell, R. C. (2000). Hierarchical dimensions of leisure stress coping. *Leisure Sciences, 22*(3), 163–181. https://doi.org/10.1080/01490409950121843

Jack, A. I., Rochford, K. C., Friedman, J. P., Passarelli, A. M., & Boyatzis, R. E. (2019). Pitfalls in organizational neuroscience: A critical review and suggestions for future research. *Organizational Research Methods, 22*(1), 421–458. https://doi.org/10.1177/1094428117708857

Jacobs, L. M., Nawaz, M. K., Hood, J. L., & Bae, S. (2012). Burnout among workers in a pediatric health care system. *Workplace Health & Safety, 60*(8), 335–344. https://doi.org/10.3928/21650799-20120726-03

Jahncke, H., Hygge, S., Halin, N., Green, A. M., & Dimberg, K. (2011). Open-plan office noise: Cognitive performance and restoration. *Journal of Environmental Psychology, 31*(4), 373–382.

Jamal, M., & Baba, V. V. (1992). Shiftwork and department-type related to job stress, work attitudes and behavioral intentions: A study of nurses. *Journal of Organizational Behavior, 13*(5), 449–464.

Jang, K. L., Thordarson, D. S., Stein, M. B., Cohan, S. L., & Taylor, S. (2007). Coping styles and personality: A biometric analysis. *Anxiety, Stress & Coping: An International Journal, 20*(1), 17–24. https://doi.org/10.1080/10615800601170516

Jarczok, M. N., Jarczok, M., Mauss, D., Koenig, J., Li, J., Herr, R. M., & Thayer, J. F. (2013). Autonomic nervous system activity and workplace stressors—a systematic review. *Neuroscience & Biobehavioral Reviews, 37*(8), 1810–1823.

Jarczok, M. N., Jarczok, M., & Thayer, J. F. (2020). Work stress and autonomic nervous system activity. In T. Theorell (Ed.), *Handbook of socioeconomic determinants of occupational health: From macro-level to micro-level evidence* (pp. 625–656). Springer International Publishing

Jebelli, H., Hwang, S., & Lee, S. (2018). EEG-based workers' stress recognition at construction sites. *Automation in Construction, 93*, 315–324. https://doi.org/10.1016/j.autcon.2018.05.027

Jewell, L. (1998). *Contemporary industrial/organizational psychology* (3rd ed.). Brooks/Cole.

Jex, S. M., & Beehr, T. (1991). Emerging theoretical and methodological issues in the study of work related stress. *Research in Personnel and Human Resource Management, 9*, 311–365.

Jex, S. M., & Bliese, P. D. (1999). Efficacy beliefs as a moderator of the impact of work-related stressors: A multilevel study. *Journal of Applied Psychology, 84*(3), 349–361.

Jex, S. M., Bliese, P. D., Buzzell, S., & Primeau, J. (2001). The impact of self-efficacy on stressor-strain relations: Coping style as an explanatory mechanism. *Journal of Applied Psychology, 86*(3), 401–409. https://doi.org/10.1037/0021-9010.86.3.401

Jex, S. M., & Yankelevich, M. (2008). Work stress. In J. Barling & C. L. Cooper (Eds.), *The Sage handbook of organizational behavior. Volume 1: Micro perspectives* (pp. 498–518). SAGE Publications.

Jiang, L., & Lavaysse, L. M. (2018). Cognitive and affective job insecurity: A meta-analysis and a primary study. *Journal of Management, 44*(6), 2307–2342.

Johns, G. (2010). Presenteeism in the workplace: A review and research agenda. *Journal of Organizational Behavior, 31*(4), 519–542.

Johns, G., & Miraglia, M. (2015). The reliability, validity, and accuracy of self-reported absenteeism from work: A meta-analysis. *Journal of Occupational Health Psychology, 20*(1), 1–14.

Johnson, R. E., Rosen, C. C., & Levy, P. E. (2008). Getting to the core of core self-evaluation: A review and recommendations. *Journal of Organizational Behavior: The International Journal of Industrial, Occupational and Organizational Psychology and Behavior, 29*(3), 391–413.

Joseph, B., Walker, A., & Fuller-Tyszkiewicz, M. (2018). Evaluating the effectiveness of employee assistance programmes: A systematic review. *European Journal of Work and Organizational Psychology, 27*(1), 1–15. https://doi.org/10.1080/1359432x.2017.1374245

Joyce, K., Pabayo, R., Critchley, J. A., & Bambra, C. (2010). Flexible working conditions and their effects on employee health and wellbeing. *Cochrane Database of Systematic Reviews* (2), 91. https://doi.org/10.1002/14651858.CD008009.pub2

Judge, T. A., & Bono, J. E. (2001). Relationship of core self-evaluations traits—self-esteem, generalized self-efficacy, locus of control, and emotional stability—with job satisfaction and job performance: A meta-analysis. *Journal of Applied Psychology, 86*(1), 80–92.

Judge, T. A., Erez, A., & Thoresen, C. J. (2000). Why negative affectivity (and self-deception) should be included in job stress research: Bathing the baby with the bath water. *Journal of Organizational Behavior, 21*(1), 101–111. https://doi.org/10.1002/(SICI)1099-1379 (200002)21:1<101::AID-JOB966>3.0.CO;2-Q

Judge, T. A., Locke, E. A., Durham, C. C., & Kluger, A. N. (1998). Dispositional effects on job and life satisfaction: The role of core evaluations. *Journal of Applied Psychology, 83*(1), 17–34.

Judge, T. A., Piccolo, R. F., & Kosalka, T. (2009). The bright and dark sides of leader traits: A review and theoretical extension of the leader trait paradigm. *The Leadership Quarterly, 20*(6), 855–875.

Judge, T. A., Zhang, S. C., & Glerum, D. R. (2020). Job satisfaction. In V. I. Sessa & N. A. Bowling (Eds.), *Essentials of job attitudes and other workplace psychological constructs* (pp. 207–241). Routledge.

Juster, R.-P., McEwen, B. S., & Lupien, S. J. (2010). Allostatic load biomarkers of chronic stress and impact on health and cognition. *Neuroscience & Biobehavioral Reviews, 35*(1), 2–16.

Jyoti, J., & Rani, A. (2019). Role of burnout and mentoring between high performance work system and intention to leave: Moderated mediation model. *Journal of Business Research, 98*, 166–176. https://doi.org/10.1016/j.jbusres.2018.12.068

Kaas, J. H. (2013). The evolution of brains from early mammals to humans. *Wiley Interdisciplinary Reviews: Cognitive Science, 4*(1), 33–45.

Kagan, J. (2016). An overly permissive extension. *Perspectives on Psychological Science, 11*(4), 442–450. https://doi.org/10.1177/1745691616635593

Kahn, R. S., & Byosiere, P. (1990). Stress in organizations. In M. Dunnette & L. M. Hough (Eds.), *Handbook of industrial and organizational psychology* (Vol. 3, pp. 571–650). Consulting Psychologists Press.

Kahn, R. L., & Byosiere, P. (1992). Stress in organizations. In M. D. Dunnette (Ed.), *Handbook of industrial and organizational psychology* (pp. 571–648). Rand McNally.

Kahn, R. L., Wolfe, D. M., Quinn, R. P., Snoek, J. D., & Rosenthal, R. A. (1964). *Organizational stress: Studies in role conflict and ambiguity.* John Wiley.

Kain, J., & Jex, S. M. (2010). Karasek's (1979) job demands-control model: A summary of current issues and recommendations for future research. In P. L. Perrewé & D. C. Ganster (Eds.), *Research in occupational stress and well-being: New developments in theoretical and conceptual approaches to job stress* (Vol. 8, pp. 237–268). Emerald Group Publishing. https://psycnet.apa.org/doi/10.1108/S1479-3555(2010)0000008009

Kalleberg, A. L., Reskin, B. F., & Hudson, K. (2000). Bad jobs in America: Standard and nonstandard employment relations and job quality in the United States. *American Sociological Review, 65*, 256–278.

Kalliath, T., Gillespie, D., O'Driscoll, M., & Bluedorn, A. (2000). A test of the Maslach Burnout Inventory in three samples of healthcare professionals. *Work and Stress, 14,* 35–50.

Kalliath, T., O'Driscoll, M., & Gillespie, D. (1998). The relationship between burnout and organizational commitment in two samples of health professionals. *Work and Stress, 12,* 179–185.

Kamerāde, D., Wang, S., Burchell, B., Balderson, S. U., & Coutts, A. (2019). A shorter working week for everyone: How much paid work is needed for mental health and well being. *Social Science & Medicine, 241.* https://doi.org/10.1016/j.socscimed.2019.06.006

Kammeyer-Mueller, J. D., Judge, T. A., & Scott, B. A. (2009). The role of core self-evaluations in the coping process. *Journal of Applied Psychology, 94*(1), 177–195.

Kam, C., Morin, A. J., Meyer, J. P., & Topolnytsky, L. (2016). Are commitment profiles stable and predictable? A latent transition analysis. *Journal of Management, 42,* 1462–1490. https://doi.org/10.1177/0149206313503010

Kamphuis, W., Delahaij, R., & de Vries, T. A. (2021). Team coping: Cross-level influence of team member coping activities on individual burnout. *Frontiers in Psychology, 12,* 1–11. https://doi.org/10.3389/fpsyg.2021.711981

Kaplan, S., Bradley, J. C., Luchman, J. N., & Haynes, D. (2009). On the role of positive and negative affectivity in job performance: A meta-analytic investigation. *Journal of Applied Psychology, 94*(1), 162–176.

Karanika-Murray, M. (2010). Work and health: Curvilinearity matters. In J. Houdmont & S. Leka (Eds.), *Contemporary occupational health psychology: Global perspectives on research and practice (Vol. 1,* pp. 151–168). John Wiley & Sons Ltd.

Karanika-Murray, M., Biron, C., & Saksvik, P. Ø. (2016). Organizational health interventions: Advances in evaluation methodology. *Stress and Health, 32*(4), 255–257. https://doi.org/10.1002/smi.2708

Karanika-Murray, M., & Cooper, C. L. (2018). Presenteeism: An introduction to a prevailing global phenomenon. In L. Lu & C. L. Cooper (Eds.), *Presenteeism at work* (pp. 9–34). Cambridge University Press.

Karasek, R. A. (1979). Job demands, job decision latitude, and mental strain: Implications for job redesign. *Administrative Science Quarterly, 24,* 285–308.

Karasek, R. A., & Theorell, T. (1990). *Healthy work: Stress, productivity, and the reconstruction of working life.* Basic Books.

Kath, L. M., Roesch, S. C., & Ehrhart, M. G. (2016). An overview of multilevel modeling in occupational health psychology. In R. R. Sinclair, M. Wang, & L. E. Tetrick (Eds.), *Research methods in occupational health psychology: Measurement, design, and data analysis* (pp. 323–348). Routledge.

Kavous, S. N., Park, K., Silpasuwanchai, C., Wang, Z., & Ren, X. (2019). The relationship between flow proneness in everyday life and variations in the volume of gray matter in the dopaminergic system: A cross-sectional study. *Personality and Individual Differences, 141,* 25–30.

Keenan, A., & Newton, T. J. (1985). Stressful events, stressors and psychological strains in young professional engineers. *Journal of Occupational Behaviour, 6,* 151–156.

Keijsers, G. J., Schaufeli, W. B., LeBlanc, P., Zwerts, C., & Miranda, D. R. (1995). Performance and burnout in intensive care units. *Work and Stress, 9*(4), 513–527. https://doi.org/10.1080/02678379508256897

Keim, A. C., Landis, R. S., Pierce, C. A., & Earnest, D. R. (2014). Why do employees worry about their jobs? A meta-analytic review of predictors of job insecurity. *Journal of Occupational Health Psychology, 19*(3), 269–290.

Kelliher, C., & Anderson, D. (2009). Doing more with less? Flexible working practices and the intensification of work. *Human Relations, 63*(1), 83–106. https://doi.org/10.1177/0018726709349199

Kelloway, E. K., & Francis, L. (2012). Longitudinal research and data analysis. In R. R. Sinclair, M. Wang, & L. E. Tetrick (Eds.), *Research methods in occupational health psychology: Measurement, design, and data analysis* (pp. 374–394). Routledge.

Kelly, S. J., & Ismail, M. (2015). Stress and type 2 diabetes: A review of how stress contributes to the development of type 2 diabetes. *Annual Review of Public Health, 36*, 441–462.

Kelly, E. L., Kossek, E. E., Hammer, L. B., Durham, M., Bray, J., Chermack, K., Murphy, L. A., & Kaskubar, D. (2008). Getting there from here: Research on the effects of work–family initiatives on work–family conflict and business outcomes. *Academy of Management Annals, 2*(1), 305–349.

Kim, M., & Beehr, T. A. (2018). Challenge and hindrance demands lead to employees' health and behaviours through intrinsic motivation. *Stress and Health, 34*(3), 367–378.

Kinnunen, U., Geurts, S., & Mauno, S. (2004). Work-to-family conflict and its relationship with satisfaction and well-being: A one-year longitudinal study on gender differences. *Work & Stress, 18*(1), 1–22.

Kirschbaum, C., Pirke, K. M., & Hellhammer, D. H. (1993). The 'Trier Social Stress Test'—a tool for investigating psychobiological stress responses in a laboratory setting. *Neuropsychobiology, 28*(1–2), 76–81.

Kivimäki, M., Nyberg, S. T., Batty, G. D., Fransson, E. I., Heikkilä, K., Alfredsson, L., Bjorner, J. B., Borritz, M., Burr, H., & Casini, A. (2012). Job strain as a risk factor for coronary heart disease: A collaborative meta-analysis of individual participant data. *The Lancet, 380*(9852), 1491–1497.

Kivimäki, M., Nyberg, S. T., Batty, G. D., Shipley, M. J., Ferrie, J. E., Virtanen, M., Marmot, M. G., Vahtera, J., Singh-Manoux, A., & Hamer, M. (2011). Does adding information on job strain improve risk prediction for coronary heart disease beyond the standard Framingham risk score? The Whitehall II study. *International Journal of Epidemiology, 40*(6), 1577–1584.

Kivimäki, M., Virtanen, M., Kawachi, I., Nyberg, S. T., Alfredsson, L., Batty, G. D., Bjorner, J. B., Borritz, M., Brunner, E. J., & Burr, H. (2015). Long working hours, socioeconomic status, and the risk of incident type 2 diabetes: A meta-analysis of published and unpublished data from 222 120 individuals. *The Lancet Diabetes & Endocrinology, 3*(1), 27–34.

Kjellstrom, T., Briggs, D., Freyberg, C., Lemke, B., Otto, M., & Hyatt, O. (2016). Heat, human performance, and occupational health: A key issue for the assessment of global climate change impacts. *Annual Review of Public Health, 37*, 97–112.

Kniffin, K. M., Narayanan, J., Anseel, F., Antonakis, J., Ashford, S. P., Bakker, A. B., Bamberger, P., Bapuji, H., Bhave, D. P., Choi, V. K., Creary, S. J., Demerouti, E., Flynn, F. J., Gelfand, M. J., Greer, L., Johns, G., Kesbir, S., Klein, P. G., Young Lee, S., ... van Vugt, M. (2021). Covid-19 and the workplace: Implications, issues, and insights for future research and action [Working paper]. *American Psychologist, 76*(1), 63–77. http://dx.doi.org/10.1037/amp0000716

Kobasa, S. (1979). Stressful life events, personality and health: An inquiry into hardiness. *Journal of Personality and Social Psychology, 37*, 1–11.

Kochan, T. A., Riordan, C. A., Kowalski, A. M., Khan, M., & Yang, D. (2019). The changing nature of employee and labor-management relationships. *Annual Review of Organizational Psychology and Organizational Behavior, 6*, 195–219.

Koen, J., & Parker, S. K. (2020). In the eye of the beholder: How proactive coping alters perceptions of insecurity. *Journal of Occupational Health Psychology, 25*(6), 385–400. https://doi.org/10.1037/ocp0000198

Koeske, G. F., & Koeske, R. D. (1989). Construct validity of the Maslach Burnout Inventory: A critical review and reconceptualizing. *Journal of Applied Behavioral Sciences, 25*, 131–144.

Koeske, G. F., & Koeske, R. D. (1993). A preliminary test of a stress-strain-outcome model for reconceptualizing the burnout phenomenon. *Journal of Social Service Research, 17*, 107–135.

Konradt, U., Hertel, G., & Schmook, R. (2003). Quality of management by objectives, task-related stressors, and non-task-related stressors as predictors of stress and job satisfaction among teleworkers. *European Journal of Work and Organizational Psychology, 12*(1), 61–79. https://doi.org/10.1080/13594320344000020

Kossek, E. E., & Ozeki, C. (1998). Work–family conflict, policies, and the job–life satisfaction relationship: A review and directions for organizational behavior–human resources research. *Journal of Applied Psychology, 83*(2), 139–149.

Kost, D., Fieseler, C., & Wong, S. I. (2020). Boundaryless careers in the gig economy: An oxymoron? *Human Resource Management Journal, 30*, 100–113. https://doi.org/10.1111/1748-8583.12265

Koutsimani, P., Montgomery, A., & Georganta, K. (2019). The relationship between burnout, depression, and anxiety: A systematic review and meta-analysis. *Frontiers in Psychology, 10*(284). https://doi.org/10.3389/fpsyg.2019.00284

Kozlowski, S. W., & Klein, K. J. (2000). A multilevel approach to theory and research in organizations: Contextual, temporal, and emergent processes. In K. J. Klein & S. W. Kozlowski (Eds.), *Multilevel theory, research, and methods in organizations: Foundations, extensions, and new directions*. Jossey-Bass.

Kristensen, T. S., Borritz, M., Villadsen, E., & Christensen, K. B. (2005). The Copenhagen Burnout Inventory: A new tool for the assessment of burnout. *Work & Stress, 19*(3), 192–207.

Kuhn, K. M., & Galloway, T. L. (2019). Expanding perspectives on gig work and gig workers. *Journal of Managerial Psychology, 34*(4), 186–191. https://doi.org/10.1108/JMP-05-2019-507

La Torre, G., Esposito, A., Sciarra, I., & Chiappetta, M. (2019). Definition, symptoms and risk of techno-stress: A systematic review. *International Archives of Occupational and Environmental Health, 92*(1), 13–35.

Lahey, B. B. (2009). Public health significance of neuroticism. *American Psychologist, 64*(4), 241–256.

Laker, B., & Roulet, T. (2019). Will the 4-day workweek take hold in Europe? *Harvard Business Review.* https://hbr.org/2019/08/will-the-4-day-workweek-take-hold-in-europe

Lamb, S., & Kwok, K. C. (2016). A longitudinal investigation of work environment stressors on the performance and wellbeing of office workers. *Applied Ergonomics, 52*, 104–111.

Lamontagne, A. D., Keegel, T., Louie, A. M., Ostry, A., & Landsbergis, P. A. (2007). A systematic review of the job-stress intervention evaluation literature, 1990–2005. *International Journal of Occupational and Environmental Health, 13*(3), 268–280. https://doi.org/10.1179/oeh.2007.13.3.268

Lanaj, K., Johnson, R. E., & Barnes, C. M. (2014). Beginning the workday yet already depleted? Consequences of late-night smartphone use and sleep. *Organizational Behavior and Human Decision Processes, 124*(1), 11–23.

de Lange, A. H., Taris, T. W., Kompier, M. A. J., Houtman, I. L. D., & Bongers, P. M. (2003). «The very best of the millennium»: Longitudinal research and the demand-control-(support) model. *Journal of Occupational Health Psychology, 8*(4), 282–305. https://doi.org/10.1037/1076-8998.8.4.282

Latack, J., Kinicki, A. J., & Prussia, G. E. (1995). An integrative process model of coping with job loss. *Academy of Management Review, 20*, 311–342.

Lazarus, R. S. (1966). *Psychological stress and the coping process.* McGraw-Hill.

Lazarus, R. S. (1990). Theory-based stress measurement. *Psychological Inquiry, 1*, 3–13.

Lazarus, R. S. (1991). Psychological stress in the workplace. *Journal of Social Behavior and Personality, 6*, 1–13.

Lazarus, R. S. (1993). From psychological stress to the emotions: A history of changing outlooks. *American Review of Psychology, 44*, 1–21.

Lazarus, R. S. (1995). Vexing research problems inherent in cognitive mediational theories of emotion – and some solutions. *Psychological Inquiry, 6*, 183–196.

Lazarus, R. S. (1996). The role of coping in the emotions and how coping changes over the life course. In C. Maletesta-Magni & S. H. McFadden (Eds.), *Handbook of emotion, adult development, and aging* (pp. 289–306). Academic Press.

Lazarus, R. S. (1999). *Stress and emotion.* Springer Publishing Company.

Lazarus, R. S. (2001). Conservation of resources theory (COR): Little more than words masquerading as a new theory. *Applied Psychology. An International Review, 50*, 381–391.

Lazarus, R., & Folkman, S. (1984). *Stress, appraisal and coping.* Springer.

Lazarus, R. S., & Folkman, S. (1987). Transactional theory and research on emotions and coping. *European Journal of Personality, 1*, 141–169.

Lazarus, R. S., & Launier, R. (1978). Stress-related transactions between person and environment. In L. A. Pervin & M. Lewis (Eds.), *Perspectives in international psychology* (pp. 287–327). Plenum.

LeDoux, J. E. (1993). Emotional memory systems in the brain. *Behavioral Brain Research, 58*(1–2), 69–79. https://doi.org/10.1016/0166-4328(93)90091-4

LeDoux, J. E. (2007). The amygdala. *Current Biology, 17*, 868–874.

Lee, C., Ashford, S. J., & Jamieson, L. F. (1993). The effects of Type A behavior dimensions and optimism on coping strategy, health, and performance. *Journal of Organizational Behavior, 14*(2), 143–157.

Lee, R. T., & Ashforth, B. E. (1990). On the meaning of Maslach's three dimentions of burnout. *Journal of Applied Psychology, 75*, 743–747.

Lee, R. T., & Ashforth, B. E. (1993). A further examination of managerial burnout: Toward an integrated model. *Journal of Organizational Behavior, 14*, 3–20.

Lee, R. T., & Ashforth, B. E. (1996). A meta-analytic examination of the correlates of the three dimensions of job burnout: Toward an integrated model. *Journal of Applied Psychology, 81*, 123–133.

Lee, C., Huang, G.-H., & Ashford, S. J. (2018). Job insecurity and the changing workplace: Recent developments and the future trends in job insecurity research. *Annual Review of Organizational Psychology and Organizational Behavior, 5*, 335–259.

Lee, H. F., Kuo, C. C., Chien, T. W., & Wang, Y. R. (2016). A meta-analysis of the effects of coping strategies on reducing nurse burnout. *Applied Nursing Research, 31*, 100–110. https://doi.org/10.1016/j.apnr.2016.01.001

Leger, K. A., Lee, S., Chandler, K. D., & Almeida, D. M. (2021). Effects of a workplace intervention on daily stressor reactivity. *Journal of Occupational Health Psychology, 27*(1), 152–163. https://doi.org/10.1037/ocp0000297

Leiter, M. P. (1990). The impact of family resources, control coping, and skill utilization on the development of burnout: A longitudinal study. *Human Relations, 43*, 1067–1083.

Leiter, M. P. (1991). Coping patterns as predictors of burnout: The function of control and escapist coping. *Journal of Occupational Behaviour, 12*, 123–144.

Leiter, M. P. (1992). Burnout as a crisis in professional role structures: Measurement and conceptual issues. Special issue: Occupational stress, psychological burnout and anxiety. *Anxiety, Stress and Coping – An International Journal, 5*, 79–93.

Leiter, M. P. (1993). Burnout as a developmental process: Consideration of models. In W. Schaufeli, C. Maslach, & T. Marek (Eds.), *Professional burnout: Recent developments in theory and research* (pp. 237–250). Taylor & Francis.

Leiter, M. P., & Maslach, C. (1988). The impact of interpersonal environment on burnout and organizational commitment. *Journal of Occupational Behaviour, 9*, 297–308.

Leiter, M. P., & Maslach, C. (2016). Latent burnout profiles: A new approach to understanding the burnout experience. *Burnout Research, 3*(4), 89–100. https://doi.org/10.1016/j.burn.2016.09.001

Leiter, M. P., & Schaufeli, W. (1996). Consistency of the burnout construct across occupations. *Anxiety, Stress and Coping, 9*, 229–243.

LePine, M. A. (2022). The challenge-hindrance stressor framework: An integrative conceptual review and path forward. *Group & Organization Management, 47*(2), 223–254. https://doi.org/10.1177/10596011221079970

LePine, J. A., LePine, M. A., & Jackson, C. L. (2004). Challenge and hindrance stress: Relationships with exhaustion, motivation to learn, and learning performance. *Journal of Applied Psychology, 89*(5), 883–891.

LePine, J. A., LePine, M. A., & Saul, J. R. (2007). Relationships among work and non-work challenge and hindrance stressors and non-work and work criteria: A model of cross-domain stressor effects. In P. L. Perrewé & D. C. Ganster (Eds.), *Exploring the work and non-work interface* (pp. 35–72). Elsevier Science/JAI Press.

Lepine, J. A., Podsakoff, N. P., & Lepine, M. A. (October 2005). A meta-analytic test of the challenge stressor-hindrance stressor framework: An explanation for inconsistent relationships among stressors and performance. *Academy of Management Journal, 48*(5), 764–775. https://doi.org/10.5465/AMJ.2005.18803921

Lesener, T., Gusy, B., & Wolter, C. (2019). The job demands-resources model: A meta-analytic review of longitudinal studies. *Work & Stress, 33*(1), 76–103. https://doi.org/10.1080/02678373.2018.1529065

Leventhal, H. (1997). Systems as frameworks, theories and models: From the abstract to the concrete instance. *Journal of Health Psychology, 2,* 160–162.

Levesque, C., Copeland, K. J., & Sutcliffe, R. A. (2008). Conscious and nonconscious processes: Implications for self-determination theory. *Canadian Psychology, 49*(3), 218–224.

Levitt, H. M., Bamberg, M., Creswell, J. W., Frost, D. M., Josselson, R., & Suárez-Orozco, C. (2018). Journal article reporting standards for qualitative primary, qualitative meta-analytic, and mixed methods research in psychology: The APA publications and communications board task force report. *American Psychologist, 73*(1), 26–46. https://doi.org/10.1037/amp0000151

Liao, H. (2017). Leadership in virtual teams: A multilevel perspective. *Human Resource Management Review, 27,* 648–659. http://dx.doi.org/10.1016/j.hrmr.2016.12.010

Lieberman, M. D. (2007). Social cognitive neuroscience: A review of core processes. *Annual Review of Psychology, 58,* 259–289. https://doi.org/10.1146/annurev.psych.58.110405.085654

Lim, V. K. G., & Chen, D. J. Q. (2012). Cyberloafing at the workplace: Gain or drain on work? *Behaviour & Information Technology, 31*(4), 343–353. https://doi.org/10.1080/01449290903353054

Lindebaum, D., Geddes, D., & Jordan, P. J. (2018). *Social functions of emotion and talking about emotion at work.* Vol. Edward Elgar Publishing.

Lindebaum, D., & Jordan, P. J. (2012). Positive emotions, negative emotions, or utility of discrete emotions? *Journal of Organizational Behavior, 33*(7), 1027–1030.

Linnan, L., & Steckler, A. (2002). Process evaluation for public health interventions and research: An overview. In A. Steckler & L. Linnan (Eds.), *Process evaluation for public health interventions and research* (pp. 1–21). Jossey-Bass Publishers.

Lin, Y.-H., Young, I. M., Conner, A. K., Glenn, C. A., Chakraborty, A. R., Nix, C. E., Bai, M. Y., Dhanaraj, V., Fonseka, R. D., & Hormovas, J. (2020). Anatomy and white matter connections of the inferior temporal gyrus. *World Neurosurgery, 143,* e656–e666. https://doi.org/10.1016/j.wneu.2020.08.058

Liston, C., McEwen, B. S., & Casey, B. (2009). Psychosocial stress reversibly disrupts prefrontal processing and attentional control. *Proceedings of the National Academy of Sciences, 106*(3), 912–917.

Li, P., Taris, T. W., & Peeters, M. C. W. (2020). Challenge and hindrance appraisals of job demands: One man's meat, another man's poison. *Anxiety, Stress & Coping: An International Journal, 33*(1), 31–46. https://www.tandfonline.com/action/showCitFormats?doi=10.1080/10615806.2019.1673133

Litt, M. D., Tennen, H., & Affleck, G. (2011). The dynamics of stress, coping, and health: Assessing stress and coping processes in near real time. In S. Folkman (Ed.), *The Oxford handbook of stress, health, and coping.* Oxford University Press. https://doi.org/10.1093/oxfordhb/9780195375343.001.0001

Liu, S., Wang, M., Zhan, Y., & Shi, J. (2009). Daily work stress and alcohol use: Testing the cross-level moderation effects of neuroticism and job involvement. *Personnel Psychology*, *62*(3), 575–597.

Lizano, E. L. (2015). Examining the impact of job burnout on the health and well-being of human service workers: A systematic review and synthesis. *Human Service Organizations Management Leadership & Governance*, *39*(3), 167–181. https://doi.org/10.1080/23303131.2015.1014122

Lizano, E. L., & Barak, M. M. (2015). Job burnout and affective wellbeing: A longitudinal study of burnout and job satisfaction among public child welfare workers. *Children and Youth Services Review*, *55*, 18–28. https://doi.org/10.1016/j.childyouth.2015.05.005

Locke, E. A. (1996). Using programmatic research to build a grounded theory. In P. J. Frost (Ed.), *Rhythms of academic life: Personal accounts of careers in academia* (pp. 99–106). SAGE Publishing.

Loued-Khenissi, L., Döll, O., & Preuschoff, K. (2019). An overview of functional magnetic resonance imaging techniques for organizational research. *Organizational Research Methods*, *22*(1), 17–45. https://doi.org/10.1177/1094428118802631

Lovallo, W. R. (2016). *Stress and health: Biological and psychological interactions*. SAGE.

Lucassen, P. J., Pruessner, J., Sousa, N., Almeida, O. F., Van Dam, A. M., Rajkowska, G., Swaab, D. F., & Czéh, B. (2014). Neuropathology of stress. *Acta Neuropathologica*, *127*(1), 109–135.

Lyons, R. F., Mickelson, K. D., Sullivan, M. J. L., & Coyne, J. C. (1998). Coping as a communal process. *Journal of Social and Personal Relationships*, *15*(5), 579–605.

Mackay, C., Palferman, D., Saul, H., Webster, S., & Packham, C. (2012). Implementation of the management standards for work-related stress in Great Britain. In C. Biron, M. Karanika-Murray, & C. L. Cooper (Eds.), *Improving organizational interventions for stress and well-being* (pp. 285–312). Routledge.

Maddi, S. R. (2007). Relevance of hardiness assessment and training to the military context. *Military Psychology*, *19*(1), 61–70.

Mak, S., & Kozlowski, S. W. J. (2019). Virtual teams: Conceptualization, integrative review, and research recommendations. In R. Landers (Ed.), *The Cambridge handbook of technology and employee behavior*. The Cambridge University Press.

Marchand, A., Blanc, M.-E., & Beauregard, N. (2018). Do age and gender contribute to workers' burnout symptoms? *Occupational Medicine*, *68*(6), 405–411. https://doi.org/10.1093/occmed/kqy088

Marchand, C., & Vandenberghe, C. (2016). Perceived organizational support, emotional exhaustion, and turnover: The moderating role of negative affectivity. *International Journal of Stress Management*, *23*(4), 350–375.

Marescaux, E., De Winne, S., & Forrier, A. (2019). Developmental HRM, employee well-being and performance: The moderating role of developing leadership. *European Management Review*, *16*(2), 317–331. https://doi.org/10.1111/emre.12168

Maslach, C. (1982). *Burnout: The cost of caring*. Prentice Hall.

Maslach, C. (1993). Burnout: A multidimensional perspective. In W. Schaufeli, C. Maslach, & T. Marek (Eds.), *Professional burnout: Recent developments in theory and research* (pp. 19–32). Taylor & Francis.

Maslach, C., & Jackson, S. E. (1981). The measurement of experienced burnout. *Journal of Occupational Behaviour, 2,* 99–115.

Maslach, C., & Jackson, S. E. (1986). *Maslach Burnout Inventory.* Consulting Psychologists Press, Inc.

Maslach, C., Jackson, S. E., Leiter, M. P., Schaufeli, W. B., & Schwab, R. L. (2017). *Maslach Burnout Inventory manual* (4th ed.). Mind Garden.

Maslach, C., Schaufeli, W. B., & Leiter, M. P. (2001). Job burnout. *Annual Review of Psychology, 52,* 397–422.

Mas, A., & Pallais, A. (2020). Alternative work arrangements. *Annual Review of Economics, 12,* 631–658. https://doi.org/10.1146/annurev-economics-022020-032512

Mathieu, M., Eschleman, K. J., & Cheng, D. (2019). Meta-analytic and multiwave comparison of emotional support and instrumental support in the workplace. *Journal of Occupational Health Psychology, 24*(3), 387–409.

Matthews, R. A., Wayne, J. H., & Ford, M. T. (2014). A work–family conflict/subjective well-being process model: A test of competing theories of longitudinal effects. *Journal of Applied Psychology, 99*(6), 1173.

Mauss, D., Li, J., Schmidt, B., Angerer, P., & Jarczok, M. N. (2014). Measuring allostatic load in the workforce—a systematic review. *Industrial Health, 53*(1), 5–20.

Mayo, M., Sanchez, J. I., Pastor, J. C., & Rodriguez, A. (2012). Supervisor and coworker support: A source congruence approach to buffering role conflict and physical stressors. *The International Journal of Human Resource Management, 23*(18), 3872–3889.

Mazzola, J. J., & Disselhorst, R. (2019). Should we be «challenging» employees? A critical review and meta-analysis of the challenge-hindrance model of stress. *Journal of Organizational Behavior, 40*(8), 949–961.

Mazzola, J. J., Schonfeld, I. S., & Spector, P. E. (2011a). What qualitative research has taught us about occupational stress. *Stress and Health, 27,* 93–110. https://doi.org/10.1002/smi.1386

Mazzola, J. J., Walker, E. J., Shockley, K. M., & Spector, P. E. (2011b). Examining stress in graduate assistants: Combining qualitative and quantitative survey methods. *Journal of Mixed Methods Research, 5*(3), 198–211. https://doi.org/10.1177/1558689811402086

McEwen, B. S. (1998). Stress, adaptation, and disease: Allostasis and allostatic load. *Annals of the New York Academy of Sciences, 840*(1), 33–44.

McEwen, B. S. (2000). The neurobiology of stress: From serendipity to clinical relevance. *Brain Research, 886,* 172–189. https://doi.org/10.1016/S0006-8993(00)02950-4

McEwen, B. S. (2001). Plasticity of the hippocampus: Adaptation to chronic stress and allostatic load. *Annals of the New York Academy of Sciences, 933*(1), 265–277.

McEwen, B. S. (2007). Physiology and neurobiology of stress and adaptation: Central role of the brain. *Physiological Reviews, 87*(3), 873–904.

McEwen, B. S. (2016). Stress-induced remodeling of hippocampal CA3 pyramidal neurons. *Brain Research, 1645,* 50–54.

McEwen, B. S. (2018). Redefining neuroendocrinology: Epigenetics of brain-body communication over the life course. *Frontiers in Neuroendocrinology, 49,* 8–30.

McEwen, B. S. (2019). Resilience of the brain and body. In G. Fink (Ed.), *Stress: Physiology, biochemistry, and pathology* (Vol. 3, pp. 19–34). Academic Press.

McEwen, B. S., Bowles, N. P., Gray, J. D., Hill, M. N., Hunter, R. G., Karatsoreos, I. N., & Nasca, C. (2015). Mechanisms of stress in the brain. *Nature Neuroscience, 18*(10), 1353–1363.

McEwen, B. S., & Gianaros, P. J. (2010). Central role of the brain in stress and adaptation: Links to socioeconomic status, health, and disease. *Annals of the New York Academy of Sciences, 1186*(190–222). https://doi.org/10.1111/j.1749-6632.2009.05331.x

McEwen, B. S., & Morrison, J. H. (2013). The brain on stress: Vulnerability and plasticity of the prefrontal cortex over the life course. *Neuron, 79*(1), 16–29.

McEwen, B. S., & Stellar, E. (1993). Stress and the individual: Mechanisms leading to disease. *Archives of Internal Medicine, 153*(18), 2093–2101.

McEwen, B. S., Weiss, J. M., & Schwartz, L. S. (1968). Selective retention of corticosterone by limbic structures in rat brain. *Nature, 220*(5170), 911–912. https://doi.org/10.1038/220911a0

McEwen, B. S., & Wingfield, J. C. (2003). The concept of allostasis in biology and biomedicine. *Hormones and Behavior, 43*(1), 2–15.

McGrath, J. E. (1976). Stress and behavior in organizations. In M. D. Dunnette (Ed.), *Handbook of industrial and organizational psychology* (pp. 1351–1395). Rand McNally.

McGrath, J. E. (1987). Stress and behavior in organizations. In M. D. Dunnette (Ed.), *Handbook of industrial and organizational psychology*. Rand McNally.

McKee-Ryan, F. M., Song, Z., Wanberg, C. R., & Kinicki, A. (2005). Psychological and physical well-being during unemployment: A meta-analytic study. *Journal of Applied Psychology, 90*(1), 53–76. https://doi.org/10.1037/0021-9010.90.1.53

McMenamin, T. M. (2007). A time to work: Recent trends in shift work and flexible schedules. *Monthly Labor Review*, 3–15. https://www.bls.gov/opub/mlr/2007/article/time-to-work-recent-trends-in-shift-work-and-flexible-schedules.htm

McNulty, J. K., & Fincham, F. D. (2011). *Beyond positive psychology? Toward a contextual view of psychological processes and well-being*. American Psychologist, Advance Online Publication. https://doi.org/10.1037/a0024572

Melamed, S., Ben-Avi, I., Luz, J., & Green, M. (1995). Objective and subjective work monotony: Effects on job satisfaction, psychological distress and absenteeism in blue-collar workers. *Journal of Applied Psychology, 80*, 29–42.

Melamed, S., Fried, Y., & Froom, P. (2001). The interactive effect of chronic exposure to noise and job complexity on changes in blood pressure and job satisfaction: A longitudinal study of industrial employees. *Journal of Occupational Health Psychology, 6*(3), 182–195.

Melrose, K. L., Brown, G. D., & Wood, A. M. (2015). When is received social support related to perceived support and well-being? When it is needed. *Personality and Individual Differences, 77*, 97–105.

Meurs, J. A., & Perrewé, P. L. (2011). Cognitive activation theory of stress: An integrative theoretical approach to work stress. *Journal of Management, 37*(4), 1043–1068. https://doi.org/10.1177/0149206310387303

Michel, J. S., Kotrba, L. M., Mitchelson, J. K., Clark, M. A., & Baltes, B. B. (2011). Antecedents of work–family conflict: A meta-analytic review. *Journal of Organizational Behavior, 32*(5), 689–725.

Miraglia, M., Cenciotti, R., Alessandri, G., & Borgogni, L. (2017). Translating self-efficacy in job performance over time: The role of job crafting. *Human Performance, 30*(5), 254–271.

Mitchell, T. R., & James, L. R. (2001). Building better theory: Time and the specification of when things happen. *Academy of Management Review, 26*(4), 530–547.

Monnier, J., Cameron, R. P., Hobfoll, S. E., & Gribble, J. R. (2002). The impact of resource loss and critical incidents on psychological functioning in fire-emergency workers: A pilot study. *International Journal of Stress Management, 9*(1), 11–29.

Moore, S., Grunberg, L., & Greenberg, E. (2004). Repeated downsizing contact: The effects of similar and dissimilar layoff experiences on work and well-being outcomes. *Journal of Occupational Health Psychology, 9*(3), 247–257.

Morgeson, F. P., Mitchell, T. R., & Liu, D. (2015). Event system theory: An event-oriented approach to the organizational sciences. *Academy of Management Review, 40*(4), 515–537.

Morley, N. L., & Luthans, F. (1984). An EMIC perspective and ethnoscience methods for organizational research. *Academy of Management Review, 9*, 27–36.

Morrison, E. W. (2014). Employee voice and silence. *Annual Review of Organizational Psychology and Organizational Behavior, 1*(1), 173–197.

Moss, J. (2018). Helping remote workers avoid loneliness and burnout. *Harvard Business Review* (November 30), 1–5. https://hbr.org/2018/11/helping-remote-workers-avoid-loneliness-and-burnout

Munk, A., Reme, S. E., & Jacobsen, H. B. (2021). What does CATS have to do with cancer? The cognitive activation theory of stress (CATS) forms the SURGE model of chronic post-surgical pain in women with breast cancer. *Frontiers in Psychology, 12*, 1–14. https://doi.org/10.3389/fpsyg.2021.630422

Murphy, L. R. (1988). Workplace interventions for stress reduction and prevention. In C. Cooper & R. Payne (Eds.), *Causes, coping and consequences for stress at work* (pp. 301–339). John Wiley.

Murphy, P., & Jackson, S. (1999). Managing work role performance: Challenges for twenty-first century organizations and their employees. In D. Ilgen & E. Pulakos (Eds.), *The changing nature of performance: Implications for staffing, motivation and development* (pp. 325–365). Jossey-Bass.

Murray, M. M., & Antonakis, J. (2019). An introductory guide to organizational neuroscience. *Organizational Research Methods* (1), 6–16. https://doi.org/10.1177/1094428118802621

Nabi, G. R. (2003). Graduate employment and underemployment: Opportunity for skill use and career experiences amongst recent business graduates. *Education+Training, 45*(7), 371–382. https://doi.org/10.1108/00400910310499947

Nagin, D. S., Jones, B. L., Passos, V. L., & Tremblay, R. E. (2018). Group-based multi-trajectory modeling. *Statistical Methods in Medical Research, 27*(7), 2015–2023. https://doi.org/10.1177/0962280216673085

Nahrgang, J. D., Morgeson, F. P., & Hofmann, D. A. (2011). Safety at work: A meta-analytic investigation of the link between job demands, job resources, burnout, engagement, and safety outcomes. *Journal of Applied Psychology, 96*(1), 71–94. https://doi.org/10.1037/a0021484

Nahum-Shani, I., & Bamberger, P. A. (2011). Explaining the variable effects of social support on work-based stressor–strain relations: The role of perceived pattern of support exchange. *Organizational Behavior and Human Decision Processes, 114*(1), 49–63.

Näswall, K., Sverke, M., & Hellgren, J. (2005). The moderating role of personality characteristics on the relationship between job insecurity and strain. *Work & Stress, 19*(1), 37–49.

Neilson, J., & Stanfors, M. (2014). It's about time! Gender, parenthood, and household divisions of labor under different welfare regimes. *Journal of Family Issues, 35,* 1066–1088. http://dx.doi.org/10.1177/0192513X14522240

Nerstad, C. G., Caniëls, M. C., Roberts, G. C., & Richardsen, A. M. (2020). Perceived motivational climates and employee energy: The mediating role of basic psychological needs. *Frontiers in Psychology, 11.* https://doi.org/10.3389/fpsyg.2020.01509

Nerstad, C. G. L., Roberts, G. C., & Richardsen, A. M. (2013). Person-situation dynamics and well-being at work: An achievement goal perspective. In R. J. Burke & C. L. Cooper (Eds.), *The fulfilling workplace: The organization's role in achieving individual and organizational health* (pp. 121–137). Gower Publishing.

Nettle, D. (2006). The evolution of personality variation in humans and other animals. *American Psychologist, 61*(6), 622–631.

Neves, P. (2014). Taking it out on survivors: Submissive employees, downsizing, and abusive supervision. *Journal of Occupational and Organizational Psychology, 87*(3), 507–534.

Newman, J., & Beehr, T. A. (1979). Personal and organizational strategies for handling job stress: A review of research and opinion. *Personnel Psychology, 32,* 1–43.

Newton, T. J. (1989). Occupational stress and coping with stress: A critique. *Human Relations, 42,* 441–461.

Newton, T. J. (1995). *Managing stress: Emotion and power at work.* SAGE.

Ng, T. W., & Feldman, D. C. (2014). Subjective career success: A meta-analytic review. *Journal of Vocational Behavior, 85*(2), 169–179.

Ng, T. W., & Sorensen, K. L. (2008). Toward a further understanding of the relationships between perceptions of support and work attitudes: A meta-analysis. *Group & Organization Management, 33*(3), 243–268.

Ng, T. W., & Sorensen, K. L. (2009). Dispositional affectivity and work-related outcomes: A meta-analysis. *Journal of Applied Social Psychology, 39*(6), 1255–1287.

Ng, T. W., Sorensen, K. L., & Eby, L. T. (2006). Locus of control at work: A meta-analysis. *Journal of Organizational Behavior: The International Journal of Industrial, Occupational and Organizational Psychology and Behavior, 27*(8), 1057–1087.

Nielsen, K. (2013). Review article: How can we make organizational interventions work? Employees and line managers as actively crafting interventions. *Human Relations, 66*(8), 1029–1050. https://doi.org/10.1177/0018726713477164

Nielsen, K. (2017). Organizational occupational health interventions: What works for whom in which circumstances? *Occupational Medicine-Oxford, 67*(6), 410–412. https://doi.org/10.1093/occmed/kqx058

Nielsen, K., & Abildgaard, J. S. (2013). Organizational interventions: A research-based framework for the evaluation of both process and effects. *Work and Stress, 27*(3), 278–297. https://doi.org/10.1080/02678373.2013.812358

Nielsen, K., Abildgaard, J. S., & Daniels, K. (2014). Putting context into organizational intervention design: Using tailored questionnaires to measure initiatives for worker well-being. *Human Relations, 67*(12), 1537–1560. https://doi.org/10.1177/0018726714525974

Nielsen, K., De Angelis, M., Innstrand, S. T., & Mazzetti, G. (2022). Quantitative process measures in interventions to improve employees' mental health: A systematic literature review and the IPEF framework. *Work & Stress.* https://doi.org/10.1080/02678373.2022.2080775

Nielsen, K., & Miraglia, M. (2017). What works for whom in which circumstances? On the need to move beyond the 'what works?' question in organizational intervention research. *Human Relations, 70*(1), 40–62. https://doi.org/10.1177/0018726716670226

Nielsen, K., Nielsen, M. B., Ogbonnaya, C., Känsälä, M., Saari, E., & Isaksson, K. (2017). Workplace resources to improve both employee well-being and performance: A systematic review and meta-analysis. *Work & Stress, 31*(2), 101–120. https://doi.org/10.1080/02678373.2017.1304463

Nielsen, K., & Noblet, A. (2018). Introduction: Organizational interventions: Where we are, where we go from here? In K. Nielsen & A. Noblet (Eds.), *Organizational interventions for health and well-being – A handbook for evidence-based practice* (pp. 1–22). Routledge.

Nielsen, K., & Randall, R. (2012). The importance of employee participation and perceptions of changes in procedures in a teamworking intervention. *Work and Stress, 26*(2), 91–111. https://doi.org/10.1080/02678373.2012.682721

Nielsen, K., & Randall, R. (2013). Opening the black box: Presenting a model for evaluating organizational-level interventions. *European Journal of Work and Organizational Psychology, 22*(5), 601–617. https://doi.org/10.1080/1359432x.2012.690556

Nielsen, K., Randall, R., & Albertsen, K. (2007). Participants' appraisals of process issues and the effects of stress management interventions. *Journal of Organizational Behavior, 28*(6), 793–810. https://doi.org/10.1002/job.450

Nielsen, K., Randall, R., & Christensen, K. B. (2017). Do different training conditions facilitate team implementation? A quasi-experimental mixed methods study. *Journal of Mixed Methods Research, 11*(2), 223–247. https://doi.org/10.1177/1558689815589050

Nielsen, K., Randall, R., Holten, A. L., & Gonzalez, E. R. (2010). Conducting organizational-level occupational health interventions: What works? *Work and Stress, 24*(3), 234–259. https://doi.org/10.1080/02678373.2010.515393

Nielsen, K., Taris, T. W., & Cox, T. (2010). The future of organizational interventions: Addressing the challenges of today's organizations. *Work and Stress, 24*(3), 219–233. https://doi.org/10.1080/02678373.2010.519176

Nilles, J. (1975). Telecommunications and organizational decentralization. *IEEE Transactions on Communications, 23*(10), 1142–1147.

Nixon, A. E., Mazzola, J. J., Bauer, J., Krueger, J. R., & Spector, P. E. (2011). Can work make you sick? A meta-analysis of the relationships between job stressors and physical symptoms. *Work & Stress, 25*(1), 1–22.

Noblet, A. J., & Lamontagne, A. D. (2006). The role of workplace health promotion in addressing job stress. *Health Promotion International, 21*(4), 346–353. https://doi.org/10.1093/heapro/dal029

Nohe, C., Meier, L. L., Sonntag, K., & Michel, A. (2015). The chicken or the egg? A meta-analysis of panel studies of the relationship between work–family conflict and strain. *Journal of Applied Psychology, 100*(2), 522–536.

Norgate, S., & Cooper, C. L. (2020). *Flexible work: Designing our healthier future lives.* Routledge.

Nyberg, S. T., Fransson, E. I., Heikkilä, K., Alfredsson, L., Casini, A., Clays, E., De Bacquer, D., Dragano, N., Erbel, R., & Ferrie, J. E. (2013). Job strain and cardiovascular disease risk factors: Meta-analysis of individual-participant data from 47,000 men and women. *PloS One, 8*(6), e67323.

Nytrø, K., Saksvik, P. Ø., Mikkelsen, A., Bohle, P., & Quinlan, M. (2000). An appraisal of key factors in the implementation of occupational stress interventions,. *Work Stress, 14,* 213–225.

O'Brien, A., Terry, D. J., & Jimmieson, N. L. (2008). Negative affectivity and responses to work stressors: An experimental study. *Anxiety, Stress, and Coping, 21*(1), 55–83.

O'Connor, D. B., Thayer, J. F., & Vedhara, K. (2021). Stress and health: A review of psychobiological processes. *Annual Review of Psychology, 72*(4), 663–688. https://doi.org/10.1146/annurev-psych-062520-122331

O'Driscoll, M. P., & Beehr, T. A. (2000). Moderating effects of perceived control and need for clarity on the relationship between role stressors and employee affective reactions. *The Journal of Social Psychology, 140*(2), 151–159.

O'Brien, K. E., & Beehr, T. A. (2019). So far, so good: Up to now, the challenge-hindrance framework describes a practical and accurate distinction. *Journal of Organizational Behavior, 40*(8), 962–972. https://doi.org/10.1002/job.2405

O'Driscoll, M. P. (1996). The interface between job and off-job roles: Enhancement and conflict. *International Review of Industrial and Organizational Psychology, 11,* 279–306.

O'Driscoll, M., Ilgen, D., & Hildreth, K. (1992). Time devoted to job and off-job activities, interrole conflict and affective experiences. *Journal of Applied Psychology, 77,* 272–279.

O'Driscoll, M., & Schubert, T. (1988). Organizational climate and burnout in a New Zealand social service agency. *Work and Stress, 2,* 199–204.

OECD. (12 June 2020). *Distributional risks associated with non-standard work: Stylised facts and policy considerations.* https://read.oecd-ilibrary.org/view/?ref=134_134518-2bfush541w&title=Distributional-risks-associated-with-nonstandard-work-Stylised-facts-and-policy-considerations

Olafsen, A. H., Niemiec, C. P., Halvari, H., Deci, E. L., & Williams, G. C. (2017). On the dark side of work: A longitudinal analysis using self-determination theory. *European Journal of Work and Organizational Psychology, 26*(2), 275–285.

Oliver, J. E., Mansell, A., & Jose, P. E. (2010). A longitudinal study of the role of negative affectivity on the work stressor–strain process. *International Journal of Stress Management, 17*(1), 56–77.

Osipow, S. (1973). *Theories of career development.* Appleton-Century-Crofts.

Padilla, A., Hogan, R., & Kaiser, R. B. (2007). The toxic triangle: Destructive leaders, susceptible followers, and conductive environments. *The Leadership Quarterly, 18*(3), 176–194.

Panatik, S. A., O'Driscoll, M. P., & Anderson, M. H. (2011). Job demands and work-related psychological responses among Malaysian technical workers: The moderating effects of self-efficacy. *Work & Stress, 25*(4), 355–370.

Parasuraman, S., & Purohit, Y. S. (2000). Distress and boredom among orchestra musicians: The two faces of stress. *Journal of Occupational Health Psychology, 5*(1), 74–83.

Pargament, K. I. (2011). Religion and coping: The current state of knowledge. In S. Folkman (Ed.), *The Oxford handbook of stress, health, and coping* (pp. 1–36). Oxford University Press.

Pargament, K. I., Koenig, H. G., & Perez, L. M. (2000). The many ways of religious coping: Development and initial validation of the RCOPE. *Journal of Clinical Psychology, 56,* 519–543.

Park, C. L. (2011). Meaning, coping, and health and well-being. In S. Folkman (Ed.), *The Oxford handbook of stress, health, and coping* (pp. 1–26). Oxford University Press. https://doi.org/10.1093/oxfordhb/9780195375343.013.0012

Parker, S. K. (1998). Enhancing role breadth self-efficacy: The roles of job enrichment and other organizational interventions. *Journal of Applied Psychology, 83*(6), 835–852.

Parker, C. P., Baltes, B. B., Young, S. A., Huff, J. W., Altmann, R. A., Lacost, H. A., & Roberts, J. E. (2003). Relationships between psychological climate perceptions and work outcomes: A meta-analytic review. *Journal of Organizational Behavior: The International Journal of Industrial, Occupational and Organizational Psychology and Behavior, 24*(4), 389–416.

Parks, K. M., & Steelman, L. A. (2008). Organizational wellness programs: A meta-analysis. *Journal of Occupational Health Psychology, 13*(1), 58–68. https://doi.org/10.1037/1076-8998.13.1.58

Parrello, S., Ambrosetti, A., Lorioi, H., & Castelli, L. (2019). School burnout, relational, and organizational factors. *Frontiers in Psychology, 10,* 6. https://doi.org/10.3389/fpsyg.2019.01695

Paul, K. I., & Moser, K. (2009). Unemployment impair mental health: Meta-analyses. *Journal of Vocational Behavior, 74,* 264–282.

Pawson, R. (2013). *The science of evaluation: A realist manifesto.* SAGE.

Pearce, J. L. (1981). Bringing some clarity to role ambiguity research. *Academy of Management Review, 6*(4), 665–674.

Pearlin, L. I., Lieberman, M. A., Menaghan, E. G., & Mullan, J. T. (1981). The stress process. *Journal of Health and Social Behavior, 22,* 337–356.

Peng, A. C., Schaubroeck, J. M., & Xie, J. L. (2015). When confidence comes and goes: How variation in self-efficacy moderates stressor–strain relationships. *Journal of Occupational Health Psychology, 20*(3), 359–376.

Pervez, A., & Halbesleben, J. (2017). Burnout and well-being. In R. J. Burke & K. M. Page (Eds.), *Research handbook of work and well-being* (pp. 101–122). Edward Elgar.

Pieper, S., & Brosschot, J. F. (2005). Prolonged stress-related cardiovascular activation: Is there any? *Annals of Behavioral Medicine, 30*(2), 91–103. https://doi.org/10.1207/s15324796abm3002_1

Pilcher, J. J., Nadler, E., & Busch, C. (2002). Effects of hot and cold temperature exposure on performance: A meta-analytic review. *Ergonomics, 45*(10), 682–698.

Pindek, S., Arvan, M. L., & Spector, P. E. (2019). The stressor–strain relationship in diary studies: A meta-analysis of the within and between levels. *Work & Stress, 33*(1), 1–21.

Pindek, S., & Spector, P. E. (2016). Organizational constraints: A meta-analysis of a major stressor. *Work & Stress, 30*(1), 7–25.

Pines, A., Aronson, E., & Kafry, D. (1981). *Burnout: From tedium to personal growth*. The Free Press.

Pines, A., & Kafry, D. (1981). Tedium in the life and work of professional women as compared with men. *Sex Roles, 7*, 117–134.

Platsidou, M., & Daniilidou, A. (2016). Three scales to measure burnout of primary school teachers: Empirical evidence on their adequacy. *International Journal of Educational Psychology, 5*(2), 164–186. https://doi.org/10.17583/ijep.2016.1810

Ployhart, R. E., & Vandenberg, R. J. (2010). Longitudinal research: The theory, design, and analysis of change. *Journal of Management, 36*(1), 94–120.

Podsakoff, N. P., Freiburger, K. J., Podsakoff, P. M., & Rosen, C. C. (2023). Laying the foundation for the challenge-hindrance stressor framework 2.0. *Annual Review of Organizational Psychology and Organizational Behavior, 10*, 165–199. https://doi.org/10.1146/annurev-orgpsych-080422-052147

Podsakoff, N. P., LePine, J. A., & LePine, M. A. (2007). Differential challenge stressor-hindrance stressor relationships with job attitudes, turnover intentions, turnover, and withdrawal behavior: A meta-analysis. *Journal of Applied Psychology, 92*(2), 438–454.

Podsakoff, P. M., MacKenzie, S. B., & Podsakoff, N. P. (2012). Sources of method bias in social science research and recommendations on how to control it. *Annual Review of Psychology, 63*, 539–569.

Porath, C., Spreitzer, G., Gibson, C., & Garnett, F. (2012). Thriving at work: Toward its measurement, construct validation, and theoretical refinement. *Journal of Organizational Behavior, 33*, 250–275. https://doi.org/10.1002/job.756

Porter, B., Hoge, C. W., Tobin, L. E., Donoho, C. J., Castro, C. A., Luxton, D. D., & Faix, D. (2018). Measuring aggregated and specific combat exposures: Associations between combat exposure measures and posttraumatic stress disorder, depression, and alcohol-related problems. *Journal of Traumatic Stress, 31*(2), 296–306.

Porter, G., & Kakabadse, N. K. (2006). HRM perspectives on addiction to technology and work. *Journal of Management Development, 25*(6), 535–560. https://doi.org/10.1108/02621710610670119

Prati, G., Pietrantoni, L., Saccinto, E., Kehl, D., Knuth, D., & Schmidt, S. (2013). Risk perception of different emergencies in a sample of European firefighters. *Work, 45*(1), 87–96.

Prem, R., Ohly, S., Kubicek, B., & Korunka, C. (2017). Thriving on challenge stressors? Exploring time pressure and learning demands as antecedents of thriving at work. *Journal of Organizational Behavior, 38*(1), 108–123.

Prince, M. M., Stayner, L. T., Smith, R. J., & Gilbert, S. J. (1997). A re-examination of risk estimates from the NIOSH occupational noise and hearing survey (ONHS). *The Journal of the Acoustical Society of America, 101*(2), 950–963.

Purvanova, R. K., & Muros, J. P. (2010). Gender differences in burnout: A meta-analysis. *Journal of Vocational Behavior, 77*(2), 168–185. https://doi.org/10.1016/j.jvb.2010.04.006

Qiao, H., & Schaufeli, W. B. (2011). The convergent validity of four burnout measures in a Chinese sample: A confirmatory factor-analytic approach. *Applied Psychology-An International Review-Psychologie Appliquee-Revue Internationale, 60*(1), 87–111. https://doi.org/10.1111/j.1464-0597.2010.00428.x

Rafferty, A. E., & Griffin, M. A. (2006). Perceptions of organizational change: A stress and coping perspective. *Journal of Applied Psychology, 91*(5), 1154–1162. https://doi.org/10.1037/0021-9010.91.5.1154

Ragu-Nathan, T. S., Tarafdar, M., Ragu-Nathan, B. S., & Tu, Q. (2008). The consequences of technostress for end users in organizations: Conceptual development and empirical validation. *Information Systems Research, 19*(4), 417–433. https://doi.org/10.1287/isre.1070.0165

Raudenbush, S. W., & Bryk, A. S. (2002). *Hierarchical linear models: Applications and data analysis methods.* SAGE.

Rau, R., Morling, K., & Rösler, U. (2010). Is there a relationship between major depression and both objectively assessed and perceived demands and control? *Work & Stress, 24*(1), 88–106.

Razinskas, S., & Hoegl, M. (2019). A multilevel review of stressor research in teams. *Journal of Organizational Behavior, 41*, 185–209. https://doi.org/10.1002/job.2420

Reb, J., Chaturvedi, S., Narayanan, J., & Kudesia, R. S. (2019). Leader mindfulness and employee performance: A sequential mediation model of LMX quality, interpersonal justice, and employee stress. *Journal of Business Ethics, 160*(3), 745–763.

Reeve, J. (2015). *Understanding motivation and emotion* (6th ed.). John Wiley & Sons.

Reinelt, J., Uhlig, M., Müller, K., Lauckner, M. E., Kumral, D., Schaare, H. L., Baczkowski, B. M., Babayan, A., Erbey, M., & Roebbig, J. (2019). Acute psychosocial stress alters thalamic network centrality. *Neuroimage, 199*, 680–690. https://doi.org/10.1016/j.neuroimage.2019.06.005

Reis, D., Hoppe, A., & Schröder, A. (2015). Reciprocal relationships between resources, work and study engagement, and mental health: Evidence for gain cycles. *European Journal of Work and Organizational Psychology, 24*(1), 59–75.

Reme, S. E., Eriksen, H. R., & Ursin, H. (2008). Cognitive activation theory of stress: How are individual experiences mediated into biological systems? *Scandinavian Journal of Work, Environment & Health, 32*(6), 177–183.

Rhee, S.-Y., Hur, W.-M., & Kim, M. (2017). The relationship of coworker incivility to job performance and the moderating role of self-efficacy and compassion at work: The Job Demands-Resources (JD-R) Approach. *Journal of Business and Psychology, 32*(6), 711–726.

Rhoades, L., & Eisenberger, R. (2002). Perceived organizational support: A review of the literature. *Journal of Applied Psychology, 87*(4), 698–714.

Richardsen, A. M., & Martinussen, M. (2005). The Maslach Burnout Inventory: Factorial validity and consistency across occupational groups in Norway. *Journal of Occupational and Organizational Psychology, 77*, 377–384.

Richardson, K. M., & Rothstein, H. R. (2008). Effects of occupational stress management intervention programs: A meta-analysis. *Journal of Occupational Health Psychology, 13*(1), 69–93. https://doi.org/10.1037/1076-8998.13.1.69

Ritter, K.-J., Matthews, R. A., Ford, M. T., & Henderson, A. A. (2016). Understanding role stressors and job satisfaction over time using adaptation theory. *Journal of Applied Psychology, 101*(12), 1655.

Rizzo, J. R., House, R. J., & Lirtzman, S. I. (1970). Role conflict and ambiguity in complex organizations. *Administrative Science Quarterly, 15*(2), 150–163.

Rodell, J. B., & Judge, T. A. (2009). Can 'good' stressors spark 'bad' behaviors? The mediating role of emotions in links of challenge and hindrance stressors with citizenship and counterproductive behaviors. *Journal of Applied Psychology, 94*(6), 1438–1451.

Roodbari, H., Axtell, C., Nielsen, K., & Sorensen, G. (2022). Organizational interventions to improve employees' health and wellbeing: A realist synthesis. *Applied Psychology: An International Review, 71*, 1058–1081. https://doi.org/10.1111/apps.12346

Roozendaal, B., McEwen, B. S., & Chattarji, S. (2009). Stress, memory and the amygdala. *Nature Reviews Neuroscience, 10*(6), 423–433.

Rosen, C. C., Dimotakis, N., Cole, M. S., Taylor, S. G., Simon, L. S., Smith, T. A., & Reina, C. S. (2020). When challenges hinder: An investigation of when and how challenge stressors impact employee outcomes. *Journal of Applied Psychology, 105*(10), 1181–1206. https://doi.org/10.1037/apl0000483

Rosenman, R. H., Friedman, M., Straus, R., Wurm, M., Kositchek, R., Hahn, W., & Werthessen, N. T. (1964). A predictive study of coronary heart disease: The Western Collaborative Group Study. *Journal of the American Medical Association, 189*(1), 15–22.

Rubino, C., Luksyte, A., Perry, S. J., & Volpone, S. D. (2009). How do stressors lead to burnout? The mediating role of motivation. *Journal of Occupational Health Psychology, 14*(3), 289–304.

Ruhle, S., Breitsohl, H., Aboagye, E., Baba, V., Biron, C., Correia Leal, C., Dietz, C., Ferreira, A. I., Gerich, J., & Johns, G. (2020). 'To work, or not to work, that is the question'–Recent trends and avenues for research on presenteeism. *European Journal of Work and Organizational Psychology, 29*(3), 344–363.

Ruotsalainen, J. H., Serra, C., Marine, A., & Verbeek, J. (2008). Systematic review of interventions for reducing occupational stress in health care workers. *Scandinavian Journal of Work Environment & Health, 34*(3), 169–178. https://doi.org/10.5271/sjweh.1240

Ruotsalainen, J. H., Verbeek, J. H., Marine, A., & Serra, C. (2015). Preventing occupational stress in healthcare workers. *Cochrane Database of Systematic Reviews* (4), 155. https://doi.org/10.1002/14651858.CD002892.pub5

Saksvik, I. B., Bjorvatn, B., Hetland, H., Sandal, G. M., & Pallesen, S. (2011). Individual differences in tolerance to shift work–a systematic review. *Sleep Medicine Reviews, 15*(4), 221–235.

Saksvik, P. Ø., Nytrø, K., Dahl-Jørgensen, C., & Mikkelsen, A. (2002). A process evaluation of individual and organizational occupational stress and health interventions. *Work & Stress, 16*(1), 37–57. https://doi.org/10.1080/02678370110118744

Saksvik, P. Ø., Olanyan, O. S., Lysklett, K., Lien, M., & Bjerke, L. (2015). A process evaluation of a salutogenic intervention. *Scandinavian Psychologist, 2*, e8.

Salanova, M., Llorens, S., & Cifre, E. (2013). The dark side of technologies: Technostress among users of information and communication technologies. *International Journal of Psychology, 48*(3), 422–436.

Salanova, M., Llorens, S., Cifre, E., & Nogareda, C. (2007). *El Tecnoestrés: Concepto, Medida e Intervención Psicosocial*. [Technostress: Concept, Measurement and Prevention]. (Nota Técnica de Prevención, Issue).

Salanova, M., Llorens, S., & Schaufeli, W. B. (2011). 'Yes, I can, I feel good, and I just do it!' On gain cycles and spirals of efficacy beliefs, affect, and engagement. *Applied Psychology, 60*(2), 255–285.

Sallinen, M., & Kecklund, G. (2010). Shift work, sleep, and sleepiness—differences between shift schedules and systems. *Scandinavian Journal of Work, Environment & Health, 36*(2), 121–133.

Salvagioni, D. A. J., Melanda, F. N., Mesas, A. E., González, A. D., Gabani, F. L., & Andrade, S. M. (2017). Physical, psychological and occupational consequences of job burnout: A systematic review of prospective studies. *Plos One, 12*(10), e0185781. https://doi.org/10.1371/journal.pone.0185781

Sapolsky, R. M., Krey, L. C., & McEwen, B. S. (1986). The neuroendocrinology of stress and aging: The glucocorticoid cascade hypothesis. *Endocrine Reviews, 7*(3), 284–301.

Sapolsky, R. M., Romero, L. M., & Munck, A. U. (2000). How do glucocorticoids influence stress responses? Integrating permissive, suppressive, stimulatory, and preparative actions. *Endocrine Reviews, 21*(1), 55–89.

Schaubroeck, J., Cotton, J. L., & Jennings, K. R. (1989). Antecedents and consequences of role stress: A covariance structure analysis. *Journal of Organizational Behavior, 10*(1), 35–58.

Schaubroeck, J. M., Shen, Y., & Chong, S. (2017). A dual-stage moderated mediation model linking authoritarian leadership to follower outcomes. *Journal of Applied Psychology, 102*(2), 203–214.

Schaufeli, W. B. (2014). What is engagement? In C. Truss, R. Delbridge, K. Alfes, A. Schantz, & E. Soane (Eds.), *Employee engagement in theory and practice* (pp. 15–35). Routledge.

Schaufeli, W. B. (2017a). Applying the job demands-resources model: A 'how to' guide to measuring and tackeling work engagement and burnout. *Organizational Dynamics, 46*, 120–132. https://doi.org/10.1016/j.orgdyn.2017.04.008

Schaufeli, W. B. (2017b). Burnout: A short socio-cultural history. In S. Neckel, A. K. Schaffner, & G. Wagner (Eds.), *Burnout, fatigue, exhaustion: An interdisciplinary perspective on a modern affliction* (pp. 105–127). Palgrave MacMillan.

Schaufeli, W. B., & Bakker, A. B. (May 2004). Job demands, job resources, and their relationship with burnout and engagement: A multi-sample study. *Journal of Organizational Behavior, 25*(3), 293–315. <Go to ISI>://000220704900001

Schaufeli, W. B., & Buunk, B. P. (1996). Professional burnout. In M. J. Schabracq, J. A. K. Winnubst, & C. Cooper (Eds.), *Handbook of work and health psychology* (pp. 311–346): John Wiley & Sons.

Schaufeli, W. B., De Witte, H., & Desart, S. (2019). *Manual burnout assessment tool (BAT)*. Unpublished internal report. KU Leuven.

Schaufeli, W. B., & Enzmann, D. (1998). *The burnout companion to study and practice a critical analysis*. Taylor & Francis.

Schaufeli, W. B., Leiter, M. P., & Maslach, C. (2009). Burnout: 35 years of research and practice. *Career Development International, 14*(3), 204–220. https://doi.org/10.1108/13620430910966406

Schaufeli, W. B., Leiter, M. P., Maslach, C., & Jackson, S. E. (1996). The Maslach burnout inventory-general survey. In C. Maslach, S. E. Jackson, & L. M. P. (Eds.), *Maslach burnout inventory* (3rd ed.). Consulting Psychology Press.

Schaufeli, W. B., & Taris, T. W. (2005). The conceptualization and measurement of burnout: Common ground and worlds apart. *Work & Stress, 19*(3), 256–262. http://search.ebscohost.com/login.aspx?direct=true&db=bth&AN=106434215&site=ehost-live18909028

Schaufeli, W. B., & Taris, T. W. (2014). A critical review of the job demands-resources model: Implications for improving work and health. In G. F. Bauer & O. Hämmig (Eds.), *Bridging occupational, organizational and public health* (pp. 43–68). Springer. https://doi.org/10.1007/978-94-007-5640-3_4

Schaufeli, W. B., & van Dierendonck, D. (1993). The construct validity of two burnout measures. *Journal of Organizational Behavior, 14*, 631–647.

Schlachter, S., McDowall, A., Cropley, M., & Inceoglu, I. (2018). Voluntary work-related technology use during non-work time: A narrative synthesis of empirical research and research agenda. *International Journal of Management Reviews, 20*(4), 825–846.

Schmidt, S., Roesler, U., Kusserow, T., & Rau, R. (2014). Uncertainty in the workplace: Examining role ambiguity and role conflict, and their link to depression—a meta-analysis. *European Journal of Work and Organizational Psychology, 23*(1), 91–106.

Schmitt, A., Borzillo, S., & Probst, G. (2012). Don't let knowledge walk away: Knowledge retention during employee downsizing. *Management Learning, 43*(1), 53–74.

Schneider, B. (Ed.). (1990). *Organizational climate and culture.* Jossey-Bass.

Schneider, T. R. (2004). The role of neuroticism on psychological and physiological stress responses. *Journal of Experimental Social Psychology, 40*(6), 795–804.

Schneider, T. R., Rench, T. A., Lyons, J. B., & Riffle, R. R. (2012). The influence of neuroticism, extraversion and openness on stress responses. *Stress and Health, 28*(2), 102–110.

Scholz, U. (2019). It's time to think about time in health psychology. *Applied Psychology: Health and Well-Being, 11*(2), 173–186.

Schonfeld, I. S., & Chang, C.-H. (2017). *Occupational health psychology: Work, stress, and health.* Springer Publishing Company.

Schonfeld, I. S., & Farrell, E. (2010). Qualitative methods can enrich quantitative research on occupational stress: An example from one occupational group. In D. C. Ganster & P. L. Perrewé (Eds.), *Research in occupational stress and wellbeing series: New developments in theoretical and conceptual approaches to job stress* (Vol. 8, pp. 137–197). Emerald.

Schonfeld, I. S., & Mazzola, J. J. (2013). Strengths and limitations of qualitative approaches to research in occupational health psychology. In R. R. Sinclair, M. Wang, & L. E. Tetrick (Eds.), *Research methods in occupational health psychology* (pp. 268–289). Routeledge.

Schonfeld, I. S., & Mazzola, J. J. (2015). A qualitative study of stress in individuals self-employed in solo businesses. *Journal of Occupational Health Psychology, 20*(4), 501–513. https://doi.org/10.1037/a0038804

Schuler, R. S. (1980). Definition and conceptualization of stress in organizations. *Organizational Behavior and Human Performance, 25*, 184–215.

Schulz, R., Greenley, J., & Brown, R. (1995). Organization, management and client effects on staff burnout. *Journal of Health and Social Behavior, 36*, 333–345.

Schwab, K. (2017). *The fourth industrial revolution.* Currency.

Schwarz, U. V., Nielsen, K. M., Stenfors-Hayes, T., & Hasson, H. (2017). Using kaizen to improve employee well-being: Results from two organizational intervention studies. *Human Relations, 70*(8), 966–993. https://doi.org/10.1177/0018726716677071

Schyns, B., & Schilling, J. (2013). How bad are the effects of bad leaders? A meta-analysis of destructive leadership and its outcomes. *The Leadership Quarterly, 24*(1), 138–158.

Sconfienza, C., Lindfors, P., Friedrich, A. L., & Sverke, M. (2019). Social support at work and mental distress: A three-wave study of normal, reversed, and reciprocal relationships. *Journal of Occupational Health, 61*(1), 91–100.

Seligman, M. E. P., & Csikszentmihalyi, M. (2000). Positive psychology: An introduction. *American Psychologist, 55*, 5–14.

Selye, H. (1956). *The stress of life*. McGraw-Hill.

Selye, H. (1976). *The stress of life* (Rev. ed.). McGraw-Hill.

Selye, H. (1983). The stress concept: Past, present and future. In C. L. Cooper (Ed.), *Stress research*. John Wiley.

Semmer, N. K., Elfering, A., Jacobshagen, N., Perrot, T., Beehr, T. A., & Boos, N. (2008). The emotional meaning of instrumental social support. *International Journal of Stress Management, 15*(3), 235–251.

Semmer, N. K., Grebner, S., & Elfering, A. (2004). Beyond self-report: Using observational, physiological, and situation-based measures in research on occupational stress. In P. L. Perrewé & D. C. Ganster (Eds.), *Emotional and physiological processes and positive intervention strategies. Research in occupational stress and well-being* (*Vol. 3*, pp. 205–263). Elsevier.

Semmer, N. K., & Meier, L. L. (2009). Individual differences, work stress and health. In C. L. Cooper, J. Campbell Quick, & M. J. Schabracq (Eds.), *International handbook of work and health psychology* (3rd ed., pp. 99–122). Wiley-Blackwell.

Shadish, W. R., Cook, T. D., & Campbell, D. T. (2002). *Experimental and quasi-experimental designs for generalized causal inference*. Wadsworth Cengage Learning.

Shieh, G. (2009). Detecting interaction effects in moderated multiple regression with continuous variables power and sample size considerations. *Organizational Research Methods, 12*(3), 510–528.

Shin, H., Park, Y. M., Ying, J. Y., Kim, B., Noh, H., & Lee, S. M. (2014). Relationships between coping strategies and burnout symptoms: A meta-analytic approach. *Professional Psychology: Research and Practice, 45*(1), 44–56. https://doi.org/10.1037/a0035220

Shirom, A. (2003). Job-related burnout: A review. In J. Campbell & L. E. Tetrick (Eds.), *Handbook of occupational health psychology* (pp. 245–264). American Psychological Association.

Shirom, A. (2010). Employee burnout and health. In J. Houdmont & S. Leka (Eds.), *Contemporary occupational health psychology: Global perspectives on research and practice* (*Vol. 1*, pp. 59–76): John Wiley & Sons Ltd.

Shirom, A., & Melamed, S. (2006). A comparison of the construct validity of two burnout measures in two groups of professionals. *International Journal of Stress Management, 13*(2), 176–200.

Shockley, K. M., Shen, W., DeNunzio, M. M., Arvan, M. L., & Knudsen, E. A. (2017). Disentangling the relationship between gender and work-family conflict: An integration of theoretical perspectives using meta-analytic methods. *Journal of Applied Psychology, 102*, 1601–1635. https://doi.org/10.1037/ap10000246

Shoji, K., Cieslak, R., Smoktunowicz, E., Rogala, A., Benight, C. C., & Luszczynska, A. (2016). Associations between job burnout and self-efficacy: A meta-analysis. *Anxiety, Stress, & Coping, 29*(4), 367–386.

Shore, L., Barksdale, K., & Shore, T. (1995). Managerial perceptions of employee commitment to the organization. *Academy of Management Journal, 38*, 1593–1615.

Shultz, K. S., Wang, M., & Olson, D. A. (2010). Role overload and underload in relation to occupational stress and health. *Stress and Health: Journal of the International Society for the Investigation of Stress, 26*(2), 99–111.

Siegrist, J. (1996). Adverse health effects of high effort/low reward conditions. *Journal of Occupational Health Psychology, 1*, 27–41. https://doi.org/10.1037/1076-8998.1.1.27

Siegrist, J. (2010). Effort-reward imbalance at work and cardiovascular diseases. *International Journal of Occupational Medicine and Environmental Health, 23*(3), 279–285. https://doi.org/10.2478/v10001-010-0013-8

Siegrist, J., Starke, D., Chandola, T., Godin, I., Marmot, M., Niedhammer, I., & Peter, R. (2004). The measurement of effort-reward imbalance at work: European comparisons. *Social Science & Medicine, 58*(8), 1483–1499. https://doi.org/10.1016/S0277-9536(03)00351-4

Simbula, S., Guglielmi, D., & Schaufeli, W. B. (2011). A three-wave study of job resources, self-efficacy, and work engagement among Italian schoolteachers. *European Journal of Work and Organizational Psychology, 20*(3), 285–304.

Singer, J. D., & Willett, J. B. (2003). *Applied longitudinal data analysis: Modeling change and event occurrence.* Oxford University Press.

Skinner, E. A., Edge, K., Altman, J., & Sherwood, H. (2003). Searching for the structure of coping: A review and critique of category systems for classifying ways of coping. *Psychological Bulletin, 129*(2), 216–269. https://doi.org/10.1037/0033-2909.129.2.216

Sliter, M. T., Pui, S. Y., Sliter, K. A., & Jex, S. M. (2011). The differential effects of interpersonal conflict from customers and coworkers: Trait anger as a moderator. *Journal of Occupational Health Psychology, 16*(4), 424–440.

Sneve, M. H., Grydeland, H., Rosa, M. G., Paus, T., Chaplin, T., Walhovd, K., & Fjell, A. M. (2019). High-expanding regions in primate cortical brain evolution support supramodal cognitive flexibility. *Cerebral Cortex, 29*(9), 3891–3901.

Snijders, T. A. B., & Bosker, R. J. (1999). *Multilevel analysis: An introduction to basic and advanced multilevel modeling.* SAGE.

Snyder, J. S., Soumier, A., Brewer, M., Pickel, J., & Cameron, H. A. (2011). Adult hippocampal neurogenesis buffers stress responses and depressive behaviour. *Nature, 476*(7361), 458–461.

Sonnentag, S., Binnewies, C., & Ohly, S. (2012). Event-sampling methods in occupational health psychology. In R. R. Sinclair, M. Wang, & L. E. Tetrick (Eds.), *Research methods in occupational health psychology: Measurement, design, and data analysis.* Routledge.

Sonnentag, S., & Frese, M. (2012). Stress in organizations. In N. W. Schmitt (Ed.), *Handbook of psychology* (Vol. 12, pp. 560–592). Wiley.

Sonnentag, S., & Fritz, C. (2007). The recovery experience questionnaire: Development and validation of a measure for assessing recuperation and unwinding from work. *Journal of Occupational Health Psychology, 12*(3), 204. https://doi.org/10.1037/1076-8998.12.3.204

Sonnentag, S., & Spychala, A. (2012). Job control and job stressors as predictors of proactive work behavior: Is role breadth self-efficacy the link? *Human Performance, 25*(5), 412–431.

Sorensen, O. H., & Holman, D. (2014). A participative intervention to improve employee well- being in knowledge work jobs: A mixed- methods evaluation study. *Work and Stress, 28*(1), 67–86. https://doi.org/10.1080/02678373.2013.876124

Sparks, K., Cooper, C. L., Fried, Y., & Shirom, A. (2013). The effects of working hours on health: A meta-analytic review. In C. L. Cooper (Ed.), *From stress to wellbeing volume 1: The theory and research on occupational stress and wellbeing* (pp. 292–314). Palgrave Macmillan. https://doi.org/10.1057/9781137310651_14

Spector, P. E. (1999). Objective versus subjective approaches to the study of job stress. *Journal of Organizational Behavior, 20*, 737.

Spector, P. E. (2009). The role of job control in employee health and well-being. In C. L. Cooper, J. Campbell Quick, & M. J. Schabracq (Eds.), *International handbook of work and health psychology* (3rd ed., pp. 173–196). Wiley-Blackwell.

Spector, P. E. (2019). Do not cross me: Optimizing the use of cross-sectional designs. *Journal of Business and Psychology, 34*(2), 125–137.

Spector, P. E., & Jex, S. M. (1998). Development of four self-report measures of job stressors and strain: Interpersonal conflict at work scale, organizational constraints scale, quantitative workload inventory, and physical symptoms inventory. *Journal of Occupational Health Psychology, 3*(4), 356–367.

Spector, P. E., & Pindek, S. (2016). The future of research methods in work and occupational health psychology. *Applied Psychology: An International Review, 65*(2), 412–431. https://doi.org/10.1111/apps.12056

Spector, P. E., Zapf, D., Chen, P. Y., & Frese, M. (2000). Why negative affectivity should not be controlled in job stress research: Don't throw out the baby with the bath water. *Journal of Organizational Behavior, 21*(1), 79–95. https://doi.org/10.1002/(SICI)1099-1379(200002)21:1<79::AID-JOB964>3.0.CO;2-G

Spicer, J. (1997). Systems analysis of stress and coping: A testing proposition. *Journal of Health Psychology, 2*, 167–170.

Spreitzer, G. M., Cameron, L., & Garrett, L. (2017). Alternative work arrangements: Two images of the new world of work. *Annual Review of Organizational Psychology and Organizational Behavior, 4*, 473–499.

Spreitzer, G., Sutcliffe, K., Dutton, J., Sonenshein, S., & Grant, A. M. (2005). A socially embedded model of thriving at work. *Organization Science, 16*(5), 537–549. https://doi.org/10.1287/orsc.1050.0153

Sprung, J. M., & Jex, S. M. (2012). Work locus of control as a moderator of the relationship between work stressors and counterproductive work behavior. *International Journal of Stress Management, 19*(4), 272–291.

Spurk, D., Hirschi, A., Wang, M., Valero, D., & Kauffeld, S. (2020). Latent profile analysis: A review and 'how to' guide of its application within vocational behavior research. *Journal of Vocational Behavior, 120*, 1–21. https://doi.org/10.1016/j.jvb.2020.103445

Stahl, S., Grim, C., Donald, C., & Neikirk, A. (1975). A model for the social sciences and medicine: The case for hypertension. *Social Science and Medicine, 9*, 31–38.

Steel, P., Schmidt, J., Bosco, F., & Uggerslev, K. (2019). The effects of personality on job satisfaction and life satisfaction: A meta-analytic investigation accounting for bandwidth–fidelity and commensurability. *Human Relations, 72*(2), 217–247.

Stetz, T. A., Stetz, M. C., & Bliese, P. D. (2006). The importance of self-efficacy in the moderating effects of social support on stressor–strain relationships. *Work & Stress*, *20*(1), 49–59.

Stiglbauer, B. (2017). Under what conditions does job control moderate the relationship between time pressure and employee well-being? Investigating the role of match and personal control beliefs. *Journal of Organizational Behavior*, *38*(5), 730–748.

Stiglbauer, B., & Batinic, B. (2015). Proactive coping with job insecurity: Is it always beneficial to well-being. *Work & Stress*, *29*(3), 264–285. https://doi.org/10.1080/02678373.2015.1074956

Stoeva, A. Z., Chiu, R. K., & Greenhaus, J. H. (2002). Negative affectivity, role stress, and work–family conflict. *Journal of Vocational Behavior*, *60*(1), 1–16.

Straus, M. A. (1973). A general systems theory approach to a theory of violence between family members. *Social Science Information*, *12*, 105–125.

Strazdins, L., D'Souza, R. M., Lim, L. L.-Y., Broom, D. H., & Rodgers, B. (2004). Job strain, job insecurity, and health: Rethinking the relationship. *Journal of Occupational Health Psychology*, *9*(4), 296–305.

Sullivan, S. E., & Baruch, Y. (2009). Advances in career theory and research: A critical review and agenda for future exploration. *Journal of Management*, *35*(6), 1542–1571. https://doi.org/10.1177/0149206309350082

Sutherland, V., & Cooper, C. L. (1990). *Understanding stress*. Chapman & Hall.

Svensen, E., Neset, G., & Eriksen, H. R. (2007). Factors associated with a positive attitude towards change among employees during the early phase of a downsizing process. *Scandinavian Journal of Psychology*, *48*, 153–159.

Sverke, M., Hellgren, J., & Näswall, K. (2002). No security: A meta-analysis and review of job insecurity and its consequences. *Journal of Occupational Health Psychology*, *7*(3), 242–264.

Swider, B. W., & Zimmerman, R. D. (2010). Born to burnout: A meta-analytic path model of personality, job burnout, and work outcomes. *Journal of Vocational Behavior*, *76*(3), 487–506. https://doi.org/10.1016/j.jvb.2010.01.003

Szalma, J. L., & Hancock, P. A. (2011). Noise effects on human performance: A meta-analytic synthesis. *Psychological Bulletin*, *137*(4), 682–707.

Tafvelin, S., Schwarz, U. V., Nielsen, K., & Hasson, H. (2019). Employees' and line managers' active involvement in participatory organizational interventions: Examining direct, reversed, and reciprocal effects on well-being. *Stress and Health*, *35*(1), 69–80. https://doi.org/10.1002/smi.2841

Tamres, L. K., Janicki, D., & Helgeson, V. S. (2002). Sex differences in coping behavior: A meta-analytic review and examination of relative coping. *Personality and Social Psychology Review*, *6*(1), 2–30.

Tarafdar, M., Tu, Q., Ragu-Nathan, B. S., & Ragu-Nathan, T. S. (2007). The impact of technostress on role stress and productivity. *Journal of Management Information Systems*, *24*(1), 301–328. https://doi.org/10.2753/MIS0742-1222240109

Taris, T. W. (2006). Is there a relationship between burnout and objective performance? A critical review of 16 studies. *Work and Stress*, *20*(4), 316–334. https://doi.org/10.1080/02678370601065893

Taris, T. W., Kessler, S. R., & Kelloway, E. K. (2021). Strategies addressing the limitations of cross-sectional designs in occupational health psychology: What they are good for (and what not). *Work & Stress*, *35*(1), 1–5.

Taris, T. W., & Kompier, M. A. J. (2014). Cause and effect: Optimizing the designs of longitudinal studies in occupational health psychology. *Work & Stress, 28*(1), 1–8. https://doi.org/10.1080/02678373.2014.878494

Taris, T. W., Kompier, M. A. J., Geurts, S. A. E., Houtman, I. L. D., & van den Heuvel, F. F. M. (2010). Professional efficacy, exhaustion, and work characteristics among police officers: A longitudinal test of the learning-related predictions of the demand–control model. *Journal of Occupational & Organizational Psychology, 83*, 455–474. https://doi.org/10.1348/096317909X424583

Taris, T. W., Le Blanc, P. M., Schaufeli, W. B., & Schreurs, P. J. G. (2005). Are there causal relationships between the dimensions of the Maslach Burnout Inventory? A review and two longitudinal tests. *Work & Stress, 19*(3), 238–255. http://search.ebscohost.com/login.aspx?direct=true&db=bth&AN=106434212&site=ehost-live18909030

Taylor, S. G., & Kluemper, D. H. (2012). Linking perceptions of role stress and incivility to workplace aggression: The moderating role of personality. *Journal of Occupational Health Psychology, 17*(3), 316–329.

Ten Brummelhuis, L. L., & Bakker, A. B. (2012). The resource perspective on the work-home interface. *American Psychologist, 67*(7), 545–556. https://doi.org/10.1037/a0027974

Tetrick, L. E. (2017). Trends in measurement models and methods in understanding occupational health psychology. *Journal of Occupational Health Psychology, 22*(3), 337–340.

Tetrick, L., & LaRocco, J. (1987). Understanding, prediction, and control as moderators of the relationships between perceived stress, satisfaction, and psychological well-being. *Journal of Applied Psychology, 72*, 538–543.

Tetrick, L. E., & Winslow, C. J. (2015). Workplace stress management interventions and health promotion. *Annual Review of Organizational Psychology and Organizational Behavior, 2*, 583–603.

Thompson, C. A., & Prottas, D. J. (2006). Relationships among organizational family support, job autonomy, perceived control, and employee well-being. *Journal of Occupational Health Psychology, 11*(1), 100–118.

Thoresen, C. J., Kaplan, S. A., Barsky, A. P., Warren, C. R., & De Chermont, K. (2003). The affective underpinnings of job perceptions and attitudes: A meta-analytic review and integration. *Psychological Bulletin, 129*(6), 914–945.

Tims, M., Bakker, A. B., & Derks, D. (2013). The impact of job crafting on job demands, job resources, and well-being. *Journal of Occupational Health Psychology, 18*(2), 230–240.

Tims, M., Bakker, A. B., & Derks, D. (2015). Examining job crafting from an interpersonal perspective: Is employee job crafting related to the well-being of colleagues? *Applied Psychology, 64*(4), 727–753.

Tims, M., Twemlow, M., & Fong, C. Y. M. (2021). A state-of-the-art overview of job-crafting research: Current trends and future research directions. *Career Development International, 27*(1), 54–78.

Toda, T., Parylak, S. L., Linker, S. B., & Gage, F. H. (2019). The role of adult hippocampal neurogenesis in brain health and disease. *Molecular Psychiatry, 24*(1), 67–87.

Toker, S., Gavish, I., & Biron, M. (2013). Job Demand–Control–Support and diabetes risk: The moderating role of self-efficacy. *European Journal of Work and Organizational Psychology, 22*(6), 711–724.

Tomas, J. M., de los Santos, S., Alonso-Andres, A., & Fernandez, I. (2016). Validation of the Maslach burnout inventory-general survey on a representative sample of Dominican teachers: Normative data. *Spanish Journal of Psychology, 19*, 9. https://doi.org/10.1017/sjp.2016.91

Törnroos, M., Hintsanen, M., Hintsa, T., Jokela, M., Pulkki-Råback, L., Hutri-Kähönen, N., & Keltikangas-Järvinen, L. (2013). Associations between five-factor model traits and perceived job strain: A population-based study. *Journal of Occupational Health Psychology, 18*(4), 492–500.

Tran, M., & Sokas, R. K. (2017). The gig economy and contingent work: An occupational health assessment. *Journal of Occupational and Environmental Medicine, 59*(4), e63–e66. https://doi.org/10.1097/JOM.0000000000000977

Truyens, M., & Van Eecke, P. (2014). Legal aspects of text mining. *Computer Law & Security Review, 30*(2), 153–170.

Tubre, T. C., & Collins, J. M. (2000). Jackson and Schuler (1985) revisited: A meta-analysis of the relationships between role ambiguity, role conflict, and job performance. *Journal of Management, 26*(1), 155–169.

Tucker, P., & Rutherford, C. (2005). Moderators of the relationship between long work hours and health. *Journal of Occupational Health Psychology, 10*(4), 465–476.

Tuckey, M. R., Searle, B. J., Boyd, C. M., Winefield, A. H., & Winefield, H. R. (2015). Hindrances are not threats: Advancing the multidimensionality of work stress. *Journal of Occupational Health Psychology, 20*(2), 131–147. https://doi.org/10.1037/a0038280

Tugade, M. M., & Fredrickson, B. L. (2007). Regulation of positive emotions: Emotion regulation strategies that promote resilience. *Journal of Happiness Studies, 8*, 311–333. https://doi.org/10.1007/s10902-006-9015-4

Turgeman-Lupo, K., Toker, S., Ben-Avi, N., & Shenhar-Tsarfaty, S. (2020). The depressive price of being a sandwich-generation caregiver: Can organizations and managers help? *European Journal of Work and Organizational Psychology, 29*(6), 862–879. https://www.tandfonline.com/action/showCitFormats?doi=10.1080/1359432X.2020.1762574

Ulrich, M., Keller, J., & Grön, G. (2015). Neural signatures of experimentally induced flow experiences identified in a typical fMRI block design with BOLD imaging. *Social Cognitive and Affective Neuroscience, 11*(3), 496–507.

Ulrich, M., Keller, J., Hoenig, K., Waller, C., & Grön, G. (2014). Neural correlates of experimentally induced flow experiences. *Neuroimage, 86*, 194–202.

Urien, B., Rico, R., Demerouti, E., & Bakker, A. B. (2021). An emergence model of team burnout. *Journal of Work and Organizational Psychology, 37*(3), 175–186. https://doi.org/10.5093/jwop2021a17

Ursin, H. (1998). The psychology in psychoneurodocrinology. *Psychoneurodocrinology, 23*(6), 555–570.

Ursin, H. (2009). The development of a cognitive activation theory of stress: From limbic structures to behavioral medicine. *Scandinavian Journal of Psychology, 50*, 639–644. https://doi.org/10.1111/j.1467-9450.2009.00790.x

Ursin, H., Baade, E., & Levine, S. (1978). *Psychobiology of stress: A study of coping men.* Academic Press.

Ursin, H., & Eriksen, H. (2004). The cognitive activation theory of stress. *Psychoneuroendocrinology, 29*, 567–592. https://doi.org/10.1016/S0306-4530(03)00091-x

Ursin, H., & Eriksen, H. R. (2010). Cognitive activation theory of stress (CATS). *Neuroscience & Biobehavioral Reviews, 34*(6), 877–881. https://doi.org/10.1016/j.neubiorev.2009.03.001

Vahle-Hinz, T. (2016). Stress in nonregular work arrangements: A longitudinal study of task- and employment-related aspects of stress. *Journal of Occupational Health Psychology, 21*(4), 415–431.

Van Dierendonck, D., & Jacobs, G. (2012). Survivors and victims, a meta-analytical review of fairness and organizational commitment after downsizing. *British Journal of Management, 23*(1), 96–109.

Van Vleet, M., Helgeson, V. S., Seltman, H. J., Korytkowski, M. T., & Hausmann, L. R. M. (2018). Communally coping with diabetes: An observational investigation using actor-partner interdependence model. *Journal of Family Psychology, 32*(5), 654–663. https://doi.org/10.1037/fam0000414

Vander Elst, T., Notelaers, G., & Skogstad, A. (2018). The reciprocal relationship between job insecurity and depressive symptoms: A latent transition analysis. *Journal of Organizational Behavior, 39*(9), 1197–1218.

Van der Doef, M., & Maes, S. (1999). The job demand-control (-support) model and psychological well-being: A review of 20 years of empirical research. *Work & Stress, 13*(2), 87–114.

Vargas Llave, O., Mandl, I., Weber, T., & Wilkens, M. (2020). *Telework and ICT-based mobile work: Flexible working in the digital age.* https://www.eurofound.europa.eu/publications/report/2020/telework-and-ict-based-mobile-work-flexible-working-in-the-digital-age

van Vegchel, N., de Jonge, J., Bosma, H., & Schaufeli, W. (2005). Reviewing the effort-reward imbalance model: Drawing up the balance of 45 empirical studies. *Social Science & Medicine, 60*, 1117–1131. https://doi.org/10.1016/j.socscimed.2004.06.043

van Vianen, A. E. M. (2018). Person-Environment Fit: A review of its basic tenets. *Annual Review of Organizational Psychology and Organizational Behavior, 5*, 75–101. https://doi.org/10.1146/annurev-orgpsych-032117-104702

Venetjoki, N., Kaarlela-Tuomaala, A., Keskinen, E., & Hongisto, V. (2006). The effect of speech and speech intelligibility on task performance. *Ergonomics, 49*(11), 1068–1091.

Vignoli, M., Nielsen, K., Guglielmi, D., Tabanelli, M. C., & Violante, F. S. (2017). The importance of context in screening in occupational health interventions in organizations: A mixed methods study. *Frontiers in Psychology, 8*(1347). https://doi.org/10.3389/fpsyg.2017.01347

Viitasalo, K., Kuosma, E., Laitinen, J., & Härmä, M. (2008). Effects of shift rotation and the flexibility of a shift system on daytime alertness and cardiovascular risk factors. *Scandinavian Journal of Work, Environment & Health, 34*(3), 198–205.

Virtanen, M., Heikkilä, K., Jokela, M., Ferrie, J. E., Batty, G. D., Vahtera, J., & Kivimäki, M. (2012). Long working hours and coronary heart disease: A systematic review and meta-analysis. *American Journal of Epidemiology, 176*(7), 586–596.

Virtanen, M., Jokela, M., Madsen, I. E., Magnusson Hanson, L. L., Lallukka, T., Nyberg, S. T., Alfredsson, L., Batty, G. D., Bjorner, J. B., & Borritz, M. (2018). Long working hours and depressive symptoms: Systematic review and meta-analysis of published studies and unpublished individual participant data. *Scandinavian Journal of Work, Environment & Health, 44*(3), 239–250.

Virtanen, M., & Kivimäki, M. (2018). Long working hours and risk of cardiovascular disease. *Current Cardiology Reports, 20*(11), 123. https://doi.org/org/10.1007/s11886-018-1049-9

Viswesvaran, C., & Ones, D. S. (2000). Perspectives on models of job performance. *International Journal of Selection and Assessment, 8*(4), 216–226.

Viswesvaran, C., Sanchez, J. I., & Fisher, J. (1999). The role of social support in the process of work stress: A meta-analysis. *Journal of Vocational Behavior, 54*(2), 314–334.

Vogt, K., Hakanen, J. J., Brauchli, R., Jenny, G. J., & Bauer, G. F. (2016). The consequences of job crafting: A three-wave study. *European Journal of Work and Organizational Psychology, 25*(3), 353–362.

Wadsworth, L. L., & Facer, R. L. (2016). Work-family balance and alternative work schedules: Exploring the impact of 4-day workweeks on state employees. *Public Personnel Management, 45*(4), 382–404. https://doi.org/10.1177/0091026016678856

Waldman, D. A., Wang, D., & Fenters, V. (2019). The added value of neuroscience methods in organizational research. *Organizational Research Methods, 22*(1), 223–249. https://doi.org/10.1177/1094428116642013

Waldman, D. A., Ward, M. K., & Becker, W. J. (2017). Neuroscience in organizational behavior. *Annual Review of Organizational Psychology and Organizational Behavior, 4*, 425–444. https://doi.org/10.1146/annurev-orgpsych-032516-113316

Walker, F. R., Pfingst, K., Carnevali, L., Sgoifo, A., & Nalivaiko, E. (2017). In the search for integrative biomarker of resilience to psychological stress. *Neuroscience & Biobehavioral Reviews, 74*, 310–320.

Walkey, F., & Green, D. (1992). An exhaustive examination of the replicable factor structure of the Maslach Burnout Inventory. *Educational and Psychological Measurement, 52*, 309–323.

Wang, M., Beal, D. J., Newman, D. A., Chan, D., Vancouver, J. B., & Vandenberg, R. J. (2017). Longitudinal research: A panel discussion of conceptual issues, research design, and statistical techniques. *Work, Aging and Retirement, 3*, 1–24. https://doi.org/10.1093/workar/waw033

Wang, Q., Bowling, N. A., & Eschleman, K. J. (2010). A meta-analytic examination of work and general locus of control. *Journal of Applied Psychology, 95*(4), 761–768.

Wang, S.-W., Repetti, R. L., & Campos, B. (2011). Job stress and family social behavior: The moderating role of neuroticism. *Journal of Occupational Health Psychology, 16*(4), 441–456.

Wang, M., Sinclair, R. R., Zhou, L., & Sears, L. E. (2013). Person-centered analysis: Methods, application, and implications for occupational health psychology. In R. R. Sinclair, M. Wang, & L. E. Tetrick (Eds.), *Research methods in occupational health psychology* (pp. 349–373). Routledge.

Watson, D. (2000). *Mood and temperament.* Guilford Press.

Watson, D., & Clark, L. A. (1984). Negative affectivity: The disposition to experience aversive emotional states. *Psychological Bulletin, 96*(3), 465–490.

Watson, D., & Pennebaker, J. W. (1989). Health complaints, stress, and distress: Exploring the central role of negative affectivity. *Psychological Review, 96*(2), 234–254.

Webster, J. R., & Adams, G. A. (2020). The differential role of job demands in relation to nonwork domain outcomes based on the challenge-hindrance framework. *Work & Stress, 34*(1), 5–33.

Webster, J. R., Beehr, T. A., & Love, K. (2011). Extending the challenge-hindrance model of occupational stress: The role of appraisal. *Journal of Vocational Behavior, 79*, 505–516. https://doi.org/10.1016/j.jvb.2011.02.001

Wells, J. D., Hobfoll, S. E., & Lavin, J. (1997). Resource loss, resource gain, and communal coping during pregnancy among women with multiple roles. *Psychology of Women Quarterly, 21*(4), 645–662.

West, C. P., Dyrbye, L. N., Erwin, P. J., & Shanafelt, T. D. (2016). Interventions to prevent and reduce physician burnout: A systematic review and meta-analysis. *The Lancet, 388*(10057), 2272–2281. https://doi.org/10.1016/S0140-6736(16)31279-X

Westman, M. (2001). Stress and strain crossover. *Human Relations, 54*(6), 717–751.

Wetherell, M. A., & Carter, K. (2014). The multitasking framework: The effects of increasing workload on acute psychobiological stress reactivity. *Stress and Health, 30*(2), 103–109.

Wheeler, L., & Reis, H. T. (1991). Self-recording of everyday life events: Origins, types, and uses. *Journal of Personality, 59*(3), 339–354.

Whitman, M. V., Halbesleben, J. R. B., & Holmes, O. (2014). Abusive supervision and feedback avoidance: The mediating role of emotional exhaustion. *Journal of Organizational Behavior, 35*, 38–53.

Widmer, P. S., Semmer, N. K., Kälin, W., Jacobshagen, N., & Meier, L. L. (2012). The ambivalence of challenge stressors: Time pressure associated with both negative and positive well-being. *Journal of Vocational Behavior, 80*, 422–433. https://doi.org/10.1016/j.jvb.2011.09.006

Wiley, J. F., Gruenewald, T. L., Karlamangla, A. S., & Seeman, T. E. (2016). Modeling multisystem physiological dysregulation. *Psychosomatic Medicine, 78*(3), 290–301.

Winwood, P. C., & Winefield, A. H. (2004). Comparing two measures of burnout among dentists in Australia. *International Journal of Stress Management, 11*(3), 282–289.

Wirtz, P. H., Ehlert, U., Kottwitz, M. U., La Marca, R., & Semmer, N. K. (2013). Occupational role stress is associated with higher cortisol reactivity to acute stress. *Journal of Occupational Health Psychology, 18*(2), 121–131.

Wohlers, C., & Hertel, G. (2017). Choosing where to work at work: Towards a theoretical model of benefits and risks of activity based flexible offices. *Ergonomics, 60*(4), 467–486. https://doi.org/10.1080/00140139.2016.1188220.

Wolff, M., & Vann, S. D. (2019). The cognitive thalamus as a gateway to mental representations. *The Journal of Neuroscience, 39*(1), 3–14. https://doi.org/10.1523/JNEUROSCI.0479-18.2018

Wong, K., Chan, A. H., & Ngan, S. (2019). The effect of long working hours and overtime on occupational health: A meta-analysis of evidence from 1998 to 2018. *International Journal of Environmental Research and Public Health, 16*(12), 2102. https://doi.org/10.3390/ijerph16122102

Worley, J. A., Vassar, M., Wheeler, D. L., & Barnes, L. L. B. (2008). Factor structure of scores from the Maslach Burnout Inventory: A review and meta-analysis of 45 exploratory and confirmatory factor-analytic studies. *Educational and Psychological Measurement, 68*(5), 797–823. https://doi.org/10.1177/0013164408315268

Wright, T. A., & Cropanzano, R. (2000). Psychological well-being and job satisfaction as predictors of job performance. *Journal of Occupational Health Psychology, 5*(1), 84–94. https://doi.org/10.1037/1076-8998.5.1.84

Wrzesniewski, A., & Dutton, J. E. (2001). Crafting a job: Revisioning employees as active crafters of their work. *Academy of Management Review, 26*(2), 179–201.

Wyller, V. B., Eriksen, H. R., & Malterud, K. (2009). Can sustained arousal explain the chronic fatique syndrome? *Behavioral and Brain Functions, 5*(10), 1–10. https://doi.org/10.1186/1744-9081-5-10

Xanthopoulou, D., Bakker, A. B., Demerouti, E., & Schaufeli, W. B. (2007). The role of personal resources in the job demands-resources model. *International Journal of Stress Management, 14*(2), 121–141.

Xanthopoulou, D., Bakker, A. B., Demerouti, E., & Schaufeli, W. B. (2009). Reciprocal relationships between job resources, personal resources, and work engagement. *Journal of Vocational Behavior, 74*(3), 235–244.

Xanthopoulou, D., Bakker, A. B., & Fischbach, A. (2013). Work engagement among employees facing emotional demands. *Journal of Personnel Psychology, 12,* 74–84.

Yang, L. Q., Che, H., & Spector, P. E. (2008). Job stress and well-being: An examination from the view of person-environment fit. *Journal of Occupational and Organizational Psychology, 81*(3), 567–587.

Yang, W.-N., Niven, K., & Johnsen, S. (2019). Career plateau: A review of 40 years of research. *Journal of Vocational Behavior, 110,* 286–302. https://doi.org/10.1016/j.jvb.2018.11.005

Yorulmaz, Y. I., Colak, L., & Altinkurt, Y. (2017). A meta-analysis of the relationship between teachers' job satisfaction and burnout. *Eurasian Journal of Educational Research* (71), 175–190. https://doi.org/10.14689/ejer.2017.71.10

Yoshii, T. (2021). The role of the thalamus in post-traumatic stress disorder. *International Journal of Molecular Sciences, 22*(1730), 1–18. https://doi.org/10.3390/ijms22041730

Yung, M., Lang, A. E., Stobart, J., Kociolek, A. M., Milosavljevic, S., & Trask, C. (2017). The combined fatigue effects of sequential exposure to seated whole body vibration and physical, mental, or concurrent work demands. *PloS One, 12*(12), e0188468. https://doi.org/10.1371/journal.pone.0188468

Zajdel, M., & Helgeson, V. S. (2020). Communal coping: A multi-method approach with links to relationships and health. *Journal of Social and Personal Relationships, 37*(5), 1700–1721. https://doi.org/10.1177/0265407520903811

Zajdel, M., & Helgeson, V. S. (2021). An experimental approach to communal coping. *Journal of Social and Personal Relationships, 38*(4), 1380–1400. https://doi.org/10.1177/0265407521992464

Zhang, X., Li, X., Steffens, D. C., Guo, H., & Wang, L. (2019). Dynamic changes in thalamic connectivity following stress and its association with future depression severity. *Brain and Behavior, 9*(12), 1–13. https://doi.org/10.1002/brb3.1445

Zhang, Y., Zhang, Y., Ng, T. W. H., & Lam, S. S. K. (2019). Promotion- and prevention-focused coping: A meta-analytic examination of regulatory strategies in the work stress process. *Journal of Applied Psychology, 104*(10), 1296–1323. https://doi.org/10.1037/apl0000404

Zhou, Z. E., Yan, Y., Che, X. X., & Meier, L. L. (2015). Effect of workplace incivility on end-of-work negative affect: Examining individual and organizational moderators in a daily diary study. *Journal of Occupational Health Psychology, 20*(1), 117–130.

Zhu, Y., Nachtrab, G., Keyes, P. C., Allen, W. E., Luo, L., & Chen, X. (2018). Dynamic salience processing in paraventricular thalamus gates associative learning. *Science, 362,* 423–429. https://doi.org/10.1126/science.aat0481

INDEX

Abildgaard, J. S., 166, 170
Absenteeism, 73, 74
Achievement Striving, 113
ACTH. *See* Adrenocorticotrophic hormone (ACTH)
Activity-based work (ABW), 207, 208
Acute stress, 41, 42, 52
Adrenal medulla, 32
Adrenocorticotrophic hormone (ACTH), 32
Adult neurogenesis, 36
Affective distress, 71
Affective well-being, 71
Ahola, K., 80
Akinola, M., 183
Alarcon, G. M., 93, 97, 100, 118
Alarm, 37, 38
Alcoholism, 1
Allen, T. D., 116
Allostatic load model, 34–36, 67 (figure), 68, 105, 124
  pedagogical mediated mode, 69
  physiological processes, 66
Alternative work arrangements, 57, 196–197
  consequences of, 198–205
Amstad, F. T., 61
Amygdala, 31–36
  functional connectivity, 42
  neural activity in, 42
Anderson, D., 95
Anger, 70, 107, 112, 113, 185
ANS. *See* Autonomic nervous system (ANS)
Antecedents, 92
Anticipatory stress, 44
Anxiety, 7, 71, 187
Appraisals, 4, 12, 19, 23, 33, 138
  brain systems in, 33
  challenge, 140
  cognitive, 139
  cognitive activation theory of stress (CATS), 142
  hindrance, 19, 140
  job demands, 127
  primary, 33, 139
  psychological, 34
  secondary, 34, 139

strain-producing, 110
types of, 11
Aronsson, G., 95
Arousal, 36, 37, 44
  short-term, 38
Arthur, M. B., 198
Ashforth, B. E., 84, 93, 99
Aspinwall, L. G., 142
Authoritarian leadership style, 55
Autocratic leadership style, 55
Autonomic nervous system (ANS), 31, 69

Baade, E., 143
Baethge, A., 183
Bakker, A. B., 16
Barley, S., 201
BAT. *See* Burnout Assessment Tool (BAT)
Bavik, Y. L., 128
Beal, D. J., 175
Beehr, T. A., 53, 54, 115, 134, 158, 164
Behavioral strain, 72–75
Bereavement, 195
Big Five personality traits, 97
Biological tradition, 3
Biomarkers, 68
Biron, C., 159, 167, 170
Bliese, P. D., 116
Blood oxygenation level dependent (BOLD) signal, 39
Blood pressure, 7, 66
Bolger, N., 106
Bond, F. W., 159
Boundaryless career, 198
Bowling, N. A., 48, 70, 72, 115
Bradley, H., 79
Brotheridge, C. M., 118
Brough, P., 128
Bunce, D., 159
Burnout, 27, 71, 182
  antecedents, 92
  Burnout Assessment Tool (BAT), 91
  consequences of, 99–101
  conservation of resources theory (COR), 85–86
  Copenhagen Burnout Inventory (CBI), 90–91
  correlates of, 92–101

definitions, 79–83
elements of, 80
individual factors, 95–99
job demands-resources model (JD-R), 86–87
Maslach Burnout Inventory (MBI), 87–89
Maslach's classic model of, 81
measurement of, 87–92
methodological issues, 101–102
models of, 83–85
Oldenburg Burnout Inventory (OLBI), 90
Shirom-Melamed Burnout Measure, 89, 90
strain and, 80
theories of, 85
work-related factors, 92–95
Burnout Assessment Tool (BAT), 91

Campbell, D. T., 174
Cardiovascular system, 67
Career advancement, 58–59
Career development, 55
job insecurity, 56–58
promotion and career advancement, 58–59
Career mobility, 59
Career plateauing, 199
Career progression, 198
Career transitions, 198
Caregiving, 62, 203
Catecholamines, 7, 32
CATS. See Cognitive activation theory of stress (CATS)
Causality hypothesis, 110
CBI. See Copenhagen Burnout Inventory (CBI)
Cell proliferation, 36
Cendales-Ayala, B., 60
Cerebral cortex, 31
Challenge appraisals, 140
Challenge-hindrance framework, 46, 50
Challenge-hindrance model of stress (CHM), 14, 16–19
Challenge stressors, 18
Charalampous, M., 52
Chawla, N., 182
Cherniss, C., 80, 83
Cheung, F. M., 62
Chiaburu, D. S., 131
CHM. See Challenge-hindrance model of stress (CHM)
Christian, P., 7
Christopoulos, G., 40
Chronic fatigue, 80
Chronic strain, 85
Chronic stress, 41
Circadian rhythms, 51
Cockburn, B., 125

Cognition, 32, 39, 44, 186
Cognitive activation theory of stress (CATS), 14, 21–23, 36, 206
coping behavior, 38, 142, 143
experience of the stress response, 37
nonspecific general stress response, 37
organizational neuroscience and, 39
organizational stress, 39
psychological mechanisms, 37
response outcome expectancies, 38
stimulus expectancies, 38
stress experience, 37
stress stimuli, 37
Cognitive appraisal, 139
Cognitive impairment, 91
Cognitive machinery, 29
Conrad, C. D., 32
Conservation of resources model (COR), 14, 19–20, 85, 179, 206
burnout, 85–86
coping, 140–142, 147
Construct validity, 163–164
Contingent workforce, 195
Contract working, 195
Cook, T. D., 174
Copenhagen Burnout Inventory (CBI), 90–91
Coping, 11, 12, 22, 38, 86, 128, 137
burnout, 96, 98
control-oriented, 99
defensive, 81
definitions, 138–143
depersonalization, 84
effectiveness, 149–150
families of, 143
methodological approaches and measurement, 150–152
problem-focused, 98
promotion and prevention focused coping, 146–148
refining measures of, 189–191
research context, 138–143
role of, 148–149
taxonomies of, 143–148
theories of, 138–143
COR. See Conservation of resources model (COR)
Core self-evaluations, 118–119
Cortisol, 66
Countershock, 7
COVID-19, 52, 185, 194, 196
burnout, 95
job insecurity, 56
work from home (WFH), 197, 204
Criticisms, 9, 10, 23
Cyberloafing coping, 144
Cynicism, 81, 93, 96

Damage limitation, 156
Datta, D. K., 57
Dawson, K. M., 127
Decision latitude model, 122
Defensive coping, 81
De Jonge, J., 119
Demands-discretion model, 122
Demerouti, E., 16, 120
Demographic variables, 6
Dependent variable, 2
Depersonalization, 81, 82, 84, 89, 92, 96, 97, 100
Depression, 80, 85
Destructive leadership, 55
Deterioration, 7
De Witte, H., 71
Differential exposure, 107, 107 (figure)
Differential reactivity, 107
Differential selection, 109
Dispositional optimism, 97
Dispositional/personality moderators, 106–108
  differential exposure, 107, 107 (figure)
  hardiness, 114–115
  negative affectivity/neuroticism, 108–112
  personal resources, 115–122
  reactivity hypotheses, 107, 107 (figure)
  Type A behavior pattern (TABP), 112–113
Disselhorst, R., 18
DiStasio, M. J., 147, 206
Divorce, 3
Dormann, C., 119, 179
Drug abuse, 1
Dual-income households, 203

EAPs. See Employee assistance programs (EAPs)
Eatough, E. M., 73
EBSCO host, 40
Economic strain, 3
Edwards, J. R., 113
EEG. See Electro-encephalogram (EEG)
Effort reward imbalance (ERI) model, 20–22, 21 (figure)
Effort-to-performance expectancy (E → P), 54
Egan, M., 159
Ego depletion, 71
Electro-encephalogram (EEG), 39–42, 184
Embarrassment, 71
Emotional energy, 81
Emotional exhaustion, 70, 71, 81, 83, 84, 87, 90, 92, 97, 100, 164
Emotional impairment, 91
Emotional responses, 43
Emotional strain, 70
  measurements of, 71

Emotion-focused coping, 145
Emotion regulation, 144
Employee assistance programs (EAPs), 157
Endocrine system, 31
Engagement, 51, 71, 75, 93, 113, 128, 182
Environmental stressors, 47
Enzmann, D., 97
Epidemiologic tradition, 3
ERI. See Effort reward imbalance (ERI) model
Eriksen, H. R., 18
Eschleman, K. J., 114
ESM. See Experience sampling method (ESM)
Event-contingent recording, 176
Exhaustion, 91, 93, 106
  cope, 84
  emotional, 81, 83
  job performance and, 100
  physical and mental, 91
  work-related state of, 82
Expectancies, 4, 6, 22
  response outcome, 38
  stimulus, 38
Experience sampling method (ESM), 175–177
External validity, 164–165

Falco, A., 110
Fan, W., 182
Fatigue, 48, 71
  chronic, 80
  physical, 81
Feedback mechanism, 14
Fenlason, K. J., 134
Fight-or-flight response, 7, 32
Firefighters, 52
Five Factor model, 97
fMRI. See Functional magnetic resonance imaging (fMRI)
Folkman, S., 23, 33, 45, 98, 144
Ford, M. T., 62, 178
Fourth Industrial Revolution, 56
Freedy, J., 95
Frese, M., 178
Freudenberger, H. J., 79, 80
Friedman, M., 112
Frustration, 80
Functional magnetic resonance imaging (fMRI), 39–42, 184

Ganster, D. C., 66, 69, 124, 183
Garden, A. M., 101
GAS. See General adaptation syndrome (GAS)
Gender, 6, 62, 185
General adaptation syndrome (GAS), 6–8

General Health Questionnaire, 205
Gilboa, S., 73
Glucocorticoids, 31, 35
Golembiewski, R. T., 83
Golkar, A., 41
González-Morales, M. G., 102
Gonzalez-Mulé, E., 125–127, 132
Google Scholar, 40, 79
Gray, P., 158
Greenglass, E. R., 142
Griffin, M. A., 179

Hakanen, J., 80, 99
Halbesleben, J. R. B., 81, 85, 89, 95, 100, 102, 120, 131
Hall, D., 198
Halpern, D. F., 62
The Handbook of Stress: Neuropsychological Effects on the Brain, 32
Handy, C., 198
Happening in reality (actual) values, 21
Harassment, 46
Hardiness, 114–115
Harrison, D. A., 131
Häusser, J. A., 125, 132
Health impairment process, 18
Heart disease, 1
Helplessness, 143
Hierarchical plateau, 59
Higgins, E. T., 143
High cost-low gain condition, 21
High performance work systems (HPWS), 94
Hindrance appraisals, 140
Hindrance stressors, 18
Hippocampus, 31, 34, 35
  new neurons in, 36
  plasticity, 43
History-by-treatment interaction, 165
Hobfoll, S. E., 23, 84, 85, 95
Hoegl, M., 180
Homeostasis, 12, 42
Home-work interface, 60–62
Hopelessness, 38, 85, 143
Hormones, 31, 35
  allostatic load, 34
  catecholamine, 32
Hou, N., 118
HPWS. *See* High performance work systems (HPWS)
Human brain, 29, 33
  amygdala, 31
  cell death, 35
  electro-encephalogram (EEG), 39
  hippocampus, 31
  hypothalamic-pituitary-adrenal (HPA) axis, 32

hypothalamus, 31
  imaging techniques, 41
  maladaptive and damaging effects, 35
  mechanisms, 35
  midsagittal view of, 31, 32 (figure)
  multiple systems and areas, 30
  ordinary stressors, 43
  organizational stress, 30
  prefrontal cortex, 31
  sympathetic-adreno-medullar (SAM) axis, 32
  thalamus, 31
Human resource management (HRM), 197
Huyghebaert, T., 106
Hyper-responsivity mechanism, 109, 111
Hypothalamic-pituitary-adrenal (HPA) axis, 32, 33, 41, 66
Hypothalamus, 31

ICT. *See* Information and communication technology (ICT)
Imbalance, 2, 12, 14, 20, 23, 80
Impatience/Irritability dimension, 113
Independent variable, 2, 12
Individual (personal) sources, 45
Industrialization, 8
Inferior temporal gyrus, 33
Information and communication technology (ICT), 51, 52
Interactional approach, 10–11
Internal validity, 162–163
International Labour Organization (ILO), 194
Interpersonal conflict, 185
Interval-contingent recording, 176
Intrinsic job characteristics, 47
  new technology, 51–52
  noise, 47
  risk and hazards, exposure to, 52
  temperature, 47–48
  vibration, 47–48
  work hours, 50–51
  workload, 48–50
Irritation, 71
Ito, J. K., 118
Ivancevich, J. M., 158

Jack, A. I., 40
Jahncke, H., 47
JDCS. *See* Job demands-control-support model (JDCS)
JD-R model. *See* Job demands-resources (JD-R) model
Jebelli, H., 42
Jex, S. M., 116, 118

Job accountability, 111
Job/career security, 198
Job control, 126–128
Job crafting, 120
Job demands-control model (JDC), 122, 128
Job demands-control-support model (JDCS), 15, 16 (figure), 46
Job demands-resources (JD-R) model, 15–19, 17 (figure), 123
    burnout, 86–87, 92, 94
Job dissatisfaction, 70
Job-family balance, 204
Job-family conflict, 62
Job insecurity, 55–58, 71
Job involvement, 99
Job loss, 57
Job performance, 73
Job-related sources of strain, 45–46, 153
    career development, 55–59
    home-work interface, 60–62
    intrinsic job characteristics, 47–52
    organizational factors, 59–60
    organizational roles, 52–54
    work relationships, 54–55
Job-related stress, 1, 27, 191
    cognitive activation theory of stress (CATS), 22–23
    conservation of resources model (COR), 19–20
    effort reward imbalance (ERI) model, 20–22, 21 (figure)
    job demands-control-support model (JDCS), 15, 16 (figure)
    job demands-resources (JD-R) model, 15–19, 17 (figure)
    McGraths stress model, 14
    person-environment fit model of, 15
    research, 205–208
    theoretical models of, 13–25
Job-related stressors, 43, 46, 80
    meta-analysis of, 48
Job-related thriving, 75–76
Job satisfaction, 70, 71, 99
Johnson, R. E., 118
Journal of Occupational Health Psychology (JOHP), 174

Kafry, D., 96
Kagan, J., 2
Kahn, R. L., 46, 52, 53
Kalliath, T., 88, 100
Kammeyer-Mueller, J. D., 118
Karanika-Murray, M., 160, 167, 170
Karasek, R. A., 15, 46, 55, 60, 122
Kelliher, C., 95

Kivimäki, M., 68
k-Means cluster analysis, 68
Knowledge, 3, 19, 57
Kobasa, S., 114
Kompier, M. A. J., 179
Kossek, E. E., 62
Kost, D., 197

LaRocco, J., 13
Latack, J., 56
Latent class analysis (LCA), 181
Latent profile analysis (LPA), 181
Lazarus, R. S., 8, 12, 23, 25, 33, 45, 138, 143, 144
LCA. *See* Latent class analysis (LCA)
Leader/immediate work group, 179
Leadership style, 55
Learning, 22
Lee, R. T., 84, 93, 99
Leger, K. A., 175
Leisure coping (beliefs and strategies), 144
Leiter, M. P., 42, 82–84, 86, 87, 98, 100, 182
Leon, M., 102
Lesener, T., 94
Levin, S., 143
Li, P., 140
LOC. *See* Locus of control (LOC)
Lock, E. A., 23
Locus of control (LOC), 117–118
Lolas, F., 7
Longitudinal research design, 177–178
Lovallo, W. R., 33
LPA. *See* Latent profile analysis (LPA)

Maddi, S. R., 114
Maes, S., 125
Marchand, A., 96
Marchand, C., 110
Maslach Burnout Inventory (MBI), 87–90, 96
Maslach, C., 42, 80–84, 81, 86, 93, 97, 100, 182
Mathieu, M., 132, 133
Mazzola, J. J., 18, 185
MBI. *See* Maslach Burnout Inventory (MBI)
McEwen, B. S., 35
McGrath, J. E., 13, 14
Meaning-focused coping, 144
Mediation, 105, 106, 130 (figure)
Mediator effect, 106, 106 (figure)
Meier, L. L., 108
Memory system, 31, 33, 57
Mental distance, 91
Mental health complaints, 71
Mesial prefrontal cortex (mPFC), 42

Meta-analysis, 15, 18, 48–50, 54, 68–70, 72, 73, 93, 94, 96, 100, 125, 126, 130, 131, 147, 179
  Big Five personality variables and burnout, 97
  burnout, 95, 98
  core self-evaluations, 118
  hardiness, 114
  instrumental and emotional support, 133
  job strain and coronary heart disease, 124
  leadership style, 55
  locus of control (LOC), 117
  organizational politics, 60
  personality variables vs. burnout, 97
  role ambiguity, 53
  role conflict, 53
  stressor–strain relationship, 177
  work-family conflict, 62
Metabolic system, 68
MeToo – movement, 46
Mindfulness-based stress-reduction training, 43
Miraglia, M., 120
Mismatch, 23
MIST. See Montreal Imaging Stress Task (MIST)
Misfit, 14, 23
Mixed methods approaches, 186–188
Moderators
  dispositional/personality, 106–122
  situational, 122–124
  social support, 129
  variables, 105, 119
Montreal Imaging Stress Task (MIST), 41
Mood, 31, 70
Moss, J., 198
Motor control, 32
Multilevel modeling, 179–180
Muros, J. P., 96

Nahrgang, J. D., 93
Negative affectivity (NA)/neuroticism, 70, 108
  causality hypothesis, 110
  differential selection, 109
  hyper-responsivity mechanism, 109, 111
  stress-creation mechanism, 109
  symptom perception hypothesis, 109
  transitory mood, 109
Nerstad, C. G. L., 59, 95
Nesdoly, N., 40
Neuroscience, 1, 29, 30, 35
Neves, P., 57
Newman, J., 158

Ng, T. W., 54, 117
Nielsen, K., 163, 166, 168, 170
Nixon, A. E., 48, 69
Noblet, A. J., 170
Nohe, C., 61
Noise, 47
Nonconscious (automatic) processing, 42, 43
Norepinephrine, 32
Normal situation (set) values, 21
Nytrø, K., 159

Objective measurement issues, 183–184
OCB. See Organizational citizenship behaviors (OCB)
Occupational stress, 1
O'Driscoll, M. P., 54, 94
O'Hara, K., 164
OLBI. See Oldenburg Burnout Inventory (OLBI)
Oldenburg Burnout Inventory (OLBI), 90
Optimism, 17
Ordinary stressors, 43
Organizational citizenship behaviors (OCB), 70, 73
Organizational commitment, 100
Organizational factors, 59–60
Organizational interventions, 154, 158
  workplace stress reduction, 158
Organizational neuroscience, 29, 30, 43
  cognitive activation theory of stress (CATS), 39
  methods of, 39–40
  organizational stress and, 30–33, 32 (figure)
Organizational politics, 60
Organizational productivity, 1
Organizational roles, 52
  role ambiguity, 53
  role conflict, 53
  role overload, 53–54
Organizational sources, 45
Organizational stress, 4, 5 (figure), 23, 30, 34
  brain, 29. See also Human brain
  electro-encephalogram (EEG), 40–42
  functional magnetic resonance imaging (fMRI), 40–42
  organizational neuroscience and, 30–33, 32 (figure)
Organizational stress theory, 195
Organizational support, 131
Outcomes, 128
Outcomes process, 1, 6, 30
  behavioral, 30
  strain and maladaptive, 4, 5 (figure)
  stressors, 18, 19

Overcommitment, 21, 21 (figure)
Overextended, 182
Ozeki, C., 62

Panatik, S. A., 117
Pedagogical mediated mode, 69
Peeters, M. C. W., 140
Peng, A. C., 117
Pennebaker, J. W., 109
Perceptions, 29, 35, 60
Performance-to-outcome expectancy
    (P → O), 54
Perseverative cognition, 39
Personal accomplishment, 81
Personal expectations, 17
Personal health threats, 17
Personality variables, 96
Personal resources, 115
    core self-evaluations, 118–119
    locus of control (LOC), 117–118
    moderating role of, 119–122
    self-efficacy, 116–117
Person-based analytical approach, 180–182
    objective measurement issues, 183–184
Person–environment (P-E) fit model, 3,
    13–15, 154
Pervez, A., 81, 85, 89, 100
Physical degeneration, 7
Physical demands, 47
Physical hazards, 52
Physiological strain, 53, 58, 65–69, 67
    (figure)
Pindek, S., 70
Pines, A., 89, 96
Pituitary gland, 32
Plasticity, 36, 43
Ployhart, R. E., 177
Portfolio career, 198
Prefrontal cortex, 31, 35
Presenteeism, 74
Preservative cognition, 44
Prevention focused coping, 146–148
Primary appraisal, 139
Problem-focused coping, 98, 145, 185
Process evaluation, 159
Productivity-related losses, 1
Professional efficacy, 81
Promotion focused coping, 146–148
Protean career, 198
Psychological distress, 91
Psychological strain, 53, 55, 58, 69–72, 79,
    82
Psychological tradition, 3
Psychosomatic complaints, 91
PsycINFO, 40
Purvanova, R. K., 96

Qualitative methodological issues,
    184–186
Qualitative workload, 48
Quantitative measurement issues
    cause and effect, 173–175
    experience sampling method (ESM),
        175–177
    longitudinal research design, 177–178
    multilevel modeling, 179–180
    time interval issues/temporal aspects,
        178–179
Quantitative workload, 48

Randomized controlled trials (RCT), 162,
    165, 166
Razinskas, S., 180
RCT. See Randomized controlled trials
    (RCT)
Reactivity hypotheses, 107, 107 (figure)
Reciprocal effects, 177
Reis, H. T., 176
Religious/spiritual coping, 144
Response-based model, 6–8, 6 (figure),
    9–10
Richardson, K. M., 158
Richelson, G., 80
Rizzo, J. R., 53
Role ambiguity, 53, 55, 92
Role conflict, 53, 92, 189
Role overload, 53–54
Rosen, C. C., 69, 124
Rosenman, R. H., 112
Rothstein, H. R., 158
Rousseau, D. M., 198
Rumination, 44, 71

Sandwich generation, 203
Schaufeli, W. B., 16, 82, 88, 89, 96, 99
Schilling, J., 55
Schmitt, A., 57
Schonfeld, I. S., 185
Schubert, T., 94
Schulz, R., 94
Schyns, B., 55
Secondary allostatic load, 68
Secondary appraisal, 139, 149
Self-efficacy, 17, 116–117, 119, 120, 122,
    149
    coping, 143
Self-report, 54, 71–74, 89, 113, 175, 189
Self-undermining, 18
Selye, H., 6–8, 18
Semmer, N. K., 108, 132
Sensory information, 33
Sexual misconduct, 46
Shackleton, G., 40

Shift work, 51
Shin, H., 98
Shirom, A., 85
Shirom-Melamed Burnout Measure, 89, 90
Short-term arousal, 38
Shoss, M. K., 147, 206
Signal-contingent recording, 176
Situational moderators, 122–124
Skinner, E. A., 145, 146
Smartphones, 51
Social/communal coping, 141
Social problems, 1
Social/relation-focused coping, 144
Social support, 133, 134, 164
    mediating variable, 130, 130 (figure)
    moderating variable, 130, 130 (figure)
    strain and, 129, 129 (figure)
Sonnentag, S., 120
Sorensen, K. L., 54
Spector, P. E., 109
Spicer, J., 180
Sprung, J. M., 118
Spychala, A., 120
Stetz, T. A., 122
Stimulus-based model, 2, 8–10
Stimulus expectancies, 38
Strain, 65, 75, 137. See also Job-related sources of strain
    behavioral, 72–75
    classifying, 65–75
    core self-evaluations on, 118
    determinants of, 45
    emotional, 70
    family-related, 71
    hardiness, 115
    job-related, 54, 79, 153
    leadership style, 55
    noise, 47
    physiological, 53, 58, 65–69, 67 (figure)
    psychological, 53, 55, 58, 69–72, 79
    refining measures of, 189–191
    self-reports of, 209
    social support and, 129, 129 (figure)
    temperature, 47
    vibration, 47
    work-related, 71, 108
Strain/thriving, 4
Stress, 85, 137, 154, 210. See also specific types
    components of, 22
    definitions, 2–6, 5 (figure)
    emerging themes in, 25–27
    experience, 22
    individual health, 1
    as interaction, 10–11
    job-related, 1

    occupational, 1
    organizational, 4, 5 (figure), 23, 29
    person-environment fit model of, 15
    process and implications, 24–25
    response-based definitions of, 6–8, 6 (figure)
    stimuli (stressor), 22
    stimulus-based definitions of, 8
    theories and models, 23–25, 42–44
    three-dimensional challenge-hindrance-threat framework for, 19
    time interval issues/temporal aspects of, 178–179
    as transaction, 11–12, 11 (figure), 33–34
    well-being, 1
    work-related, 1
Stress-buffering hypothesis, 123
Stress contagion, 203
Stress-coping process, 11, 27, 46, 71, 107, 119, 193
Stress-creation mechanism, 109
Stress management interventions
    conceptual framework for, 154–158, 155 (table)
    construct validity, 163–164
    external validity, 164–165
    guidelines for, 165–171, 167 (figure)
    internal validity, 162–163
    intervention process, 159–161
    primary interventions, 154
    problems in, 161–165
    research on, 158–159
    secondary interventions, 156
    tertiary level of, 157
Stress management training, 156, 157
Stressors, 4, 7, 26, 37, 46, 52, 54, 73, 75, 92, 137, 185
    absenteeism and, 74
    allostasis, 34
    cell death, 35
    challenge, 18, 147
    characteristics of, 36
    core self-evaluations on, 118
    e-mail, 202
    endocrinological changes in, 31
    environmental, 47
    experimental, 41
    functions, 45
    hindrance, 18, 147
    interpretation, 29
    job-related, 43, 80
    ordinary, 43
    organizational citizenship behaviors (OCB), 73
    outcomes, 18, 19, 46
    pedagogical mediated model, 69

...rception, 29
   physiological responses to, 66
   prevalence of, 75
   prevalent and pervasive, 8
   refining measures of, 189–191
   self-reports of, 209
   social support, 129
   structural plasticity, 36
   thermal, 48
   three-dimensional challenge-hindrance-
      threat framework for, 19
   toxic effect on, 35
   work-related, 37, 45, 66
Stressor-strain relationships, 105–106, 175,
   177, 178
   dispositional/personality, 106–122
   perceived control over environment,
      124–128
   situational, 122–124
   social support on, 128–134
   sources of support, 131–132
   support provided, 132–133
   unresolved issues, 133–134
Structural manipulations, 10
Structured Interview (SI), 113
Subject-by-treatment interaction, 164
Survivor syndrome, 57
Swider, B. W., 97
Sympathetic-adrenal–medullary (SAM)
   axis, 32, 33, 66
Symptom perception hypothesis, 109, 110

TABP. See Type A behavior pattern (TABP)
Taris, T. W., 84, 140, 179
Task content factors, 47
Taylor, S., 142
Technoaddiction, 201
Technostrain, 201
Technostress, 201
Tedium, 89
Temperature, 47–48
Temporality, 121
Tetrick, L., 13
Thalamus, 31, 32
   dominant coordination center, 33
   functional connectivity, 42
Theorell, T., 15
Threatening experiences, 31
Three-dimensional challenge-hindrance-
   threat framework, 19
Tobacco use, 73
Toker, S., 117
Transactional approach, 11–12, 11 (figure)
Transactional theory of stress, 33–34, 46,
   138
   emotion focused, 144
   problem focused, 144

Transitory mood, 109
Treatment-by-setting interaction, 164
Trier Social Stress Test (TSST), 41
TSST. See Trier Social Stress Test (TSST)
Tuckey, M. R., 19
Type A behavior pattern (TABP), 112–113

Ulrich, M., 42
Underemployment, 194, 195
Unemployment, 3, 56, 194
Ursin, H., 18, 143

Vandenberghe, C., 110
Vandenberg, R. J., 177
Van der Doef, M., 125
Van Dierendonck, D., 89
Vibrations, 47–48
Virtanen, M., 68
Virtual teams, 200
Vogt, K., 120

Walker, E. J., 121
Watson, D., 109
Web of Science, 79
Webster, J. R., 19
Well-being, 50, 51, 56, 59, 65, 80, 159, 170
   affective, 71
   burnout and, 85
   coping, 142
   job-related, 125
   physical and psychological, 53
   social support, 164
   strain and, 54
West, C. P., 158
WFH. See Working from home (WFH)
Wheeler, A. R., 120
Wheeler, L., 176
Workaholism, 17
Work-family conflict, 61
Workforce ecosystems, 200
Work hours, 50–51
Working from home (WFH), 194, 197,
   201–204
Work-life balance, 51
Work-life conflict, 60
Workload
   issue, 49
   meta-analysis, 48, 49
   qualitative, 48
   quantitative, 48
Work/nonwork conflict, 60
Work overload, 92, 189
Work-related commitment, 21
Work-related strain, 108
Work-related stress, 1, 21
Work-related stressors, 37, 45
Work-related support, 131

Work relationships, 54
  leadership style, 55
Work schedules, 50
Work & Stress (WS), 174
Work Tension Scale, 70
Worries, 44, 71

Xanthopoulou, D., 116, 120, 121

Zapf, D., 178
Zhang, Y., 146
Zimmerman, R. D., 97
Zuckerman, A., 107